For Anna

in appreciation of
all your achieved and
with admiration for
your work.

John

February 2007

ELY JACQUES KAHN, ARCHITECT

C.1 Ely Jacques Kahn,
"Market Place, Tangiers,"
watercolor, 1911

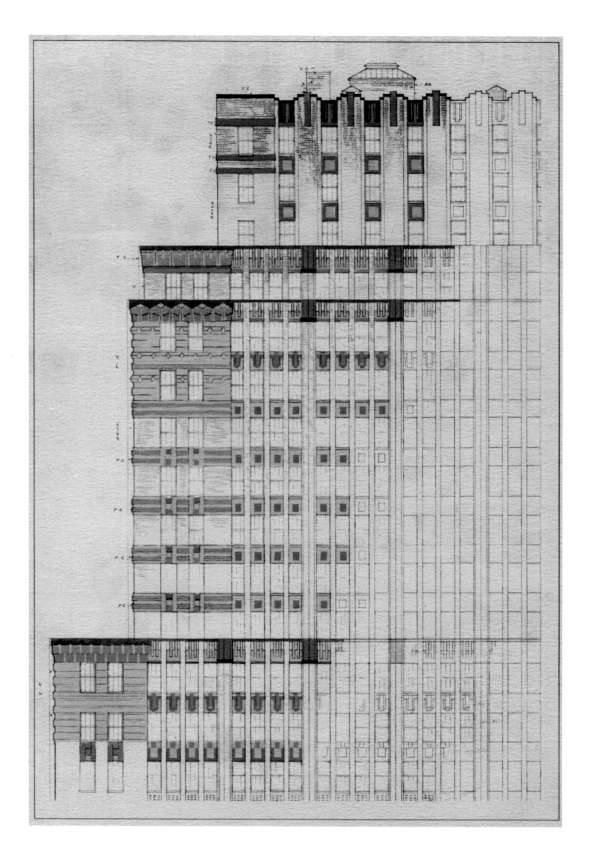

C.2 Park Avenue Building, polychrome study, 1928, B&K

C.3 Park Avenue Building,
polychrome at first setback,
1928, B&K

C.4 Park Avenue Building,
polychrome scheme, 1928,
B&K

C.5 42 West 39th Street, second to fourth story polychrome decoration, 1927, B&K

C.7 261 Fifth Avenue,
pier polychrome ornament
on entrance base, 1929,
B&K

C.6 261 Fifth Avenue,
pier polychrome ornament,
upper stories, 1929,
B&K

5

C.8 Film Center Building, lobby, 1929, B&K

C.9 530 Seventh Avenue, Building number, 1929, B&K

C.10 Ely Jacques Kahn
and William
Muschenheim, Marine
Transportation Building,
"New York World's
Fair," 1939, Arthur
Frappier rendering

ELY JACQUES KAHN, ARCHITECT
BEAUX-ARTS TO MODERNISM IN NEW YORK

JEWEL STERN AND JOHN A. STUART

Ely Jacques Kahn, 1926

W. W. NORTON & COMPANY

NEW YORK • LONDON

To Liselotte Hirschmann Myller Kahn.

Abbreviations used in captions

B&K   Buchman & Kahn
EJK   The Firm of Ely Jacques Kahn
K&J   Kahn and Jacobs

FIRST EDITION

For information about permission to reproduce selections from this book,
write to Permissions, W. W. Norton & Company, Inc., 500 Fifth Avenue,
New York, NY 10110

Composition and book design by Abigail Sturges
Manufacturing by Quebecor World Kingsport
Production Manger: Leeann Graham

Library of Congress Cataloging-in-Publication Data

Stern, Jewel, date-
   Ely Jacques Kahn, architect : beaux-arts to modernism in New York /
Jewel Stern and John A. Stuart.
      p. cm.
   Includes bibliographical references and index.

   ISBN 0-393-73114-6

   1. Kahn, Ely Jacques, 1884–1972. 2. Architects—United States—
Biography. 3. Architecture—New York (State)—New York—20th century.
I. Stuart, John A. II. Title.

NA737.K3S74 2006

720.92—dc22
2005054395
[B]

W. W. Norton & Company, Inc., 500 Fifth Avenue, New York, N.Y. 10110
www.wwnorton.com
W. W. Norton & Company Ltd., Castle House, 75/76 Wells St.,
London W1T 3QT
0 9 8 7 6 5 4 3 2 1

CONTENTS

ACKNOWLEDGMENTS

This book is the product of many years of research that began in the mid-1970s with Jewel Stern's master's thesis on Ely Jacques Kahn and culminated in a five-year writing partnership with John Stuart that evolved from their meeting at the home of Wendy Kaplan in Miami Beach, Florida, in 2000. Many individuals aided in Jewel's research, but none more than Liselotte Kahn, her late husband Ely Jacques Kahn's most ardent champion. Liselotte gave Jewel complete freedom to examine and use Kahn's private papers, and she has been a source of encouragement over the decades required to realize this book. The authors also thank Liselotte's son Rolf Myller and his wife Lois, and Kahn's children, Ely Jacques Kahn Jr. and Joan Kahn (both deceased); and Olivia Kahn.

Many who contributed significantly to early research are now deceased. They were: Adèle Maximilian, Kahn's first cousin; Jean Heyman of Brussels, a nephew of Kahn's sister Rena Rosenthal; Mrs. Robert S. (Margaret) Bookman, Kahn's sister-in-law; Aline MacMahon Stein, the wife of Kahn's close friend Clarence S. Stein; members of the Buchman & Kahn firm: Shamoon Nadir (also of Kahn and Jacobs), John Theodore Jacobsen, and Otto John Teegen; and Willis Messiah, Pierre A. "Pete" Bezy, and Lloyd Doughty, of Kahn and Jacobs; Mrs. Maurice Benjamin (Edith Bry), a Kahn client; Isabel M. Crocé, formerly of the Lord & Taylor department store; and Donald Deskey, Lewis Mumford, and Isamu Noguchi.

The recollections of the late Robert Allan Jacobs, Kahn's partner in Kahn and Jacobs, and those of Sheldon Fox and Irving Kaplan, former partners in the Kahn and Jacobs firm, provided important details of Kahn's later life and work.

Colleagues whose support has been substantial are Rosemarie Bletter, Jan Hochstim, William H. Jordy, Victoria Newhouse, Arlene Olson-Muravchick, Peter Papademtriou, Susan Tunick, and Mary Woods. Others who have contributed are Anne Boyer Cotten, Andrew Dolkart, Edgar Kaufmann Jr., Karen Davies Lucic, Eduard F. Sekler, Carol Willis, and Kees Somer of the Netherlands. In addition, Jewel thanks Daniel Cowin of United National Corporation, a former owner of 745 Fifth Avenue (formerly the Squibb Building); and Carola (Teegen) and Guy Walton for access to Otto John Teegen's papers. John thanks his former dean William G. McMinn, his current dean Juan Antonio Bueno, his program director Adam Drisin, and his colleagues at the Florida International University School of Architecture for their encouragement and unwavering support during the long process of writing the book.

At the Avery Architectural and Fine Arts Library of Columbia University, Janet Parks has been tireless in her assistance and cooperation. Thanks also to her assistant, Julie Tozer. Leonore F. Bona, a manager in the Columbia Records Division, was especially helpful. Sarah ("Sally") Wiener, director, and Jeanette Silverthorne, assistant director, of the Miriam and Ira D. Wallach Art Gallery at Columbia University are recognized with appreciation for mounting the exhibition on the work of Ely Jacques Kahn. A debt of gratitude is extended to archivists Tony P. Wrenn and Nancy Hadley, at the American Institute of Architects; Carolyn A. Davis at the George Arents Research Library of Syracuse University; Bruce Brooks Pfeiffer and Indira Berndtson at Taliesen West; Kathleen Jacklin at the John M. Olin Library of Cornell University; Elaine Massena at the White Plains City Archives; and Barbara J. Niss at Mount Sinai Hospital in New York. Others who have helped locate materials and provided invaluable assistance are Terence Riley and Mackenzie Bennet at the Museum of Modern Art; Melanie Bower at the Museum of the City of New York; Joan A. Daby, historian of the Town of Moriah; Kamal Farah at Columbia University; Julie Nicoletta at the University of Washington; Nancy Robinson at the office of I. M. Pei; Despina Stratigakos at Harvard University; and Suzanne Stevens at Architectural Record. Thanks also to David Kaplan, Judy Fox, and Norman McGrath for various forms of support and encouragement.

The authors have benefited from research at the Richter Library of the University of Miami with the help of Felipe Aragon, and Eduardo Abella, among others, and at the Steven and Dorothea Green Library at the Florida International University.

The assistance of Roberta Prevost of the Canadian Centre for Architecture and Marjorie McNinch and Richard Jones of the Hagley Museum and Library has been invaluable for the study of the Seagram Building.

Several individuals and institutions were involved in providing the photographs for this book: C. Ford Peatross at the Library of Congress; Steven Miller, Nancy Kessler-Post, Bob Shamis, and others at the Museum of the City of New York; Marilyn F. Symmes and Gail S. Davidson at the Cooper-Hewitt, National Design Museum; Nicholas Blaga, Cathy Leff, Frank Luca, and Silvia Ros at the The Wolfsonian-Florida International University; William Palin at Sir John Soane's Museum; Susan Tunick and the Friends of Terra Cotta; and photographers Jacob Getz, Peter Mauss and Lawrence Cashman of New York, and Richard Chimelis of Miami.

Those who have followed the process of realizing this book with interest are: Sal J. Fusaro, Leila Marcus, Dahlia Morgan, Barbara Pine, and Laurie Wilson. Jewel also acknowledges the support of her late husband Edward A. Stern, and of her children, Lori Schainuck and James Schainuck. She extends her deep appreciation to John Stuart for the perspective he brought to the study of Kahn's architecture and for the innumerable scans of illustrations he graciously made. In turn, John offers Jewel a heartfelt acknowledgment for suggesting a partnership, for access to her extensive research files, for her remarkable attention to detail, and for her warm hospitality during many long nights of work at her kitchen table. John also thanks Joel Hoffman for his loving support, encouragement, and companionship that continues to enrich life on all levels, personal and intellectual. Finally, the authors jointly recognize Margaret Ryan, copy editor, Abigail Sturges, book designer, and Nancy Green, their adept and patient editor at W. W. Norton, whose vision and enthusiasm made this book a reality. Research for the project was supported by a generous grant from the Graham Foundation for Advanced Studies in the Fine Arts.

INTRODUCTION

Ely Jacques Kahn (1884–1972), preeminent twentieth-century architect of commercial buildings in the United States, was one of the most prolific architects in New York City. While his career spanned nearly half a century—from his partnership in 1917 in the Buchman & Kahn firm, through the 1930s independently as The Firm of Ely Jacques Kahn, until his retirement from the Kahn and Jacobs firm in 1965—his most widely known work is associated with the 1920s building boom in New York City in which the setback skyscraper emerged as a potent symbol of modern America. This is the first major, critical study of his work, and surveys his immense output. By presenting his built work and a close reading of his texts, a portrait of Kahn emerges that highlights the complex urban social issues and business and professional practices of his day. Unlike his contemporaries, Raymond Hood and William Van Alen, Kahn's achievement does not rest on individual buildings, but on a large body of work created over a long career. Kahn's buildings have endured. Over fifty from the 1920s through the early 1960s are extant and in use in New York City.

Clusters of Kahn's buildings are located throughout the city, significantly in the garment and financial districts, on corporate Park Avenue, and in the midtown business and shopping sectors. Like 120 Wall Street at the East River, which has an iconic presence, Kahn's buildings help define the rugged skyline of New York, one of the most recognized symbols of American democracy and free enterprise today.

In this book we establish Kahn's place in the successor partnerships of the firm founded by Hermann Joseph Schwarzmann, architect-in-chief of the 1876 International Centennial Exhibition in Philadelphia. During Kahn's career, phases of which paralleled two periods of intense building activity in the city, he created two aesthetically distinct yet closely related bodies of work that we address in depth. Through our chronological approach to Kahn's oeuvre, we bring to light the record of Kahn's clients—many of whom were immigrant Jewish developers—building contractors, the team of designers in his firm, and the artists who realized his vision. In contextualizing Kahn's architectural production, we emphasize Kahn's passionate belief in a uniquely American modernism founded upon "honesty" between materials and form in all design fields.

Like most of his peers in the 1920s—a time when debates that would continue for the rest of the century were raging over the nature of modernism and the role of tradition in American architecture—Kahn's position was colored by the character of his architectural education. Kahn belonged to the last wave of Americans to attend the Ecole des Beaux-Arts at the acme of its prestige and influence in the United States. Considered progressive but not radical, he sanctioned experimentation, heralded artistic freedom, yet adhered throughout his entire career to Beaux-Arts methodology and planning. An early exponent of modern polychrome building facades, Kahn rapidly evolved an abstract, geometric decorative style that alluded to his classical training and was inspired partly by such diverse sources as the machine, exotic cultures, and the innovations of Josef Hoffmann and Frank Lloyd Wright. Kahn's building entrances and lobbies were dazzling and attracted tenants and the public alike. They are distinguished for their coordination of detailing, inventiveness of patterns, use of fine materials, and overall precision and elegance. These qualities helped maintain the commercial value of his buildings long after they opened, evidenced by the number of original Kahn lobbies that are relatively intact today.

As one of the fabled "three Napoleons" of New York (the other two were Hood and Ralph T. Walker), Kahn made rich and varied contributions to architectural culture that extend beyond his many constructed buildings and luxury retail facilities. He played a prominent role in the Metropolitan Museum of Art's groundbreaking Contemporary Industrial Arts Exhibitions of 1929, 1934, and 1940; participated in the 1933 Chicago Century of Progress Exposition and the 1939 New York World's Fair; led the Department of Architecture of the Beaux Arts Institute of Design in the early 1930s; and served as president of the Municipal Art Society during World War II.

After 1925, Kahn's work was frequently published in architectural periodicals with lavish photographic illustrations, many of which have been reproduced here for the first time. The wide exposure of Kahn's work to the public was primarily the result of glowing critical reviews. The legendary architecture critic Lewis Mumford, whose career and period of greatest influence roughly paralleled that of Kahn, was one of his greatest advocates. Mumford later wrote: "I followed his work closely & [sic] still consider him one of the major figures in the period from 1914 to 1940."[1]

One of Kahn's most important skills was his ability to adapt to the changing world of the twentieth century. Kahn was one of the very few of his successful prewar colleagues to rekindle a prolific career after World War II. Although critical acclaim for his buildings never again reached the height of the pre–World War II period, Kahn renewed his early contacts, relied upon loyal design staff, and utilized his prior experience in space planning and building technologies to create an impressive body of postwar work in partnership with Robert Allan Jacobs. For example, during this second major period of architectural production the Municipal Asphalt Plant on the East River was exhibited by the Museum of Modern Art; the firm designed the first postwar high rise in Manhattan, the Universal Pictures Building; and Kahn served as the architect of record for the Seagram Building by Mies van der Rohe. The best recorded and most well known of Kahn's postwar production, however, was a series of midtown corporate buildings on and around Park Avenue. With his training in the Beaux-Arts process of architectural design and his successful history of brick and terracotta facades, Kahn often satisfied these clients with simplified exteriors that did not fully embrace the tenets of the International Style. The trajectory of Kahn's entire body of work, however, exposes and highlights in the career of one architect the many connections that join the seemingly distant and often critically disconnected points between Beaux-Arts and modernism in New York.

CHAPTER ONE

THE SHAPING OF AN AMERICAN ARCHITECT

For more than half a century Ely Jacques Kahn practiced architecture in New York, the place of his birth on June 1, 1884, and his lifelong residence.[1] The vicissitudes of the metropolis molded his life and career, every stage of which was affected by the city's commercial development, economic cycles, stylistic taste, and growth. Kahn grew up in the period epitomized by Lewis Mumford as "the brown decades."[2] A tumultuous celebration hailed the completion of the Brooklyn Bridge in 1883, the year prior to his birth, and the cornerstone of the Statue of Liberty was laid on Bedloe's Island in New York's harbor late in 1884 when he was an infant. The city was slow to adopt electricity, and gaslight still flickered on most streets and in most interiors, but a web of telephone and telegraph wires now loomed overhead in populated districts. Other than carriages, the common conveyances were horse-cars and the older omnibuses. Trolleys would arrive before the end of the decade. By the early 1880s Madison Square at 23rd Street had supplanted Union Square at 14th Street as the focus of fashionable metropolitan life and entertainment and the hub of the city's leading hotels, restaurants, theaters, private clubs, and stores. A string of theaters dotted Broadway north of Madison Square to 42nd Street and "Ladies Mile," the deluxe shopping promenade, stretched from Madison Square south to 8th Street—below which a crazy patchwork quilt of ethnic neighborhoods coexisted with governmental, financial, and commercial enclaves. Here buildings occasionally soared to an unprecedented twelve stories! Fifth Avenue north from Madison Square to 42nd Street was solidly lined with stately brownstone mansions. Some incursions had been made in the area between 42nd Street and 59th Street, the northern boundary of the exclusive residential quarter. McKim, Mead & White's Villard Houses (1884) on Madison Avenue and 49th Street were indicative of the trend. Elevated railway lines, erected in the late 1870s, provided public transit and opened the largely uninhabited upper reaches of the city above 59th Street to the burgeoning population of more than one million. The advent of the "El," the elevated train line, led to wild real estate speculation on the Upper East Side after the economic depression of 1873–79 had run its course. At first residential development clung to the routes of the El along Second and

Third Avenues. It was here, in a brownstone rowhouse at 221 East 60th Street, that Kahn was born.

Family History

Ely Jacques Kahn, an only son, was the third and youngest child of Eugenie Maximilian Kahn (1858–1953) and Jacques Kahn (1855–1918). Kahn's birth into an enterprising, cultivated, French and Austro-German Jewish New York family that had strong European ties provided him with economic advantages and emotional support for his creative potential (fig. 1.1). Moreover, the family's way of life gave his childhood and youth a distinctive cast that shaped his developing sensibilities. Kahn's paternal grandfather, Elias Kahn (1806–58), left his home in Fellheim, Germany, as an adult and moved to his mother's birthplace in Hohenems, Austria, a Tyrolean Alpine village a few kilometers from the Rhine River border between Austria and Switzerland.[3] Better economic prospects and religious tolerance probably brought Elias Kahn to Hohenems, a market town where Jews had contributed to the community's thriving trade since 1617. Records show that Elias Kahn became a merchant, a director of the Israelite Congregation, and an imperial lottery collector. That Elias Kahn was entrusted with an imperial appointment signified considerable social standing in Hohenems. Ely Jacques Kahn's father, Jacques, was the third of Elias Kahn's five children with his younger wife, Regina Bernheimer (1825–77). Little is known of Jacques's early years, but they were undoubtedly troubled by Elias Kahn's death when the boy was only three. His mother's remarriage two years later and the arrival of three half-sisters in rapid succession further complicated his childhood. During the 1860s, while Jacques Kahn was educated in a French-language school in neighboring Switzerland,[4] mounting Italian and German nationalism shook the Austro-Hungarian Empire. The turbulence of the period induced him to leave Hohenems at age sixteen for the security and opportunity America offered. Jacques Kahn arrived in New York a year after the War of 1870, between Germany and France,

ended.[5] Of the period before his marriage to Eugenie Maximilian in 1879, virtually nothing is known, but the depressed economy in the 1870s thwarted any hope of rapid advancement.[6]

Eugenie Maximilian, a second-generation American, was born in New York. During a visit to her cousin, a *couturière* in Paris, Eugenie's mother, Rosalie Lazard of French Alsace and Luxembourg, met her father, Maximilian Kahn Maximilian, a German-born Parisian decorator.[7] Soon after their Paris wedding in 1850, Rosalie and Maximilian, Kahn's maternal grandparents, sailed for New York. They settled in a brownstone at 79 Third Avenue, a short distance west of Tompkins Square, the center of "Little Germany," and close to bustling 14th Street. Eugenie, the youngest of three children, was born here in 1858 and attended Public School Number 35 on 13th Street near Sixth Avenue when the renowned educator Thomas Hunter was its principal.

Declaring himself a *"Tapissier Français,"* Maximilian opened a shop at 73 Third Avenue, adjacent to their home. The tapissier's traditional role of making or supplying floor, window, and furniture coverings had expanded in nineteenth-century France to include the arrangement and adornment of entire rooms. Consequently, the profession exerted substantial influence in determining taste; indeed, a certain status had been attached to Maximilian's position in Paris.[8] In New York, Maximilian became a popular decorator of private and public halls for concerts, balls, and special events, and of exterior facades for parades and ceremonies. Shortly before his accidental death in 1871 at age forty-four, Maximilian had applied for a patent on a "sofa bed," one of the earliest versions of its kind.[9] Late in his life Kahn wrote that his grandfather Maximilian had been an "architect and decorator and famous in my mother's eyes because he had arranged the decorations for the reception of President Lincoln at Cooper Union in 1862 [1860]."[10]

Kahn's creative streak sprang from the Maximilian line. Within the traditional context of her generation's feminine role, Eugenie expressed her artistic talent through the design and fabrication of puppet theaters for gifts and by teaching sewing to indigent children at the Hudson Guild Settlement House.[11] Her older sister, Clementine, was a highly regarded pianist within the family and her older brother, Ferdinand, produced several patented innovations for the mirror and glass trade.[12] Ferdinand's three daughters, Kahn's first cousins, became designers. Modern table linens designed by Rosalie Maximilian Campbell, the oldest daughter, were shown in the Metropolitan Museum of Art's 1934 and 1940 "Contemporary American Industrial Art" exhibitions.[13] Adèle Maximilian designed and manufactured a custom line of children's apparel under the "Caradèle" label, and Carrie Maximilian, the youngest of the three sisters, was a millinery designer. As for Kahn ancestors, a lone reference has been found to his grandfather Elias Kahn's musical talent.[14]

Following their marriage in 1879, Eugenie and Jacques Kahn, who were reportedly cousins, lived for over ten years at 221 East 60th Street in the home of her sister Clementine and brother-in-law Ferdinand Kahn, Jacques's Parisian-born cousin who owned a flourishing artificial flower business. Within the household, smartly decorated with furniture from Paris and staffed with servants, French was spoken by family members. Kahn's long-lasting affinity with France and its culture was rooted in these formative years: "My main recollection as a child was to visit the building on 6th Avenue near 8th Street where my mother's grandmother then lived. This old lady was 96 when I knew her in my fifth year and I still [in 1962] recall the impression made on me, even after her death, of the typically French household—no windows open, odors of cooking, and everyone speaking French."[15] It was a comfortable environment into which Kahn and his two sisters, Rena (1880–1966) and Adele (1882–1963), were born and where Kahn passed his first six years.

During these years Kahn's father established himself financially. The first entry found for Jacques Kahn in the *New York City Directory* listed him as a "clerk" in 1882. Near the time of Kahn's birth in 1884, he ventured into business on his own, importing mirror and glass. Jacques Kahn's European background and fluent French

were valuable assets in the trade. His company grew rapidly and in 1889 manufacturing began in a leased seven-story building at 27 Bleecker Street in the downtown mercantile district (fig. 1.2).[16] As early as 1890 the company maintained

1.2 *Jacques Kahn Company, 27 Bleecker Street, New York, c. 1890*

offices in Brussels and Paris to expedite trade in Belgian and French mirror and glass plates, the company specialty. By 1905 Jacques Kahn employed three hundred men and conducted business from his own eight-story building at 533 West 37th Street.[17]

Jacques's prosperity made possible the purchase of a home in the new luxury residential neighborhood on the Upper East Side, and in 1890 the family moved to an understated Renaissance revival brownstone rowhouse at 50

Glück auf!

1.3 *Jacques Kahn and Ferdinand Kahn families, Salt Mine, Berchtesgaden, Bavaria, c. 1892. From left: Ely, Adele, Clara, Rena, Clementine, Jacques, Eugenie, Ferdinand*

East 83rd Street between Park and Madison Avenues, close to Central Park and the Metropolitan Museum of Art on Fifth Avenue. Initially illuminated by gaslight, modernized later with electricity, the Victorian home boasted a wine cellar for the family's dining pleasure, a parlor furnished as a Louis XV salon, an inviting upstairs room that Kahn remembers as "pleasant and unpretentious, full of books and deep sofas," and on the third floor the ubiquitous "Turkish room" of the period, where Rena and Adele entertained their friends.[18] A governess tutored the Kahn children in German; French was spoken at the dinner table, and English at other times.[19]

Jacques Kahn's business on the continent added another dimension to family life: annual travel abroad. One sightseeing expedition in Germany *en famille* was preserved in a photograph (fig. 1.3). Although only five on his first voyage to Europe, in his memoirs Kahn recalled touring the 1889 Paris Exposition Universelle,[20] which celebrated the centennial of the French Revolution and unveiled two remarkable feats of engineering, the Eiffel Tower and the Galerie des Machines. Throughout Kahn's youth the family regularly returned to Hohenems to visit relatives and friends. The family ties there were strengthened in 1901 when Rena, Kahn's elder sister, married Rudolf Rosenthal (1871–1954), scion of an old Austrian textile house whose mills were located in Hohenems and nearby Liechtenstein.[21] Rena and Rudolf's formal wedding reception, held at the fashionable Sherry's Restaurant, was emblematic of the social consciousness, sophistication, and affluence of the family at the turn of the century.[22] The continuity of European contact during childhood and adolescence molded Kahn into an urbane man whose polish was more than a veneer.

A Predisposition for Art

In contrast to Kahn's cosmopolitan experience abroad, his public school education was commonplace. Given the family's finances and worldliness, it is surprising that he was not enrolled in a private preparatory school such as Dr. Julius Sachs's School for Boys, or later in its upper-level extension, the Sachs Collegiate Institute, a rigorous institution for sons of the German-Jewish establishment seeking admission to Harvard and other elite Eastern colleges.[23] Kahn, however, was unburdened by academic pressure. His parents' expectations were shaped by different values: a high regard for creativity and mercantile pragmatism superseded a focus on academia. Kahn had demonstrated a strong predisposition for art at an early age and had considered painting as a career: "As the youngest member of the family, I was the last to choose my vocation. My elder sister, Rena, was studying painting; I was entranced by her palettes and brushes, and by the copies of famous paintings that she had made. . . . My younger sister, Adele, was an accomplished violinist; she had studied in Brussels with [Eugène] Ysaye. My own decision to study art met with no surprise or opposition . . . though my father had expected that, as the only son, I would take over his business."[24]

Kahn's identification with Rena influenced his aesthetic development. Exposed to progressive European design while living in Austria from 1901 to 1910, Rena became one of the earliest importers and dealers in modern European applied art. In the 1920s her Madison Avenue shop in New York became a beacon for American aficionados of modernism and a haven for European émigré artists and designers. Kahn's inborn attraction to the decorative arts was bolstered by Rena's example. Kahn's perspective was broadened by Rena's passion for modern applied art and her close association with its designers well before its popular acceptance in America.

After finishing public school Kahn attended City College of New York for a year before applying for admission to Columbia College. In October 1899, at age fifteen, Kahn was accepted as a special student on the condition that he compensate for his deficiency in Latin (which he did), and the next year he was elevated to full-fledged student status.[25] Kahn's undergraduate academic performance at Columbia College was unexceptional. The only high mark he earned was for the first semester of comparative literature in his jun-

ior year.[26] Although his four-year transcript did not list a single art course, Kahn later mused that most of his time at Columbia was spent drawing.[27] Another distraction from academics was extracurricular activities. "King's Crown" membership, the highest honor for nonathletic service, was awarded to Kahn for his associate editorship of *The Columbia Jester*, a semimonthly student publication. The Chess Club challenged him, too, and he also competed in the Tennis Club and Track Athletic Association.[28]

In June 1903 Kahn received a Bachelor of Art degree from Columbia College. Although "Art is the child of Nature" was the quotation he selected to accompany his senior class picture in the school yearbook, Kahn had abandoned the notion of a career in painting by the end of the term, deciding instead to study architecture.[29] Reflecting back on this period in his memoirs, Kahn revealed that architecture had been "a foreign field, for I knew no architects, had no first hand acquaintance with any phase of it beyond the memory of my mother's father who had been active as a decorator in the time that the profession had hardly been known to exist under the dignity of a profession."[30] Kahn never disclosed the reason for his shift to architecture; it may simply have been pragmatic.

Jacques Kahn expected Ely to enter the family business and eventually take it over, but he did not insist on it. The option was left open to Kahn. His father's willingness to underwrite his aspirations may be attributable to the influence of late nineteenth-century Austrian values as well as to assimilation of American values. Carl Schorske's depiction of the Austrian middle class's preoccupation with "aesthetic cultivation and personal refinement," and the relationship of this cultural obsession to assimilation, suggest a reason for Jacques Kahn's acceptance of his son's vocation: "In Austria, where higher culture was so greatly prized as a mark of status by the liberal urban class, the Jews of that class merely shared the prevalent values, holding them perhaps more intensely because the taint of trade had stained their lives more deeply. . . . Assimilation through culture as a second stage in Jewish assimilation was but a special case of the middle-class phase-ology of upward mobility from economic to intellectual vocations . . . many bourgeois intellectuals acquired aesthetic culture as a substitute for rank."[31]

Notwithstanding its hybrid roots, the Kahn family exhibited the high standards and capacity for assimilation associated with New York's German-Jewish community. The family's liberalization dated from the 1840s when Eugenie's mother, Rosalie Lazard, was exposed to the teaching of Luxembourg's chief rabbi, Samuel Hirsch, a pioneer of the German reform movement.[32] In 1855, when Jacques Kahn was born, the Hohenems Jewish community was also "German reform."[33] To what extent Kahn's parents practiced Judaism during his youth is unknown. The evolution of given names of Kahn males, however, charts the trend toward assimilation. By the turn of the century, Jacques had shed his given name, "Jacob," entered on his 1879 marriage certificate, Ely's birth certificate, and the 1890 census. Rena and Rudolf's 1901 marriage certificate named the father "Jacques." Ely's given name on his birth certificate was "Eli," after grandfather Elias Kahn. In 1899 he registered at Columbia College as "Ely J. Kahn." Four years later the transformation to "Ely Jacques Kahn" was recorded on his Columbia University School of Architecture transcript.[34] Kahn was mute on his religious background, but the overall impression from his life and writing is that religion and the observance of ritual were not an issue, the parental position having been more or less laissez-faire.[35] Kahn never drew attention to his Jewish ethnicity. Neither did he deny it or attempt to "pass" as a gentile. One can conclude from his accomplishments that he objected to a classification that would narrow his self-perception and limit his possibilities.

Columbia School of Architecture

In September 1903, after a summer holiday in Europe, Kahn, boyish at nineteen, entered Columbia University School of Architecture (fig. 1.4). The school was in crisis over the forced retirement the previous June of Professor William Robert Ware (1832–1915), its organiz-

er and guiding light since 1881. Ware's removal culminated a protracted struggle between him and the influential architect Charles Follen McKim (1847–1909) over the role of design, technical mastery, and professional preparation in the curriculum. Kahn's years at the Columbia School of Architecture, from 1903 to 1907, spanned the transition from Ware's culturally oriented, noncompetitive regime that stressed the historic styles and their delineation to the modified Beaux-Arts system inaugurated for the 1905–6 school year. Given the role of Beaux-Arts planning in Kahn's work and the strength of his commitment to Beaux-Arts values, the background of his introduction to its theory and methods at Columbia and the influence of his teachers are critical factors to understanding Kahn and evaluating his place in American architecture. Kahn described Ware's legacy in his memoirs: "We had instruction in drawing and delved into some technical subjects, but mostly we spent our time in a thorough study of history—as much of it as we could absorb. Greek, Roman, Gothic, and Renaissance forms were drilled into us because it was likely that when we graduated we would be required to know any or all of these styles. We were provided with a smattering of information on a large number of subjects which, it was felt, would mature and develop under the direction of the master architects for whom we would be working."[36] Students were not informed, however, of the work being accomplished by progressives in Chicago and the Midwest. The structural experiments of Midwestern architects were outside of the Columbia context: "We were aware of the work of Louis Sullivan and Frank Lloyd Wright and of their point of view regarding architecture, which was, of course, completely different from that which we were taught. The obviously placid and traditional attitude with which we were inculcated made it very difficult for us to fully appreciate what these two men from the west advocated."[37]

Kahn found his metier in the Columbia School of Architecture and finally measured up to his potential. He applied himself vigorously to first-year work[38] and before long, he became impatient to learn about the operation of a real architectur-

1.4 Ely Jacques Kahn, Adele Kahn, Rudolf and Rena Rosenthal, Zurich, 1903

al office: "While I was at Columbia in 1904, in my second year, I had the urge to see what an architect's office did look like. One firm then, a very busy one, Clinton and Russell, had sent out word that a job was open. They were preparing plans for two large buildings on Vesey Street, the terminal of the Hudson and Manhattan Railroad. The drawings were large, needed juniors to fill in the details, and—if I recall correctly—[we] were paid fifty cents an hour."[39] The Columbia School of Architecture's reorganization, implemented in Kahn's third year, 1905–6, gave design prominence in the curriculum and brought the school more in line with the atelier system and methods of the Ecole des Beaux-Arts in Paris. The method of study at the Ecole had several distinctive features. Design was taught in ateliers directed by practicing architects. In exchange for their guidance, the new students helped the older, more experienced members with their drawings. Advancement was determined by accomplishment in the competitions, not by years of enrollment or by course work. The design section at Columbia was entirely revamped and coordinated into ateliers that were taught by actively practicing Beaux-Arts-trained architects. It was hoped that the teacher's example, rigorous methodology, and competition would sharpen student work and foster closer relations between the school and the profession. Several distinguished architects were enlisted to direct the new ateliers. The significance of a student's choice of master in the minds of professionals and educators was passionately noted in a report (endorsing the modified French atelier system) to the 1907 convention of the American Institute of Architects: "We are of the opinion that this passion for beauty and this instinctive good taste may be inculcated if at all not through methods of scientific pedagogy, but by the close personal relations and the keen enthusiasm that arises through the association of a group of students with a practicing architect chosen by the free will of the student because of his admiration for and sympathy with his principles, his personality and his achievements."[40]

For the school year 1905–6, in addition to the existing campus studio headed by faculty members William A. Delano (1871–1940) and Alfred Gumaer (dates unknown), two additional official ateliers, each led by a design partner of the preeminent architectural firms in the northeastern United States—McKim of McKim, Mead & White and Thomas Hastings (1860–1929) of Carrère & Hastings—were maintained downtown (close to the administering architects' offices), with the assistance of John Russell Pope (1874–1937) and John Vredenburgh Van Pelt (1874–1963), respectively. The ideas of McKim and Hastings were similar in outline but differently shaded.[41] In selecting an atelier these differences would have been considered by Kahn and other students.[42] The desire to rescue American architecture from the stylistic confusion, indiscriminate copying, and idiosyncratic designs generally characteristic of the post–Civil War period had united McKim and Hastings in the 1880s and 1890s.[43] Their mission became the reinstatement of discipline, order, and unity in the practice of American architecture and the raising of its standards to a uniformly high level. McKim, the older of the two men, studied at the Ecole des Beaux-Arts in the late 1860s and recognized the benefits of the Ecole's system and academicism. Nevertheless, McKim was critical of the modern direction taken by the Ecole and French architecture, which he viewed as a watered-down classicism.[44] More suited to McKim's taste and ideals were the order, dignity, restraint, and sober beauty inherent in the monumental neoclassicism of the Italian Renaissance. In the mid-1880s, the McKim, Mead & White firm initiated the Renaissance revival in American architecture, which they popularized by their example in the 1890s and at the turn of the century.

Hastings, almost a generation younger than McKim, came of age during the intellectual and artistic awakening of the 1880s, a time when greater numbers of aspiring American architects sailed off to Paris. He and others returned home determined to bring the sophisticated French system to native institutions and to enlighten public taste to its standards.[45] Hastings was unequivocally committed to the Ecole and its educational system. The consistent practice of making the plan the pillar upon which his designs were built became a hallmark of Hastings's work. Differing stylistic and methodological priorities set the architects and their firms apart; the Columbia ateliers of Hastings and McKim reflected the contrasts.

Kahn left no record—not even a clue—to identify his Columbia atelier(s), nor was this information preserved on his transcript or in the school's yearbooks. One obscure document, noting all students' ateliers, has survived: "Classbook

1905–1906." Under "Design, Intermediate II, A.21.3," for 1905–6, an abbreviation of "Hastings" appears next to Kahn's name on the class roll. Kahn entered the Hastings downtown atelier as an intermediate design student in the fall of 1905.[46] Although Kahn's background and familiarity with Paris from childhood predisposed him to alignment with Hastings rather than McKim, another factor was relevant. Hastings was more progressive than McKim. His evolutionary theory of architecture implied progress, however slow; and Hastings accepted the modern French Beaux-Arts architecture that McKim rejected.[47] McKim may have been too restrained and archaeological, even too idealistic, to satisfy Kahn's rich sensibility and pragmatism. Comparatively, the Hastings atelier would have offered Kahn more latitude and play and a greater sense of modernity than the McKim atelier.

The small enrollment of the intermediate design class—Kahn and six others—and the absence of older, experienced students in the atelier's first year would have encouraged the development of a close working relationship with both design teachers.[48] The reliance on Van Pelt, the younger associate charged with the daily work, was greater than on Hastings, who was expected in the atelier only "three or four times a week for personal desk-to-desk criticism."[49] The extent of Hastings's role in the atelier is undocumented, but two posthumously published essays of lectures delivered to architectural students strongly suggest that he was more than a figurehead.[50] The positive results of the design section's reorganization into ateliers were reported early on with satisfaction by A. D. F. Hamlin, Ware's successor: "In all this work, pupil and teacher get close together. The teacher's personality counts; his enthusiasm kindles that of his students; they, on their part, feel that they are learning from one who is no mere pedagogue, but a man who has done and is doing 'real architecture.'"[51]

Hastings's teaching of composition benefited from the lucidity of his analytical mind. The method he employed relied on reason and logic and was underscored by his strict observance of Beaux-Arts principles of architectural composition.[52] The plan was the focus of composition and the generator of architecture. First the problem was analyzed and reduced to its simplest form from the utilitarian aspect. Only after a thorough study of the practical requirements of the building's program, especially circulation (the "first principle" of Jules André, Hastings's Beaux-Arts *patron*), was the floor plan determined.[53] Hastings was known for successfully meeting the practical needs of clients without sacrificing his own interest in design or eschewing aesthetics—a quality that would later be attributed to Kahn. Hastings's methodology contributed to the development of Kahn's strength in practical planning and proved to be the most beneficial and enduring legacy of the Hastings atelier. The potentially stultifying effect of academicism on Kahn was mitigated by Hastings's approval of controlled personal expression and his conviction that the architect should represent his own time. Kahn continued in the atelier for a second semester of advanced design; he was the only student during this period to take two or more consecutive classes with Hastings.[54] An early identification with Hastings was established during these formative years at Columbia and would resonate in Kahn's mature architectural writing. A comparison of excerpts from two essays, the first by Hastings in 1894, and the second by Kahn in 1930, are illustrative:

> We must demand, while holding to precedents and traditions as much as possible, perfect freedom in composition, and above all avoid copying or adapting entire motifs or parts of other buildings we have seen, to these new conditions. We must compose, and not copy. . . . New conditions have always demanded of contemporaneous architects, a modern architecture expressive of the times, and every honest solution of this new and difficult problem should be allowed to have its proper and natural influence upon our architecture.[55]

> Nothing is modern other than it represents its own time . . . let the individual realize that: the day when originals were made men were designing not copying. Problems were solved. . . . In copying there is complete failure, whether it be imitation of our ancestors or modern Europe. . . . The theory of the modern designer consists very

simply in the answering of a problem . . . the result should be no more than an honest solution.[56]

In architectural practice Kahn would maintain a balance between respect for time-honored principles and the respect for the inner necessity of creative expression appropriate to his time. Was Hastings a role model for Kahn? In drafts of his unpublished memoirs, Kahn named Hastings three times, each reference saluting Hastings's accomplishments. Although no mention of Hastings in this context has been found in Kahn's published papers, Kahn's neglect of Hastings in later years does not preclude the master's influence on him.[57] Given that there was no other architectural figure in Kahn's experience to set an example prior to his enrollment in the Columbia School of Architecture, Hastings was probably Kahn's earliest, if unacknowledged, role model.

The design teacher with whom Kahn seems to have had a personal rapport was Hastings's younger assistant, John Vredenburgh Van Pelt, who had a strong fine arts background and believed that some degree of painting and sculpture was essential to understanding the application of architectural ornament.[58] Like Kahn, Van Pelt had shown an early predilection for painting. He attended the Ecole des Arts Décoratifs in Paris before turning to architecture, and he continued to paint during and after his matriculation at the Ecole des Beaux-Arts, where he earned a *diplôme* in 1895.[59] At the Cornell University College of Architecture Van Pelt managed the school's radical shift to the Beaux-Arts system and wrote *A Discussion of Composition Especially as Applied to Architecture,* based on his lectures.[60] One of the earliest of its kind in English, Van Pelt's textbook became an important guide for architectural students. From a reading of *A Discussion of Composition,* it is clear that Van Pelt and Hastings were perfectly matched. The exercise of reason was as crucial to Van Pelt as it was to Hastings. Van Pelt introduced Kahn to the foremost synthesizer of academic doctrine in the period, Julien Guadet (1834–1907), professor of architectural theory at the Ecole des Beaux-Arts, whose monumental four-volume work, *Eléments et théorie de l'architecture* (1901–4), reigned for years as the Beaux-Arts student's "bible."[61] Guadet skirted the issue of eclecticism and avoided a purely stylistic evaluation of any historical period by isolating an underlying body of unchanging organizational laws, or principles, a formal "common denominator" of good architecture in all ages.[62] Guadet's theory set the tone as Van Pelt expounded on time-honored principles in the atelier. Unlike many Columbia students who tried two or more ateliers, Kahn continued with Hastings and Van Pelt.[63] He was content with his mentors' French bias, the disciplined atmosphere ruled by reason, and Van Pelt's tempering aesthetic empathy.

The other important professor during Kahn's years at Columbia was A. D. F. Hamlin (1855–1926), Ware's assistant and his successor as executive head of the school from 1903 to 1912.[64] Hamlin's scholarship was well recognized from the publication of *A Text-Book of the History of Architecture* in 1896.[65] Outside of the atelier, Kahn was enrolled in at least eight courses taught by Hamlin. Kahn never referred to Hamlin in his architectural writing, but in his memoirs he indirectly acknowledged Hamlin's influence: "What did impress me [at Columbia] was the course in history where we were urged to look at masterpieces and draw constantly. I feel that the time I spent on producing so many drawings marked the beginning of a love of art in some form that has persisted throughout a long life."[66] Although Kahn received the highest mark in the 1905–6 modern ornament class (Hamlin's courses on architectural ornament, his specialty, became the basis of a later two-volume work), in an interview near the end of his life, Kahn depicted Hamlin as an "uninteresting person who had no imagination, no spark whatsoever," and who "meant nothing at all" to him.[67] An exception was Hamlin's recognition of the progressive Austrian architect and educator Otto Wagner (1841–1918), whose work he viewed as informed with a "striking originality and an exuberant imagination, held in bounds by a cultivated taste and the discipline of a thorough training in construction."[68] Hamlin's high regard for Wagner would have been transmitted to Kahn in the

modern architectural history and modern ornament classes. He probably discussed the work of Wagner's students, Joseph Maria Olbrich and Josef Hoffmann, who exhibited at the 1904 Louisiana Purchase International Exposition held in St. Louis, Missouri, where Hamlin addressed the Congress of Arts and Science in a speech titled "The Problems of Modern Architecture."[69] Hamlin's classes were doubtless Kahn's only exposure at Columbia to Austrian progressives, because they were outside Hastings and Van Pelt's orbit of interest.

After achieving the required points in advanced design, Columbia students undertook a thesis—a demanding design problem with an accompanying written explanation and structural computations.[70] The subject of Kahn's thesis was "The Improvement of Columbus Circle," for which he proposed an expansion of the site into what appears to have been a cultural complex composed of an opera house, a school of fine arts, and galleries (figs. 1.5 and 1.6). His design embodied City Beautiful concepts and reflected the current popular taste for monumental civic architecture in the Beaux-Arts tradition.[71] The catalyst of the Columbus Circle idea may have been Columbia's 1905 McKim Travelling Fellowship Competition for the proposed Brooklyn Public Library on a site facing a large ovoid plaza at the entrance to Prospect Park. The competition drawings were exhibited at Columbia, and Lucien E. Smith's winning plan was illustrated in the periodical *Architecture*.[72] By working with an actual site rather than the imaginary one that was typical of Beaux-Arts programs, Kahn revealed a willingness to wrestle with real problems instead of fantasies of paper architecture. By virtue of the site's location in New York, Kahn established an early identification with the city and a sense of civic concern. He may also have realized that this project would flatter and impress Hastings, a known City Beautiful acolyte, as were McKim and Hamlin.

Kahn's thesis demonstrated his adherence to and mastery of Beaux-Arts academic principles of composition and design. In plan, a biaxial symmetrical hierarchic ensemble of seven buildings defined the circle. The ensemble's centerpiece, an

1.5 *Ely Jacques Kahn,*
"Improvement of
Columbus Circle,"
General Plan, Columbia
University School of
Architecture thesis, 1907

1.6 *Ely Jacques Kahn,*
"Improvement of
Columbus Circle,"
partial perspective

1.7 *Charles Garnier,*
Nouvel Opéra, Paris,
1861–75

opera house, terminated the main axis, a boulevard connecting Columbus Circle with Central Park. The opera's climactic placement at the top of the plan accorded with Beaux-Arts composition, in which the most important element was reached at the end of the processional axis. Kahn's obvious model was Charles Garnier's Nouvel Opéra in Paris (1861–75), doubtless motivated by Hastings's outspoken admiration of the building (fig. 1.7). Kahn also quoted the rounded corner pavilions and horizontal layering of facades in the Carrère & Hastings New Theatre (1906). The stylistic unity, clarity, harmonious scaling of parts within the whole, uniform cornice line, and elegant neoclassic urbanity of Kahn's thesis design paid homage to the City Beautiful movement and the Beaux-Arts principles upheld by Hastings and Van Pelt.

Outside of classes and the atelier, Kahn's activities were less varied than at Columbia College. His involvement with the editorial staff of *The*

Columbia Jester continued; in addition, he held an editorial post on *The Morningside*, a literary monthly.[73] Kahn's professional service and leadership began in his third year as treasurer of the Architectural Society.[74] Near the conclusion of his studies, for a short time before going to Paris, Kahn worked as a draftsman in the Schickel & Ditmars office, a conservative firm led by the German-born and trained design partner, William Schickel (1850–1907), and widely known for its design of Catholic churches.[75] Schickel, a Catholic who had many "wealthy Hebrew" clients, was a next-door neighbor of the Kahn family at 52 East 83rd Street; he made it possible for Kahn to gain some practical experience.[76] Shortly after Kahn left for Paris, Schickel died, and any prospect for the future Kahn may have envisioned faded. Even if Schickel had lived, Kahn, after his sojourn at the French school, would have found Schickel's rigidity stifling and his outspoken contempt of the Beaux-Arts intolerable.[77]

The Columbia School of Architecture's reorganization replaced class divisions based on a strict four-year schedule with advancement dependent upon satisfaction of requirements. Although four to five years was regarded as average, it was possible for a talented, industrious student to complete the program in three to three and a half years.[78] Kahn seized this opportunity. Eager to prepare for the entrance examinations to the Ecole des Beaux-Arts, Kahn bypassed the class of 1907's graduation exercises and departed for Europe early in 1907. In his memoirs, he was unenthusiastic about his training at Columbia. He gave the program credit for little more than his mastery of the historic styles and his acquisition of skill in delineation, and he cited the school's failure to bring students in contact with construction, complaining that the practice of architecture was still a "mystery" when he left Columbia.[79] This omission was largely true, but in retrospect Kahn failed to recognize the roots of his preparation for the rigors of the Ecole and his strength in planning. Although he would call for the rejection of historicism and the freedom to experiment, Kahn's core values remained the traditional, time-honored principles of design firmly implanted at Columbia by Hastings, Van Pelt, and Hamlin and fortified at the Ecole. In his 1929 essay "The Architect and the Industrial Arts," Kahn would eloquently integrate these values into a modern context: "The constant cry of the modern is for freedom of expression, independence of thought, emancipation from the fetters of the past. It is obvious that intelligent artists can no more discard the strong truths of their traditional education than they could willfully destroy the works of the great masters. It is conceivable, however, that starting from the problem and working towards a solution with little artificial aid from either European novelties or traditional recollection, the artist may approach fresh results with the confidence that he has at least been honest to his work and himself."[80]

CHAPTER TWO

ECOLE DES BEAUX-ARTS

Paris, 1907–11

For an ambitious American architectural graduate at the turn of the twentieth century, particularly one from the Northeast, further study at the Ecole des Beaux-Arts under a French master, supplemented with travel to historic European monuments, was *de rigueur.* Sermonizing on its attributes in 1901, Thomas Hastings declared that the Beaux-Arts should be the architectural student's "Mecca."[1] No wonder at the pressure on Kahn and his peers to attend the French school: "When we, as young architects, thought of our future, it was automatic, that no matter what the problems, financial or otherwise, Paris was our goal and study at the Ecole des Beaux-Arts practically required."[2]

Hastings, Van Pelt, and Kahn represented three waves of American attendance at the Ecole between the founding of the French Third Republic in 1871 and the outbreak of World War I in 1914, the period in which the school attained its greatest eminence. During the 1870s and 1880s, about thirty Americans sailed for Paris each decade, as Hastings did in 1880, and undertook the arduous preparation for the semiannual entrance examinations. Once accepted, they remained only long enough to learn the school's

principles and master its method—usually a year or two in an atelier. There was no incentive yet among Frenchmen or Americans to earn a *diplôme*, the recently instituted equivalent of a degree. The prestige accorded the *diplôme* in 1887 by the French government's award of one to each living Grand Prix de Rome winner gradually altered the attitude of French and American students toward the investment of four to six years or more for its achievement.[3] As American enrollment burgeoned five-fold in the 1890s, prompting architectural critic Montgomery Schuyler to remark that Americans were no longer returning from the Ecole as "single spies" but in "battalions [*sic*]," some diligent students earned the degree.[4] In 1895 the first three Americans were granted *diplômes*; Van Pelt, admitted in 1890, was one of them.[5] By the first decade of the twentieth century, the fulfillment of the program leading to the *diplôme* was a common objective.

The exact date of Kahn's departure from New York is unknown, but in his memoirs he recalled that "the damp cold of winter was a bit hard to take" when he arrived in Paris early in 1907 and found temporary lodgings at 22 rue Jacob near the Ecole.[6] He soon joined the company of coun-

31

*2.2 Ely Jacques Kahn,
identification card
(Carte d'Elève), Ecole
des Beaux-Arts, Paris,
1908*

trymen in the hotel nearby at 50 rue Jacob, where he collected autographs of friendly visitors on the backs of his sketches. Signatures from 1907 confirm his relationships with Columbia men William F. Lamb, MacDonald Mayer, and Alexander D. Seymour.[7]

Kahn immediately began preparing for the entrance examination. Although he was conversant in French, improved comprehension was a priority. The examination was largely oral, and a departure from French would eliminate the candidate. Simultaneously, Kahn arranged for tutoring in the *atelier préparatoire* of Eugéne Chifflot, who catered mainly to Americans. Competition for the fifteen places allotted to foreigners semiannually was fierce. Consequently, Kahn and his compatriots applied themselves unsparingly: "We Americans, probably because we could afford to tutor and knew there was no fooling permitted, if we wanted seriously to get by, went at the examinations as though our lives depended on them."[8] With the traditional letter of introduction from the American Ambassador in Paris to the Ecole, Kahn was formally registered as an *aspirant*, a candidate for admission to the school.[9] Crucial to passing the examinations was the quick formulation of a *parti* (viable solution) to the design problem outlined in the program and the effective rendering of its presentation in the time allotted. After taking the June 1907 entrance examination for practice, Kahn successfully passed in December, demonstrating his virtuosity by responding clearly and correctly to Guadet's qualifying program (fig. 2.1).[10] An unidentified and undated newspaper clipping saved by Kahn reads: "Ely Jacques Kahn admitted to L'Ecole des Beaux-Arts [on January 6, 1908] standing 3rd among the 600 competitors, most of whom were Frenchmen" (fig. 2.2).[11] The relief and elation after so much effort and uncertainty were vividly described by Kahn's closest friend at the Ecole, Clarence S. Stein (1883–1975), a New Yorker and fellow student at Columbia who preceded him to Paris by two years and whose name would be made in urban and regional planning: "But yesterday it was over. The results of the examination were posted. Happiness reigned. . . . But after dinner was the

real celebration. It is the custom at the Près [restaurant Près aux Clercs] for the successful candidates for the School to set up the drinks. Of course nothing else than champagne would suffice for such an event—Ely Kahn and I, who were the only ones of the Près bunch [American *aspirants*] to 'make it' lived up to the best prestige. Everyone drank to their heart's content."[12]

Kahn's relationship with Stein flourished at the Ecole. Enthusiasm and mutual interests engaged them in cultural, social, and academic activities. They heard Beethoven's Fifth and Ninth Symphonies at the Concert Colonne; saw the Ballet Russes at the Théâtre du Châtelet; attended dramatic plays, an occasional "cinematograph show," and a salon at the Grand Palais. They celebrated holidays such as Thanksgiving and New Year's Eve, dined all over Paris, and hosted a farewell dinner for Stein's roommate, Henry Klaber (1883–1971), at Foyet, a well-known Latin Quarter establishment. They enjoyed escapes from academic routine on a carriage ride through the Bois de Bologne, a boat ride to Sevres, and a weekend excursion to Versailles.[13] Kahn and Stein shared many adventures, often traveling together and sketching. The later divergence of their careers strained at times but never severed the close personal bond that had been forged in the Beaux-Arts years.

The Atelier Redon

Students (*élèves*) of the Ecole learned design in ateliers headed by architects who were almost always Grand Prix de Rome winners. Kahn entered the atelier Redon, celebrated for its success in decorative work and the high ranking its members maintained in competitions. Kahn knew of Redon's reputation as a painter and master of exterior and interior architectural decoration, and chose Redon for that reason.[14] The atelier Redon at 15 rue de L'Abbé Grégoire, a brisk walk from the Ecole, was situated above a furniture factory on the second floor of a dingy building. The drafting room was bare except for work tables, and the only source of illumination on dark days was oil lamps that hung from the ceiling and dripped on drawings at inopportune moments.[15] Despite the absence of amenities, the atelier was the center of the *élèves'* world. The atelier Redon fostered comradeship among its fifty members and a keen sense of competition with other ateliers. The more prizes garnered, the greater the prestige of the atelier and *patron*. The esprit de corps was intense. Kahn and other new students (*nouveaux*) initially received little or no attention from Redon and were dependent on the older students (*anciens*) for direction. Although this format was common in all ateliers, Gaston Fernand Redon (1853–1921), the brother of the painter Odilon Redon, was especially remote from Americans. Kahn remembered that it took a few years before Redon recognized an American student or showed any interest in his work. If you were an American, you had to prove yourself: "And the average American meant nothing to him [Redon] whatsoever. In other words, if you weren't serious about trying to do your work in Paris, not in sort of a hit-and-miss fashion, but really do it seriously, if you were interested in the *diplôme*, for example, or really stayed there for many years, then he would begin to take the trouble to want to know who you were. But I don't think he ever looked at me for the first two or three years. . . . I'm sure that quite a few Americans who came to our atelier went out without ever having met him."[16]

Kahn remembered Redon as a tall, frail, dignified yet autocratic gentleman who visited the atelier irregularly and seldom with prior notice. Whenever he arrived, a hush would fall over the studio and students would follow him around, listening attentively to his critiques, which were reserved for major projects and competitions.[17] The key to engaging Redon in conversation was music, for he relished such discussions. His method of analyzing architecture and decoration reflected his musical bent: "The 'patron' criticized frequently in terms of his favorite musicians, and we learned more by his referring to the masters for inspirations than by any inconsequential word as to detail."[18] In his mature writing, Kahn adopted Redon's metaphor of music to explain modern decorative design: "In the new mood the designer essays to introduce in his work precisely that quality of interest that the musi-

cian understands by rhythm, accent or colour."[19] Another aspect of Redon's teaching recounted by Kahn was stylistic freedom: "Our own patron, Redon, and the strong men of our atelier who today [1955] are the key men of France—Expert and Laprade, understood their background thoroughly but never for a moment gave the slightest intimation that a particular style was necessary or that classical examples had to be copied. . . . You could be as classical or modern as your whimsey [*sic*] dictated, always remembering that your work stood next to many others and the juries were coldly impersonal."[20] Redon rejected overblown decoration and was considered an exponent of understated elegance, "*la petite saveur.*"[21] Neither Redon's penchant for decoration nor his stylistic independence, however, prevented him from teaching the importance of planning. Kahn emphasized this point in his memoirs: "What impressed me particularly [in the atelier Redon] was the constant search for solutions to problems by planning rather than by searching for decorative design features. Far more time was spent on plan studies in the competitive designs than on pretty pictures. Despite charges that Beaux-Arts design involved surplus decoration of small value I did not find this to be true."[22] Kahn never regretted choosing the atelier Redon. Neither did his esteem for Redon wane: "With Redon it was always something a little more sparkling, a little more interesting, a little more dramatic. Of course he brought this atmosphere into the atelier. Well, you felt it anyway; you felt that here was a man with artistic interests."[23] Interestingly, Hastings, Redon, and Deglane (Van Pelt's *patron*) had been members of the atelier André around 1880 where intuitive, hence more personally creative design, was accepted.[24]

Although Kahn's life in Paris revolved around the atelier, his gregarious nature prevented him from becoming one-dimensional. While living at 50 rue Jacob and preparing for the entrance examination, Kahn had befriended two young men, outside of his Columbia coterie, who became his roommates: William E. Groben and William "O. K." Shepard. The threesome declared themselves "*Les trois camrades {sic} de Rue*

Jacob" on the back of a Kahn sketch of Chartres Cathedral on June 8, 1907.[25] Kahn's association with Groben (1883–1961), a Philadelphian admitted to the Ecole in January 1906 and an *élève* of Chifflot, was brief. Groben was back home late in 1907 or early 1908 without having completed the program. Less is known of Shepard, who was named Kahn's roommate by Clarence Stein in a letter to his parents on September 20, 1907. Shepard was not accepted into the Ecole, and he returned home.[26] At the end of 1907, Kahn moved out of 50 rue Jacob and into permanent lodgings on the seventh floor of an eighteenth-century stone building at 7 rue Corneille opposite the Odeon Theatre and near the Luxembourg Gardens.[27] The apartment, which Kahn shared, at a cost of $100 a year, with Walter Henry Cassebeer (1884–1963), a member of his atelier, and another American (probably Shepard initially), consisted of a large all-purpose living room and three tiny bedrooms—no bathroom or heating (fig. 2.3). A small gas stove was used mainly for morning coffee. Afternoon tea was often a means of socializing and entertaining.

When in Paris, relatives and friends from the United States were invited to tea, the young ladies accompanied by their mothers. Stein described one occasion: "A week ago Ely gave a tea in his new apartment. He is very nicely situated, way up towards the heavens in a house near the Odeon. His roommate is a Rochesterian and a former Columbia man."[28] Like Kahn, Cassebeer was of German descent, and read and spoke German fluently, but he was not Jewish (fig. 2.4).[29] Kahn lived well, if modestly, on his annual allowance of $1,000. He had more funds available than others—Clarence Stein, for one—but less than some privileged Americans.[30] In his memoirs Kahn revealed his distance from the latter: "Among the Americans . . . there were a number from wealthy families who managed to pass the tests. They could afford to live as they might at home and enjoy fine apartments and servants. They looked down the nose at the many fellow students who lived on precarious budgets and on the French boys, some of whom were rather rough. They doubtless felt socially superior to these types. As I look back on those years it

2.4 *Ely Jacques Kahn,
Walter H. Cassebeer
and Clarence S. Stein,
Paris, c. 1908*

is interesting to note that few of this type ever came to light as professional architects."[31]

The "Prés," or *Prés aux Clercs*, the cafe near the Ecole mentioned in Stein's letter to his parents, had been a meeting place for Americans many years prior to Kahn's arrival. Kahn recalled: "American students had a long table that was ours and ours alone. For two francs twenty (the franc was worth 20 cents then), one dined splendidly, with wine ad lib. The hors d'oeuvres, fresh vegetables, the confiture with thick cream, were standbys. After dinner, green almonds and glasses of brandy started endless discussions that dealt mercilessly with individuals, politics or our own work."[32] Kahn's acquaintance with Lee Simonson (1888–1967), who became a leading stage set designer, founder of the Theatre Guild after World War I, editor of *Creative Art*, and an author and critic, added spice to his social life. Simonson arrived in Paris in September 1908 after graduating with honors from Harvard University. He entered Kahn's Parisian circle through Clarence Stein, whom he knew from their affiliation with the New York Society for Ethical Culture. Simonson originally planned to be a mural painter, but "with my passion for galaxies of brilliant color, I realized that any hope of becoming a mural decorator when I returned to the United States was a forlorn one. The American architects, busily turning the Baths of Caracalla into museums and railway terminals and perversions of Greek and Roman temple fronts into libraries and banks, needed decorations that gibed with their inflated classicism. Nothing could be in key with their interiors but the iconography of the Renaissance, seemingly dusted with talcum powder by way of remaining decoratively flat. Like Gauguin, I might cry for walls, but I would not be given them."[33]

Simonson's independence of the "establishment" was accepted by Stein and Kahn, who found their flamboyant friend fascinating. It was probably Simonson, a habitué of the Stein avant-garde Saturday evening salon, who introduced Kahn to Gertrude Stein and her brother Leo.[34] On his first visit to their home at 27 rue Fleurus,

Kahn and his companions were puzzled by the art works of Matisse, Picasso, and other cubists. A harmless remark from Kahn to his hostess prompted Gertrude Stein to assail the Beaux-Arts system she so detested: "I recall that I complimented Miss Stein on a superb gold chain fashioned beautifully from ancient fragments. I was entranced with the skill of the goldsmith and the beauty of the ensemble. This was her cue for sailing into us as young old fogies who assembled bits of ancient architecture just as her craftsman had put her chain together. I didn't like the jolt at the time but had the sense enough to realize that she had put her finger on a rather sensitive spot. American architecture at that precise moment and later, unfortunately, was still rummaging about the attic for satisfactory remnants that could carry on, desperately and in a losing fight, a false tradition of the Renaissance that was as foreign to us, actually, as Chinese ornament."[35]

Kahn's years in Paris corresponded with the advent of cubism, the movement ushered in by Picasso's 1907 painting "Les Demoiselles d'Avignon." The next year Tahitian images from Gauguin's retrospective painting exhibition sparked impassioned discussions of esoteric cultures—perhaps the catalyst of Kahn's intrigue with Moorish decoration. Meeting Gertrude Stein, examining the Stein art collection, and studying Leo Stein's analytical aesthetics and philosophy deepened Kahn's Parisian experience. So did the European debut of the Ballet Russes at the Théâtre du Châtelet, which took Paris by storm in the spring of 1909 and impressed Kahn indelibly: "This was a brilliant and startling thing, entirely different and completely devastating. The setting of Leon Bakst, the dancing of Nijinski, the vastly different conception of a ballet presented as a work of art in superb color, music and moving plastic form, swept the Quarter. The Quarter saw them when . . . the shock of new beauty could be compared with the grey platitudes of the Place del'Opéra."[36] Clearly, the cultural ferment of the Paris art world stimulated Kahn and enriched his sojourn at the Ecole.[37]

In architectural terms, the structural clarity of reinforced concrete used by Auguste Perret (1874–1954) in the Théâtre des Champs-Elysées of 1911–12 made it the most progressive Parisian building erected in Kahn's Beaux-Arts years. Perret, originally engaged as the building contractor, swiftly wrested the 1910 commission away from the esteemed Belgian architect Henry van de Velde (1863–1957) by claiming that the latter's design was uneconomical and structurally unsound.[38] This turn of events early in 1911 caused a flurry in architectural circles. Unlike the young Le Corbusier (1887–1965), who worked part-time for Perret in Paris from midsummer 1908 through late 1909, Kahn was not responsive to Eugène-Emmanuel Viollet-le-Duc's (1814–79) structural rationalism, nor did he demonstrate an interest in advanced building techniques.[39] Kahn stood with his teachers between the poles of art and science, balancing formal, intuitive composition and aesthetics with logical planning. Although Kahn was not at the cutting edge of cultural events in Paris, he observed them close up and probed their meaning. Kahn's orientation may not have changed significantly; however, exposure to early modernism in Europe had a residual effect and contributed to his mature work in the late 1920s.

Kahn initially remained within the tightly knit American colony but soon befriended several French students in his atelier: "After a while, I got to know the French boys much better than I did the Americans. I travelled a great deal with the French boys and, of course, I spoke French . . . fluently, and I was accepted as a Frenchman . . . which was very satisfactory, because an American was immediately looked down upon as something curious and uninteresting."[40]

Kahn's intimate French atelier comrades, Roger Expert (1882–1955) and Albert Laprade (1883–1978), were talented students who later rose to prominence. Expert, a Grand Prix de Rome in 1912, set his course for academia and became a *patron*. The Grand Prix eluded Laprade, but his election to the French Academy in 1959 recognized a long and distinguished practice of architecture.[41] In France, Expert, Laprade, and Michel Roux-Spitz (1888–1947) were ranked as Redon's most illustrious French *élèves*. Their American counterparts, named by Laprade in a

weekends Kahn and his friends made trips to Fontainebleau, Versailles, or Chartres.[43] Although his repertory of French travel sketches was typical of the genre, Kahn's technique of representation was expressive and pictorially sophisticated. For example, in his sketch of Chaumont (fig. 2.5) Kahn deliberately set up tension in the contrasts between foreground and background, positive and negative space, and action and repose (which was actuated by varying the pencil strokes—active in the natural landscape and quiet in the articulation of the architecture). There is an overall looseness to his drawing, without loss of control, and a sense of spontaneity and enjoyment in the act itself.

Surviving sketches of the same building by Kahn and those of his friends Walter Cassebeer and Clarence Stein invite comparison and demonstrate Kahn's virtuosity. Comparing Kahn's (fig. 2.6) and Cassebeers's (fig. 2.7) drawings of Amboise chapel, for example, Kahn's more complex composition, selection of view, and variety of line stand out, whereas the men's technical skill was similar. In the drawings of the Loches city gate, Stein's version (fig. 2.8) lacks the solid expression of form, firmness of line, and attention to detail of Kahn's version, which shows a more dramatic conception and greater contrast operating on all levels (fig. 2.9).

A group of sketches from February 1909 recorded a trip to the south of France and across the border to Gerona, Spain. Like the one at Carcassonne (fig. 2.10), these were more subdued but have in common with the Loire sketches intimations of influence from Japanese prints—a source of compositional ideas for one of Kahn's favorite painters, James Abbot McNeill Whistler (1834–1903),[44] as well as for Degas, van Gogh, Gauguin, and Monet, impressionists whose paintings, Kahn remembered, had "aroused great excitement among students in Paris."[45] Kahn had the ability to absorb and assimilate complex compositional and stylistic strategies outside of his formal training, and he may have distilled ideas from these artists as well as from Whistler.

An enduring fascination with Moorish and Persian art resulted from Kahn's travels to Spain in 1911: "Starting on foot across the Pyrenees,

1957 tribute to Redon, were William Welles Bosworth (1869–1945), John Auger Holabird (1886–1945), and Ely Jacques Kahn.[42] Kahn's gravitation toward men of great promise, and they toward him, became a pattern first in Paris and later in New York. Kahn's talent, his powerful drive for accomplishment, and his personal charm were all factors. In the American colony and the atelier Redon in Paris, Kahn was part of an elite professional milieu as he would be as a member of the Architectural League of New York during the 1920s.

Traditional Study Trips and Modernism

Study trips were another facet of student life at the Ecole. During his first year Kahn bicycled out of Paris with a backpack for overnight stays at small *auberges*. On these excursions Kahn sketched many renowned and picturesque *châteaux* and cathedrals along the Loire River, including Amboise and Chaumont. On other

FAR LEFT
2.6 *Ely Jacques Kahn,*
"Amboise,"
c. 1907–8

LEFT
2.7 *Walter H.*
Cassebeer, "Amboise,"
1910

FAR LEFT
2.8 *Clarence S. Stein,*
"City Gate Loches,"
1906

LEFT
2.9 *Ely Jacques Kahn,*
"City Gate Loches,"
c. 1907–8

2.10 *Ely Jacques Kahn, "Carcassone," February 19, 1909, Cooper-Hewitt, National Design Museum, Smithsonian Institution*

FACING PAGE
2.11 *Ely Jacques Kahn, "Faculty of Medicine, Zaragoza," c. 1911*

through the grey olive groves, the northern cities, and eventually to the south and across North Africa, left deep impressions on me. In fact, visits to Arabic Spain in Cordova and Seville led to a more serious interest in the origins of the culture of Persia and of the middle East."[46] A Kahn watercolor painting dated 1911 and a written reminiscence document this as a study trip with Clarence Stein: "We travelled to Spain and Morocco, where, in Tangiers [*sic*], we sat next to each other facing the market place with the bustle of dust, camels, and turbanned merchants" (see fig. C.1).[47] An undated sketchbook contains dozens of drawings executed in Italy as well as Spain. In these drawings Kahn's focus shifted from the general to the particular and from the romantic to the pragmatic. He examined, select-

ed, and drew details of architectural decoration, making notes on color, materials, and construction for future reference. One drawing from Zaragoza, Spain, is exemplary (fig. 2.11).

Another consequence of travel was Kahn's encounter with the work of Frank Lloyd Wright. He saw the first of two extensive Wright portfolios, published in Berlin by Wasmuth: "One book published in beautiful format in Holland [*sic*] at that moment was a collection of drawings by Frank Lloyd Wright. Interesting too, for while we had seen photographs of his Buffalo tower [Larkin Building] and some of his houses, here was a European publication that noted Wright in Amsterdam in 1910."[48] Kahn's concern for exterior and interior surface pattern and texture drew him to Wright, a master of both. Kahn would later recognize Wright's impact on the Amsterdam School and his effect on the rich decorative flowering of Dutch brick architecture—influences that flowed back and forth in both directions.[49]

As he traveled it became apparent to Kahn that European architects were "searching for a free expression," and that travel was the means of keeping abreast of these developments and partaking in the "excitement of a new world about to emerge where artists were being encouraged by patrons as well as by their governments, to produce in the very centers of old world, fresh work with little restraint. I must not exaggerate the extent of the acceptance of this new spirit but I can, without question, state that Europe, at least, was being prepared for a renaissance of a different variety, that eventually recognized . . . among a brilliant entourage, craftsmen like Joseph Hoffman [*sic*] in Austria."[50] Kahn's openness to innovative German and Austrian work was not shared by his French comrades. Relations between France and Germany were tense, in part due to lingering animosity over France's loss of Alsace and Lorraine to Germany in the War of 1870. Kahn remembered that there were "plenty of Belgians, Russians, Poles, Rumanians, a few English, but nothing Germanic" at the Ecole.[51] Clarence Stein wrote to his parents of the overtly hostile attitude toward Germans in his atelier: "One can be anything in the atelier Laloux and

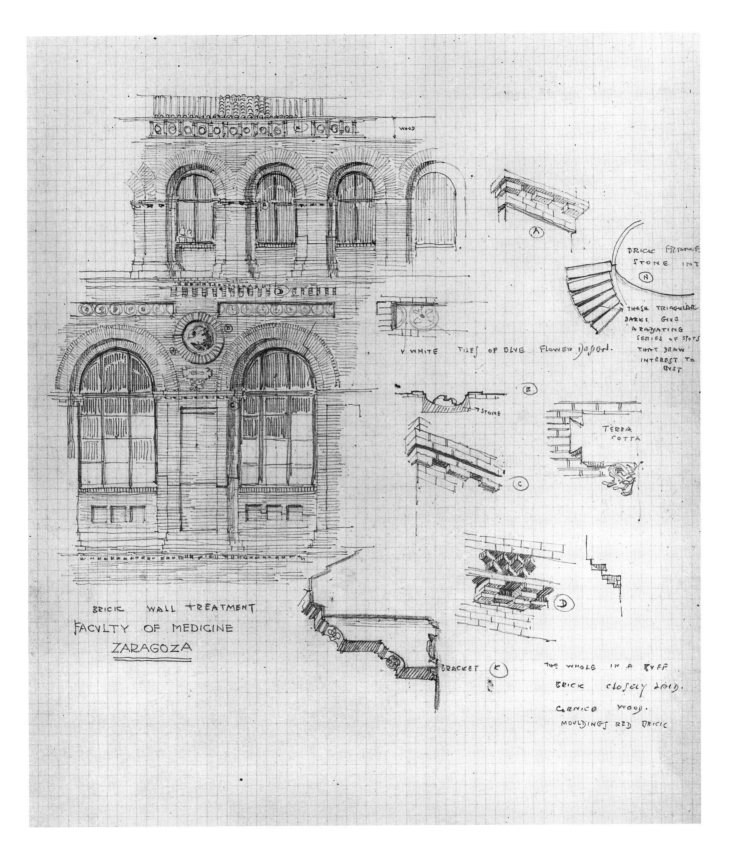

WOOD

V WHITE TILES OF BLUE FLOWER DESIGN.

A

STONE

C

N

DRICK FRAMES STONE INT

THESE TRIANGULAR DARKS GIVE A RADIATING SERIES OF SPOTS THAT DRAW INTEREST TO BUST

E

TERRA COTTA

D

BRICK WALL TREATMENT
FACVLTY OF MEDICINE
ZARAGOZA

BRACKET K

THE WHOLE IN A BVFF BRICK CLOSELY LAID. CORNICE WOOD. MOVLDINGS RED BRICK

welcome; anything but a German."[52] Because of this bias, modern German and Austrian architecture and design were not well known in France—and, if known, were not viewed objectively. One exception to French policy was an invitation extended to a group from Munich to participate in the 1910 Salon d'Automne in Paris. The greater part of the Munich exhibit—furnished interiors by Richard Riemerschmid, Bruno Paul, and others—caused quite a stir among the French, whose eyes were opened to the thrust of German design.[53] Kahn surveyed the Munich work with a "very French Frenchman, who begrudgingly admitted how interesting it was."[54]

Kahn actively sought to see German and Austrian architecture and design. He and a few friends visited and were "intrigued with new buildings that were far from any established idea." Kahn recalled that the Darmstadt artists' colony in Germany, the largest concentration of innovative architecture and design in Europe during Kahn's Beaux-Arts years, was evidence of "fresh design," and that the Wiener Werkstätte was a "lively indication that the old shell of conservatism was cracking."[55] From the distance of age, Kahn remembered that the work of Josef Hoffmann had "aroused great excitement" when he was at the Ecole.[56] The principle of *Gesamtkunstwerk*—that each project, regardless of function, should be planned and executed as a unified whole—prevailed among early European progressives and was embraced by the colony. It was not a new idea, but the rejection of historicism differentiated it from the Beaux-Arts and prior examples of ensemble. Kahn's knowledge of the Darmstadt colony may have contributed to his championship of experiment and freedom of expression in American architecture, concepts outside of Beaux-Arts doctrine, yet associated with Kahn by the end of the 1920s. Kahn's exposure to the work and ideas of Hoffmann and Olbrich differed from that of other American architects of his generation because of the Kahn family's interest in, and ongoing contact with, Austrian decorative arts. In Hohenems, a vacation retreat during the Beaux-Arts years, Kahn must have experienced his sister Rena's enthusi-

asm for Austrian applied art. It was a subject that inevitably led to lively discussions of the Wiener Werkstätte's philosophy, designs, and leaders. In his memoirs, Kahn wrote of Rena's involvement: "Many people will remember her as an exponent of the movement that developed early in the century in Austria where she had lived for a long period."[57]

At the Ecole, however, it is doubtful that avant-garde European architecture caused the young Kahn to seriously question his direction. American architecture, especially in New York, was dominated by the Beaux-Arts and any hope of getting ahead professionally rested on acceptance of the status quo. Nonetheless, Kahn's observation of progressive design in his travels, reinforced by subsequent trips abroad after 1911, and his affinity with the decorative arts, expanded by Rena and later contact with Austrian and German émigré designers at home, made Kahn a conduit for *art moderne*–derived modernism following the 1925 Paris Exposition.

The Prix Labarre and the Diplôme

Many requirements for graduation needed Kahn's attention at the Ecole. In between various projects and competitions, he earned a few extra francs as a draftsman in the office of Albert Tournaire, architect of the city of Paris, who would succeed Redon as patron in 1921. In contrast to the aesthetic air that permeated the Redon atelier, Tournaire's operation of a large office was pragmatic, as was Kahn's work there on the Paris morgue.[58] The design competitions consumed most of Kahn's time. In a letter to his parents, Clarence Stein described the intense pressure at the end of a competition and the camaraderie of Kahn, Stein, and his fellow *élève* in the atelier Laloux, William Van Alen (1883–1954), later designer of the Chrysler Building (1929): "I am writing this on top of my drafting board. Van Alen and Kahn are working in the same room—my room—and here we have been for the past week—past two weeks I guess. Our competition must be sent off next Wednesday, and there is no end of work to be done before then. We are steadily at it from early morn until late at night, just stopping for meals and tea—'le five o'clock' as the Frenchmen call it—has become quite an institution with us. I have even started making my own breakfast—so as to save time re-climbing six flights. . . . Christmas Eve we did stop long enough to take a good meal at the Voltaire, just Ely and I alone."[59] Less than a month later Kahn won the prestigious Prix Labarre over hundreds of competitors, among whom Expert and Laprade received "Mentions." It was the first time since the Concours Edmond Labarre was instituted in 1881 that the prize had gone to a non-Frenchman.[60]

The 1911 Labarre program proposed a national immigrant station, to be located on a small island near a large seaport, whose purpose would be to receive, sort out, examine (detain or hospitalize, if necessary), legally process, and finally release and direct to their destinations large shiploads of immigrants.[61] Required structures were docking facilities in a sheltered cove, a broad platform for disembarkment in front of the principal building, and a number of outer support buildings connected to each other and the principal building by corridors or small roads. Kahn correctly analyzed the essence of the problem: orientation and circulation, the movement of masses of people smoothly and systematically through the procedure. Logic guided him to a clear and efficient *parti*. He organized his composition around the principal building by placing it in the center of the plan on the primary vertical axis in the form of an inverted T (fig. 2.12). In turn, he organized the principal building around its most important element, the immense examination hall, and centered it on the vertical axis. He directed the flow of circulation from entrance to exit sequentially, by wrapping an exceptionally wide, continuous aisle in an inverted U around an examination triage, the hall's core. Apart from the restaurant pavilion, all departments fell either to the left (incoming) or right (outgoing) of the vertical spine. The administration offices occupied the wings of the entrance pavilion on the left; on the right at the exit, Kahn placed a ticket office for transportation and a waiting room for relatives

and friends of arriving immigrants. Two annexes, connected to the principal building on the plan's horizontal axis, housed the detention room on the left and bathrooms on the right. On the same axis, somewhat removed, as required, were three small hospital structures on the left side and a power plant, a garage, and a laundry on the right.

In the French architectural journal, *La Construction Moderne*, Kahn was congratulated for his successful *parti*, the principal building cited as "*le point brillant*." The *parti* so clearly articulated the program, the reviewer continued, that in spite of a "*fantastique*" array of entries, the jury hardly hesitated to award Kahn the prize.[62] At home the *American Architect* also gave a glowing account of Kahn's accomplishment: "His plan (the La Barre [*sic*] is given essentially for planning) is not only an example of amazingly brilliant study, executed in the brief space of three days, but it is one of the most excellent plans the competition has brought forth during its existence. The problem was an Immigrant Station, somewhat on the lines of the one at New York built ten or twelve years ago by Messrs. Boring & Tilton. . . . It was a problem such as an American, especially a New Yorker, might be expected to grasp thoroughly, but it is none the less satisfactory that an American rose, properly, to the occasion and won a much coveted honor."[63] The Ellis Island Immigrant Station by Boring and Tilton undoubtedly was the program's precedent. As the project was nearing completion in 1901 (well before Kahn decided to study architecture), the general plan was illustrated in *Architects' and Builders' Magazine*.[64] Comparison of the general plans of Kahn's Prix Labarre and Boring and Tilton's Immigrant Station supports Kahn's independence of the latter (fig. 2.13). Kahn did adopt a triple-arched entrance like that of the Ellis Island pavilion. However, such an entrance was a Beaux-Arts formula for monumental civic buildings. Other similarities, such as the examination hall's huge size relative to other rooms, arose from the requirements of the program. If Kahn knew the Boring & Tilton plan, he did not rely on it for his Labarre scheme.

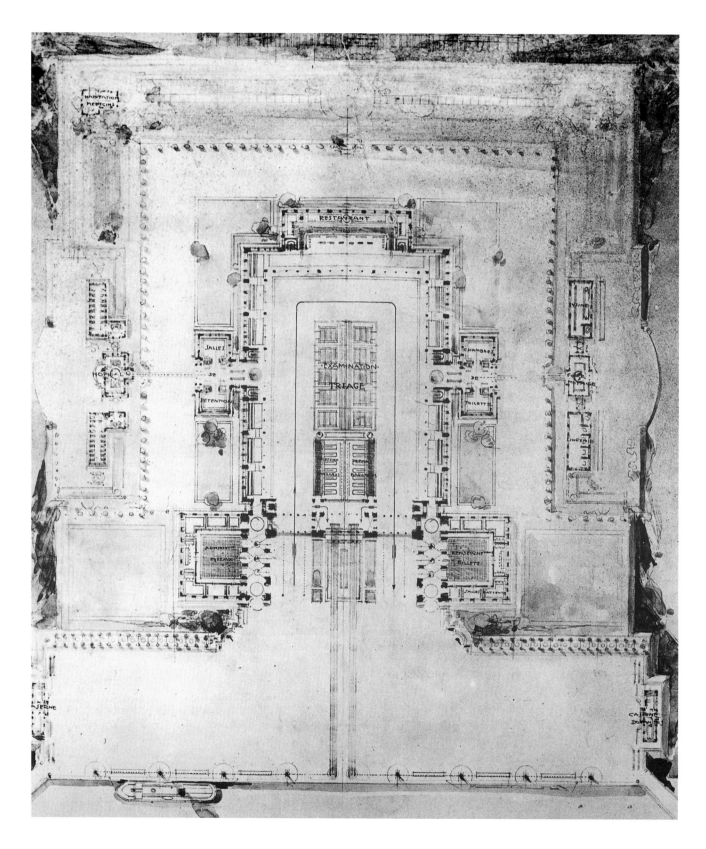

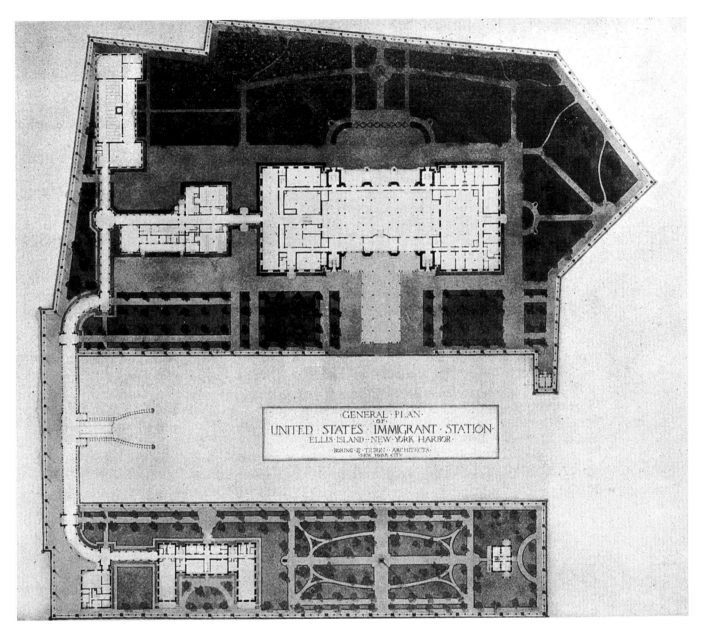

Encouraged by friends, Kahn entered a small group of watercolors from his travels through France, Italy, and Spain, in the salon of the Société des Artistes Français in 1911. To his delight, his submission was honored: "I was happy to be able to view the gold card on my exhibit giving me the highest award for the first appearance at the Salon, 'Honorable Mention.'"[65] Kahn was initially attracted to watercolor paint-ing at Columbia, and he claimed to have been self-taught in the medium.[66] His interest was intensified by the Tate Gallery exhibition of J. M. W. Turner (1775–1851) watercolors, which he saw in 1910 on a visit to London with Laprade and two other French students.[67] Kahn's enthusi-asm for watercolor painting fostered a friendship with a notable watercolorist of the day, Pierre-Paul-Louis Guidetti (1878–?), a practicing archi-

FACING PAGE
2.12 Ely Jacques Kahn, Concours Labarre, "Une Station d'Immigrants," General Plan, 1911

ABOVE
2.13 Boring & Tilton, United States Immigrant Station, general plan, Ellis Island, New York City Harbor, 1900

tect and former Redon *élève*.[68] Kahn referred to watercolor painting as a "form of relaxation and glorious release" as well as a valuable professional tool.[69] In architectural practice he would often communicate ideas to his draftsmen with spontaneous watercolor sketches.

Kahn had earned a sufficient number of credits (*valeurs*) by the spring of 1911 to become eligible for the *diplôme*. The final requirement was an independent thesis project and another set of oral examinations. The thesis involved an elaborate presentation with full studies and a defense before a jury of *patrons*. The thesis subject he chose was an American prison. Although the drawings, some over twenty feet long, were not preserved, Kahn's retrospective description has survived: "The building consisted of a masonry shell in the center of which [was a] many tiered arrangement of cells—back to back, a steel fenced corridor giving access on every level. The professors were surprised and entertained by my version of a prison."[70] Kahn's thesis was approved, he passed the oral examinations, and the *Architecte Diplômé par le Gouvernement Français* was officially conferred on November 16, 1911.[71] Looking back at the end of his life, Kahn summarized the benefits of his years at the Ecole des Beaux-Arts: "It was interesting, very inspiring, and very educational. Believe me, I got a great deal out of it. It broadened my mind enormously. It was fine for music and theatre and the arts as a whole, and traveling I gained so much. It was a very broadening experience, which was the important thing finally."[72]

Early in the summer of 1911, Kahn and Clarence Stein began preparing for their return home that autumn. A six-week Italian tour was planned as the finale to the years spent abroad.[73] Stein moved in with Kahn and Cassebeer at 7 rue Corneille. On August 2, Kahn and Stein boarded a train for Turin, Italy, where they saw the industrial exhibits of the 1911 International Exposition that commemorated the fiftieth anniversary of Italy's unification. Five days later, after making brief stops in Pisa, Lucca, and Siena, the young men reached Rome and settled in for a month of

sketching and sightseeing. There they met other American students on leave from the Ecole; Van Alen, "Adams," and John Klaber joined them on an expedition to Tivoli and the Villa d'Este. More interesting to them than the industrial exhibits in Turin was the cultural aspect of Rome: the historical sections in the Baths of Diocletian, the medieval Papal City in the recently restored Castel Sant'Angelo, and the sixteen stunning regional Italian pavilions erected for the event on the Piazza d'Armi.[74] Kahn and Stein enjoyed the paintings and sculptures in the national pavilions near the Villa Borghese, where Josef Hoffmann's Austrian pavilion—a building that exemplified Hoffmann's unorthodox, recognizable, but freely interpreted approach to classicism—commanded a strategic location near the main entrance (fig. 2.14).[75] The monumentality of Roman antiquity finally overwhelmed Kahn and Stein, who wrote his parents: "Yesterday we started making studies of some of the frescoes in the Museum of the Baths of Diocletian. . . . These Roman frescoes are wonders—the Renaissance never outdid them. In fact, has any age since theirs approached them in the arts? After each visit to the museums we answer no. What sculpture! What is the use anyhow: Two thousand years ago they did what we can never hope to outdo. So we said last night, after we had finished a watercolor in the Forum—as we saw it all lit up by that most glorious light, a Roman sunset. And so we say every time we pass the Colosseum, or the Column of Trajan or—what is the use? Well, anyhow, we are going home in October to see. Until then we will take in as much Roman inspiration as possible."[76]

Kahn and Stein's memorable Italian holiday ended in Verona on September 17th when they boarded a train going north, through the scenic Tyrolean Alps, to Innsbruck, Austria. A few days later the young men were received in Hohenems as houseguests of Rudolf's parents, Charlotte and Anton Rosenthal, who entertained them for a week. Stein left Le Havre on October 14, 1911 aboard the SS *Rochambeau*, sharing a stateroom with Kahn's roommate Walter Cassebeer for the voyage to New York.[77] Kahn returned on December 2, 1911 aboard the SS *Lorraine*.[78] Some time later, Stein considered the thoughts that had

2.14 Josef Hoffmann, Austrian Pavilion, perspective, Italian International Exposition, Rome, 1911

occupied him and Kahn as they prepared for the journey home, especially their concern about the economy, which had not recovered completely from the depression of 1907–8: "Our last night we had other things to think of. What chance had we of getting a job: Our studies at the Beaux Arts might be of help in an architectural office—it might, we didn't know. We were very uncertain then. We had much competition not only from the many who had studied and traveled as we had, but also from the unemployed draftsmen who had spent years in practical office work."[79]

Kahn left the Ecole des Beaux-Arts with a distinguished record. Adjustment to the French system had come easily, for he had been well prepared at Columbia and comfortable in a French milieu. Moreover, Kahn respected authority and was conscientious, disciplined, and motivated to excel. The atelier Redon had offered an ideal balance between art and reason for him. Redon's scintillating and poetic pondering of aesthetics was offset by the grip he retained on rational composition and design. The balance was mirrored in Kahn's affirmation of reason and traditional values, on the one hand, with a striving for artistic autonomy and a fresh viewpoint, on the other—a polarity that reflected the character of Kahn's family, at once conservative yet tolerant of creative expression. Development in such an environment enabled Kahn to negotiate these polarities without inner conflict, an aspect of his personality that suited him to lead, with others, the transition to a modern idiom in the latter half of the 1920s. Notwithstanding his attraction to exotic Moorish architecture he encountered in Spain, and his appreciation of early European progressives, Kahn outwardly emerged from the Ecole in 1911 as a model of early twentieth-century Beaux-Arts training. Now, homeward bound after twelve preparatory years, he would soon commence the practice of architecture. As he crossed the Atlantic somewhat apprehensively, the prospect nonetheless must have been exhilarating.

CHAPTER THREE

HOMECOMING: BUCHMAN & KAHN

The Early Years, 1917–21

Kahn returned home to face the task of establishing himself in practice. Although his father's business had suffered a serious setback following the 1907 stock market collapse, unwavering financial support at the Ecole had shielded him from the impact. The young architect was now ready to pull his own weight. Finding a job was another matter—and a frustrating one, at that. In his memoirs Kahn recalled with some resentment, the dashed hope of employment in an important firm: "I had two degrees from Columbia University, one from the Ecole des Beaux-Arts, I could draw, make color studies, and was eager to proceed. . . . Whatever my ideals, that hope of finding a job in one of the well established and highly respectable firms was abruptly shattered.[1] The tone of the major offices was aristocratic; the architects themselves were from prominent families, and unless one's social position was considerable, the secretary might well be the first and last person one would meet."[2] Although Kahn did not identify the patrician firms, they most likely included those of Beaux-Arts practitioners who had led Columbia ateliers during Kahn's years, and others, such as York & Sawyer, and William Welles Bosworth, whose principals had been members of the atelier Redon.

Logically, Kahn would have approached Carrère & Hastings. Given Hastings's esteem for the French School, and Kahn's accomplishment there, it is surprising that Kahn was not accepted into the firm after receiving the *diplôme*. Another Hastings student, William F. Lamb, a schoolmate of Kahn at both Columbia and the Ecole, entered Carrère & Hastings about 1911–12. Although their school achievements were comparable, Lamb clearly had a social advantage: He came from an influential Brooklyn family, the only son of William Lamb, a successful building contractor and banker (and an official of two Presbyterian churches), and Mary Louise Wurster Lamb, sister of a former Brooklyn mayor. By 1920 Lamb was a partner in Carrère & Hastings.[3]

The Struggle for Employment

Anti-Semitism may have been the reason for Kahn's rejections. Unlike his friend, Lee Simonson, who wrote of discrimination encountered as a young man, Kahn never complained of bias.[4] Yet numerous historians have documented the upsurge in anti-Semitism in the United States between 1910 and 1916. Prejudice was intensified at the top levels of society by the rapid

3.1 Buchman & Fox,
Browning Tower
(World's Tower), 1914

economic rise and assimilation of American Jews of German descent, who were competitors for position and power. "Invisible barriers" were discreetly erected in the upper classes.[5] The barriers in the workplace, described by historian Moses Rischin, were less subtle: "Increasingly the great [concerns] rejected or ignored Jewish applicants. Like social exclusion earlier, economic discrimination became overt. 'Help wanted' ads specified 'Christians' and thus singled out Jews from all other New Yorkers."[6] Kahn's frustration over the failure to find a suitable position caused him to have second thoughts about the family business. In his memoirs he noted: "[Father] had hoped that I would take over his business, and though I was strongly tempted, I decided to continue in architecture."[7]

The aftermath of the economic depression of 1907–8 made competition even more difficult for the available jobs. During 1912 an upturn in commercial and industrial activity nationally raised hope of a full recovery, especially in New York, where building increased 15 percent over the previous year.[8] The resurgence, however, was brief. A decline in the economy in 1913 bordered on a recession. At year's end, A. D. F. Hamlin reported grimly: "Never since the great strikes and lockouts of the building trades in 1903–4 had the volume of building fallen so low in New York City, where many architects either closed their offices or reduced their drafting-rooms to a mere skeleton of the usual staff."[9] Unemployment in the building industry and allied trades continued as the city suffered a 38 percent decrease in the total value of plans filed during 1914.[10]

Nevertheless, between 1911 and 1915 Kahn managed to find intermittent employment as a draftsman. His Prix Labarre carried weight with the architects of the Ellis Island Immigrant Station, Boring and Tilton, who gave Kahn his first freelance job in 1911. Kahn was assigned to their Alfred University Library project in Alfred, New York, and he may have had a hand in the design of the entrance elevation.[11] The brick relief above the doorway recalls his sketches of Moorish art in Spain and his interest in its Persian roots (fig. 3.2). Other architects for whom Kahn worked were George B. Post, Clinton MacKenzie,

and the Clinton & Russell firm. Kahn recalled that the entrenched eclecticism he encountered wherever he had worked was stifling: "What concerned me was not the few [fine] examples that characterized their day but the overwhelming display of banal copying. Any glimpse at the magazines that were on every architect's desk would state clearly that inspiration from the past was primarily a species of reproduction. . . . Originality was taboo. I emphasize this because there were no symptoms of desire to see change." Kahn depicted his acceptance of eclectic practice during these years as safe cover. He "teamed up with the group in power" and suppressed his true values because success depended upon it.[12]

In 1912 Kahn joined the Society of Beaux-Arts Architects, an organization of former Ecole students that was devoted to teaching and extending its principles in the United States. His service as a judge for competitions brought him into contact with other members, who then offered him part-time work.[13] Although he was not formally affiliated with the Architectural League of New York until 1918, Kahn gained some exposure for his European travel drawings by entering them in the league's annual exhibitions of 1912, 1913, and 1914.[14] In a 1931 profile of Kahn, Henry Saylor, editor of *Architecture*, recognized this stage in his career as a "period of finding oneself," a time when Kahn "was known in architectural circles" only as "a man who could render presentation drawings, a man to be called in for a special job."[15]

While Kahn struggled professionally, his personal life took shape under the strong influence of Clarence Stein. Inspired by Stein and his close friends Lee Simonson and the Klaber brothers, Kahn embraced the nonsectarian Ethical Culture movement, whose humanistic principles of moral conduct and responsibility for others, and its emphasis on independent, reasoned judgment, appealed to Kahn. In the spring of 1912, Stein proposed Kahn for membership in the New York Society for Ethical Culture; he was admitted. Kahn's decision to join the society was in keeping with his drift toward assimilation. The ideal of fellowship advanced by the Ethical Culture movement also offered a supportive social and

professional network. The society gradually became a small but steady source of clients for Kahn's practice.[16]

Shortly after his affiliation, Kahn was introduced by Stein's sister Lillie to her friend, Elsie Plaut (1889–1952), a Columbia University graduate student known in her circle as "a brilliant bluestocking."[17] Nothing is known of their courtship, but within a year Kahn and Elsie, whose father was a trustee of the New York Society for Ethical Culture, were married by Assistant Ethical Leader John Lovejoy Elliot on May 16, 1913, in the society's meeting house at 64th Street and Central Park West. After an extended European honeymoon, the newlyweds sailed home from Hamburg, Germany aboard the SS *Imperator*.[18] The Kahns began domestic life in an apartment at 54 Morningside Avenue, a short distance from the Columbia campus. About 1917 they moved to a larger apartment at 35 Claremont Avenue, across from Barnard College, where the couple lived for twenty years with their children, Joan Plaut Kahn (1914–94), Ely Jacques Kahn Jr. (1916–94), and Olivia Kahn (born 1920). Kahn would benefit professionally

from the influence and financial help of his wealthy father-in-law. Elsie's German-born father Joseph Plaut (1859–1939) and his younger brother Albert owned Lehn & Fink, one of the largest wholesale pharmaceutical companies in the United States (known for its highly successful Lysol disinfectant). The Plaut brothers had connections in business, civic, and philanthropic spheres and were capable of directing substantial commissions to an architectural office.

During the first year of his marriage Kahn struck out on his own in a small office at 381 Fourth Avenue. Unfortunately, stalled construction and a depressed economy early in 1914 meant few commissions. The only Kahn design on record that year was a commission from the Society for Ethical Culture for a small one-story shower house.[19] Ironically, the outbreak of World War I in August 1914 brought Kahn relief. Replacements for French design faculty in American institutions were needed immediately. On September 15 the College of Architecture at Cornell offered Kahn the position of Professor Georges Mauxion, who had been detained in France. Kahn jumped at the chance to earn

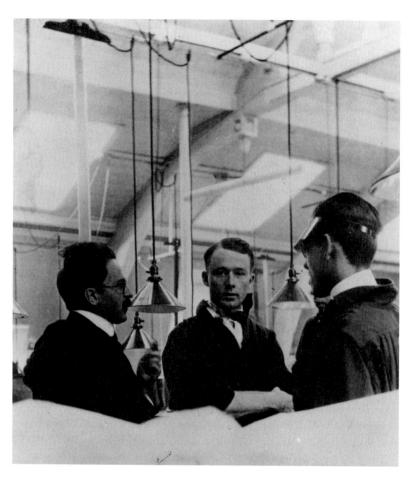

3.3 *Drafting room,*
Cornell University
College of Architecture,
Ely Jacques Kahn,
Slocum Kingsbury, and
Ralph Potter Ripley,
1914

of construction, but Kahn and his peers faced a tighter, more competitive market than had the previous generation. A. D. F. Hamlin summarized the past twenty-five years of American architecture and dramatized the present predicament (in 1916) of young architects: "There are a hundred capable architects now where there were ten in 1891—and the ranks are beginning to be overcrowded. . . . The relatively diminished demand for new buildings falls upon a greatly increased army of capable architects, among whom the prizes are very unequally distributed. It is much harder now than in 1891 for a young architect to start in independent practice, and his chances of securing important commissions are relatively smaller. . . . Undoubtedly the prospects are less certain, less alluring than they used to be."[24]

After returning from Cornell in 1915, Kahn practiced from an office in the Sinclair Building at 373 Fourth Avenue, a Carrère & Hastings design of 1910.[25] Commissions for a cluster of residences in Elmsford, a Westchester County village of country estates sixteen miles northeast of New York City, kept him occupied. Kahn remodeled the 1909 residence of Augustus T. Gillander, a prominent New York City attorney, and his father-in-law's house on Knolltop, the Plaut's Elmsford estate. On the grounds of Knolltop he designed, for his own family, a picturesque half-timbered stucco cottage reminiscent of English architect M. H. Baillie Scott's (1865–1945) domestic work. Herman Younker, a member of the Society for Ethical Culture and a Plaut friend and neighbor, engaged Kahn to design a large country house and garage.[26] The progress of Kahn's career was nonetheless disappointing. By 1917, at age thirty-three—six years after graduation, with honors, from the Ecole des Beaux-Arts—he still had not found a position with a major firm or procured a significant commission. Unexpectedly, an opening that materialized in the middle of 1917 transformed his professional life.

Predecessors to Buchman & Kahn

Buchman & Fox, an established firm that specialized in commercial design, was seeking a young associate to succeed Mortimer J. Fox, a partner of

$3,000 for the school year. Arrangements were made for him to live in Ithaca weekdays and to commute home on weekends and holidays.[20] Shortly after he accepted the Cornell post he was invited by MIT, on the recommendation of Van Pelt, his Columbia atelier mentor, to fill the place in design left vacant by Professor Albert Le Monnier's return to France.[21] Barely older than his students, Kahn found teaching at Cornell a challenge. He was stimulated by lively exchanges and attentive to the problems of students (fig. 3.3). A tribute signed by sixty-two students urging him to continue a second year affirmed his success as their mentor.[22] Although the administration's persistence matched student fervor, Kahn declined. Elsie was pregnant with their second child, and Kahn was eager to return to practice.[23]

The escalating economy, buoyed by Europe's demands for industrial products, fueled a revival

seventeen years and the primary business producer, who was about to retire. Recognizing a unique opportunity, Joseph Plaut bought a partnership interest for Kahn, assuring Albert Buchman that he would personally generate new business. Kahn acknowledged that the contacts and influence of his father-in-law figured in the partnership with Buchman, and that the prospect of Plaut's bringing work into the office was decisive.[27] Indeed, Buchman & Fox business had declined considerably from a peak in 1912.[28]

Buchman, who was in his late fifties, turned responsibility over to Kahn, who assumed leadership of the firm as designer and responsible head at the end of 1917.[29] His experience of office management and knowledge of commercial planning was limited, but the transition was eased by the loyal, well-trained organization Buchman had honed over thirty-three years. Veterans within the firm gave Kahn their full support. Office manager John Miller Montfort (1867–1936) kept a low public profile but played a key role throughout the 1920s, as did head draftsman Ernest H. Graesser (dates unknown). Kahn recalled: "I . . . had the rare good fortune to become associated with a group of seasoned men of the old school, who knew how to proceed without fanfare and without fumbling. Under their firm guidance, I very quickly learned the importance of team play, how many details arise in the study and evolution of an enterprise, the amount of permissible freedom and the rigid limitations as well. From this beginning I did absorb information."[30] Buchman withdrew into the background, but his majority interest (Kahn owned about 30 percent) gave him fiscal control until 1926.[31] Kahn inherited a fine-tuned organization with an excellent reputation among entrepreneurial merchants and real estate developers. Kahn's professional accomplishment was inseparable from the Buchman legacy that provided him with a solid base from which to grow. A reconstructed history of the firm demonstrates its value to Kahn.[32]

The founder of the partnerships that preceded Buchman & Kahn was German-born Hermann Joseph Schwarzmann (1846–91), the charismatic architect-in-chief of the 1876 Philadelphia Centennial Exhibition and creator of its plan in Fairmont Park, Memorial and Horticulture halls, and numerous pavilions (fig. 3.4). Two years after his triumph in Philadelphia, Schwarzmann moved to New York City and opened an office in the prestigious Tribune Building designed by Richard Morris Hunt. The German-American community became the main source of commis-

3.4 Hermann J. Schwarzmann, Memorial Hall, 1876 Centennial Exhibition, Philadelphia

3.5 Buchman & Deisler, 580–590 and 594–596 Broadway, East Side between Prince and Houston Streets

1879, he entered the Schwarzmann office as a draftsman; in 1884 he became a name partner.[35] A year later the volume of work ballooned; one job, a retail store on Third Avenue and 59th Street, initiated the long-term relationship the successor firms maintained with the Bloomingdale brothers. At the height of his career, Schwarzmann became ill and was forced to retire in 1887. Buchman carried on alone for about a year before joining forces with Gustav Deisler (1858–1927), a draftsman in the firm who, like Schwarzmann, was a German-born Catholic.[36]

The Buchman & Deisler partnership lasted twelve years and survived the economic depression of 1894. A highly regarded commercial practice evolved under Buchman's leadership. In a turn-of-the-century history of New York City real estate, the firm was cited for planning highly successful commercial buildings and for its contribution on Broadway, below 14th Street, to the "artistic appearance of the city."[37] A number of these buildings were designed for the firm's major client, Jeremiah C. Lyons, a self-made general contractor and real estate developer. In a fifteen-month stretch during 1896 and 1897, eight commissions originated with Lyons (fig. 3.5).[38] Although most of the seventy-five buildings erected from Buchman & Deisler plans have been demolished, one exception is the boldly arcaded East 59th Street "Modern French" addition to Bloomingdale's Department Store (1893; fig. 3.6).[39] At the end of 1899, just as the firm was recognized in the architects' section of Moses King's *Notable New Yorkers 1896–1899*, Deisler left the partnership for reasons not known.[40]

Buchman's next partner was Mortimer J. Fox (1874–1948), a native New Yorker and son of Joseph Fox, a prominent Jewish banker of German descent. Fox began as a draftsman in the firm after his graduation from the Columbia School of Mines in 1895. Four years following Deisler's departure Buchman & Fox was formed.[41] Fox's impressive connections were reinforced by his marriage in 1906 to Helen Morgenthau, the daughter of Henry Morgenthau, a client of the firm. Morgenthau, a real estate titan, was the founder and president of the Central Realty Bond and Trust Company, which had merged in 1902

sions. The Liederkranz Clubhouse (1881), somewhat reminiscent of Memorial Hall, was a highly visible example.[33]

Two characteristics of the Schwarzmann firm and its successors stand out sharply: the German ancestry of its leaders and their Columbia University architectural education. All the name partners were either born in Germany or were children or grandchildren of German-born immigrants. Some but not all were German-Jewish (the nineteenth-century leadership was mixed), and the firm's roster—partners as well as staff—has always been nonsectarian.[34] The educational influence of the Columbia University School of Architecture on the firm was strong in the twentieth century. Partners Fox, Kahn, and Robert Allan Jacobs were Columbia men, as were many designers, among them MacDonald Mayer, Arthur Norman Clough, Edward Raymond McMahon, and Pierre A. Bezy.

Albert Buchman (1859–1936), of German-Jewish roots, was a native of Cincinnati, Ohio. After graduation from the Cornell University College of Engineering and Architecture in

with the Chicago-based George A. Fuller Company and the New York Realty Corporation to form the colossal United States Realty & Construction Company.[42] Having amassed a personal fortune, Morgenthau's interest turned to national politics. After serving as the finance committee chairman for Woodrow Wilson's 1912 presidential campaign, he was rewarded with an ambassadorship to Turkey. Morgenthau's contacts generated considerable new business for the firm.

Buchman & Fox produced a diverse mix of buildings that included warehouses, factories, and lofts downtown; apartment buildings and hotels in midtown; attached and freestanding residences above 59th Street; and an occasional health facility, school, and bank.[43] Retail merchants and office building developers constituted a growing segment of the firm's work. Following the example of R. H. Macy at the turn of the century, department store owners began to relocate from "Ladies Mile" between 14th and 23rd Streets and Broadway and Sixth Avenue to 34th Street and north on Fifth Avenue.[44] Leading merchants enlisted the firm to design their deluxe new quarters: Saks &

Company, Greeley Square between 33rd and 34th Streets (1902, demolished); Oppenheim, Collins & Company, 31–39 West 34th Street (1906); L. P. Hollander & Company, 550 Fifth Avenue (1909); and Bonwit Teller & Company, 417 Fifth Avenue (1910). Between 1911 and 1913, Buchman & Fox planned four large office buildings. The original Buchman & Fox eleven-story New York Times Annex, 217–29 West 43rd Street, was enlarged in 1924 by Ludlow & Peabody and is often mistakenly attributed, in its entirety, to the latter. At twenty-five stories, the white terra-cotta, Woolworth-inspired Browning Tower (renamed World's Tower) at 110–12 West 40th Street, was the firm's tallest skyscraper (see fig. 3.1). The other two buildings were located on the East Side, the twenty-story Kaye Building, 105–17 Madison Avenue at 30th Street, and the twenty-story Forty-Second Street Building, 30 East 42nd Street (fig. 3.7). The latter, strategically located on the southwest corner of Madison Avenue, a block from the new Grand Central Terminal, became the home of the Buchman & Fox office. A well-publicized road and viaduct to the Fort

3.6 Buchman & Deisler and Buchman & Fox, Bloomingdale's Department Store, engraving, c. 1908

*3.7 Buchman & Fox,
42nd Street Building
(Union Carbide and
Carbon Building), 1913*

Firm History

Hermann J. Schwarzmann
1878–1884
New York City

Schwarzmann & Buchman
1884–1887

Albert Buchman
1887–1888

Buchman & Deisler
1888–1899

Buchman & Fox
1899–1917

Buchman & Kahn
1917–1930

Firm of Ely Jacques Kahn
1930–1940

Kahn & Jacobs
1940–1973

Kahn & Jacobs/Hellmuth Obata &
Kassabaum
1973–1975

Hellmuth Obata & Kassabaum (HOK)
1975–present

EMPIRE STATE NOTABLES

ARCHITECTS AND HOTEL MEN

ALBERT BUCHMAN
Buchman & Fox, Architects
New York City

MORTIMER J. FOX
Buchanan & Fox, Architects
New York City

3.8 Albert Buchman and Mortimer J. Fox, c. 1914

Tryon estate of multimillionaire Cornelius K. G. Billings, chairman of the board of Union Carbide and Carbon Corporation, was a commission that came through Henry Morgenthau.[45] Buchman and Fox's substantial production was recognized in the 1914 edition of *Empire State Notables* (fig. 3.8).[46]

Despite the firm's enormous commercial output up to 1917, and the quality of individual buildings, the names of Schwarzmann, Buchman, Deisler, and Fox rarely appear in the professional literature. Although the firm of Schwarzmann and his successors spanned the period of the American Renaissance, the principals were not leaders of the movement. Once the firm's mantle was laid on the shoulders of Ely Jacques Kahn, however, the young partner would receive considerable exposure and recognition in architectural journals for his work in the emerging Garment

District and for championing modernist design after the 1925 Paris exposition. At first, though, Buchman & Kahn tightened its belt, vacated the former Buchman & Fox office in its prestigious 42nd Street Building, and relocated in 1918 to a small, serviceable building at 56 West 45th Street, a sober move dictated by Fox's withdrawal and wartime conditions.[47]

On August 15, 1918, in the middle of Kahn's first year in the Buchman & Kahn partnership, his sixty-three-year-old father succumbed to heart disease at the family summer home in White Plains, New York. A surviving sketch, signed "E. J. Kahn, Dordrecht" and dated 1918, suggests that Kahn went abroad, after the November Armistice that ended World War I, to settle his father's affairs.[48] With the aid of Eugenie Kahn's brother, Ferdinand Maximilian, her brother-in-law Louis Kahn, and son-in-law

Rudolf Rosenthal, the Kahn mirror and glass company operated profitably until 1926, when the factory site was sold and the business was acquired by a competitor.[49] Family supervision of the business left Kahn free to pursue his architectural career.

Lehn & Fink Commissions

During the inflationary year of 1919, when skyrocketing costs deferred many previously scheduled plans, Kahn's father-in-law delivered three Lehn & Fink commissions to Buchman & Kahn. Two were factories, one in Brooklyn and the other in Bloomfield, New Jersey; the third was an office building–warehouse in Lower Manhattan.[50] The

seven-story Lehn & Fink Building, designed and erected in 1919 on the northeast corner of Greenwich and Morton Streets, offered Kahn his first commercial decorative experiment. "My work on these projects was confined to ornamental details," he recalled, "but I had the opportunity to learn about reinforced concrete construction and modern industrial processes."[51] Kahn's early work for the firm demonstrates that he focused his attention at this time partly on practical planning, partly on ornament. Although the solutions Kahn explored were tentative or inconsistent, his interest in ornament was constant. The sources varied, but most important for his future career were experiments that illustrated alternatives in architectural decoration.

*3.11 Lehn & Fink
Building, cornice,
1919, B&K*

For the Lehn & Fink Building Kahn indulged his taste for Moorish and Persian geometric patterning. An exterior terra-cotta latticed banding has a diagonal diaper in relief with contrasting floral and geometric motifs (fig. 3.9). Brick facing of the rounded-corner entrance bay, executed in diamond-within-a-diamond bond, subtly echoed the diaper pattern of the latticed banding (fig. 3.10). The scheme was weakened by a five-foot overhanging cornice with an undulating, arabesque lower edge that was out of sync with the dominant geometrical elements (fig. 3.11). Although Kahn abandoned this scheme, he continued to experiment with commercial facades, with uneven success, during the early Buchman & Kahn years. Abstraction of classical motifs and the use of geometric patterns in relief to achieve contrasts of light and shadow, however, persisted.

Expert in Store Planning

For a different building type and client—a luxury store in a prestigious location for a flourishing merchant—Kahn produced a unified scheme that demonstrated his mastery of the modern French style and recalled his student work at Columbia and the Ecole des Beaux-Arts. In 1919, Charles J. Oppenheim Jr., scion of the Oppenheim Collins retail department store chain, turned to Kahn to design an exclusive women's apparel shop that would be smaller and more lavish than the flagship store on West 34th

Street designed earlier by Buchman & Fox. The building permit application for the Jay-Thorpe store at 24 West 57th Street was filed on November 29, 1919, and construction, which commenced early in 1920, was completed before the end of the year. The store was awarded the prestigious Fifth Avenue Association Gold Medal in 1920 for the best exterior of a new building in the Fifth Avenue District, an honor that publicized Kahn as the new design partner of the firm (fig. 3.12).[52]

The Jay-Thorpe facade was a study in classical restraint. Clarity, proportion, planarity, symmetry, and stylized ornament, sparingly applied, were characteristics of the elegant Louis XVI style evoked by Kahn. On the third story, French doors that opened onto delicate metal-railed balconies were capped with slender "eyebrow" pediments, gracefully arched above applied terracotta garlands. Similar balconies punctuated the high windows of the eighth floor, where paired Corinthian pilasters framed the windows and gave the impression of support for the balustraded parapet. There was no sense of experiment here. Kahn was in full command of this composition. The growth and expansion of the Oppenheim Collins chain in the early 1920s produced additional projects for Buchman & Kahn. Unlike Jay-Thorpe, these branch stores were uniformly designed. The entrance facade of the 1919 Pittsburgh branch, for example, was almost identical to the flagship store on West 34th Street in New York.[53]

Kahn soon became known as an expert in store planning. His strategies were enumerated in his first published article, "Essential Details in Store Designing," which appeared in *Architectural Forum* in 1924. Kahn explained that a merchant's success depended upon first attracting the customer to the show window, which is why he analyzed show-window design for various types of merchandise. Dresses should be shown in the "normal relation of the customer's eye to the [mannequin]," whereas jewelry and similar small articles needed to be "nearer the eye, and not dwarfed by the scale of a large window setting." The type of merchandise also determined the depth of the window: shal-

FACING PAGE
3.12 Jay-Thorpe Building, 1920, B&K

low for small items, eight feet for apparel, and about twelve feet for furniture. Protecting the store from the liability of careless customers by making all fixtures "foolproof" was another priority. Kahn's emphasis on beauty in commercial design—a recurring theme in his writing—was introduced in this article: "It is fortunate that in recent years a clear recognition has developed of the actual value of a beautiful store, since the main difference between the attractive and the unattractive result lies in the direction that an intelligent designer can give to the work, and the cost is likely to be approximately the same. Let the solution be practical, and the owner will be interested in seeing a new arrangement of his goods in an attractive setting."[54] Kahn pressed for excellent craftsmanship, still economically feasible, and managed to satisfy practical demands while squeezing enough out of commercial budgets to realize his aesthetic goals. One after another, high-class Fifth Avenue stores became clients: Bergdorf Goodman (1927–28), Lord & Taylor (1928), Van Cleef & Arpels (1929), Yardley & Company (1929), Bonwit, Teller and Company (1930), Richard Hudnut (1931), and Léron (1931), a couture linen shop.

The Kahn and Feldman Mill: A Modern Industrial Plant

During these early years, the firm designed several industrial buildings outside Manhattan. Period photographs and some plans survive for the Kahn and Feldman silk throwing mill (c. 1921–23), a Brooklyn factory at 360 Suydam Avenue. The mill demonstrated Kahn's grasp of modern industrial design. Nothing remotely like it had been designed by the firm before Kahn became a partner. The reinforced concrete, flat-slab construction, stark white walls, and gridded expanses of glass contrasted startlingly with Kahn's previous work (fig. 3.13). Published in front and rear elevations and shown with floor plan and cross section in a special *Architectural Forum* issue on industrial buildings in 1923, Kahn's design appeared closer to the work of German functionalists.[55] In *The New World Architecture* (1930),

3.13 Kahn and Feldman factory, Brooklyn, New York, c. 1921–23, B&K

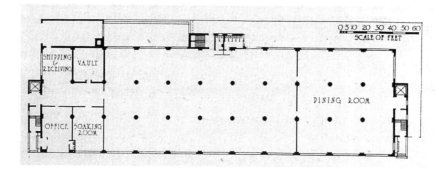

3.14 Kahn and Feldman factory, Brooklyn, New York, plan, c. 1921, B&K

Sheldon Cheney illustrated and discussed the mill in the context of the industrial work of Norman Bel Geddes, and of the German architects, Peter Behrens, Emil Fahrenkamp, and Walter Gropius. On the one hand, Cheney asserted that the Kahn and Feldman factory "is typical of thousands of checkerboard designs: glass, steel-casemented, set into the simplest arrangement of concrete piers and floors." On the other hand, he lauded the design for the "notable expressiveness of the separation of the manufacturing space from two units of grouped service elements."[56] This was the feature that received favorable review in the architectural press: the reduction of corridor space to a minimum by the separation of service elements into three narrow towers that abutted

each end of the main structure and the center entrance (fig. 3.14).[57] No other New York industrial building designed by Buchman & Kahn later in the 1920s matched the Kahn and Feldman mill for functional purity.

The Setback Style

The work that made Kahn a major architectural figure in New York in the 1920s were the sixteen-to-forty-three-story skyscraper loft and office buildings in the new "setback" style. The advent of setback massing, which revolutionized the scheme of the skyscraper in the 1920s, was precipitated by a pioneering 1916 New York zoning law that forced a new formula of design upon architects. Following the requirements demanded by the law, Kahn and his peers recast the skyscraper into a three-dimensional study of mass and silhouette. Ornament remained important but was simplified and subordinated to the overall effect of mass and profile. Many critics reacted positively to the transformed skyscraper. Lewis Mumford commented dryly that a "virtue" had been made of a "necessity."[58] Architectural critic Talbot Faulkner Hamlin (1889–1956) proclaimed the "necessity for mass composition" an "architectural blessing."[59] Kahn responded more romantically: "Almost unknown to the New Yorker himself, a new style of architecture is being created that is so characteristic of New York that it would be more logical, by far, to call it a New York Style, although it is also something essentially American. . . . While this new style is born . . . of legal and economic circumstances, it has yet become the soul and spirit of some of the most notable buildings of today. The New York laws protecting property rights, light and air, have encouraged a new art by reason of the very restrictions they contain. . . . The fact that the zoning law performed its artistic feat without premeditation is merely one of the curious tricks of fate that makes the new style doubly fascinating."[60] The soaring pyramidal masses and bold receding profiles of 1920s skyscrapers changed the city's skyline. The "New York Style," soon imitated nationwide, offered one solution to the search for an indigenous American style.

The legislation that had profound aesthetic and economic consequences for skyscraper design was, in large measure, a reaction to unbridled commercial development in Lower Manhattan. The lack of controls had caused alarming congestion, turned many narrow streets into canyons lacking air and light, and jeopardized property values. The drive to control growth began in the 1890s and came to a head in 1915 with the erection of Ernest R. Graham's massive forty-five-story Equitable Building (1913–15) on a square block at 120 Broadway. The 1916 zoning law divided the city into districts based on use (residential, business, or unrestricted), and placed controls on the height, bulk, and area that a

building could occupy on a lot.[61] The restrictions critical to the design of loft and office buildings were those of height and bulk. Maximum building height above the property line was dictated by the street width and the height zone in which the lot was located. Most commercial lots fell into either the "one and a half times" or "two times" zones.[62] Buchman & Kahn's Borden Building at 350 Madison Avenue, for example, was in a "two times" zone on a street eighty feet wide. Therefore, the limit of its height above the property line was one hundred sixty feet. In order to build higher, a setback was required. For each foot set back from the street line, four additional feet of height were allowed, provided that the setbacks fell within the angle of a line drawn from the center of the street through the point of limiting height at the street line. Towers of unlimited height were allowed to rise on 25 percent of a lot. The "setback principle" was illustrated diagrammatically in published texts of the zoning resolution (fig. 3.15).

As the post-war construction revival began, the problems of conforming to the new zoning regulations preoccupied commercial architects, animated professional discussions, and provoked

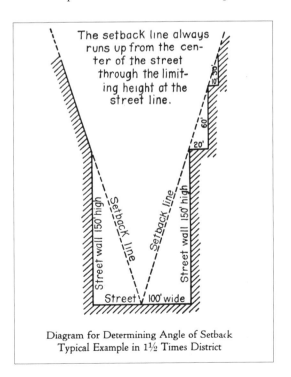

Diagram for Determining Angle of Setback
Typical Example in 1½ Times District

3.15 *"Diagram for Determining Angle of Setback," 1916 New York zoning law*

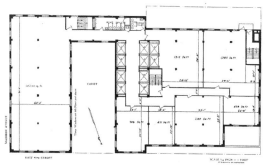

3.16 *Borden Building,
early scheme, 1921,
B&K*

3.17 *Borden Building,
thirteenth floor plan,
1921, B&K*

abundant analyses in newspapers and architectural journals. The intricacies of the law spawned a new profession of "consulting expert[s] in zoning" to interpret regulations, advise architects and builders, and mediate between them and the New York City Building Department.[63] Kahn recalled how the restrictive "envelope" was bitterly received by property owners and developers, who realized that their privileges had been diminished.[64] Clients pressured their architects, demanding the maximum allowed by the law. Financial return on investment—always a factor in skyscraper design but now threatened by zoning restrictions—made economics more of a determinant in 1920s design and was a challenge to New York's commercial architects.

The relationship of pre-Columbian pyramidal structures to the setback skyscraper was an issue discussed as early as 1925 in the *American Architect* by transplanted English architect Alfred C. Bossom (1881–1965), an unabashed admirer of Mayan architecture. Cognizant of American dependence on European tradition and the longstanding desire for a national American architecture, Bossom raised the question, "*hasn't America got an artistic heritage of her own?*" (emphasis in original), offering Mayan composition as the ideal model for American skyscraper design.[65] In another essay a year later Bossom connected these issues to the zoning law: "Compare these Mayan pyramids . . . with the present day, set-back American skyscraper. The resemblance is a startling one. . . . In fact, a comparison of . . . the Tikal pyramid . . . in Guatemala with a combination loft and office building thirty stories in height shows that America is doing by law what originally man in Mexico did by desire."[66] Chilean architect, archaeologist, and educator Francisco Mujica (1899–1979), a researcher of ruins in Mexico and Central America, ardently argued the existence of a relationship between pre-Columbian architecture and the setback skyscraper. Like Bossom in the *American Architect*, he noted, in his *History of the Skyscraper* (1929), the resemblance of the lines and proportions of setback skyscrapers to "elements of primitive American architecture," which he claimed had "approached us miraculously through modern skyscrapers." Mujica ventured that this so-called "miracle" applied to Buchman & Kahn's Park Avenue Building of 1927–28: "The skyscraper and modern art have arrived at this likeness without any influence of primitive American art having been brought to bear upon it. The example of [Two Park Avenue] is a point in fact. Mr. Ely J. Kahn of the firm Buchman & Kahn asserts that the forms of primitive American art have not furnished the slightest inspiration for this building."[67] Furthermore, at the time Kahn bluntly stated that it was inappropriate and "absurd to foist the . . . Maya naivete on a new building."[68] The possible influence of pre-Columbian architecture on the form of the 1920s setback skyscraper has been debated and discussed by a number of authors, and the consensus does not support a significant connection.[69] Rosemarie Bletter summed up the situation in *Skyscraper Style* (1975): "If architects in New York ever had in mind Pre-Columbian architecture, it came as an afterthought."[70]

The Borden Building

An office building commission in 1920 from the Borden Company for its new executive headquarters in the Grand Central Terminal District marked Kahn's emergence as a skyscraper architect. The deluxe twenty-three-story Borden Building, 350 Madison Avenue at 45th Street, his first major design in conformance with the new zoning law, was a milestone in Kahn's career. The initial, unexecuted scheme that was illustrated in the *New York Times* reveals the skillful manipulation of setbacks that Kahn planned and that distinguished his later 1920s work (fig. 3.16).[71] The unified, telescoping setbacks and bold, vertical continuity contrasted with contemporaneous massing such as that of the Aronson Building by Schwarz & Gross, in which a pedimented dormer—a motif favored early in the decade—accented the upper setbacked mass (fig. 3.18).[72] Although the zoning law permitted dormers, Kahn chose not to use them until 1925, when his treatment was simplified and without historical allusions.

The process of assembling the 95- by 175-foot southwest corner of Madison Avenue and 45th Street was complicated and prolonged.

3.18 *Schwartz & Gross, Aronson Building, 1921*

Ultimately a residential holdout caused a thirty-foot gap on 45th Street that forced an idiosyncratic plan (fig. 3.17). Because the office building was constructed in two stages,[73] costs escalated, the plan was inefficient, and the building appeared awkward. Despite the unified organization of the floors below the first setback, the fifteen-story Madison Avenue corner block and the connected twenty-three-story 45th Street annex failed to mesh, although the annex was

3.19 *Borden Building, bases of piers, 1922, B&K*

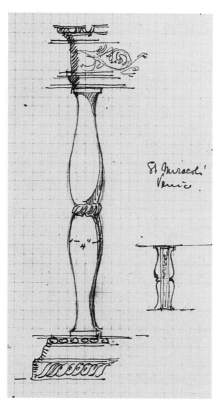

3.20 *Ely Jacques Kahn, Santa Maria dei Miracoli, Venice, detail, c. 1910–11*

effective on its own. The handling of setbacks in the annex was noted by architect Harvey Wiley Corbett (1873–1954), New York's most vocal theorist on the implications of zoning. Corbett praised the Borden Building's annex as an "excellent example of a high building on one of the narrower streets . . . [in which the] 'setbacks' are cleverly adjusted to an economical steel framing and yet keep almost the maximum floor area at each stage that the enclosing 'envelope' would permit."[74] What impressed Corbett was the unusual strategy of setting back almost all of the 45th Street annex six feet from the building line on the street elevation. By decreasing the depth of the street front bays, the need for costly steel for setbacks taken between bays was minimized.

The quality and abundance of decoration and attention to detail in the exterior treatment of the Borden Building attest to an ample budget, the importance of facade to a corporate client's commercial image, and the value of the property. Deference to its context on a prominent busi-

*3.21 Borden Building,
Madison Avenue corner,
twelfth and thirteenth
stories, 1922, B&K*

ness avenue near Grand Central Terminal and to the client's conservative image set the tone. Kahn used the conventional tripartite division into entrance base, office shaft, and terminating capital and organized the eight-story shaft sections into a pier–spandrel system of single-window bays, doubled at each corner. Both the Madison Avenue and 45th Street elevations were treated uniformly to the first setback and faced above the entrance base in variegated "tapestry" brick.[75] Except for entrances, brick rather than costly limestone was the fireproof material Kahn and his clients preferred for cladding the steel frame. The eclectic decoration suggested quattrocento sources. The inspiration for the double baluster, a recurring motif, was probably Santa Maria dei Miracoli, an early Venetian Renaissance church designed by Pietro Lombardo, which Kahn had sketched during his school travels (figs. 3.19 and 3.20). Unusual were the colossal pleated brick pilasters that rose from flared stone bases above the fourth-floor balustrade. For the decorative stone enrichment

Kahn continued his experiments with abstract geometric forms (fig. 3.21). The most innovative motifs and the least conspicuous from the street occurred on the parapets of upper setbacks. Here, under projecting canopies, are triangular brick pendants with faceted stone tips that prefigured Kahn's modernist ornament (fig. 3.22). Rich ornamental brickwork, either inlaid in the wall or in low relief, became a Buchman & Kahn hallmark.

Kahn's interest in brickwork paralleled the revival of brick vernacular traditions in Holland and Germany before and after World War I. The revival in Holland was influenced by architects of the Amsterdam School, most notably, its senior figure Hendrik Petrus Berlage (1856–1934). The work in Hamburg of Fritz Hoger (1877–1949), the major exponent of the post–World War I Hanseatic brick vernacular revival, and that of Hans Poelzig (1869–1936) in Berlin, as well as Peter Behrens's "medievalized" brick I. G. Farben Dyeworks in Frankfurt-Hoechst (1920–24), were undoubtedly known to Kahn.[76] As his work

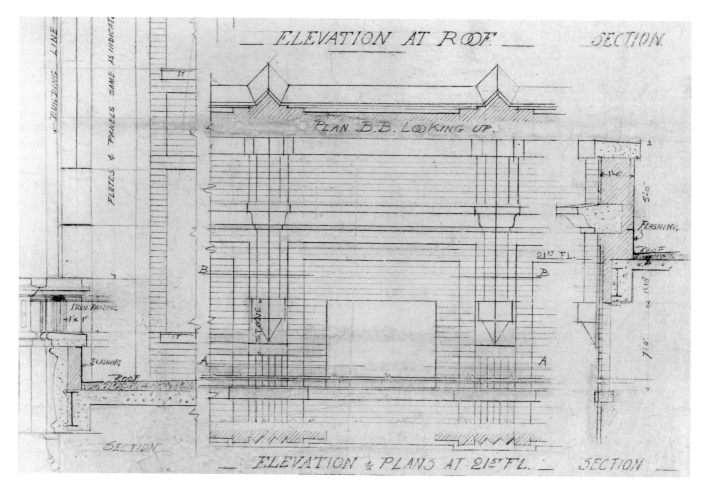

3.22 Borden Building
plan, detail of upper
setback, 1921, B&K

matured, the texture and patterning of the exterior brick wall assumed greater importance in Buchman & Kahn work.

Professional Networks

During the early years of the new partnership, Kahn's pursuit of professional contacts was considerable. In 1918 he affiliated with the Architectural League of New York, an organization that provided a strong social and creative mix of architects, artists, and other allied professionals and businesses. Kahn's relations with his peers were cordial and he valued their affirmation of him as "a mark of esteem."[77] He gravitated toward Raymond Hood and Ralph T. Walker, who joined the league in 1921 and 1922, respectively, and they became his closest colleagues.

The men, nicknamed the "Three Little Napoleons of Architecture," were frequently observed at lunch in the league dining room, "marking up many a table cloth between them with soft pencils." Fridays drew them downtown to the so-called "Four-Hour Lunch Club" at Mori's Italian Restaurant, where the Austrian émigré architect-designer Joseph Urban (1872–1933) and invited guests such as Frank Lloyd Wright joined them for lively exchanges of ideas.[78] The celebrated trio's relationship intensified as the decade progressed and each architect experienced success in commercial practice.

For the league's thirty-sixth annual exhibition in 1921, Kahn served on the "committee on catalogue" with Leon V. Solon (1872–1957), the transplanted English ceramic designer who later influenced Kahn's use of exterior polychrome, particularly in the Park Avenue Building. The exhibition included drawings of Buchman & Kahn's Borden and Jay-Thorpe Buildings, the Kahn and Feldman factory, and the Elmsford country houses of Kahn and Herman Younker.[79] Elevated to chairman of the committee on catalogue for the league's annual exhibition the following year, Kahn undoubtedly knew of Hugh Ferriss's (1889–1962) provocative "zoning envelope" studies before the exhibit opened at the Fine Arts Building on February 5, 1922. Ferriss's influential drawings, which were based on Harvey Wiley Corbett's diagrams hypothesizing four stages of the evolution of an envelope under the 1916 zoning law, dramatized the three-dimensional possibilities of pyramidal form and the awesome sculptural power of simple masses.[80] In his writing Kahn never mentioned Ferriss, nor is there evidence of anything more than a superficial relationship between the men. Judging from the limited patronage of Ferriss by the firm, Kahn did not warm to Ferriss's brooding, visionary constructions. The firm preferred delineators Schell Lewis, Francis Keally, and J. Floyd Yewell.[81]

In 1921 Kahn became a member of the American Institute of Architects, and two years later he was elected by the board of directors to the Allied Arts Committee.[82] The mission of the committee was to foster a close relationship between architects and the artists allied to architecture, a role that fit well with Kahn's aesthetic propensity for architectural decoration. Kahn's expanding network of contacts through his father-in-law, as well as the New York Society for Ethical Culture, the Society of Beaux-Arts Architects, the Architectural League of New York, and the American Institute of Architects helped consolidate his position of leadership in the firm. Moreover, he had garnered an award for the Jay-Thorpe department store in the Fifth Avenue District and designed an office building for the Borden Company, a major corporation, in the Grand Central Terminal District. Although Kahn's work was mixed and evolving, by 1922 he was poised to benefit from the upcoming building boom, especially in the burgeoning Garment District along Seventh Avenue.

CHAPTER FOUR

BUILDING BOOM

Garment District Developers and Design,

1921–25

The frenzied pitch of the 1920s building boom was vividly portrayed at the end of 1925 in a *New York Times* article titled "Titanic Forces Rear a New Skyline":

The remaking of New York is at full tide. . . . A host of workers is striving to complete before snow fall the 350 buildings under construction on Manhattan Island. Another army of workmen is engaged in altering no less than 900 buildings. . . . Relatively new structures of eight to ten floors are demolished and skyscrapers put up. . . . Rents rise even faster than do buildings. . . . This activity finds its greatest expression in the garment centre around Thirty-seventh Street and Seventh Avenue, where a dozen buildings are under way, varying from fifteen to twenty-odd floors. . . . Sixth Avenue, long under blight of the elevated railroad, is joining in the movement. . . . Buildings of twenty floors and more rise as a matter of course. . . . They have even ceased to attract any particular notice.[1]

The greatest concentration of Buchman & Kahn commercial work—twenty office and loft buildings, all extant—were erected between 1919 and 1931 in the new Garment District (fig. 4.1). Its development shaped a remarkable chapter in the city's history and decisively affected Kahn's career. By 1915 the incursion of clothing manufacturers into loft buildings on side streets off Fifth Avenue had reached above 34th Street. Sidewalks jammed with immigrant factory workers blocked the carriage trade's access to retail establishments during the fashionable shopping hour between noon and one o'clock. Property owners feared the ruin of Fifth Avenue and adjacent residential neighborhoods north to 59th Street. After anguishing over the problem for several years without resolution, a number of retail merchants from the Fifth Avenue Association, a private interest group organized in 1907, met early in 1916 to deal decisively with the threat. Determined to act, thirteen merchants, three of whom were Buchman & Fox clients (Bonwit Teller; Saks; and L. P. Hollander), joined together under the militant leadership of J. Howes Burton, and declared themselves the "Save New York Committee." An ambitious plan was formulated to create a large area free of manufacturing in the heart of the city, dubbed the "Save New York Zone," the borders of which were initially 59th Street, north; 32nd and 33rd Streets,

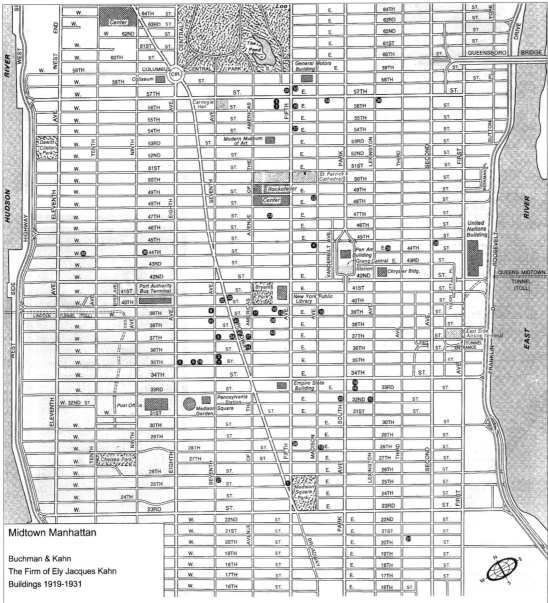

Midtown Manhattan

Buchman & Kahn

The Firm of Ely Jacques Kahn

Buildings 1919-1931

Key to Map

1. Cusack Building (1919)
2. Armion Building (1920)
3. Jay Thorpe Building (1920/1929)
4. Borden Building (1922)
5. Rubin Building (1924)
6. Ludwig Baumann Building (1922)
7. Arsenal Building (1925)
8. Banco Building (1925)
9. 550 Seventh Avenue (1925)
10. Scientific American Building (1925)
11. Millinery Center (1925)
12. 15 West 39th Street (1926)
13. 79 Madison Avenue (1925)
14. Lefcourt-Empire Building (1926)
15. Furniture Exchange Building (1925)

16. Lefcourt-Madison Building (1925)
17. 1001 Sixth Avenue (1926)
18. 271 Madison Avenue (1927)
19. 247 West 35th Street (1926)
20. Park Avenue Building (1927)
21. Pinaud Factory (1927)
22. 424 Madison Avenue (1926)
23. Federation Building (1928)
24. Lefcourt-State Building (1928)
25. Bergdorf Goodman Building (1927)
26. Grand Central Terminal Building (1927)
27. Lefcourt Clothing Center (1928)
28. 261 Fifth Avenue (1928)
29. Allied Arts Building (1929)
30. Film Center Building (1929)

31. 530 Seventh Avenue (1929)
32. Bricken Textile Building (1930)
33. Squibb Building (1930)
34. Rolls Royce Building (1930)
35. Bonwit Teller Building (1930) (demolished)
36. 136 East 57th Street (1931)
37. Richard Hudnut Building (1931) (demolished)
38. Paramount Publix Warehouse (1931)
39. Commerce Building (1931)
40. 1400 Broadway (1931)
41. Bricken Casino Building (1931)
42. Continental Building (1931)
43. Bomzon Building (1925)

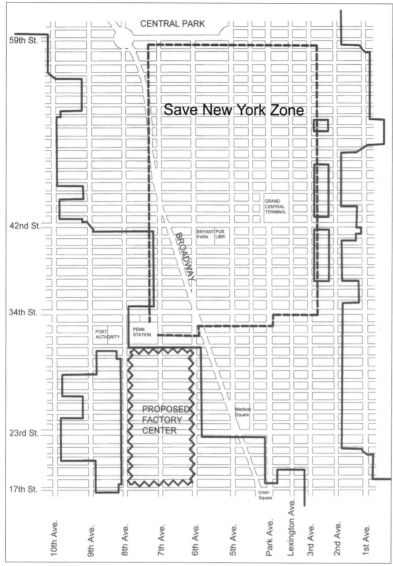

4.2 "Save New York Zone,"
1918

south; Third Avenue, east; and Seventh Avenue, west (fig. 4.2). At the end of January, the *New York Times* applauded the plan in an editorial, and early in March an advertising campaign was launched in the daily newspapers.[2] The pressure of an economic boycott persuaded manufacturers to move out of the zone when their leases expired, prevented others from entering the zone, and halted new factory and loft construction there. Remarkably, by midsummer 1916, 95 percent of the manufacturers affected by the boycott had

agreed to move. The inducement to the nation's largest body of ready-to-wear manufacturers was the promise of a stable, centralized enclave elsewhere in the city, where cheaper rents, more light and air, and better equipped space would be available to them and accessible to out-of-town buyers arriving by rail at Pennsylvania Station and Grand Central Terminal. Less than a year after the Save New York Committee had mobilized, its goal, with adjusted boundaries to the zone, was assured. The campaign's outcome ultimately benefited all parties: Fifth Avenue retained its status, manufacturers' rents were reduced, and labor conditions were improved. Seventh Avenue (between 34th and 42nd Streets) became the Garment District's main artery—and a synonym for the women's fashion industry. The massive rebuilding and revitalization along this spine between Sixth and Ninth Avenues would take more than a decade, a period that, for the most part, coincided with the 1920s building boom.

The building boom of the 1920s was propelled by speculators who profited from plentiful finance capital at low interest rates and a stabilized market for labor and materials. Overbuilding of office space had caused intense rental competition for ten years prior to World War I. The wartime construction moratorium and sluggish postwar revival, along with an expanding population and economy, created an urgent need for modern, efficient space conveniently located to the city's new business and manufacturing centers. However, conditions for new construction were unfavorable during 1919, 1920, and 1921. Building loans were costly and difficult to obtain, and labor and materials were expensive. The situation began to improve in 1921, and by early 1922, interest rates had descended to about 5 percent—from a mid-1920 high of almost 9 percent.[3] The major obstacle to a construction boom in 1922 was the high cost of labor. Although demands for higher wages and union turmoil persisted through 1923, investors regained confidence, the commercial real estate market boomed, and all previous construction records were broken.[4] At the end of 1923, a two-year labor settlement was reached with thirty-eight of the forty-eight New York building trades. Reduction of interest rates, lower at the end of 1924 than at any time since 1915, further stimulated building. Real estate transactions in 1925 shattered the 1923 record. The boom produced new buildings at a fantastic rate. Office space increased a staggering 92 percent from 1925 to 1931 in New York, where the vacancy factor, normal at 9.85 percent, was 5.5 percent in 1925.[5] Between 1923 and 1931 no fewer than forty-five buildings were erected from plans of Buchman & Kahn and following Buchman's retirement in 1930, its successor, The Firm of Ely Jacques Kahn.

The rapid spread of mortgage bond financing and the proliferation of speculative builders fueled this building boom. Traditionally, real estate and building projects had been financed primarily by savings banks or insurance companies, both extremely conservative lenders. In the 1920s the mortgage business was revolutionized by specialized mortgage and real estate security underwriting firms known as "bond houses." The sale of mortgage bonds to small investors all over the country tapped an enormous source of capital that flowed into New York real estate during the decade. Banks and insurance companies only offered partial financing of a project, but mortgage bond issues could provide full value with longer and more flexible terms—a boon to developers. Many of Kahn's clients used this method to fund operations, often through S. W. Straus and Company, the largest underwriter of real estate bonds in the United States.[6]

Before World War I and the boom, association with speculative builders, or "promoters," would tarnish an architect's reputation. The boom caused many architects to compromise their standards, however, because the bulk of big commercial work came from "promoted jobs." Consorting with promoters had advantages other than financial: These commissions were thought by some in the field to have produced the period's best buildings.[7] The promoter gave the commercial architect more freedom to express himself than the traditional client, who generally was a noted individual, trustee, or building committee. Kahn's experience affirmed this perspective: "In the earlier days of New York, buildings were

erected by men of capital as sound investment to which these solid men of affairs affixed their names. They were essentially conservative and insisted on traditional designs. Today [1926] the owner is a shrewd real estate operator who visualizes the type of development that made a Jewelry Center appear in a year's time, a Garment Center out of nothing. He seldom insists on discussing architectural detail. He realizes that the trained man who is paid to do a certain thing knows more of that particular detail than he does. The architect is more free to strike new paths than ever before."[8] Nonetheless, the architect had to satisfy the practical requirements and the speculator's assurance of an ample return on investment. Many of Kahn's speculative clients were self-made Jewish garment manufacturers, often of German, Eastern European, or Russian origin, although sometimes native-born, who had come up "the hard way." From their vantage point in the trade, they foresaw the demand that the industry's relocation to a centralized district would bring, and they plunged into speculation. Kahn competed with other Jewish architectural firms, particularly the offices of Schwartz & Gross and George & Edward Blum, who specialized in speculative commercial work.

The Rubin and Arsenal Buildings: Establishing a Reputation in the Garment District

Following the firm's sixteen-story Armion Building, 469 Seventh Avenue (a minor design erected from 1919 to 1920 on the southeast corner of 36th Street), two commissions for massive Seventh Avenue lofts nearby—the Rubin and Arsenal Buildings—established Kahn's reputation in the Garment District. Lofts, a building type indigenous (but not exclusive) to New York, were multistory structures built as rental properties that catered to the needs of the apparel industry. In the district zoned for business, the 1916 zoning law allowed a maximum of 25 percent light manufacturing use; the remaining space accommodated storage of merchandise, showrooms, offices for tenants, and in desirable locations, street-level stores. In the summer of 1922 developer Hyman B. Rubin and builder Joseph

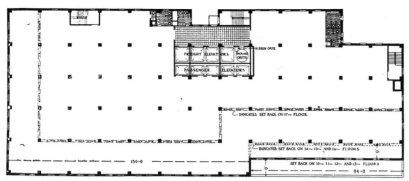

4.3 *Rubin Building, typical floor plan, 1922, B&K*

4.4 *Rubin Building, 1923, B&K*

E. Gilbert purchased the lot on the northeast corner of Seventh Avenue and 37th Street for a millinery center. Months of negotiations between the Save New York Committee and the leadership of the millinery trade had led to an endorsement of this industry's centralization in the new district. Upon acquiring the property, Rubin and Gilbert engaged Buchman & Kahn to plan a mixed office–loft building for light manufacturing, showrooms, millinery organizations, and a club for the trade.[9] The seventeen-story Rubin Building, 501 Seventh Avenue, also known as the Millinery Center, was the first of several for this trade in the Garment District; two were designed by Buchman & Kahn. Although plans in Avery Library designated Julius Gregory (1875–1955) as associate architect, his role remains vague and seems to have been minor; published references attributed the building solely to Buchman & Kahn.[10]

Practical planning was the prime consideration in the design of rental lofts. As in all commercial properties, the objective was an efficient building at minimum cost that yielded the maximum income over the longest possible period. The two most important factors in the ratio of cost to income were, first, the "plot solution"— that is, the configuration of the building on the lot, which the firm projected in a composite plan that superimposed setbacks in relation to the lot—and, second, the typical floor plan. In the Buchman & Kahn office intensive study was concentrated on the formulation of both. The firm made a practice of analyzing and categorizing sites, and developing plot solutions and floor plans for each type of lot.[11] Because the expense of the enclosing wall was the major construction cost, the firm's plot solutions tended to take on simple shapes (as close to square or rectangle as possible) that limited the wall's length.

On the long, narrow, rectangular corner sites of the Rubin and Arsenal Buildings, a favorable distribution of floor area was attained by placing the passenger and freight elevators back to back in a group at the rear center, and by dividing the other services along the party walls. This was an ideal layout—without freight and passenger crossover—for one or two tenants per floor (fig.

4.3). The Rubin and Arsenal plans were Kahn's typical arrangement for loft floors of approximately 20,000 square feet.[12] According to Kahn, column spacing, determined by the need for economical steel construction and the desire for uninterrupted open space, was "the most important consideration" in the planning of factory buildings.[13] If the bays became too large (from fifteen to twenty-two feet was the optimal range), the cost of steel mounted precipitously, and deeper girders lowered ceiling heights. In terms of function, structural columns spaced eighteen to nineteen feet apart and two-window bays made subdivision flexible and economical for manufacturing, showrooms, and perimeter offices. The rule of thumb for column spacing in Buchman & Kahn lofts was eighteen to twenty feet on center.[14]

Because the Rubin and Arsenal Buildings occupied corner lots fronting 100 feet on Seventh Avenue, with depths of 244 feet on 37th Street and 200 feet on 35th Street, respectively, all parts of the buildings that were more than 150 feet from the Seventh Avenue corners were subject to the zoning regulations for narrower streets and were set back accordingly (fig. 4.4). The Rubin Building's facade combined historical decoration on the lower floors with an experimental decorative treatment of the upper floors. A simple base from a preliminary scheme (fig. 4.5) would have harmonized better with the composition's strong interplay of verticals and horizontals and powerful corner masses, but the client doubtless demanded the highly embellished, eclectic entrance zone. The motifs of the Rubin Building's third-story transitional banding, however, were simplified to layered and framed squares that alternate at angles to each other (fig. 4.6). Kahn's source may, again, have been a drawing from his Beaux-Arts sketchbook, the Venetian Gothic Addolorata Chapel cornice in the Dominican church of Santi Giovanni e Paolo (fig. 4.7). The crisply stacked and staggered squares also recall the early twentieth-century ornament of the Wagner School architect Robert Farsky in Vienna (fig. 4.8).[15] Variations on these motifs became standard in Kahn's post-1925 decorative vocabulary.

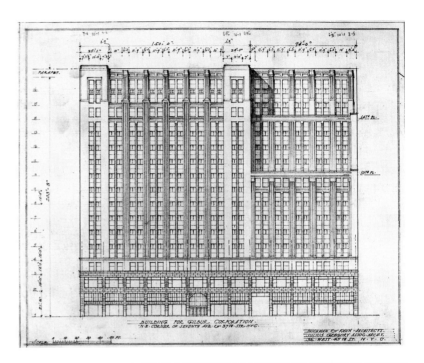

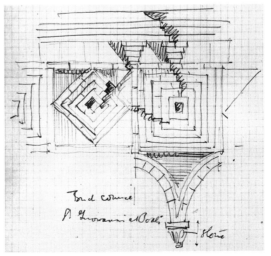

TOP

4.5 Buchman & Kahn, Architects, and Julius Gregory, Associated Architect, "Building for Gilbur Corporation," preliminary scheme, 1922

ABOVE

4.6 Rubin Building, detail of transitional frieze, 1923, B&K

LEFT

4.7 Ely Jacques Kahn, brick cornice, St. Giovanni e Paolo, Venice, detail, c. 1910–11

4.8 Robert Farsky, apartment house, Vienna, c. 1904

4.9 York & Sawyer, Bowery Savings Bank, entrance, 1923

FACING PAGE
4.10 Arsenal Building, 1925, B&K

The facade above the third-story frieze was organized by piers and spandrels into shallow, two-window bays and faced in two tones of brick. The spandrels and the stripes that delineate each load-bearing column received the reddish-brown accent color; the rest of the wall was faced in the background color, a light buff. This bold yet economical manipulation of brick produced a rhythmic pattern that flows across the elevations and helps relieve the sheer bulk of the mass. Except for the end bays, the two-story attic was slightly recessed to produce an effect of corner pylons. Kahn's treatment evoked praise from architectural critic Talbot F. Hamlin who found the Rubin Building's "ornament of an unconventional character" and its "new feeling for mass" especially interesting for an inexpensive building.[16]

The Rubin Building's layered and outlined ornament and dark banding were details associated with Josef Hoffmann, who influenced Kahn's work in the 1920s and 1930s. The opening in New York City in 1922 of an American branch of the Wiener Werkstätte, directed by the Austrian émigré architect-designer Joseph Urban, may have inspired Kahn. Its elegant galleries, at 581 Fifth Avenue, were decorated with dark rectilinear banding reminiscent of early Hoffmann.[17] Kahn's attempt at a progressive decorative scheme in the Rubin Building was innovative for New York in 1922. More typical was York & Sawyer's Bowery Savings Bank on 42nd Street between Lexington and Park Avenues (fig. 4.9). Completed in June of 1923, the architects' use of Italian Byzantine and Romanesque architectural decoration precipitated a vogue for those styles that swept the city and prompted this observation from a speaker at the convention of the American Institute of Architects in 1924: "And just now in New York, because presumably of the notable success of a certain splendid bank building inspired by the Romanesque of Lombardy, there are signs of a coming epidemic."[18] Although the Rubin and Arsenal Buildings, designed only a year apart, were comparable in site, purpose, scale, and plan, their exterior schemes differed significantly. Unlike the Rubin Building, the Arsenal Building was emphatically medieval in spirit (fig. 4.10). The reversion to a historical revival, after the success of the moderately progressive Rubin Building, suggests the pressure of clients who demanded the popular style.

In the summer of 1923 the New York State Arsenal was sold to three builders for $1,350,000—a record high for the location.[19] The new owners, Henry Greenberg, Maurice Blenstock, and Louis Bergias, moved quickly to develop the property, a choice location near Pennsylvania Station. Early in November they applied for a building permit from Buchman & Kahn plans.[20] The demolished arsenal was recalled by the new building's name and its sixteenth-story battlement, but the inspiration for the decorative program was York & Sawyer's Bowery Savings Bank. To attract tenants willing to pay higher rents, the owners made a substantial investment in decoration; the high price of the land required rentals greater than those of neighboring buildings in order to meet carrying costs.

The imposing four-story entrance base of the twenty-one-story Arsenal Building, 463 Seventh Avenue, one of the most lavish in the Garment District, was the primary focus of the building's exterior decoration (figs. 4.10, 4.11). The distinctive element in the richly plastic scheme was the treatment of the structural piers. From the sidewalk to the mezzanine, piers were faced with rose-color granite. At the mezzanine, single rows of variegated buff brick laid in stack bond were alternated with vertical terra-cotta infills to simulate column fluting. These applied columns were topped at the fourth floor by projecting terra-cotta basket capitals of entwined plant and animal forms. The spandrels between the second and third floor held interlaced terra-cotta panels. Alternating with fourth-floor windows and recessed between paired pilasters were niches covered with abstract Byzantine motifs. The building's Seventh Avenue entrance featured four niches with sculpted figures (an unusual treatment for the firm) surmounted by a frieze of grotesque mascarons. A projecting terra-cotta belt course repeated details from the capitals and defined the separation of entrance base from shaft. Byzantine ornament carried over into the lobby, where Tennessee marble covered the floor, mottled

Botticino marble paneled the walls, and the light tracery of the barrel-vaulted ceiling was described as "time colored plaster work."[21] The tour de force of the lobby was the bronze elevator doors, which featured a motif based on a tenth-century Byzantine panel from St. Mark's Cathedral in Venice and was surrounded by sparkling mosaic glass. The building's letterbox carried the popular Byzantine and Islamic "Tree of Life" motif with an interlaced border. Interior details were coordinated and designed specifically for the building.

In his 1924 *Architectural Forum* essay, "The Office Building Problem in New York," Kahn rejected the use of ready-made stock designs and noted a growing desire among owners of commercial buildings for original, custom-made equipment, such as elevator cars and doors, letterboxes, and directories. In the same issue, architect William Lamb observed that clients were becoming more receptive to "an investment in beauty" for entrances.[22] C. H. Blackall, writing in the *American Architect* a few years later, commented that an expenditure on beauty that earlier would have seemed a "reckless extravagance . . . now is accepted as a matter of course . . . and the public realizes as never before that beauty in architecture is an asset, that a good looking building, a successful architectural design rents better, sells better, and wears better than one in which the artistic element is subordinate to the so-called practical requirements."[23] Kahn was certainly an exponent of this approach. For commercial projects after the Arsenal Building, when the budget permitted it, the Buchman & Kahn firm devoted considerable energy to the design of sumptuous entrances and lobbies.

The vertical organization of the Arsenal Building differed from that of the Rubin Building. For example, Kahn abandoned the pier–spandrel system for a treatment that emphasized planarity. The simplicity of the shaft's vast surfaces acted as a foil for the richly plastic base and the parapets of the upper setbacks (see fig. 4.10). Although smooth brick facing was not unprecedented in Kahn's work, he no doubt paid attention to Arthur Loomis Harmon's (1878–1958) thirty-four-story Shelton Hotel on

FACING PAGE
4.11 Arsenal Building, Seventh Avenue entrance, 1925, B&K

4.12 Arthur Loomis Harmon, Shelton Hotel, 1924

Lexington Avenue at 49th Street, which was nearing completion (fig. 4.12). Although Kahn admired the powerful setback massing, which elicited critical acclaim, and praised it publicly, the height and massing of the Shelton were inappropriate for Kahn's loft buildings.[24] Nonetheless, a relationship can be seen between the Shelton Hotel and the Arsenal Building. The latter is more static than soaring and less complex in its massing than the Shelton, but, like Harmon, Kahn employed simple forms and emulated the Lombard Romanesque architecture strategy from of contrasting austere wall planes of brick with smaller areas of concentrated decoration.

Kahn's disregard for the expression of the steel skeleton in the Arsenal Building scheme was in line with a pervasive change in outlook among architects. The struggle to express the steel frame, which had preoccupied professionals at the turn of the twentieth century, had become a "dead issue" by 1924 according to architect-educator Fiske Kimball.[25] As a result of the 1916 zoning law, mass design became the focus of architectural thought in the 1920s. Powerful sculptural form expressed, for example, in the romantic visions of renderer Hugh Ferriss, inspired dramatic compositions and became the ideal as architectural theories were temporarily laid to rest. The function of the "skin" of a building changed conceptually from that of covering a frame to that of containing the bulk of a building. It was not surprising to read of "hiding" the steel frame, instead of expressing it, and "dressing" the envelope.[26] In 1924 Kahn wrote that the facade of a modern skyscraper office building was simply a "question of clothing," a metaphor that would resonate with his Garment District clients.[27]

The Arsenal Building, Kahn's first unified setback scheme, brought him critical recognition. C. Matlack Price, a former editor of *Architectural Record*, praised the building in the same breath as the Shelton Hotel for its "interesting lines" and "towering, receding masses."[28] The building was featured in the *American Architect* and was selected to illustrate the editorial "Office Buildings of Today and Tomorrow" in the January 1928 issue of *Architectural Forum*, evidence of how distant American architecture was from European modernism during this period.[29]

The Arsenal Building brought to a close Kahn's "apprenticeship" years with the Buchman organization. He had worked hard and fast to distance himself from Buchman & Fox formulas. Relying at first on those around him, he rapidly overcame his deficiencies and mastered the new zoning regulations. His published writing widened his exposure and enhanced his reputation as an expert in his field. He contributed to the Architectural League of New York and earned the respect of his peers. Kahn was his own man now and ideally positioned to reap the benefits of

the commercial building boom. The trajectory of his rise to prominence would parallel the era of Coolidge prosperity.

Buildings for Adler, Adelson, and Shroder & Koppel

Kahn attracted and retained as clients four of the most influential New York real estate entrepreneurs of the 1920s, whose business proved the major factor in the realization of his mature work: Louis Adler, Abe N. Adelson, Abraham E. [A. E.] Lefcourt, and Abraham Bricken.[30] During the building boom, Buchman & Kahn designed nineteen office and loft buildings (two unrealized) for these four clients. Their buildings are the most outstanding the firm produced. During the planning of the Arsenal Building at the end of 1923, builders Millard Shroder (1890–1971) and Arthur Koppel (1891–1974) of Shroder & Koppel Construction Company introduced Kahn to Louis Adler (1883–1959), an Austrian-born dress manufacturer, and to Abe N. Adelson (1884–1949), a native New York millinery manufacturer. Both men were eager to profit from escalating values in the Garment District. How Kahn met the builders is not known, but Shroder had worked for seven years before the war in the Bing & Bing Real Estate Company, where he likely had had contact with Buchman & Fox.[31] Certainly, the builders were acquainted with Buchman & Kahn's earlier Garment District work, the Armion and Rubin Buildings and the projected Arsenal Building. Kahn remembered the builders as young men of integrity and energy.[32] Energetic, indeed. By the early 1930s Shroder and Koppel were ranked with construction industry giants George A. Fuller, Thompson-Starrett, and the Starrett Brothers and Eken Companies, on a short list of seven "Outstanding Building Contractors" in *New York: The Wonder City*.[33]

Louis Adler, a prototypical self-made man, had emigrated from Austria as a boy and at sixteen had started work in a wholesale house selling ladies shirtwaists for three dollars a week.[34] Ten years later Adler launched his own dress-manufacturing business, and by 1923, at age thirty-nine, he had amassed enough capital to speculate in real estate. Experience had taught Adler what made a loft building work, and he began with the building type he knew best. Adler was in the process of negotiating a leasehold with the Trinity Church Corporation for the northwest corner of Seventh Avenue and 39th Street, on which he and Adelson planned to develop a loft building for manufacturers of quality ladies wear.[35] The design of the twenty-three-story 550 Seventh Avenue Building began a prolific collaboration of eight years between Kahn, clients Adler and Adelson, and builders Shroder and Koppel. All of Adler's projects (two in partnership with Adelson) were designed by the firm and constructed by Shroder and Koppel. What cemented Adler's patronage of Kahn? Looking back, Kahn declared: "At no time do I remember Adler becoming difficult, for he concentrated on what he did so well, in finances, in the handling of tenants, always honest with contractors." Although Kahn admired his client's shrewd sense of value, ambition, and the courage to take risks, personal relations appear to have had little influence—Kahn described Adler in retrospect as a "man with very little of social grace, no glitter of education."[36] Adler, for his part, appreciated Kahn's expertise, especially in the aesthetics of architecture, and it may well have been the crucial factor in Kahn's ability to retain the client. Because Adler's loft and office buildings were tailored to attract high-caliber professionals and manufacturers of exclusive apparel—tenants who needed to project an image of taste and discernment—the quality of design and location was paramount. For that reason, Adler developed only corner sites. Renting strictly to high-level manufacturers became an undeviating policy of his that established a distinctive identity for a building and its occupants with out-of-town buyers. (The current roster of manufacturers at 550 Seventh Avenue includes Donna Karan International, Bill Blass Couture, Ralph Lauren, and Oscar de la Renta, among others, and attests to the enduring success of Adler's strategy.)

Independently, Adelson matched—and at times exceeded—Adler's enterprise. Whereas Adler confined his building operations to the Garment District and the West Side, Adelson shifted his focus to the East Side and other locations. For the most part, but not exclusively, Adelson remained a client of the firm and built with Shroder & Koppel. Contemporaneous press coverage of Adelson's real estate transactions reveals little of the man other than his ambition and astute investments.[37] The fact that two of Kahn's most significant works—the polychrome Park Avenue Building (2 Park Avenue, 1927) and the elegant Squibb Building (745 Fifth Avenue, 1930)—were Adelson projects suggests a synergy that inspired Kahn creatively and brought Adelson profit and prestige.

In his memoirs Kahn mentioned that he had often been asked how business had been generated. Had clients been intimate friends? Had he entertained them? Were commissions to others involved? Kahn, perhaps referring to Shroder and Koppel, stated that initially jobs had come from "friendly contacts of young men at the start of their careers," yet he claimed to have had "no social life with contractors or clients," mainly because of time constraints. Kahn believed that prospective clients chose him because of their confidence in his record of service and integrity[38]—ideally, perhaps, but business relationships were clearly more complex than Kahn described. However much downplayed, partnering with clients, especially in the Garment District, involved a network of connections and negotiation of sensitive issues involving comfort with religious and ethnic backgrounds.

At the end of 1923 Adler concluded his deal with the Trinity Church Corporation for the leasehold on the northwest corner at Seventh Avenue and 39th Street, the nearly 100-foot-square site of St. Chrysostom's Chapel, a mid-nineteenth-century Gothic revival landmark that was demolished to make way for the twenty-four-story loft.[39] Although the venture, ambitious in its day, met with skepticism from many veteran manufacturers, it was fully rented before completion.[40] The immediate success of 550 Seventh Avenue led Adler and Adelson to their next acquisition: the northeast corner of Sixth Avenue and 39th Street, a site with old stores and rooming houses in a rundown section near the Sixth Avenue El. In real estate and building circles the

4.13 550 Seventh
Avenue Building, 1925,
B&K. Pictorial Review
Building, partial view

pioneering move was hailed as the "forerunner of the development of [Sixth Avenue] north of 34th Street." Plans by Buchman & Kahn for a new Millinery Center loft on the site were filed at the end of March 1925, less than three months after the formal opening of 550 Seventh Avenue. In order to complete the building before the end of the year, three construction shifts were scheduled for the summer months.[41] After successfully completing these two Garment District lofts, Adler and Adelson separated as partners.

Of Buchman & Kahn's work between 1923 and mid-1925, the first two lofts designed for real estate entrepreneurs Adler and Adelson (550 Seventh Avenue and the Millinery Center on Sixth Avenue at 39th Street), and the loft developed and built by Shroder & Koppel (Sixth Avenue at 37th Street), epitomize the skyscraper model evolved by Kahn at this stage. On equivalent corner lots, these three twenty-three-story Garment District lofts demonstrate that Kahn's starting point was the Arsenal Building and his focus was the

ABOVE LEFT
4.14 *Millinery Center, 1925, B&K*

LEFT
4.15 *Building at Sixth Avenue and 37th Street, 1926, B&K*

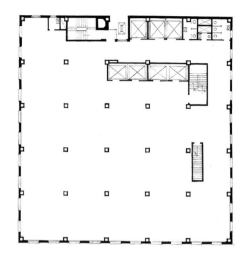

4.16 *Building at Sixth Avenue and 37th Street, typical plan, 1926, B&K*

designing of decoration and the modeling of upper setbacks (figs. 4.13, 4.14, 4.15). Kahn described the challenge of skyscraper design as "a search for forms allied to the rigid and powerful block of the building itself: shapes that are more a series of planes that become attractive through the play of light and shadow." In this quest he identified with cubist painters and sculptors.[42]

Flexibility of plan—a major concern of clients and their financiers—was a Buchman & Kahn strength. In order to secure the most open floor area and fully utilize light and ventilation from street fronts, passenger and freight elevators and other service facilities were widely separated and

4.17 *Millinery Center, setbacks, 1925, B&K*

banked along party walls in the 550 Seventh Avenue plan. This plan (typical for Buchman & Kahn lofts housing one tenant per floor on a square corner lot) was repeated for the Millinery Center. The ground floors—as generators of substantial revenue—differed, however. In contrast to the 550 Seventh Avenue Building, which provided for one major street-front tenant (the Bank of the United States), the Millinery Center was designed for multiple street-front tenants. Because the loft on Sixth Avenue at 37th Street was planned to accommodate more than one tenant per floor, passenger elevators were moved parallel and closer to freight elevators for greater flexibility of subdivision—a type of planning the firm called "safety of investment through diversification," the ability to convert from one type and occupancy to another (fig. 4.16).[43]

The massing of the three twenty-three-story lofts was similar and followed the Arsenal model: three horizontal divisions composed of entrance base, planar shaft, and upper setback stories. The uniformly fenestrated walls of the midsection were faced in tapestry brick and given strong terminals. Proportioned setback tiers crowned the buildings. What distinguished each loft were Kahn's decorative programs and experimental setback treatments. The 550 Seventh Avenue Building receded in four stages above the sixteenth-story parapet arcade. Fenestration was kept consistent with the shaft and the setbacks, which graduated crisply as they ascended and were differentiated at their taut edges by brick corbelling. As building height increased in the 1920s, patterning in "shadow brick" became an economical means of harmonizing sidewalls with the main elevation.[44] On the predominantly blank north wall of 550 Seventh Avenue a bold horizontal and vertical interplay of shadow brick continued the lines of corbelling and accented the fenestration. The striking composition caught the eye of German architect Erich Mendelsohn (1887–1953), who photographed it on his visit to the United States in 1926. The image, titled "New York *Hochhaus*," shows the setbacks to their best advantage and appeared in Mendelsohn's book, *Amerika*, two years later. Another photograph, "*Nachbild*," captured the

4.18 Eliel Saarinen, second prize rendering, Chicago Tribune competition, 1922

dramatic nocturnal illumination of the firm's Cusack Building (25th Street between Fifth Avenue and Broadway).[45]

With the exception of the upper stories, where Kahn switched to a pier–spandrel system to achieve vertical continuity, the general massing of the Millinery Center was identical to that of 550 Seventh Avenue (fig. 4.17). Vertical telescoping setbacks were new in Kahn's work and may have been influenced by the celebrated design of Finnish architect Eliel Saarinen (1873–1950) for the *Chicago Tribune* competition in 1922 (Kahn did not enter). Although John Mead Howells and Raymond Hood of New York

4.19 Building at Sixth Avenue and 37th Street, setbacks, 1926, B&K

flared outward on the upper setbacks. These were undecorated except for triangular or flat pilasters along the parapets. Abstract motifs, such as these that alluded to classical triglyphs, became standard in Kahn's repertoire after 1925. From the street, the flared setbacks appear as bold serrated diagonals that give the building a dramatic visual lift. In the chapter on "stripped architecture" in *The New World Architecture*, Cheney illustrated the setbacks and called them "'proportioned boxes,'" adding that the building honestly expressed the shallowness of wall on steel frame.[46]

Kahn's experiments with tower features continued. In the loft building on Sixth Avenue and 37th Street he employed a strategy that emphasized the corner site. Utilizing the dormer provision of the 1916 zoning law for the first time, Kahn broke the horizontal setbacks with smaller, box-like volumes stacked at each side (fig. 4.19). The result was a sharp, clean profile that heightened the interplay of surface planes. The setbacks were unified with decorative horizontal bands that belted each story and parapet. Within these bands rhythmic, geometric patterns in relief were accented with a reddish brick that contrasted with the otherwise neutral buff-colored cladding. Kahn continued to develop the boxlike dormer to relieve and accent massing, and it became one of the hallmarks of his mature work. Although unusual for a New York building designed early in 1925, the treatment of setbacks in this loft was consistent with Kahn's testing of geometric decoration. The tight horizontal bands and crisp, outlined edges suggest the influence of Josef Hoffmann. Because Kahn kept abreast of progressive architecture and design in his post–World War I travels to Europe, a more likely source of inspiration would have been the horizontally striped and decoratively banded setbacks in the Dutch architect K. P. C de Bazel's (1869–1923) Amsterdam office building for the Dutch Trading Company (*Nederlandse Handelsmaatschappij*, 1919–26; fig. 4.20).[47] Notwithstanding the innovative upper setbacks, the decorative program of Sixth Avenue and 37th Street, unlike those of 550 Seventh Avenue and the Millinery Center, was not consistently integrated. The setbacks were attached to a conven-

won the first prize for their Gothic tower, Saarinen's second-prize entry was the one widely applauded by American critics, who were impressed with its organic unity, soaring vertical composition, and telescoping masses (fig. 4.18).

The unified treatment of the Millinery Center setbacks began at the fifteenth- and sixteenth-story terminus of the building's shaft, where applied terra cotta in deep relief was concentrated on the spandrels (see fig. 4.17). Ascent was forcefully expressed by a series of straplike piers that

tional base and shaft that was embellished with brick corbelling and other historical elements, including traditional Islamic motifs (such as the chevron) on the fourteenth-story arcade (see fig. 4.19).

A Medieval Revival in New York

Decoration was an outlet for experiment in these lofts. The medieval revival triggered by the Bowery Savings Bank and the Shelton Hotel, which drew inspiration mainly from the Lombard Romanesque and Byzantine styles, also freed Kahn to realize his passion for Persian and Islamic decoration. The Persian roots of Islamic, Byzantine, and Romanesque art had fascinated Kahn since his travels during the Beaux-Arts years. His adaptations of Persian and Islamic motifs in the architectural decoration of Garment District loft buildings in the 1920s emanated from these experiences. He wrote: "My visit to Spain made me curious to know more of the history of these Moors . . . the clue to their

4.20 K. P. C. de Bazel, Dutch Trading Company Headquarters, Amsterdam, 1919–26

artistic competence, for there must have been some powerful creative source deep in their past. It was the search for these origins that led me to Persia where I collected a library on the introduction of the Moslems, the reactions of the cru-

4.21 Ely Jacques Kahn's office, 49 West 45th Street, 1924

sades, fall of the Byzantine empire, and the ascendency of the Turks who at one time seemed likely to conquer Europe. There were also books on Egypt and Sicily where the Saracens had taken root, in short, the complicated record of wars and shifting powers that ultimately gave the Moslems complete mastery of the Mediterranean."[48] The decor of Kahn's personal office in 1923, after the firm had moved to 49 West 45th Street, reveals the extent of his absorption with Persian and Islamic decorative arts (fig. 4.21) and his predilection for pattern. Several examples of Islamic tilework, Persian pottery, and a vivid textile shared space with Windsor chairs, other period furniture, a Kahn watercolor cityscape, and a rendering by Hugh Ferriss of the proposed Scientific American Building (24 West 40th Street) on the fireplace mantel—an eclectic mix favored by Kahn at this time.

Kahn's struggle to imbue 550 Seventh Avenue with, in his words, the "spirit of Persian decorative forms" is apparent in the projecting parapet arcade (fig. 4.22). Like the lozenge

4.24 *Building at Sixth Avenue and 37th Street, entrance, 1926, B&K*

RIGHT
4.25 *Gaston Lachaise, zodiac elevator door, 1924, in 550 Seventh Avenue Building, B&K*

FACING PAGE TOP
4.26 *New York Furniture Exchange, cornice at first setback, 1925, B&K*

FACING PAGE BOTTOM
4.27 *L. H. Boileau, Pavillon des Magasins du Bon Marché, Paris, 1925*

lobby vestibule, glass mosaic, a decorative medium Kahn frequently employed during this period, formed a thematic six-part wall mural, executed by Ravenna Mosaic Incorporated (designer unknown) and still intact, that symbolizes the city as a center of learning, trade, commerce, building, medicine, and transportation. Both Sixth Avenue lofts, which have been remodeled at street level, originally featured open entrance vestibules with mosaic ceiling decoration. The Millinery Center vestibule was vaulted and surfaced with pictorial mosaics.[50] The flat ceiling of the 37th Street loft had a radiating pattern accentuated with six-pointed stars (fig. 4.24).

In a 1928 essay Lewis Mumford lamented the dearth of quality in architectural decoration and cited Kahn as the exception; he demonstrated his point with an illustration of an elevator door from 550 Seventh Avenue by the French émigré sculptor Gaston Lachaise (1882–1935).[51] Kahn had recommended Lachaise, who accepted a few architectural commissions in the 1920s for financial reasons, and Adler agreed to engage the sculptor to design bronze elevator doors for 550 Seventh Avenue and the Millinery Center.[52] For the former Lachaise depicted the twelve signs of the zodiac in rondels, three to a door (fig. 4.25), and he also designed the letterbox, which, like the elevator doors, is extant. For the Millinery Center elevator doors the sculptor draped female figures in diaphanous garments to allegorically represent the four seasons of fashion. Often published, the Lachaise doors brought attention to Kahn's lobbies.[53] Whether Lachaise did more than the elevator doors for the Millinery Center is uncertain because metalwork from this building has not survived. The only Buchman & Kahn buildings for which Lachaise's work is documented are 550 Seventh Avenue and the Millinery Center. Thesis research in 1949 led architectural historian Walter L. Creese to conclude that Kahn was the only New York architect during the 1920s to routinely collaborate with artists and craftsmen of stature.[54] When asked by Creese about his motivation, Kahn replied that it "seemed so obvious to me at the time, that the best crafts-

columns, perforated work, and Moorish lily details in the arcade, Islamic and Persian motifs dominated the four-story entrance base of the building (fig. 4.23). Designed by sculptor Maxfield Keck, the terra-cotta frieze was in the style of eleventh-century Islamic ivory openwork.[49] Underneath the frieze, Persian cypress motifs flanked by pilasters alternate with fourth-floor windows. Eight-pointed Islamic stars adorned the metal grilles over the main entrance doors (no longer extant).

The lobbies of the three lofts were comparable. Floors and walls were sheathed in marble, and typical Persian and Islamic motifs were adapted and applied to wall friezes and coffered plaster ceilings. In the 550 Seventh Avenue

men were the only ones to use, when they were available."[55] His response clearly showed the influence of his sister Rena.

Work Outside the Garment District

From its inception in 1917 through 1924, the Buchman & Kahn firm had filed no more than three new building plans per year. The eleven commissions of 1925 reflected both the momentum of the building boom and the reputation the firm had achieved under Kahn.[56] Work poured in for a variety of locations beyond the Garment District. Among the Buchman & Kahn buildings under construction late in the year were the fifteen-story New York Furniture Exchange, 206 Lexington Avenue between 32nd and 33rd Streets, developed by Max N. Natanson,[57] and a sixteen-story office–loft for the silk industry at 79 Madison Avenue, the northeast corner of 28th Street, developed and built by Harris H. Uris.[58] The persistence of decoration from Persian and Islamic sources was pronounced in both buildings, where the richest exterior decoration was focused on the attic zones of the main blocks. For the battlemented cornice of the Furniture Exchange, Kahn claimed that he had the "texture of fabric" in mind (fig. 4.26).[59]

Construction in New York City peaked in 1925 as the "*Exposition Internationale des Arts Décoratifs et Industriels Modernes*," an eye-opening international showing of modern decorative and industrial arts, was held in Paris. The new style, *art moderne*, was presented in full force (fig. 4.27). Reverberations from Paris would soon influence American architects and designers. Kahn toured the exposition and was deeply affected by what he saw. A comparison of the decorative programs of the buildings he designed after the Paris exposition with those highlighted in this chapter clearly demonstrates the impact of the event. Beginning in the latter half of 1925 references to medieval, Persian, and Islamic sources diminished in Buchman & Kahn work. Within a year the vigorous, abstract decoration associated with Kahn's mature style predominated. The catalyst of release was the Paris exposition.

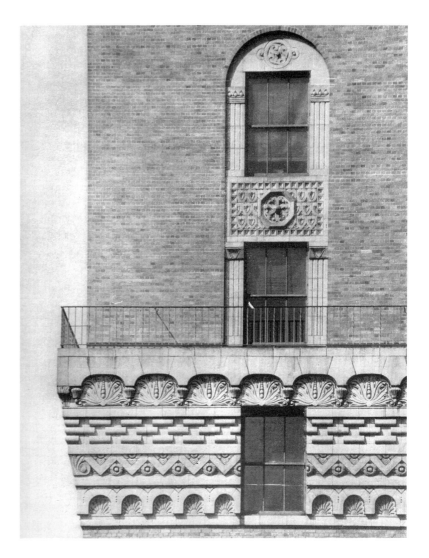

CHAPTER FIVE

TOWARD AN AMERICAN MODERNISM

1925–28

Originally slated for 1915, but postponed because of World War I and reconstruction, the *Exposition Internationale des Arts Décoratifs et Industriels Modernes* held in Paris in 1925 was the first international exposition limited to decorative and industrial arts of "new inspiration and real originality"—which meant that reproductions or derivations of historic styles were officially proscribed. Although the United States was invited to participate, and a choice site was reserved for a pavilion on the right bank of the Seine, the invitation was declined by the government on the grounds that "American manufacturers and craftsmen had almost nothing to exhibit conceived in the modern spirit, and in harmony with the spirit of the official specifications." Instead, Secretary of Commerce Herbert Hoover appointed an American Commission drawn from art and industry and headed by Professor Charles R. Richards, director of the American Association of Museums, to visit, study, and report on the exhibits for their effect upon American manufacture. The American Institute of Architects was represented by Charles Butler, William Emerson, Howard Greenley, and D. Everett Waid.[1] Although the Paris exposition

was deemed international and twenty-six nations exhibited, France alone was comprehensively represented. Prior to World War I France had lagged behind Germany and Austria in design. The exposition was a national effort to showcase the renaissance in French design and to reassert French leadership in the field. Ironically, French *art moderne* had assimilated much from earlier progressives, especially Josef Hoffmann and the Wiener Werkstätte.

With the Paris exposition as his destination, Kahn sailed for Europe early in September of 1925 and spent a month abroad.[2] In his memoirs Kahn remembered the exposition as an "awakening" and the Austrian and German pavilions as "especially striking," but he did not disclose which aspects of the innovative architecture engaged him at the time. Kahn revealed more about the French exhibits, which, he recalled, provoked discussions with craftsmen: "I spent quite some time in talking to French craftsmen, visiting their shops, for this show seemed to me to register a good deal of change from other shows not so long past. I returned with photographs of what seemed to be worthwhile, also samples that I could refer to."[3]

Even before Kahn left for Europe, detailed accounts of the event had been widely published in the United States. In August, Helen Appleton Read, the *Brooklyn Daily Eagle* art critic, a proponent of modernism attached to the American Commission, wrote a series of Sunday features on the importance of the exposition to American artists and designers. She observed that a "deep-seated urge to create forms in harmony with the Zeitgeist" was evident in Paris and that "those who look for the influences which have determined the new movement lay it either to the door of cubism or the age of the machine."[4] For Read, the importance of the exposition lay in its potential to stimulate American creativity in the modern spirit, and she predicted correctly that the effect of the exposition would be enormous.[5]

Like most American architectural professionals, architect Alfred Bossom's first impression of the French pavilions and exhibits was one of shock. Nonetheless, he applauded the controversial event in his review for the *American Architect*, and in an article in the *New York Times* Bossom acknowledged that a "vital creative impulse" operated throughout the exposition.[6] Others were less open. Architectural decorator W. Francklyn Paris

(1871–1954) viewed the event negatively in the *Architectural Record*: "The angular details of many of the Exposition's temporary structures beat against the retina with painful insistence. . . . The dreary iteration of angles, triangles, cubes, octagons, squares, and rectangles does not so much create a spirit of revolt as one of amusement. . . . It cannot be that this art is meant to endure."[7] Architect Kenneth Murchison's (1872–1938) appraisal was mocking: "The idea of the architects in charge was evidently to throw all old precedents into the Seine and to do something awfully simple, or simply awful, or both."[8]

The first American exhibition of material from the Paris exposition was the sampling of drawings and photographs exhibited at the Architectural League of New York's Forty-first Annual Exhibition, which opened January 30, 1926.[9] The French exhibits prompted a debate at the league over the new style. Kahn participated, and in published excerpts from the debate he predicted that established architects of the old school would sooner or later abandon "bogus" period design and turn the same "intelligence and vigor to a new expression."[10] In his report on the exhibition for *Architectural Record*, Kahn contrasted the "sober maturity" of American work with the "curious lighthearted daring" of that from the Paris exposition, and he endorsed the designs of "bolder spirits." Kahn also questioned why Americans challenged existing theories in science or commerce but rigidly held on to "blandly conservative" artistic policies.[11] By the end of the year Kahn had applied for membership in the Art-in-Trades Club and commented in his diary that it was "due to interest in 'modern art.'"[12] This interest led Kahn to belong to the little known Architectural Study Associates, organized by Donald Deskey (1894–1989) after he returned from France in 1926. The intimate group included Wallace K. Harrison, William Lescaze, Raymond Hood, and Henry S. Churchill and met informally during 1926 and 1927.[13]

As the Architectural League exhibition closed at the end of February 1926, the American Association of Museums' traveling exhibition of selected works of decorative art from the Paris exposition opened at the Metropolitan Museum of Art. Read reviewed the show and measured the impact to date of the Paris exposition: "The American public was strangely inert to the fact that a modern movement, a distinct period of style, was taking its place beside the historic periods. Many who visited the Paris Exposition came away entirely unaware of what it was all about— saw only the bizarre and the ultra. But such is the germinating quality of ideas that all unbeknown the idea took root. . . . The new decor has crept into our consciousness unawares, and there is no designer who can create in quite the same spirit from now on than if the Exposition had not existed.[14] Whereas Austrian and German progressive design had failed to take root earlier in the United States, French art moderne succeeded, in part, because of the alliance of American artists with French schools and fashion, and American admiration of French taste. Although reviews were mixed at first, art moderne found immediate credibility in many chic New York circles, and the style spread swiftly. Assisted by the talented émigré design colony centered in New York, department stores (which emulated the promotional role of their French counterparts), museum-organized exhibitions, and proselytizing journalists, art moderne was rapidly popularized throughout the United States. It was primarily a decorative style, and its influence after the 1925 exposition on New York skyscraper architecture was confined to the character of applied exterior and interior decoration. The popular appeal of art moderne inspired architects to create a "new dress" for the skyscraper, one in step with the spirit of the age. It was a trend noted by architectural critic Talbot F. Hamlin: "Everywhere architects seemed to be seeking freedom for their creative impulses."[15] Setback form dictated by the 1916 zoning law continued.

In the American architectural press of the 1920s, "art moderne" was rarely used to indicate the stylistic influence of the Paris exposition. The terms *modern*, *modernism*, and *modernist*, were generally employed for all manner of new thought and application, including the French *moderne* and European functionalism. Kahn associated *modern* with fresh design of contemporary relevance. He considered himself a *modernist*, as did the architectural press. *Modernistic*, a descriptive term occasionally used in the 1920s and 1930s, was disdained by Kahn, for whom it had a superficial connotation. The designation "art deco," an abbreviation of the title of the exposition, was coined in the mid-1960s to label the style brought into focus internationally by the 1925 event. This text conforms to the terminology of the 1920s with one distinction: "art moderne" refers to the French style at the 1925 Paris exposition and its permutations.

The Paris exposition heightened the battle in architectural circles between the traditionalists and the modernists, a struggle that polarized the profession in the 1920s. During the exposition, Eugene Clute, the editor of *Pencil Points*, addressed the conflict in an essay entitled "Modernism and Tradition." Clute searched for a middle ground: "Somewhere between the extremes of ultra-conservation and of radicalism, undoubtedly lies the right path, which men all over the country are trying to find and follow. It is one of the live questions of the day, this matter of modernism and tradition."[16] Sides were drawn between those who defended historical evolution, firm in the conviction that the cumulative wisdom of civilization should not be swept aside, and others who were impatient with inherited forms and eager to experiment freely. The latter was described by the conservative educator Fiske Kimball, director of the Philadelphia Museum of Fine Arts, in his book *American Architecture* (1928) as an experimental eclecticism that emphasized stylistic freedom rather than the consolidation of a unified national style with theoretical underpinnings.[17] This was, in fact, the thrust of American modernism in the second half of the 1920s and early 1930s. Yet the division between traditionalism and modernism was not yet clear. Hamlin, for example, observed that in the greater part of American work in 1926 that was "distinctively modern in style," tradition was not completely eschewed.[18] Although Kahn challenged the conservative position, like most of his peers in the 1920s he deemed European functionalism outside of the development of a modern American idiom. Nor were social reform and ethical convictions, inherent in European mod-

ernism, an issue. As early as 1924, Kahn had voiced his stance in the essay "The Office Building Problem in New York," in which he referred to the "spirited struggle now ensuing between the purists, who have more books than imagination, and the other brave souls who are fighting for a logical architectural expression."[19] Kahn passionately believed in expressing his own time, but he was not an extremist. He was in accord with moderates such as Randolph W. Sexton, author of *The Logic of Modern Architecture* (1929), who called for logical solutions grounded in the fundamental principles of architectural design.

In the year following the Paris exposition several tendencies became pronounced in Kahn's work. After the loft building at Sixth Avenue and 37th Street, Kahn abandoned his characteristic use of the planar wall punched with windows and reverted to a pier–spandrel system, which he often combined with end bays in an A-B-A rhythm. The spandrel decoration as surface enrichment, either applied or integrated with the wall, became an important element in design. Massing was frequently divided into a number of ascending setbacks and varied by introducing dormers for vertical accent. On midblock lots, a new and complex system of massing upper setbacks was formulated for small lofts. Although Kahn's fascination with decoration of Persian and Islamic inspiration continued, abstract geometric motifs began to dominate.

15–19 West 39th Street

The massing and vigorous decoration of a minor building, the sixteen-story loft at 15–19 West 39th Street on a midblock lot, is of interest from the standpoint of Kahn's evolution. A complex, sculptural massing was developed in order to bring more natural light into the upper floors of the narrow street-front elevation. The dormer provision of the zoning law was utilized, and the dormers were chamfered (fig. 5.1). At the first setback four small freestanding pylons served as capitals of the end-bay piers. The pylons conjure the Liggett Building, completed in 1921, by Carrère & Hastings and Shreve (Richmond

ABOVE
*5.2 15–19 West 39th
Street, attic stories main
mass, 1926, B&K*

RIGHT
*5.3 15–19 West 39th
Street, typical plan,
1925, B&K*

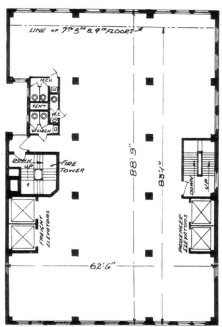

Harold Shreve, 1877–1946), but the source of reference for this design may well have been the Egyptian vogue sparked by the discovery of Tutankhamen's tomb in 1922. The building stepped back at the fourteenth floor and the end bays above it have flat vertical brick bands applied to the solid brick-faced wall—a treatment reminiscent of the ancient burial ground of the Egyptian King Zoser at Saqqara.

The geometric patterning and abstract classicism of the exterior decorative program, established before the Paris exposition opened in April 1925, have an uncanny affinity with art moderne—so much so that scholars recently mistook them for "one of New York's earliest reflections of the 1925 Paris exposition" when, in fact, the conception preceded the event.[20] Allusions to Egyptian, Persian, and modern Viennese sources are also discernible in the decoration. The most

elaborate terra-cotta reliefs were concentrated at the top of the main mass (fig. 5.2). Details from earlier buildings were combined to make a bold mix of geometric ornament: A honeycombed diaper recalled the Lehn & Fink Building; fluted brackets, the Borden Building; and stacked and staggered square plaques, the Rubin Building. Prismatic strips introduced in the Borden Building reappeared on the dormer parapet above the main mass. From this point forward, variations on this motif occur regularly on Buchman & Kahn setbacks and rooftop parapets.

The plan was the conventional one the firm had developed for loft buildings on interior lots with one street front (fig. 5.3). Passenger elevators and general stairs were placed on one side; freight elevators, fire tower stairs, and toilet rooms on the other. Elevators and stairs were located near the center of the plan and closer to

the front to facilitate entry into the building, and for convenient access to showrooms on each floor.[21] The flexible arrangement left the light area unobstructed and provided an open floor for a single tenant, or a front and back loft for two tenants, free of freight and passenger crossings.

247 West 35th Street and 424 Madison Avenue

Following his return from Paris in the fall of 1925, Kahn designed two small buildings with noteworthy exterior decoration: the sixteen-story loft at 247 West 35th Street, and the fifteen-story office building at 424 Madison Avenue. The loft was commissioned by Sylvan Froelich and C. Ludwig Baumann, furniture manufacturers and owners of the twelve-story Ludwig Baumann & Company Building, a Buchman & Kahn design of 1921 at 500 Eighth Avenue, a half-block from the

5.5 *424 Madison Avenue, upper setback at corner, 1926, B&K*

Commissioned for investment by Meyer Liberman, the owner of Arnold Constable, the fashionable Fifth Avenue department store, the 424 Madison Building, on the southwest corner of 49th Street, occupied a site about seventy feet square. *Architectural Forum* singled out the otherwise austere building for the "modernistic" decoration of its thirteenth-story setback and terminating parapet, on which elongated, triangular brick pilasters with faceted tips are the principal motifs (fig. 5.5).[22] The alternation of contrasting geometric pilasters on upper parapets, which Kahn initiated here, became an essential element in his modern decorative vocabulary.

Branching Out: Buildings for Harris H. Uris

During 1925 and 1926, in addition to the sixteen-story building for the silk industry at 79 Madison Avenue, Buchman & Kahn designed three twenty-one-story office buildings for syndicates organized by Latvian-born Harris H. Uris (1872–1945), a savvy Jewish builder and real estate developer whose earlier business, an ornamental iron foundry, had supplied metal for the Ritz-Carlton Hotel and many of the city's elevated train stations.[23] The Uris commissions (all designed after the Paris exposition) were the Court Square Building in the civic center at 2 Lafayette Street, 271 Madison Avenue in the Grand Central Terminal District, and 60 Broad Street in the Financial District. Uris revealed his formula for success to a *New York Sun* reporter in 1927: He shrewdly recognized that modern buildings with reasonable rentals would draw tenants from old offices if the requirements of average business concerns were met, and that an almost inexhaustible supply of prospective tenants would be guaranteed if he satisfied their needs. Uris knew from experience that there was a demand for office space in small units at prices ranging from $3.00 to $4.50 a foot, and in larger units for even less, and he met the demand. Uris explained the advantage of narrow inside lots, such as those of his 60 Broad Street (about fifty feet) and 271 Madison Avenue (about seventy feet), which produced small office floors: "The dignity and economy of an entire floor, or half

site of the new loft. The massing of setbacks was similar to that of 15–19 West 39th Street. An assortment of decoration, some experimental, enlivened the elevation. Most spandrels had layered and staggered applied brick slabs, a variation on an early theme of Josef Hoffmann. Parapets at the ninth- and eleventh-story setbacks featured projecting and undulating terra-cotta canopies accented with square plaques. The decorative treatment of the two-story entrance base and transitional story was outstanding. Below the zigzag frieze, geometric ornament, layered to contrast solids with voids and suggestive of folds, seemed strikingly modern (fig. 5.4).

floor for one's business is widely appreciated among executives, and the kind of office space at No. 60 Broad Street [and No. 271 Madison Avenue] at the price we are able to offer has practically no duplicate in the financial section."[24]

The Court Square Building, designed for Uris at the end of 1925, faces Foley Square on an oddly shaped lot fronting Lafayette, Reade, Elm, and Duane Streets. The building catered to the legal profession and was planned to accommodate large firms with suites of offices as well as individuals in smaller spaces. A conference room and law library were provided for tenants, and a club for lawyers, judges, civic officials, and businessmen occupied the top two floors.[25] The massing of Court Square was undistinguished. The only recession was a three-story walk-up penthouse that was not visible from the street. The effect was that of the old-fashioned, upended box.

The exterior decorative program was an art moderne-Persian-Islamic hybrid. Circular art moderne motifs embellished upper spandrels and entrance base mullions. Apart from these motifs and the faceted triangular pilasters around the rooftop parapet, all terra-cotta ornament had a distinctly Persian-Islamic cast. The original octagonal outer lobby (no longer extant) with its jazzy zigzag patterned dome, fluted walls, and stylized flame-shaped wall brackets, was the earliest Kahn interior to emulate the French moderne (fig. 5.6). Walter W. Kantack, a New Yorker who had been a delegate on the Hoover Commission to the Paris exposition, made the lighting fixtures. Most of the firm's subsequent lighting fixtures were fabricated by Kantack, including those in Kahn's own apartment.[26] Sophisticated art moderne lighting became the hallmark of the Kahn–Kantack collaboration.

The Uris building at 271 Madison Avenue, on a midblock lot between 39th and 40th Streets, has a dizzying series of identical setbacks on both street-front endbays (fig. 5.7). A vibrant scheme was wrought using two contrasting parapet motives—taut coping and corbelled arcades on the end-bay setbacks and, on the front-court setbacks, layered coping and pilasters combined with abstract openwork. The conservative lobby contained one innovation: an illuminated glass

TOP
5.6 *Court Square Building, entrance lobby, 1927, B&K*

ABOVE
5.7 *271 Madison Avenue, setbacks, 1927, B&K*

5.8 *Insurance Center, 80 John Street, Gold Street elevation, 1927, B&K*

ter half of 1926, in Avery Library, show that the original twenty-one-story building for Uris had exterior and interior art moderne decoration.

The Insurance Center Building

Kahn's next important commission—and his first in the Insurance District near Wall Street—was the Insurance Center, a twenty-three-story office building at 80 John Street, for clients Henry Greenberg and Morris Bienenstock, developers of the Arsenal Building. The Insurance Center occupied an irregular, three-sided corner site in the shape of a parallelogram, with a frontage of 94 feet on John Street, 120 feet on Gold Street, and 86 feet on Platt Street, on which had stood eighteenth-century landmark residences (they were demolished).[27] Although the main entrance was on John Street, greater emphasis was given to the wider Gold Street elevation that faced east and was relatively unobstructed at the time. In a period photograph the building emerges from a welter of rundown structures (fig. 5.8) as a beacon of modernism. It is emblematic of the redevelopment that took place in the boom years of the 1920s, which added complexity to the fabric of the city, especially in the Financial, Garment, and Grand Central Terminal Districts, and on upper Fifth Avenue, zones in which Kahn buildings figured prominently.

The primarily geometric design of the exterior demonstrated several new directions in Kahn's work. In the massing of the building, additional setbacks were taken and stepped back in six graduated stages. Squared dormers were introduced to break up and give interest to the setbacks and to accentuate and dramatize the vertical thrust of the massing. The boxlike setbacks ascend in harmonious proportions and culminate in a sharply squared tower. With some variations, this type of massing became the prototype for several major commissions, including 111 John Street (1929), 120 Wall Street (1930), and the Bricken Textile Building (1930) at 1441 Broadway (see Chapter Six). A zigzag belt course at the top of the five-story granite base defines the transition to the brickwork of the stories above, where a taut pier–spandrel system orders the elevations, and

ceiling (see fig. 5.22). For economy the elevator doors in 271 Madison were the same as those in the Court Square Building, the only instance of such duplication in Kahn's work of the period. Dominating the small entrance vestibule is a geometric ceiling mosaic executed in three different shades of blue, ochre, black, silver, and gold and featuring prismatic motifs.

All vestiges of Buchman & Kahn's design for 60 Broad Street, on a forty-seven-foot midblock lot, were obliterated in a 1962 renovation and enlargement of the building. Plans from the lat-

5.9 *Insurance Center, upper setbacks from Gold Street, 1927, B&K*

the patterning of the brick spandrels furnishes texture. On the upper-story piers, brickwork in narrow, triangular rows gives a pleated effect, an allusion to classical columns that was adapted from the Borden Building (fig. 5.9). Some rounded and cantilevered parapet details seem mechanistic; not surprisingly the Insurance Center (as well as the Park Avenue Building described below) was one of the buildings selected by Hugh Ferriss (who chose the American architecture) for the *Machine-Age Exposition* in 1927.[28] Photographed from the east, the building stood

proud, elegant, and aloof from its neighbors—the most progressive elevation Buchman & Kahn had produced.

Even prior to the *Machine-Age* show the design of the Insurance Center had earned Kahn professional recognition when a model of it was exhibited simultaneously at the Architectural League of New York's Annual Exhibition in January 1926 and a photograph of the same model and an additional drawing appeared in an exhibition of American work in Berlin, curated by Harvey Wiley Corbett and Alfred Bossom.[29] In the spring

RIGHT
5.10 Park Avenue Building, "Progress Sketch A," 1926, B&K

FAR RIGHT
5.11 Park Avenue Building, "Progress Sketch B," 1926, B&K

RIGHT
5.12 Park Avenue Building, "Progress Sketch C," 1926, B&K

FAR RIGHT
5.13 Park Avenue Building, "Progress Sketch D," 1926, B&K

FACING PAGE
5.14 Park Avenue Building, 1928, B&K

of 1926, during the erection of the Insurance Center, Kahn's essay "Our Skyscrapers Take Simple Forms" was published in the *New York Times*. In it Kahn articulated the current situation in skyscraper design: "Traditional decorations . . . now retreat before the advance of forms that respond to the bulk and simplicity of the skyscraper itself. . . . New York of the moment is definitely ignoring theories." He described the decoration of the skyscraper as a "means of enriching the surface with a play of light and shade, voids and solids," and he stressed the importance of proportion in relation to the height and location of the decoration—issues of utmost concern to Kahn in the design of tall buildings.[30]

The Polychrome Park Avenue Building

The project that confirmed Kahn's reputation as a modernist was 2 Park Avenue. His client Abe Adelson was ripe for a new deal after the completion of the Millinery Center on Sixth Avenue and 39th Street at the end of 1925. Four months later the developer bought the old Park Avenue Hotel, built in the 1870s by New York merchant A. T. Stewart as a hotel for women, and located on the west side of Park Avenue between 32nd and 33rd Streets, and Buchman & Kahn began making sketches for a new building.[31] The large site embraced the full block frontage of almost 200 feet on Park Avenue and extended west 200 feet on both streets—a square plot almost an acre in area. Late in August the *New York Times* reported the impending demolition of the old landmark and illustrated the Buchman & Kahn rendering of the proposed twenty-five-story office building.[32] Design development had evolved over four months, through at least four schemes before the resolution depicted in the *New York Times* (figs. 5.10–5.13). In Scheme A (fig. 5.10) a central tower core (a new concept for the firm) emerged out of a complex mass of setbacks. In Scheme B (fig. 5.11) the corners of the massing were recessed and angled and the tower was cropped. In Scheme C (fig. 5.12) the termination of the tower in Scheme A was restored and the rectilinear massing of dormers and corner pylons around the tower recalled the 15–19 West 39th Street

loft. In Scheme D (fig. 5.13) the setbacks were simplified. In the final version, the tower was given up and the remaining three blocks were squared (fig. 5.14). In an article published soon after the building was completed, Kahn discussed the rationale for the massing and explained that the additional light obtained from the "deep indentations on the street frontages" in the early schemes could not offset the loss of space and the lack of flexibility of plan. Furthermore, a study of the location had shown the need for large floor areas. As a result the twenty-five stories and three-story penthouse were massed in three simple stepped-back blocks. The point where the ratio of rentable area to service area became economically unproductive had determined the height of the building.[33]

The building initially was intended for offices and showrooms. However, because the neighborhood was rundown and redevelopment was early, the structure was provided, as a safety measure, with floor–load capacity, freight elevators, and services sufficient for the 25 per cent manufacture permitted by zoning in the area. During construction high-caliber tenants appeared, and leases promptly prohibited manufacture.[34] In the event that property values declined in the future, the building could convert flexibly. On the entrance floor, twenty-six elevators (services were centered in the plan) were grouped at the intersection of the passages to the three entrances. Structural piers, spaced twenty-one to twenty-two feet on center (smaller in the rear), and twelve-foot ceiling heights yielded large four-window bays that brought maximum light to the deep space planned for showrooms in the main mass. The upper block, which set back one bay, provided the shallow space desirable for small offices; four-window bays facilitated their interior subdivision.

The resounding artistic success of the Park Avenue Building was primarily due to the innovative exterior polychromatic treatment, an experiment influenced by Kahn's friendship with English-born Leon Victor Solon, an architectural writer and expert in ceramics with whom he had served on the Architectural League's Committee on Catalogue, chaired by Solon in 1921. Solon

was descended from a French family of ceramic artists, associated in the nineteenth century with the Minton Company, an esteemed English manufacturer of quality pottery and porcelain. Solon's grandfather had been responsible for the introduction of majolica ware at the Great Exhibition of 1851. His father brought the *pâte-sur-pâte* technique to Minton; and Solon designed the first Minton "Secessionist Ware" in 1898.[35] In 1917, a decade after he emigrated to the United States, Solon became a contributing editor to *Architectural Record*; by the close of 1926 he had over fifty published essays to his credit.[36] An essay of his in 1918 on Greek polychrome led the architects of the Philadelphia Museum of Art (Borie, Trumbauer, and Zantzinger) to seek his advice in 1921 for the Greek revival pedimental sculpture in their plan. Solon was retained as "polychromist," and he collaborated with the architects and sculptors, John Gregory and Paul Jennewein, both of the American Academy in Rome.[37] The commission precipitated a series of *Record* articles by Solon on Greek polychromy in 1922; these were published two years later as a book, *Polychromy*. The articles, book, and Philadelphia Museum of Art project generated considerable interest in architectural circles and made Solon the nation's leading authority on architectural polychromy.

The revival of color in commercial architecture began in 1924 with Raymond Hood's black brick and gold terra cotta American Radiator Building on East 40th Street across from Bryant Park. Herbert Croly, Solon's colleague at the *Architectural Record*, wrote enthusiastically of the gilded upper stories of the new building, which suggested to him the possibility that color might convert the New York skyline into a "wonderland of vivid masses and patterns."[38] Soon the *American Architect* described and illustrated Peter Behrens's lofty entrance hall in brick, shaded from cool blue at the bottom to bright orange, for the I. G. Farben administration building.[39] Kahn's idea to use color broadly in the Park Avenue Building probably crystallized in the fall of 1926. The firm's perspective, published at the end of August in the *New York Times*, did not show the final polychromatic scheme.[40] Kahn may have been emboldened by the article "Modernism in Architecture," in the September *Record*, in which Solon forcefully advocated color for towering masses: "It will be necessary to devise a technique in ornament which has the capacity for a new decorative emphasis and for long range visibility. This requirement causes us to feel confident that color will be employed. Color will render low relief capable of any exquisite measure of decorative force. There seems no doubt that polychromy will prove the logical solution of the decorative problem."[41]

Kahn asked Solon to study the entire scheme of the Park Avenue Building and to advise him on colors for the terra-cotta decoration (see fig. C.2). A large model was made in cardboard with details carried out in plaster and painted in colors. Kahn was satisfied with the result, but the clients hesitated, then consulted architect Raymond Hood for his opinion. Kahn later learned that Hood had reassured them that "they were in perfect hands," and the building went ahead with the polychromatic scheme intact.[42]

Kahn also overcame the qualms of Mr. S. W. Straus, from whom the Adelson syndicate sought financing. Kahn remembered his meeting with Straus in the latter's "serenely classic" building, designed by Warren and Wetmore, and the strategy that won the day: "Mr. Straus had a magnificent office at 46th Street and [565] Fifth Avenue, had seen my drawings, and in a fatherly way tried to calm me down. . . . Why did I affront the clients and endanger my own career by such outrageous experiment?" But Kahn was prepared. He knew the amount of Straus's projected loan and that his scheme would not require a loan that large. After he informed Straus of the savings, "the design, the lower loan, the entire scheme proceeded with no change."[43] What had impelled Kahn to stand firm? Was the polychrome experiment compensating for the scrapped tower, a concession to pragmatism? Was he competing with Hood? Some evidence suggests competition (such as the interview in the *New York World* quoted below). However, Kahn's assimilation of Persian-Islamic decorative art and architecture, in which color in surface ornament had deep cultural roots and was expressed in its architectural

tilework, was a factor. His close association with Solon provided the impetus.

The year 1927 witnessed a rising popularity of polychrome, and Solon and Kahn were its champions. Kahn was interviewed in January for an article headlined "Big Splashes of Color to Adorn Skyscrapers" in the *New York World* in which he credited Hood for taking "the first step in using color itself, in frank definite contrasts" for the American Radiator Building. Kahn then raised the stakes, announcing: "In the past few days my own firm has decided to go still further in this experiment and use big masses of primary colors, three hundred feet up in the air, in the new buildings we are engaged on. . . . We are going to put on strong reds and blue, in big masses, and I think the effect will be wonderful."[44] In February the Architectural League of New York's Annual Exhibition opened at the Grand Central Palace on Lexington Avenue at 46th Street. Critiques of the exhibition made special mention of the Park Avenue Building model, replete with color details, and of the polychrome scheme of the Philadelphia Museum of Art. One reviewer reported that color was the outstanding feature of the entire display, and he predicted that skyscrapers would soon "dazzle the eye by their brilliance."[45] In conjunction with the exhibition Solon led a panel, "Principles of Architectural Polychromy as Established in Ancient Practice," and in commentary on the panel in the *New York Times* Kahn foresaw the beautification of American cities through the implementation of color.[46] The promise of color in architecture was underscored in July 1927 when the Architectural and Allied Arts Exposition exploded with color applications. Reviews cited the work of Kahn and architects Frederic C. Hirons, John Sloan, Joseph Urban, and Raymond Hood, and prophesized the extensive use of color in architecture.[47]

For the innovative polychrome treatment of the Park Avenue Building Kahn departed from the conventional use of terra cotta by breaking up the exterior surface into areas of color compatible with both the scale of the building as a whole and the pier–spandrel system (see fig. C.4). Most of the polychrome terra cotta in the program was integral with the wall and was actually the surface material of the building. Unlike applied decoration, removing the polychrome meant destroying parts of the exterior wall. Kahn called his method "modeling the building itself," and he considered it analogous to a sculptor "cutting into a block of clay and letting the cuts make the surface interesting."[48] Parker Morse Hooper, editor of *Architectural Forum*, agreed that in the best modern designs for architectural decoration the detail was "an integral part of the composition," and he emphasized the importance of the wall surface.[49] The terra-cotta tile colors for the Park Avenue Building included bright magenta red, deep blue, green, and ochre in mat glazes, and black in a luster finish. After their placement was determined, full size plaster models, sprayed to match the glazes, were set on the roof of the Federal Terra Cotta Company and evaluated from a distance of about 250 feet. The testing led to some refinements.[50]

Terra cotta is a durable, fireproof material, less expensive than ornamental stone and lighter in weight than masonry. The physical properties of terra cotta—its plasticity and capacity to retain crisp definition—make it an ideal material for architectural ornament. Since the 1870s monochromatic or subtly colored terra cotta had been used in New York to articulate details in brick-clad buildings and to complement the brick. In the 1890s terra cotta began to be used as an exclusive monochromatic cladding for steel frame construction.[51] Examples in New York City were Louis Sullivan's Bayard Building (1898), Cass Gilbert's Woolworth Building (1912), and Buchman & Fox's World's Tower Building (1914). McKim, Mead & White had used glazed terra cotta in the Madison Square Presbyterian Church (1900), but polychrome was rare until Hood's American Radiator Building. One of the earliest skyscrapers following Hood's to exhibit a comprehensive polychrome program, and one of the most elaborate, was the Fred F. French Building (1925–27), 551 Fifth Avenue at 45th Street, by H. Douglas Ives, a French Company architect, and Sloan and Roberston, consulting architects.[52] Ancient Assyrian figures and motifs were revived and stylized in the exterior and interior decorative program. At the top of the north

and south elevations, forty-foot wide polychrome terra-cotta panels prominently depicted progress allegorically in the form of a rising sun that is flanked by winged griffins that represent integrity and watchfulness and beehives, symbols of thrift and industry.[53] Although it was a prime example of exterior polychrome, the historical motifs of the French Building contrasted with the pure abstract geometry that governed the Park Avenue Building.

The principal cladding material of the Park Avenue Building is brick, and the entrance base, two stories and a mezzanine, is smoothly faced in travertine to blend with the buff-color brick of the walls above it. Window bays over the street level stores originally had cast-iron spandrels, mullions, and sills in a geometric pattern. A powerful *cyma reversa* of travertine at the transitional third floor terminates the entrance base. Stone corbels support colossal, triangular brick pilasters that are capped with blue and black terra-cotta tiles, and they articulate the structural piers of the main mass from the third to the seventeenth story. In the spandrels of the four-window bays between the piers, flat brick stretchers alternate with projecting headers to create a relief pattern of solids and voids that give texture to the wall. Smooth, brick-faced corner end bays provide contrast. Buff-color brick is used overall, but with subtle variations. The spandrels, end bays, and pilasters are each a slightly different tone. The lighter shade of brick on the corners helps to minimize the bulk of the building. The use of different colors of brick or graduating shades of brick in the same building is a method of injecting color that Kahn and other architects employed.

The polychromatic program begins at the sixteenth story and extends to the topmost parapet. The decoration was organized in accord with the massing of the building, its tripartite divisions, and the pier–spandrel system. The decoration— abstract and geometric in character, in repetitive shapes and vivid colors—charges across the elevations. Paradoxically, a work of splendid sensuousness issues from a rational system in which the highly active surface enrichment contrasts with the severity of the massing. In each mass

5.16 Park Avenue
Building, main entrance
doors, detail, 1928,
B&K

5.17 Park Avenue
Building, elevator doors,
1928, B&K

the upper stories were treated as attic zones, and
the flanking corner end bays were differentiated
from the intervening bays with elaborate ornamentation. In the spandrels, superimposed
motifs were layered and staggered. The only
curvilinear shapes in the scheme occur in the corner banding at the first setback and are highly
suggestive of wheels in motion (see fig. C.3 and
fig. C.4). (These motifs were later adopted by
William Van Alen for the elevator cab interiors
of the Chrysler Building.) At the second setback
the projecting bands in the corners are incised to
give the effect of deep relief (see fig. C.4).
Triangular pilasters figure strongly on all four
parapets, and the piers of the terminating parapet step up against the sky (see fig. C.4).

The polychrome treatment of the Park
Avenue Building—unsurpassed in New York by
Kahn or his peers—was widely recognized in
architectural circles.[54] Solon brought Michael A.
Mikkelsen, editor of the *Architectural Record*, and
an advocate of color experiments, to see the
building as it neared completion. Afterward
Mikkelson wrote to Kahn: "In my opinion this
building begins a new chapter in the history of

sky-scraper design. It has my unqualified admiration."[55] The visit led to the publication, in April 1928, of a twenty-two page "Portfolio of Current Architecture," exclusively covering the Park Avenue Building with a full-page color study of the polychrome treatment and an accompanying analysis of the building by Solon.[56] Mikkelsen believed that the tendency to simplify the form and line of the skyscraper impelled architects to seek richness through texture and color, and he supported color experiments until the end of the decade.[57] In its editorial policies and as a sounding board for new ideas, the *Record* was the leader among professional journals during the period 1927–32, the years that paralleled Kahn's most intensive period of skyscraper design.[58] His rapport with Mikkelsen and the editorial staff proved a tremendous professional asset. Kahn's work received excellent coverage in the journal, and several essays by him were published.[59]

The jewel in the crown of the Park Avenue Building was the sumptuous entrance hall and elevator lobby, which became a permanent showcase for the firm when it moved its offices there in 1928. Extraordinary effort went into the coordinated design of public spaces—more than in any previous Buchman & Kahn project. A lush modern decor was created by applying repetitive, layered, and overlapping abstract motifs to quality materials, primarily bronze, marble, and mosaic. Above the polished gray marble walls in the Park Avenue entrance vestibule, a bright mosaic of red, blue, and black tesserae, accented with gold, glazed the ceiling in a pattern that echoed the forms of the molded plaster ceiling of the main lobby (fig. 5.15). Slim louvered lighting brackets were originally mounted across the marble walls of the vestibule. The tour de force is the gilt bronze entrance portal that has an ornamental panel between the revolving doors, evoking machine imagery and decoration in the manner of Frank Lloyd Wright (fig. 5.16). The motif above each revolving door repeats on the bronze elevator doors (fig. 5.17). Travertine paved the floors of the vestibule and the lofty inner hall leading to the elevators. Shallow octagonal glass and bronze art moderne chande-

5.18 *Park Avenue Building, main entrance hall, 1928, B&K*

liers, their light diffused by planes of cantilevered glass, hung from the hall ceiling on long metal rods (fig. 5.18). The high wainscot of polished gray marble was surmounted by a gilded plaster frieze, in which the relief decoration displayed an intricate and exotic medley of stylized interlocking and overlapping shapes: abstract plant motifs (such as the lotus palmette), volutes, prisms, chevrons, and inventive tubular, stepped columnar forms.

On the cross axis of the main hall, passages to the side street entrances and the elevators were vaulted and illuminated by elaborate fixtures suspended from ornamental bronze cagelike shafts

(fig. 5.19). The chandeliers were composed of staggered tiers of glass in an octagonal framework, from which hung eight bronze openwork pendants. Color was introduced in a pair of twelve-foot-high mosaic panels in the tympana below the vault penetrations on the main entrance axis. Every detail, from radiator grilles (fig. 5.20), building directories, letterbox (fig. 5.21), and mosaic clock to the subway signpost, was coordinated. The quality of design and execution of the Park Avenue Building entrance and lobbies became a benchmark for Buchman & Kahn work.

The Park Avenue Building received enthusiastic reviews. More was written about this building than any other in Kahn's career.[60] Surprisingly, Lewis Mumford, the strong foe of skyscrapers, was the most complimentary. Mumford commented on the beauty and unity of the building's exterior and interior decoration, the precision of execution of both, and the synthesis of structure and feeling. His response to the building was published in the April 1928 issue of *Architectural Forum*:

> In the building that strikes the boldest and clearest note among all our recent achievements in skyscraper architecture, the Park Avenue Building [Kahn], has kept the exterior and the interior in unity: the first has become more warm, the second has become more rigorous and geometrical—and handsome. With a warm buff brick as a foundation, the Park Avenue Building works up into bands of sunny terra-cotta [*sic*], broken and accentuated with red, green, bright sky-blue. The pattern is abstract; and every part, down to the lighting fixtures, has the same finish, rigor, swiftness, perfection. In this building, structure and feeling are at last one: the directness and simplicity of the first have not been forfeited in the decoration; the warmth and human satisfaction of the decorative forms have not been overpowered in the structure itself, for they are expressed there, too.

Mumford continued, holding up the building as an ideal model: "One swallow may not make a summer; but one building like this, which faces the entire problem of design, and has a clean,

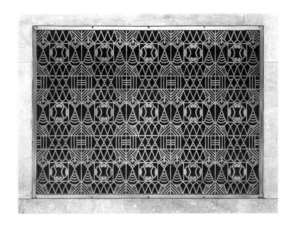

FACING PAGE
5.19 *Park Avenue Building, vaulted passage from entrance hall, 1928, B&K*

LEFT
5.20 *Park Avenue Building, radiator grille, entrance, 1928, B&K*

5.21 *Park Avenue Building, letterbox, 1928, B&K*

unflinching answer for each question, may well serve to crystallize all the fumbling and uncertain elements in present-day architecture. The success of the Park Avenue Building is not due to the fact that it is a tall tower or that it is a setback building. It is not a tower and the setback is trifling. *Its success is due to its unique synthesis of the constructive and the feeling elements*" (emphasis added).[61]

Around 1926 to 1927, Kahn began to attract a number of young, talented architects and designers of different nationalities to the office, including German, Austrian, Turkish, Japanese, Siamese, French, Chinese, Parsee, and Dutch men. Word had spread that Kahn encouraged experimentation, and those with a modern bent who had met with little enthusiasm elsewhere came to him. In the late 1920s the drafting room, like the atelier Redon earlier, had a pronounced international cast and, from all reports, excellent esprit de corps.[62] Two designers, Shamoon Nadir, a young Indian architect, and Engelbartus Van der Woerd, a Dutchman, stood out above their peers and contributed significantly during their employment from 1926–29.

Born in Bombay, India, of Persian parents, Nadir (1899–1984) came to the United States to study architecture at the University of Pennsylvania under Paul Cret and received his bachelor of architecture degree in 1926.[63] Greek, Roman, and Persian art and architecture influenced his development. After graduation Nadir entered the Buchman & Kahn firm and stayed for two years. He recalled that Kahn was sympathetic to young people who approached him for advice or help and encouraged those who displayed some talent or originality. When Nadir joined the firm in December 1926, the Park Avenue Building was under construction. His first assignment involved the lobby and entrance decoration. Nadir described the sources of his inspiration: "The decorations, which I tackled in the design of the entrance and lobbies of the 2 Park Avenue Building, were primarily based on Classical proportions. But the Classical motifs, such as Acanthus leaf, egg-and-dart, and various forms of moldings were replaced by rhythmic arrangement of simple forms to create a pleasing composition. Here, there was a slight influence of pattern one would find in Indian architecture. But there was no definite period of architectural development I had in mind. Of course, the machine did lend some exquisite forms as gears and such."[64]

Engelbartus (Bart) Van der Woerd (1893–?) was another important figure in the interior decorative program of the Park Avenue Building. The initials "E. V. D. W." appear on drawings of five lighting fixtures and the lobby letterbox. Born in Deventer, Holland, Van der Woerd, the son of a building contractor, received his architectural education from 1917 to 1922 in Amsterdam at the *Voortgezet en Hoger Bouwkunstonderricht* (VHBO; now the Academy of Architecture), at the time a stronghold of the Amsterdam School. In Paris in 1925 Van der Woerd mingled with Dutch modernists Theo van Doesburg (1883–1931) and Cornelis van Eesteren (1897–1988), and he doubtless visited the Paris exposition.[65] His visa was issued in Paris at the end of July 1926, and he sailed from Rotterdam to New York, arriving on September 12, 1926, at age thirty-three.[66] In less than two months he was employed by Buchman & Kahn and had submitted a sketch of a cast-glass ceiling lobby fixture for the building at 271 Madison Avenue (fig. 5.22). The rigid geometric design has the repetitive overlapping shapes and angularity that were softened and elaborated on for the Park Avenue Building interiors, and it seems reasonable to conclude that Van der Woerd's input may have affected more than the design of lighting fixtures and the letterbox in the Park Avenue Building. The influence of Frank Lloyd Wright on the Dutch architect is apparent from his ceiling fixture sketch. It is ironic, but not surprising, given Wright's influence on the Amsterdam School, that earlier Wrightian motifs were reintroduced in America in the work of Buchman & Kahn by a Dutch architect who came of age shortly after Wright's Wasmuth portfolio was published in Europe. Kahn, who shared Wright's affinity for surface pattern and texture, was receptive to Van der Woerd, but according to Nadir, the Dutchman was usually given work on smaller buildings and lobbies because he was considered so "radical."[67]

The recollections of Nadir and architect John Theodore "Ted" Jacobsen (1903–98), a designer in the firm between 1929 and 1930, of their employment provide a rare glimpse into Kahn's working relationship with his designers at the

SKETCH FOR RELIEF GLASS CEILING.
½" SCALE.

NOV. 26/26
(SEE GLASS CONTRACTORS DRAWING.)
C.F.B.

269-271 MADISON AVENUE
SCALE
MADE BY E.v D.W.
CHECKED
DATE 29 Oct.
GLASS RELIEF CEILING
FILE
SET
SHEET
BUCHMAN & KAHN - ARCHITECTS
49 WEST 45th STREET   NEW YORK CITY

time. Nadir pointed out that Kahn first determined the "lay-out" (plan) of a building; then other designers developed the exterior to enhance Kahn's plan by "manipulating setbacks and introducing dormers." Jacobsen remembered that Kahn "took particular interest in the design and material of each project" and that he "set the theme and function—then turned it over to the design department for development." Jacobsen added that Kahn "followed all phases closely as the planning and exterior form and materials progressed." He recalled that Kahn led members of the design department on a "tour of most of his high rise loft buildings in New York to discuss and demonstrate his methods and results," an exercise that Jacobsen found "very informative."[68] According to Nadir, "Kahn never influenced his designers by injecting any definite decorative style into their thinking. He was quick to see a new idea displayed by his boys and encouraged them to get [the] most out of it." Nadir regarded Kahn primarily as a Beaux-Arts man who especially admired the Wiener Werkstätte and other designers of ornament "with [a] fresh point of view," among them,

"Frank Lloyd Wright, Louis Sullivan, and Leo[n] V. Solon."[69]

The operation of the firm and the process of design that made the volume of work in the second half of the 1920s possible can be reconstructed, in part, from a few key sources. The financial balance of power shifted in 1926 through an agreement that increased Kahn's share in the firm to 45 percent—the majority position and indicative of his leadership—and reduced Albert Buchman's position to 30 percent in keeping with his diminishing role; it gave John Montfort, the managing partner, a 25 percent interest, a sign of the expansion of business.[70] At the height of the building boom in the late 1920s, the office had a staff of over 120.[71] Organization and an efficient division of labor facilitated its productivity. Kahn was known to conserve time through organization, delegation of authority, and decisiveness. As a service to clients a real estate research department was created to accumulate data on the availability and value of sites, the maximum volumes allowed under the zoning law, and construction financing.[72] Intensive study and analysis by a committee, which included

5.22 *271 Madison Avenue, "Sketch for Glass Ceiling," October 29, 1926, B&K*

Kahn, members of the design staff, the client, realtor, builder, and banker, determined the development of a site (and exerted influence throughout a project). A zoning diagram was prepared, costs estimated, and a preliminary sketch, based on the typical plan, developed. If the scheme appeared financially viable after computations, the design process went forward.[73] Nadir described the process: "A package of preliminary drawings was prepared under Kahn's close cooperation and submitted to the client for his consideration. This package consisted of a plan of the lot, first floor, typical floor and floors at set-backs, a cross section and a perspective sketch of the building by the designer who was assigned for the job. Cubage for a rough estimate of cost and rentable area made the package complete."[74] Kahn, who claimed exclusive control of design, met with his departmental heads weekly to resolve each job, as it progressed, in a conference system that maintained communication within the office.[75]

AN ARRAY OF BUILDINGS, 1926–27

The Lefcourt-State Building

In mid-1926, when plans for the Park Avenue Building were underway, on the drawing boards, too, was the firm's first major building for real estate developer Abraham E. Lefcourt (1877–1932), the Lefcourt-State Building, a twenty-three-story loft at 1375 Broadway on a choice northwest corner at 37th Street. Early in 1925 the firm had received the first commission from Lefcourt: a pedestrian twenty-story loft on East 34th Street between Madison and Fifth Avenues, named the Lefcourt-Madison Building.[76] The saga of Lefcourt's relentless rise from rags to riches has been retold many times. Reared on Delancey Street in the Lower East Side, he sold newspapers and saved his earnings to open a bootblack stand on Grand Avenue. After working in a retail dry goods store, he found a job with a wholesale manufacturer, first as a clerk, then as bookkeeper, buyer, and travel-

ing salesman. When his employer retired, Lefcourt took over the business on credit. In less than ten years he was a leading figure in the garment industry, helping settle the 1921 strike of 55,000 garment workers, and leading the postwar Garment District development. From 1919 to 1923, Lefcourt maintained his business in the garment trade while building lofts and accumulating them as rental property. In 1923 he gave up manufacturing to concentrate on real estate development. References to himself as a "real estate operator" angered Lefcourt: "I buy and keep," he boasted in a *New York Times* profile.[77] Lefcourt's success was phenomenal; his holdings, estimated at ten million dollars in 1923, rose to a hundred million five years later. Of the twenty-four buildings he built and owned by 1929, six were designed by Buchman & Kahn. Of the six, two were important works of the firm, the Lefcourt Exchange and the Lefcourt Clothing Center (discussed below). Other Lefcourt architects were George and Edward Blum and Schwartz & Gross—Buchman & Kahn competitors in the Garment District—and Shreve, Lamb & Harmon.

The massing of the Lefcourt-State was standard for the firm. The loft has a bold five-story base and five well-proportioned setbacks; its presence is powerful, if not innovative. The planning, nonetheless, was a financial success; the loft was 100 percent rented six weeks before completion.[78] It was the decoration that distinguished the building. This mid-to-late-1926 scheme exemplifies the progress of Kahn's consolidation of an abstract, geometric idiom that identified him in the period as a modernist. Focused on the upper setbacks, the terra-cotta ornament was expressed in a vocabulary of form reduced to square, rectangle, prism, and flutes (fig. 5.23). On the end bays of the main mass, however, Persian-inspired brickwork appeared in the spandrels. Kahn was not yet ready to relinquish earlier ornamental predilections: It would take another year for him to be free of them. Drawings of the Lefcourt-State lobby in the Avery Library show art moderne details. The interior has been completely remodeled. The firm also designed the modern Schrafft's Restaurant on the main floor.

5.23 Lefcourt-State Building, detail, upper setbacks, 1928, B&K

Bergdorf Goodman Block

During 1927 Kahn continued to mix historical and art moderne motifs in a bewildering array of projects scattered throughout the city. A row of French townhouses was emulated for the west-side block on Fifth Avenue between 57th and 58th Streets, a rental complex in which Bergdorf Goodman was the anchor store. In 1926 the German-born real estate mogul Frederick Brown, hailed by the *Real Estate Record and Builder's Guide* as "New York's boldest and largest real estate operator," had purchased the site, originally the French renaissance chateau designed by Richard Morris Hunt and George B. Post for Cornelius Vanderbilt II.[79] The commission arrived through the auspices of contractor G. Richard Davis, a close friend of Edwin Goodman, the president of Bergdorf.[80] The previous year Davis had built two Buchman & Kahn buildings, the Furniture Exchange and the loft at 15–19 West 39th Street.[81] Kahn seems to have had minimal control over the design of the project. Looking back in his memoirs, he wrote: "I cannot recall that my

5.24 Bergdorf Goodman Building block, 1927, B&K

opinion as to the entire scheme was called for."[82] A committee of experts, composed of the owners, architects, builders, engineers, and attorneys, chose to emulate an elegant Parisian avenue in an unusual plan that consisted of eight individual but joined buildings. Interior buildings were six stories high; those forming the corners were eight and nine stories (fig. 5.24). The French style of green tile mansard roofs was adopted, with green bronze trim for the windows, and the facades were faced in white South Dover marble. Although the nine-story section on 58th Street was rented at the outset by Bergdorf Goodman, anxiety over the commercial viability of the project was such that even when construction was finished, the wisdom of luxury stores was still questioned. To meet the needs of one tenant, the Dobbs Restaurant, three buildings at the southwest corner of 57th Street were altered and consolidated, and the ornate arcade that pierced the complex from 57th to 58th Street was eliminated.[83] Published photographs of the Bergdorf Goodman interiors attributed them to Buchman & Kahn, but the interiors were designed and executed by Theodore Hofstatter & Company.[84]

42 West 39th Street
(Grand Central Terminal Building)
and the Federation Building

During the first half of 1927, Kahn's polychrome and other decorative experiments were confined to two commissions for small midblock buildings: an eighteen-story office-loft structure at 42 West 39th Street for Milton M. Blumenthal (1885–1942), an importer and exporter of millinery who occupied space in the building, and the Federation Building, the new headquarters of the Federation for the Support of Jewish Philanthropic Societies, a sixteen-story part rental office-loft at 71 West 47th Street, on a site donated by Frederick Brown.[85] The builder, G. Richard Davis, with whom Kahn had previously collaborated, may have brought the Federation commission to the firm. The general massing of setbacks at 42 West 39th Street (fig. 5.25) was similar to that of 271 Madison Avenue. However, an asymmetrical scheme was developed for the

narrower Federation Building property. Both buildings featured tightly banded stepped volumes. The loft at 42 West 39th Street provided Kahn with an opportunity for polychrome experiment. The three stories above the street entrance were treated with glazed terra cotta in shades of rose, gray, and sand (see fig. C.5). Allusions to Frank Lloyd Wright, the Amsterdam School, and non-western cultures in the friezes and the complex decorative motifs of this loft and the

5.25 42 West 39th Street setbacks, 1927, B&K

5.26 *Federation Building, 71 West 47th Street, belt course decoration, 1928, B&K*

FACING PAGE
5.27 *International Telephone & Telegraph Building, 1928, B&K*

this size. The small lobbies received coordinated schemes with prominent horizontal moldings that bring to mind the Austrian pavilion in the 1925 Paris exposition. Outstanding details included the lighting fixtures, a cast-glass ceiling in 42 West 39th street, and faceted wall brackets in the Federation Building. Greater simplification overall characterized both lobbies.

Lefcourt-Exchange Building (International Telephone and Telegraph Building)

The Lefcourt-Exchange Building at 67 Broad Street, in the heart of the Financial District near Wall Street, had a complicated history. Lefcourt's purchase of the Consolidated Stock Exchange at Broad and Beaver Streets and his intention of demolishing it to make way for a skyscraper office building were announced on June 22, 1926. At the end of August, Buchman & Kahn began plans for which a variance in height regulation was granted, and on October 31 a rendering of the new building, a twenty-one-story block surmounted by a four-story setback, appeared in the *New York Times*.[87] The zoning variance precipitated a lawsuit from seven prominent Financial District firms who contended that the Board of Appeals had exceeded its authority in allowing the building to rise 258 feet at the street before the first setback—at least 103 feet higher than was legal.[88] As a result of the litigation, a completely new scheme was developed: a thirty-one-story building that stepped back in several stages and was crowned with a three-story penthouse tower. In July 1927, before construction of the Lefcourt-Exchange began, the building was leased to International Telephone and Telegraph Corporation and renamed.[89]

In the new skyscraper Kahn expressed his abiding passion for Islamic Spain (fig. 5.27). The International Telephone and Telegraph Building rose in five setbacks to a tower. Kahn recalled his inspiration: "I saw an opportunity to create a design of a tower with recollections of Spain, for I had sketch books and drawings of Spain far more important to me than some of the notes of other countries including Italy. The terra cotta tower with dots of color was inspired by the

Federation Building (which did not have polychrome) suggest that Kahn was invigorated by the influx of young foreign designers into the firm (fig. 5.26). Otto John Teegen (1899–1983), a graduate of Harvard Architectural School, previously employed by York & Sawyer, who joined the firm in April 1929, attributed the inspiration for the decoration of these buildings to Van der Woerd.[86] Judging from detail drawings in Avery Library that have Van der Woerd's initials—60 Broad Street, 271 Madison Avenue, the Park Avenue, Park-Murray, and United States Appraisers Buildings, the Film Center, and the Lefcourt Clothing Center—this could well have been the case. Both buildings had lavish entrance and lobby decoration exceptional for projects of

Giralda of Seville."[90] The romantic conception was lauded by "T-Square" (George Sheppard Chappell), the architecture critic of *The New Yorker*: "The odd-shaped corner at Beaver and Broad Streets, with its oblique angle, offered difficulties which have been picturesquely surmounted by Buchman & Kahn, the architects."[91] Light green terra-cotta tiles discreetly accent the brick details at the first two setbacks, corner oriels at the twenty-first story, idiosyncratic in Buchman & Kahn work, were emphasized with a row of cobalt blue terra-cotta tiles, and geometric details in the tower use tiles of the same color. The upper setbacks and tower have exceptionally rich brickwork patterning. The far-reaching dominion of the megacorporation was impressed upon the visitor by the scale of the imposing entrances and lobbies, which were endowed with luxurious metalwork, marbles, mural paintings, and mosaics, all traditional in character. The vaulted corner entrances at Broad and Beaver and Broad and Williams Streets received colorful mosaic ceilings (unsigned). The latter symbolically glorified the corporation's global reach. The IT&T Building, designed in mid-1927, was Kahn's final attempt to revive medieval Spain.

United States Appraisers Building

The firm's commission for the United States Customs Court and Appraisers Stores, commonly known as the United States Appraisers Building (or United States Appraisers Stores), was the result of several years of concerted effort by frustrated merchants to replace the outdated facility at 641 Washington Street. An increase in the volume of imports had created the demand for larger, more efficient space, but little was accomplished to improve conditions until early 1927, when the developer Louis Adler, who had an option to purchase the entire square block, bounded by Varick, King, Hudson, and West Houston Streets, from the Trinity Church Corporation, offered to construct a new building and lease it to the government. After prolonged negotiations, an agreement was reached whereby Adler would construct the building, the govern-

ment would purchase it from Adler, and ultimately the Trinity Church Corporation would transfer the property to the government.[92] After a long debate, the House of Representatives passed the bill authorizing the purchase of the building, as planned by Adler, the total cost of which, including the land, was not to exceed $8,000,000. Among the stipulations in the contract, signed on October 26, 1927 by the secretary of the treasury, was an occupancy date of January 1, 1929.[93] Another stated that if construction cost less than the contractual figure, the builder had to refund the difference to the government. Adler astonished everyone by completing the building over a month earlier than required and returning $410,000 to the government.[94]

The United States Appraisers Building at 201 Varick Street occupied a very large site, 200 by 400 feet, and contained more than a million square feet of space in its twelve floors. The customs facility for examining imported goods and determining duty had, in addition to storage space, almost 300 offices, three courtrooms, and a laboratory.[95] The highly specialized, budgeted program, overseen by government officials, precluded decorative experiments on Kahn's part. The minimal decoration was concentrated on the corner pylons of the upper stories. Corbelled arcades emphasized the tenth and eleventh floors and the slightly battlemented roof parapets. In the end-bay spandrels and the parapet decoration, stepped motifs contrasted curiously with the corbelling. The classically modern entrance was simple but elegant (fig. 5.28). The prismatic geometric motifs of the building directory and letterbox (fig. 5.29) were more in keeping with Kahn's exuberant modernist decoration.

Lefcourt Clothing Center

Early in November 1927, just days after the United States Appraisers Building contract had been formally signed, Kahn began a new project, the Lefcourt Clothing Center at 275 Seventh Avenue, on the east side of the block between 25th and 26th Streets. For over a year Lefcourt had promoted the relocation and consolidation of the mens and boys clothing industry from scat-

tered locations below 14th Street to an area on Seventh Avenue between 22nd and 26th Streets. Although Lefcourt's proposal failed to materialize, the centerpiece of it, his Lefcourt Clothing Center, went forward.

The massing of the twenty-six-story building was modeled on that of the Park Avenue Building. The overall effect was strengthened by the elimination of the side-street setbacks which

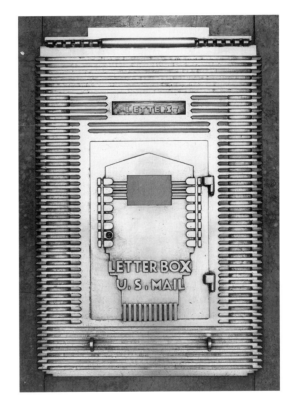

FACING PAGE
5.28 *United States Appraisers Building, Varick Street entrance, 1928, B&K*

5.29 *United States Appraisers Building, letterbox, 1928, B&K*

were not required because the site was only 112 feet deep (fig. 5.30). Like the Park Avenue Building, the elevations were organized into a pier–spandrel system with corner end bays in an A-B-A rhythm, but three-window instead of four-window bays were used throughout, except for the top tier. On the three stories of the base above the street-level stores, the columnar treatment of flat horizontal brick with narrow vertical channels of terra cotta was revived from the Arsenal Building entrance. However, the exterior decoration was primarily adapted from the Park Avenue Building but executed without polychrome, for economy. The brick spandrels are uniformly patterned except in the attic stories and corner end bays. Decoration—repetitive, rectilinear, and layered motifs—was focused on the attic stories and parapets of the three masses (the ornamental flagpole tower one bay wide on Seventh Avenue is an awkward afterthought; it does not appear on the plans). Overall, the surface enrichment is flatter and plainer than in the Park Avenue Building. Greater simplification is also reflected in lobby details such as the elevator doors (fig. 5.31) and the restrained letterbox (fig. 5.32).

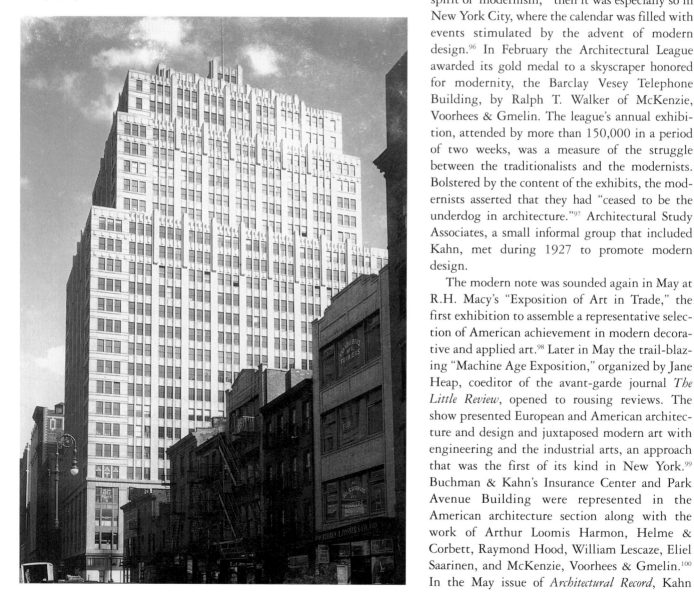

5.30 Lefcourt Clothing Center, 1928, B&K

"Electric With the Spirit of 'Modernism'"

Buchman & Kahn commercial highrises of 1927 stand out for their diversity. The year was a pivotal one in which Kahn finally relinquished his historical predilections and fully embraced a modern idiom. With the Lefcourt Clothing Center, begun at the end of 1927, Kahn turned a corner and never looked back. What transpired during the year to bring about the resolution? If, as Robert A. M. Stern has asserted, the American architectural scene in 1927 was "electric with the spirit of 'modernism,'" then it was especially so in New York City, where the calendar was filled with events stimulated by the advent of modern design.[96] In February the Architectural League awarded its gold medal to a skyscraper honored for modernity, the Barclay Vesey Telephone Building, by Ralph T. Walker of McKenzie, Voorhees & Gmelin. The league's annual exhibition, attended by more than 150,000 in a period of two weeks, was a measure of the struggle between the traditionalists and the modernists. Bolstered by the content of the exhibits, the modernists asserted that they had "ceased to be the underdog in architecture."[97] Architectural Study Associates, a small informal group that included Kahn, met during 1927 to promote modern design.

The modern note was sounded again in May at R.H. Macy's "Exposition of Art in Trade," the first exhibition to assemble a representative selection of American achievement in modern decorative and applied art.[98] Later in May the trail-blazing "Machine Age Exposition," organized by Jane Heap, coeditor of the avant-garde journal *The Little Review*, opened to rousing reviews. The show presented European and American architecture and design and juxtaposed modern art with engineering and the industrial arts, an approach that was the first of its kind in New York.[99] Buchman & Kahn's Insurance Center and Park Avenue Building were represented in the American architecture section along with the work of Arthur Loomis Harmon, Helme & Corbett, Raymond Hood, William Lescaze, Eliel Saarinen, and McKenzie, Voorhees & Gmelin.[100] In the May issue of *Architectural Record*, Kahn

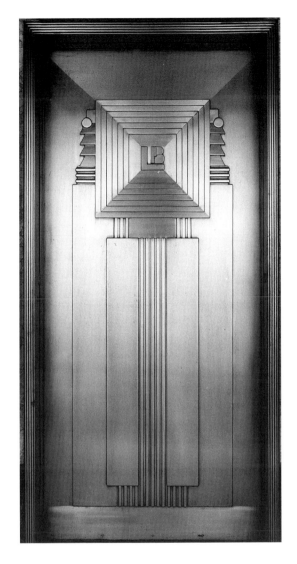

FAR LEFT
5.31 *Lefcourt Clothing Center, elevator door, 1928, B&K*

LEFT
5.32 *Lefcourt Clothing Center, letterbox, 1928, B&K*

reviewed Joseph Urban's new Ziegfeld Theatre on Sixth Avenue at 54th Street and praised its modernity: "Mr. Urban has been willing to experiment freely and boldly, and the result, irrespective of minor criticisms, will be stimulating to those who realize that archeology and design are not necessarily synonymous."[101] Kahn's circle of progressive Austrian émigrés expanded through Urban to include Wolfgang Hoffmann, son of Josef Hoffmann, and his wife Pola, who joined the interior design department of Buchman & Kahn in October.[102]

In December, as the new year approached, Kahn anticipated three major commissions:

an office building on Fifth Avenue, a building for the Film Center on Ninth Avenue, and a second insurance building downtown on John Street.[103] At the same time, he was engaged in designing the art moderne setting for the Lord & Taylor Department Store's exhibition of deluxe French furniture and decorative art, scheduled for early 1928. Throughout 1927 the massive Park Avenue Building rose and revealed its glorious pattern of color. What an exhilarating year 1927 had been for Kahn! Like other American progressives, he had become intoxicated with the idea of a New Age.

CHAPTER SIX

SKYWARD

The Major Works, 1928–31

Energized by the events of 1927 and implemented by the speed of construction during the building boom, modernist commercial architecture and design in New York City began to flower in 1928, and the fruits were soon apparent. Kahn became identified with the momentum early in 1928 as a result of the critical success of the Park Avenue Building and the rave reviews of his stunning art moderne installation for the Lord & Taylor Department Store's "Exposition of Modern French Decorative Art" in February (fig. 6.1). Dorothy Shaver, the director of fashion and decoration and the niece of Samuel Rayburn, the store's president, was the organizer and had invited Kahn to collaborate on the project with the Parisian editor and publisher Lucien Vogel. Lewis Mumford lauded the result for its "breadth, sweep, and élan," and in a salute to Kahn he added that "the space " had been "generously disposed." Continuing, Mumford contrasted the "muted palette" of the French designers with the "keen colors" found in an earlier work by Louis Sullivan and in "Mr. Ely Kahn's new Park Avenue building."[1] The demand for Buchman & Kahn swamped the firm with work in 1928. Fortuitously, the office had moved into

spacious leased quarters: the entire twenty-seventh and twenty-eighth floors of its new Park Avenue Building.[2]

The scope of Kahn's practice broadened considerably in 1928. During the year applications for five new commercial building permits were filed: an office building at 261 Fifth Avenue; the Film Center, 630 Ninth Avenue; an insurance building at 111 John Street; the mammoth Allied Arts Building, 304 East 45th Street, which offered manufacturing, showrooms, and offices; and a loft in the Garment District at 530 Seventh Avenue. At the end of 1927 merchant Charles Oppenheim had returned to the firm for a modern ten-story addition to the Jay-Thorpe store fronting on West 56th Street, and that job was in process.[3] Five new buildings were commissioned: the Bricken Textile Building, 1441 Broadway; the Holland Plaza Building, 431 Canal Street; the 120 Wall Street Building; the Rolls Royce Building, 32 East 57th Street; and the Squibb Building, 745 Fifth Avenue.

In the past Buchman & Kahn had occasionally designed traditional apartments, stores, and restaurant interiors, such as the Maillard Restaurant at 385 Madison Avenue (1922), and

6.1 Ely Jacques Kahn,
Salon of Decorative
Accessories, detail,
"Exposition of Modern
French Decorative Art,"
Lord & Taylor
Department Store, 1928

more recently the Schrafft's Restaurant in the Lefcourt-State Building (1927).[4] The success of the Lord & Taylor installation was pivotal to the firm's specialization in modern interiors. The association of émigré Pola Hoffmann with Buchman & Kahn's interior design department from 1927 through 1929, and of her husband, Wolfgang Hoffmann, who reportedly designed furniture for the firm, intensified this aspect of production.[5] The firm was commissioned to design the Yardley & Company showrooms (fig. 6.2), 452 Fifth Avenue, and a store for the luxury French jeweler Van Cleef & Arpels, 671 Fifth Avenue, both completed in 1929, and apart-

ments for several prominent New Yorkers, among them Charles J. Liebman, 907 Fifth Avenue; Alfred L. Rose, 1009 Park Avenue; and Maurice S. Benjamin, 211 Central Park West. It is likely that Van Cleef & Arpels was impressed with Kahn's installation for Lord & Taylor and his fluency in French. Kahn's design of the high-class establishment was praised as "an example of utter restraint in the design of a sumptuous show-room."[6] The walls of the posh main salon were largely walnut from floor to ceiling and veneered in squares turned to create a checkerboard pattern of vertical and horizontal graining (fig. 6.3). The pattern was relieved by carved panels in a stylized

ABOVE LEFT
6.2 *Yardley & Company, entrance gallery to salesrooms, 1929, B&K*

ABOVE RIGHT
6.3 *Van Cleef & Arpels Jewelry Store, 1929, B&K*

floral art moderne openwork motif. The lighting fixtures, executed by Kantack, were of fused quartz and clear cast glass with metalwork in a silver finish. Kahn's reputation for elegant, refined store interiors expanded with these commissions and soon led to two others on Fifth Avenue: the Bonwit Teller (1930) exterior and interior renovation and the new Hudnut Building (1931).

In June 1928 a group of prominent architects, among them, Kahn, Hood, Walker, Urban, and Eliel Saarinen, were invited to organize the exhibition and design the rooms for the Metropolitan Museum of Art's exhibition, "The Architect and the Industrial Arts," the eleventh in a series of industrial arts exhibitions and the only one to focus on contemporary architects. Kahn served on the nine-member "Co-operating Committee" and had a vital role in the realization of the exhibition. He developed and extended the general scheme that was first "laid out" by Saarinen and oversaw

the details of the installation.[7] Kahn was also on the New York committee to help organize "The First Exposition of Modern American Decorative and Industrial Art" held at the Mandel Brothers Department Store in Chicago that opened in January 1929.[8] In the landmark Metropolitan exhibition of 1929, Kahn's backyard garden and stunning bath and dressing room in the dramatic combination of black and peach, which was said to "satisfy the most confirmed Sybarite" and was singled out for its innovative materials, would bring him extensive publicity and enormous prestige (fig. 6.4).[9] An immediate consequence of the appointment was an opportunity to design for industry. Kahn entered the field of product design in 1928 when Sidney Blumenthal (1864–1948), the president of Shelton Looms, a textile manufacturing company founded in the 1800s, engaged him as "professional adviser and critic on design," a position that involved the selection of designs, weaves, and materials for production.[10] A genera-

6.4 *Ely Jacques Kahn,*
Bath and Dressing
Room, "The Architect
and the Industrial Arts,"
Metropolitan Museum of
Art, 1929

tion older than Kahn, Blumenthal was a permanent member of the Metropolitan Museum's Advisory Committee on Industrial Arts whom Kahn had befriended earlier in the Society of Ethical Culture and the Architectural League of New York. Unusually receptive to contemporary design, Blumenthal hired talented modernists such as Winold Reiss and Ruth Reeves. In 1929 Kahn designed the new Shelton Looms executive office and showrooms at One Park Avenue, which featured a room display by industrial designer Raymond Loewy.[11] Kahn negotiated a retainer in 1928 with Walter J. Kohler, president of the Kohler of Kohler Company of Wisconsin, a manufacturer of plumbing fixtures. Not surprisingly, Shelton Looms would supply the fabrics and Kohler the fixtures in Kahn's bath and dressing room for the Metropolitan exhibition. Kahn's association with Kohler was harmonious and led to numerous Wisconsin visits, where technical details of design and production were resolved. Kahn also

designed Kohler's Long Island City showroom and its pavilion at the 1933 Chicago "Century of Progress Exposition" (see Chapter Seven).[12]

261 Fifth Avenue

Kahn realized bold exterior polychromatic effects in only one important commission after the Park Avenue Building: the twenty-six-story office building at 261 Fifth Avenue, on the southeast corner of 29th Street. As the Park Avenue Building was readied for occupancy early in 1928, plans were in progress for this building on a small site, 98 by 160 feet, which would have less than half the rental space of the former (fig. 6.5). The building was eagerly anticipated by the architectural critic of *The New Yorker*: "We have noticed enough of the work of this firm to feel sure that this new enterprise will include many laudable features. . . . They will probably do something to make us sit up and take notice."[13]

Deemed a "glass skyscraper" in the announcement of its construction, the light for this high-quality office building on Fifth Avenue was maximized by employing Chicago windows, an unusual treatment for Kahn.[14] Structural bays between piers were entirely glazed in the tripartite division characteristic of Chicago-style fenestration, thus guaranteeing a minimum of three windows for each office on a typically divided floor. The primary cladding of the exterior is

6.5 261 Fifth Avenue, rendering, 1929, B&K

buff-color brick laid in American bond. The massing above the eighteenth floor features a series of layered asymmetrical setbacks that evoked the treatment of the loft at 37th Street and Sixth Avenue and recall the horizontally striped and banded setbacks in de Bazel's office building in Amsterdam (see fig. 4.20). The edges of the setbacks on both street elevations were articulated with triple bands of gold terra cotta that wrap around the corner of the building and across both street elevations. On the piers of the thirteenth, fourteenth, and fifteenth floors, applied layered and stepped geometric pendant-like medallions, in brilliant shades of red, blue, and gold terra cotta, serve as metaphoric capitals (see fig. C.6). The piers of the entrance base were embellished with compatible medallions, also in terra cotta, but the palette changed to light gray, charcoal gray, and gold (fig. C.7). The metal ornament between bays feature abstract repetitive patterns in a woven effect.

The exterior polychrome decoration has a strong affinity with the geometric layering of conventionalized plant forms in the work of Frank Lloyd Wright, especially the hollyhock motif in the capitals of the Unity Church, Oak Park, Illinois (1904–8), and in the Hollyhock House in Los Angeles, California (1920, fig. 6.6). Many of the abstract patterns for the brick spandrels and exterior terra-cotta ornament that figured in the work of the firm have a strong interplay of horizontals and verticals, and as such, relate to the abstract relief decoration in other buildings by Wright, for example, the City National Bank in Mason City, Iowa (1909, fig. 6.7), and the A. D. German Warehouse in Richland Center, Wisconsin (1915, fig. 6.8). They may have been precedents, because two members of the firm at the time later named the Dutch architect Van der Woerd, who was influenced by Wright, as the lead designer of the decorative program.[15] Taken separately, each polychrome zone has strength. Unfortunately, the differing colorations weaken the unity and integration of the exterior decorative program.

In contrast to the exterior, the small but sumptuously decorated entrance lobby was conceptually coordinated with an amalgam of vigor-

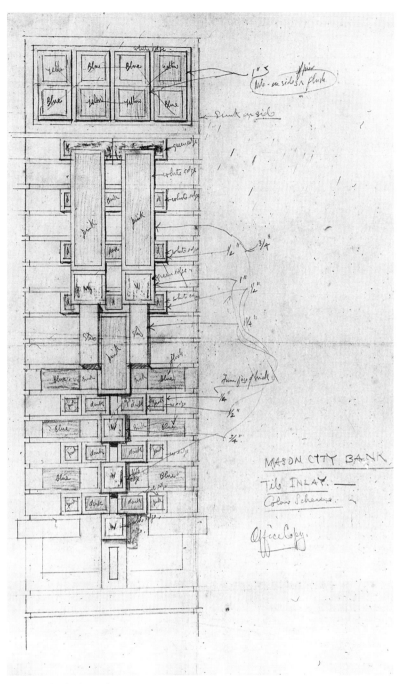

TOP
6.6 *Frank Lloyd Wright, Hollyhock House, Los Angeles, detail of ornament, 1920*

BOTTOM
6.8 *Frank Lloyd Wright, A.D. German Warehouse, detail of cornice, 1915*

6.7 *Frank Lloyd Wright, Drawing, "Mason City Bank, Tile Inlay-Color Schemes," c. 1909*

ous abstract forms in intricate, exotic patterns. The entrance (fig. 6.9) and lobby of 261 Fifth Avenue ranks with those of the Park Avenue Building, the Film Center, and the Holland Plaza Building as the most richly ornamented interior ensembles produced by the firm in 1927, 1928, and 1929, and they exemplify the efflorescence in the decoration of these public spaces during the period. In the lobby (fig. 6.10), above the highly

polished, variegated gray St. Genevieve marble wainscot, the surfaces of the ceiling and wall friezes were gold leafed over silver and softened to a matte finish.[16] The design of the brass-bonded terrazzo floor, in three shades of pink, two shades of gray, and sand color, mirrors the motifs in the pair of vibrant multicolored mosaic panels on the wall across from the elevators. The colors—red-oranges, blues, lavender, gold, black, brown, and silver gray—were repeated in a mosaic that originally enhanced the entrance vestibule. The bronze elevator doors (fig. 6.11), radiator grilles (fig. 6.12), and the panels above the original entrance doors were characteristic of the Park Avenue Building. The design element that captured the attention of the architectural press was the ceiling lighting of the lobby, which paired integral and suspended fixtures (figs. 6.10 and 6.13).[17] One elevator door was exhibited in November 1928, before the building opened, in the inaugural exhibition of the American

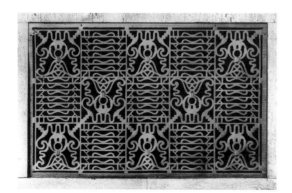

*6.12 261 Fifth Avenue,
radiator grille, 1929,
B&K*

6.10 *261 Fifth Avenue, lobby, 1929, B&K*

6.13 261 Fifth Avenue, vestibule doors and integral lighting fixtures, 1929, B&K

Designers' Gallery, organized for the purpose of promoting indigenous modernist design and comprising a group of fifteen contemporary American designers, among them Kahn, Hood, Walker, and Urban, and Donald Deskey, Winold Reiss, Ilonka Karasz, and Wolfgang Hoffmann. Kahn's participation in this venture is another instance of his central place in the advent of modernism in the 1920s.[18] Organized with the financial backing of the banker Edgar A. Levy and held on the fifth floor of the Chase National Bank Building at 145 West 57th Street, the ambitious but short-lived endeavor was quashed by the Great Depression. The pressure of his practice may have prevented Kahn from contributing in 1929. Kahn also belonged to, but was not active in, the American Union of Decorative Arts and Craftsmen organized in 1928, known by its acronym AUDAC. The organization's main accomplishments were an exhibition at the Brooklyn Museum in 1931 and a book. Kahn did not exhibit in the museum show, but the Park Avenue Building was illustrated in the publication.[19]

The Film Center

A few months following the completion of the Park Avenue Building, Abe Adelson, ever eager for a new venture, purchased the blockfront on the east side of Ninth Avenue between 44th and 45th Streets for a building to service the film industry, and he chose Kahn to design it.[20] The Film Center, known in the trade as a film exchange, was a technical facility that included processing and sound laboratories, projection rooms, graphic art studios, and steel film vaults for storage, as well as office space. Receiving returned films, storing them, and preparing new shipments daily was an important function.[21] Tenants would include the Metro Goldwyn Film Corporation, Universal Pictures, and First National Pictures. The thirteen-story utilitarian building on a 200- by 91-foot site is a bulky, rectangular block with no setbacks and minimal exterior ornamentation. The top three floors and roof parapet received the firm's simplified but characteristic geometric applied decoration (fig.

6.14 *Film Center Building, 1929, B&K*

6.14). The entrance vestibule and lobby are in startling contrast to the low-key exterior. The small space is packed with exuberant and colorful decoration that exploits three-dimensional geometric and interlocking forms and is appropriately "theatrical" (see fig. C.8). A bold mix of Viennese, Wrightian, and machine imagery was reprised from earlier lobbies and elaborated. The metalwork, especially the elevator doors (fig. 6.15), letterbox (fig. 6.16), and radiator grilles, demonstrates the attention paid to these elements. The main designer of the building was Edward "Eddie" Raymond McMahon (1895–

1971), of whom little is known.[22] According to Shamoon Nadir, McMahon was the "top designer" when he entered the firm at the end of 1926. Nonetheless, Nadir suggested that the lobby was the conception of Van der Woerd, whose initials are on the wall mosaic drawing in Avery Library.[23]

111 John Street

Another early 1928 project was a building for the trade in the Insurance District in Lower Manhattan near Wall Street. The site, 111 John Street, which fronted on the entire block between Pearl and Cliff Streets, was across the street and close by the firm's earlier Insurance Center Building at 80 John Street, and like the latter, it occupied an irregular site, trapezoidal in shape. The parcel was one of the largest assembled in the

district at the time, and demolition of the nine existing buildings, some a century old, began in May 1928.[24] Kahn appears to have had a financial interest in the project. His name as president of the 111 John Corporation, the owner of the building, is on the application for the new building permit (the real estate agent Lewis W. Flaunlacher was the corporation vice-president).[25] The scheme developed for the massing of this twenty-six-story building (fig. 6.17) became a formula, with minor variations, for sites with a full block frontage, such as the Bricken Textile Building and 120 Wall Street (see figs. 6.24 and 6.33). Above a two-story base and rusticated transitional story, 111 John Street is set back in powerful blocks with a sequence of dormers that carry the focal exterior decoration. The pair of dormers at the third major setback received the most elaborate pier decora-

*6.17 111 John Street,
Schell Lewis, rendering,
1929, B&K*

tion: art moderne pendant-type triangular pilasters that were framed with layered plaques. Apart from the six-story section on Cliff Street, a strong bilateral symmetry organized the main elevation on John Street. Single-window bays (except at the corners) traverse the elevations and offer tenants flexibility in dividing space into large or small offices. The scheme received critical notice in a trade journal: "In meeting the setback requirements of the Building Code the architects have developed an ingenious design which features a broken facade treatment that relieves the monotony of straight lines usually found in this type of structure."[26] Although the entrance and lobby were not as elaborate as those of the Park Avenue Building, 261 Fifth Avenue, and the Film Center, the distinctive character of the decoration, most of which was designed by Nadir, and especially the bronze elevator doors and panels that

punctuate the entryway, were equivalent (figs. 6.18 and 6.19).

530 Seventh Avenue

Even before the completion of his United States Appraisers Building in 1928, Louis Adler began negotiating for a property that would enhance the reputation of the firm in the Garment District. Adler ultimately purchased the twelve-story Pictorial Review Building at the southwest corner of Seventh Avenue and 39th Street (see fig. 4.13) with the intention of demolishing it to make way for 530 Seventh Avenue, a thirty-story building to be designed by Buchman & Kahn. At a height of 450 feet, it would be the tallest manufacturing building in the city when completed in 1929.[27] The scrapping of a quality building that had been erected as recently as 1919 stunned

RIGHT
6.18 111 John Street, elevator doors, 1929, B&K

FAR RIGHT
6.19 111 John Street, entrance detail, 1929, B&K

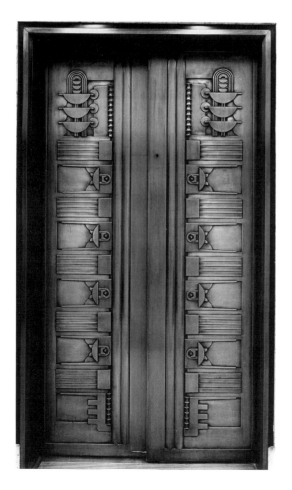

the community and dramatized the transition of Seventh Avenue in less than ten years from a midtown thoroughfare, tenanted largely by seedy second-hand clothes shops and dilapidated tenements, to one of the most important business centers in Manhattan. Adler's enterprise was widely covered by the press, and he responded to the issues in an interview: "Many factors must be considered in this project, the most important of which is land values. The Pictorial Review building was erected as a model printing plant, and its eighteen- and twenty-foot ceilings and special style of heavy construction condemn it for any other purpose. To remodel it would have been a costly and unprofitable operation. In the meantime land values on Seventh Avenue have been mounting almost daily owing to the fact that there are no sites available for improvement between 34th and 42nd Streets at any price. Coupled with this is the increasing demand for space on the avenue by the textile and apparel trade."[28] Land values had escalated in the garment district to the point that, given taxes and other carrying charges, a minimum of twenty-five stories became essential for a profitable investment. Practical features were updated by Adler to attract upscale tenants. Consequently, a new record for midtown Manhattan was set when the building was 75 percent leased before the demolition of the Pictorial Review Building. Most floors were occupied by one tenant because Adler made it a practice to lease no less than eight thousand square feet, and to have no more than two tenants on a floor.[29]

The developer was determined to make 530 Seventh a modern, high-quality sister to his successful 550 Seventh Avenue Building, located on the corner across the street and designed by Kahn only four years earlier with medieval, Persian-Islamic references. These were eschewed in the new building, and a variant of the firm's strategy for corner sites was formulated. The setback corner was chamfered, and in the uppermost zone bold, triangular pilasters projected above the parapets and alternated with the flat piers to give the impression of folds or pleats at street level (fig. 6.20). The wraparound effect was a harbinger of 1930s streamlining and the only instance

6.20 530 Seventh Avenue Building, 1929. B&K

of this corner treatment in Kahn's oeuvre. Another departure in this project was the sleek, modernist entrance and lobby. It was announced to visitors and occupants by the stepped and layered plaque bearing the building number (see fig. C.9). In contrast to the flamboyant treatment of

6.21 530 Seventh Avenue Building, lobby, 1929, B&K

the Film Center and the exoticism of the 261 Fifth Avenue Building, in this lobby smooth, marble-sheathed walls ascend to meet a geometric cast-glass ceiling lighting fixture (fig. 6.21). The radiator grilles and the elevator doors, equally subdued, comprise an elegant ensemble that demonstrates the assimilation of art moderne in America (figs. 6.22 and 6.23). The retention of these decorative components to the present is a testament to their modernity and to the vision of Adler and Kahn. In response to a description of the building as "modernistic," Kahn bristled and defined the distinction he drew between modern and modernistic: "By the word *modern* I mean original. . . . On the other hand, my idea of modernistic is borrowing conceptions from recent art practiced in other countries. For example, were I to take a modern 13-story building in Berlin and try to imitate its architecture in a 45-story building in New York, the result would be modernistic, that is, imitative."[30]

Bricken Textile Building

As construction began on 530 Seventh Avenue, developer and builder Abraham Bricken acquired an irregular site with three street frontages (41st Street, Seventh Avenue, and Broadway) in the northern end of the Garment District for a building to accommodate the nonmanufacturing needs of companies in the textile trade.[31] During the demolition of the old Broadway Theatre and other structures on the property in January 1929, Buchman & Kahn filed plans for the thirty-three-story Bricken Textile Building. The massing of the building and the organization of the elevations into bays and dormers were closely modeled on the twenty-six-story building at 111 John Street. However, bold modifications to express the greater height of the newer building were made (fig. 6.24; see also fig. 6.17): the addition of a story to the base and the application (except at the corners) of colossal triangular pilasters to the load-bearing piers above the transitional fourth story to the first setback at the seventeenth floor. The gold-color brick piers are a counterpoint to the buff-color brick walls and to the gray stone cladding of the base. The narrow flat piers

6.23 *530 Seventh Avenue Building, elevator door, 1929, B&K*

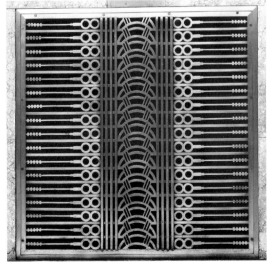

6.22 *530 Seventh Avenue Building, radiator grille, 1929, B&K*

between the triangular pilasters are in gold brick, too, as are each vertical stripe in the spandrels. These elements contribute to the perception of height and provide contrast and interest to the three street elevations. At the corners of the first setback (the sixteenth through the nineteenth stories) the terra-cotta ornament is noteworthy for its deep relief, geometry, and the rhythmic simplicity of the forms (fig. 6.25). In his summation of architecture for the year 1930, Talbot Hamlin observed that one of the general types

emerging in the treatment of the skyscraper involves "rectangularity as the basis for design," and in this category he singled out for mention "much of the work in New York by the firm of Ely Kahn, such as the Bricken Building and the Holland Plaza Building."[32] A shopping arcade spans the main floor between the Seventh Avenue and Broadway entrances, and a significant investment was made in decoration that included mosaic ceilings at the entrances, elaborate metalwork, intricate bronze paneling on the elevator

6.26 Bricken Textile Building, entrance, 1930, B&K

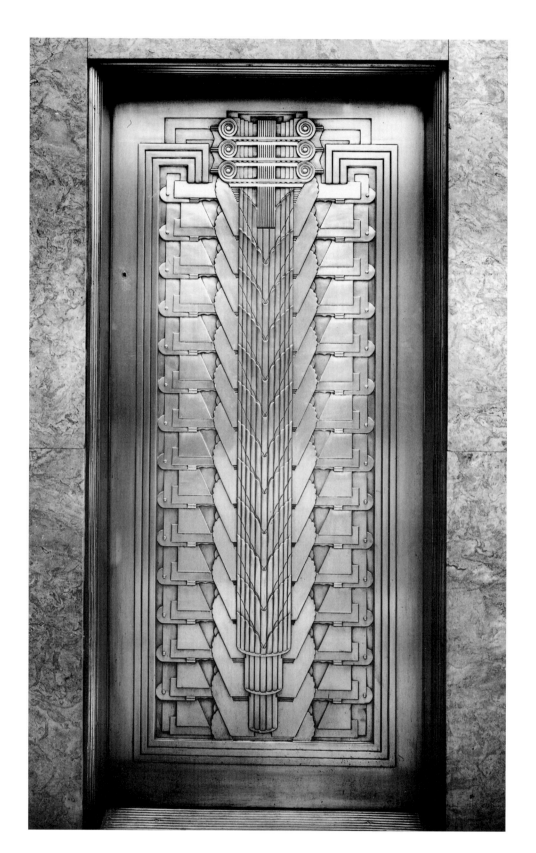

*6.27 Bricken Textile
Building, elevator door,
1930, B&K*

*6.28 Bricken Textile
Building, letterbox,
1930, B&K*

6.29 *Holland Plaza Building, 1930, B&K*

government for the United States Appraisers facility.[33] Although a rendering by Buchman & Kahn of the proposed building was published, another property about six blocks north and also owned by Trinity—the block bounded by Varick, Hudson, King, and West Houston Streets—ultimately became the site developed by Adler and designed by Kahn for the United States Appraisers (see Chapter Five), and the Canal Street site was leased by Adelson from Trinity in November 1928 for an industrial and office building.[34] Adelson's Film Center, designed by Kahn, was nearing completion on Ninth Avenue and 44th Street, and he maintained his relationship with the firm for the Canal Street project. In February 1929 plans were filed for a new sixteen-story industrial structure: the Holland Plaza Building.[35]

Because it was designed to house industries requiring high ceilings, large areas, and floor construction to accommodate heavy machinery, the frame of the building is of reinforced concrete and the columns are in a tightly spaced grid. Those of the lower six stories have steel cores. In keeping with the scale and function of the building, the transitional story between the base and shaft was treated with a bold, abstract rustication that was repeated on the colossal piers of the Canal Street elevation, over the entrance on Varick Street, and on the terminal attic of the building. The apex of the odd-shaped building was emphasized by chamfering the meeting point of the Canal and Varick Street elevations, and by the flagpole at its summit (fig. 6.29). The outward appearance of the building was described as commensurate with a "fine office" building.[36] In fact, there were offices on the upper floors. Kahn described the lobby (fig. 6.30) as "somewhat unusual for a structure located in this particular neighborhood, but [it] indicates in some measure a tendency that seems to be progressing—the realization that the approach, the public corridors, the elevators, must be attractive if the tenant is to maintain a high standard of consideration for a building." Continuing, he injected his rationale for the lavish decoration: "It is illuminating to see how quickly the trite and colorless structure loses prestige and, incidentally, income,

doors and wall friezes, and a coordinated letter-box (figs. 6.26, 6.27, and 6.28).

The Holland Plaza Building

An unusual deal in the Holland Plaza District near the Holland Tunnel, completed in November 1927, involved, at different stages, developers and former partners Adler and Adelson, who had done pioneering work in the Garment District. In 1926 Adler had independently optioned, from the Trinity Church Corporation, a full block in the burgeoning industrial area along Varick and Hudson Streets, between Clarkson and Vestry Streets, and he offered the site, bounded by Varick, Hudson, Canal, and Watts Streets, to the

6.30 Holland Plaza
Building, lobby, 1930,
B&K

so that the apparent luxury of this Holland Plaza Building may develop into being a reasonably intelligent investment."[37] Unfortunately, not a vestige remains of this extraordinarily beautiful interior entrance and lobby in which the elevator doors had an affinity with the relief motifs on a pair of teak doors in the Berlin Sommerfeld house (1921) by Gropius and Meyer. The character of the entrance and lobby, documented in surviving photographs, suggests that Adelson wanted an interior decor similar to that of his Film Center. At the same time that plans for the Holland Plaza Building were in process, a small nineteen-story project at 32 East 57th Street, named the Rolls Royce Building, was on the drawing boards, and in its lobby remain the refined elevator doors (and directory) with motifs similar to those for the original plasterwork in the Holland Plaza lobby (fig. 6.31).

6.31 Rolls Royce Building, elevator door, 1930, B&K

120 Wall Street

Kahn's ability to satisfy the demands of his clients was demonstrated by their loyalty to the firm. Henry Greenberg and David Malzman, the youthful partners who at age twenty-four had developed the Arsenal Building, and afterward the Insurance Center Building at 80 John Street, returned to Buchman & Kahn for the planning of their most ambitious project: a thirty-three-story office building in the Financial District at 120 Wall Street. The corner property, fronting also on South and Pine Streets and overlooking the harbor and the East River, was acquired at the end of 1928 from the American Sugar Refining Company.[38] The site has a historic significance. Before the land was filled in, Murray's Wharf, at the foot of Wall Street, was located on it; there General George Washington landed on April 23, 1789 to take his oath of office as the first president of the United States. A bronze tablet commemorating the event was provided by the Daughters of the American Revolution and installed later in the entrance to the new building.[39] Plans were filed on February 13, 1929, and in March the twelve-story building on the property and other warehouses and commercial structures, some over fifty years old, were torn down.[40] The construction of the foundation was reported to have been "one of the most difficult foundation problems in engineering history." In order to resist the tidal uplift from the East River, fifty-one pneumatic caissons were sunk—the deepest, ninety-two feet—through layers of brick, stone, and wood fill to the original riverbed and below it, to rock bottom.[41]

More than any other Kahn building, 120 Wall Street has an iconic presence associated with the city. The outline of its pristine white massing, which soars thirty-three stories in seven setbacks and is punctuated with dormers on the South Street elevation, is in the foreground of images of lower Manhattan looking west over the East River. Its development constituted pioneering work in the lower Wall Street area, and it serves as a lasting reminder of the glory years of 1920s setback skyscrapers. Although 120 Wall Street is now a part of the dense concentration in lower

Manhattan, at its completion in 1930 it stood out with striking prominence among its older neighbors (fig. 6.32). The massing is similar to other buildings by the firm that have a full block frontage, such as 111 John Street and the Bricken Textile Building. However, contrasting end bays were eliminated, the walls are smooth, and fenestration is uniformly in single units. The treatment may have been prompted by the design of the recently completed fifty-six-story Chanin Building on 42nd Street and Lexington Avenue that was garnering much attention. Although subdued, 120 Wall Street, like the Chanin Building, has a decorative buttressed crown, and it would not be surprising if the clients wanted to emulate this new landmark. As early as June 1930 James Blaine Newman (1892–1973), the firm's building manager, speculated that had there been "a positive certainty that the building would rent as rapidly as it did, it would have been made 50 stories at least."[42] The seven setbacks of the main elevation on South Street, facing the East River, ascend in three major stages. Each is articulated with identical paired dormers that step up in two symmetrical lines beginning at the sixth floor and terminating at the twenty-ninth. Intervening centered dormers create a secondary rhythm within the overall massing. In contrast to the marked differentiation of the base from the shaft in 111 John Street and the Bricken Textile Building, the five-story base was faced in flat stone in a color similar to the walls above it (fig. 6.33). The organization of the massing and fenestration, the harmonious proportions, brilliant glazed white brick cladding, and the muted base make 120 Wall Street one of Kahn's finest works.

The lead designers of the interiors were Shamoon Nadir and Otto John Teegen. Like Nadir, Teegen stressed Kahn's encouragement of experiment, his magnetic appeal to "young people," the "opening [of] his office to young designers," and his willingness to "give them freedom."[43] Kahn's sympathetic attitude to young talent was highlighted in the autobiography of the Viennese architect Ernst A. Plischke (1903–92). In 1929 Plischke and the America architect William Muschenheim (1902–90), whom he had befriended while the latter was

6.32 120 Wall Street Building, 1930, B&K

studying at the Behrens Master School of Architecture of the Academy of Fine Arts in Vienna, planned to open a practice in New York. The partnership never materialized, and Plischke found himself in New York looking for a job. While pounding the streets, he noticed a Buchman & Kahn building under construction. He applied to Kahn for work without a formal recommendation and was hired conditionally. According to Plischke, Kahn ran a tight shop, the work was hard, and the rules strict. Neither conversations with fellow draftsmen nor private telephone calls were permitted during work

6.33 120 Wall Street Building, Wall Street entrance, 1930, B&K

his autograph that epitomizes his receptivity to and respect for young, talented designers, qualities that attracted many to his practice: "It has been a real privilege to have had your association in the design of so much that has been of vital interest to me—you have done much to develop a fresh view point and we are all of us richer for the experience. I inscribe myself in true gratitude and friendship. Ely J. Kahn."[45]

Like the exterior decoration that was simplified, the entrances and lobby, with the exception of the intricately patterned Wall Street entrance grille, exhibited the more subdued direction that had been initiated for the 530 Seventh Avenue interiors (fig. 6.34). The walls of the lobby and entrances were smoothly faced in marble, and the floors feature a geometric pattern with rectangular and circular accents. The lighting fixtures were integrated into the ceiling and soffits in flush rectangular panels that were noted for the "original treatment" that provided "good general illumination without glare."[46] In general, the layering of the molded plaster ceiling and other decorative motifs were considerably toned down, giving a light and airy elegance to the interior. The complexity of the bronze elevator doors (fig. 6.35), in which the primary motif alludes to setback skyscrapers, as well as that of the radiator grilles (fig. 6.36), which evoke aerodynamic machines, add enrichment to the relatively plain interior. A mural by D. Putnam Brinley on the ceiling of the Wall Street entrance vestibule depicts the harbor of the quaint Dutch settlement of Manhattan on one side and on the other, from the same viewpoint, the modern skyline of Manhattan replete with stepped-back skyscrapers.[47] The 120 Wall Street building was an immediate financial success and exceeded the expectations of the developers. In October 1930 it was reported that the income was 40 percent greater than originally estimated.[48]

A Visionary Rendering

An intriguing commission for a skyscraper of at least sixty-five stories that Kahn pursued—and one that kept him in suspense most of 1929 and early 1930—was a project that ultimately did

hours, and office manager Newman enforced the rules. At the end of the month Plischke was surprised that his paycheck was twice the amount he had expected. However, because prospects were dim after the stock market crash in October 1929, he returned to Vienna. Before he left the office, he asked Kahn the reason why he had hired him. Plischke never forgot Kahn's reply: "I wanted to give you a fair chance."[44] When Nadir left the firm in December 1929, Kahn wrote a note in

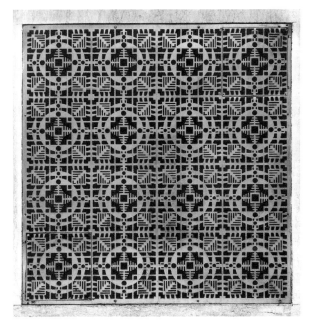

6.34 *120 Wall Street Building, elevator lobby, 1930, B&K*

ABOVE RIGHT
6.35 *120 Wall Street Building, elevator doors, 1930, B&K*

RIGHT
6.36 *120 Wall Street Building, radiator grille, 1930, B&K*

6.37 Ely Jacques Kahn, "Skyscraper," 1930, Cooper-Hewitt, National Design Museum, Smithsonian Institution, B&K

Chanin Building, of a parcel that had been assembled and included the Century Theatre (formerly the New Theatre by Carrère & Hastings, 1909) on a full block between 62nd and 63rd Streets, bounded by Central Park West and Broadway, was announced. Chanin planned to erect a sixty-five-story commercial building on the property.[49] Word had leaked out because Kahn had already approached Chanin. In his diary on May 28th he entered: "Talked with Chanin about C. P. West 62 to 63rd St—65 to 75 stories Wow."[50] Kahn was studying the project; on June 14th he jotted down in his diary: "Working on Chanin C. P. West & 63rd St—."[51] All along Chanin was negotiating with the French government and on August 13 the "Palais de France"—a sixty-five-story mixed-use building to be "a cradle of culture and the centre of permanent relations and economic exchange between France and the United States"—was heralded. In addition to accommodating official French agencies such as the French Consulate and the National Tourist Bureau, several other ambitious projects were planned to cement the Franco-American culture and friendship": a 1,200 room, thirty-story studio apartment hotel, a three-story permanent industrial exhibition, floors for displays of automobiles, boats, and small yachts, stores and showrooms, and the establishment of an Academie des Beaux-Arts. The project was regarded as a personal triumph for the French Consul General Pierre Mongendre, who had bucked the opposition to the proposal. Chanin proudly proclaimed: "Under government patronage . . . the Palais de France will be a great commercial clearing house for quality wares and merchandise. It will be a permanent exhibit of monumental proportions for the exploitation of the world's finest creations of everything appertaining to that culture, beauty and luxury wherein France has established herself supreme."[52]

Less than a week later Kahn was still involved and hopeful: "Palais de France Central Park West to Broadway—whole block 75 stories—maybe?"[53] Kahn had reason to be optimistic about snagging the commission until January 1930, when he entered in his diary: "still alive."[54] However, the financial recession that followed the

not materialize. Lost in history, it is a story that had a fascinating cast of characters, one of whom was Kahn. A mysterious rendering of an unidentified visionary skyscraper, unsigned but attributed to Kahn, is a key piece of evidence (fig. 6.37). On May 29, 1929, the acquisition by Irwin S. Chanin, president of the Chanin Construction Company and developer of the

stock market crash late in 1929 quashed the project. On October 24, 1930 the Chanin organization stated that "they were not renewing a lapsed contract with the Palais de France Corporation" and that the "failure to carry out the plan" was due to "the tariff law and general economic conditions, as well as to changes in the French Ministry which resulted in delays not anticipated by the French interest."[55] Instead the Chanins erected the mammoth thirty-story Century Apartments, named for the demolished theater, on the site, and it opened in December 1931.

In 1932 the Architectural League of New York gave Kahn a solo exhibition. Of the works on view, a reviewer observed that: "Two of the most striking designs must remain, unfortunately, in the limbo of 'paper architecture': Kahn's drawing for the Appomattox Monument competition, awarded recently to Harry Sternfeld of Philadelphia, and the French Government Building in Central Park West, which had the project been carried through, would have topped the Empire State and provided New York with probably the first skyscraper planetarium in existence."[56] It is our hypothesis that the visionary rendering reproduced here (fig. 6.37) was, in fact, the one in the description of the 1932 exhibition, and that it was Kahn's preliminary proposal for the Palais de France, often referred to as the French Government Building. Kahn never identified the building in the drawing, which clearly overlooks a park, nor have any drawings or plans for the Palais de France that Kahn worked on come to light. Notwithstanding the precedent in Kahn's work of a tower emerging from a complex mass of setbacks in schemes A and B for the Park Avenue Building (see figs. 5.10 and 5.11), the skyscraper in the drawing was an extraordinary leap for Kahn and has a kinship with the earlier, visionary rendering by Hugh Ferriss of "Verticals on Wide Avenues" (fig. 6.38) in *The Metropolis of Tomorrow* (1929). The Palais de France rendering shows Kahn at his most daring.

The Squibb Building

Meanwhile, the pace in the firm had quickened in 1929 with another commission from Adelson,

6.38 *Hugh Ferris, "Verticals on Wide Avenues," 1926.*

a luxury thirty-two-story showroom and office building named for its location, 745 Fifth Avenue, on the northeast corner at 58th Street, across from the Bergdorf Goodman store and close to Central Park, an area that was evolving into a high-quality shopping center. In the summer of 1928 Adelson had subleased the property, 120 feet on Fifth Avenue and 200 feet on 58th

Street, owned by the Mary Mason Jones estate, from the realtor Frederick Brown. The six-story Mason Apartment House, built in the 1890s, and other structures on the site were razed early in May 1929.[57] By July, E. R. Squibb & Sons, manufacturers of chemical and pharmaceutical products, leased the twelve upper floors of 745 Fifth Avenue and the name was changed to the Squibb Building. Analyzing the lease, Adelson commented: "Aside from the large amount of space involved, which makes it one of the most impor-

tant deals in that respect this year, the choice of this location by so notabel [sic] a concern is added evidence of the desirability of this upper Fifth Avenue district as a prestige location. Possessing, as it does, the advantages of freedom from noise and congestion and outstanding accessibility for the executives and personnel of large organizations, this immediate district assures 'quality surroundings' for those who desire a business home in an exclusive neighborhood."[58]

The planning of the Squibb Building

6.41 Squibb Building, detail of top stories, 1930, B&K

required intensive study and concentration, especially on the floor plans and on the distribution of courts in the massing. Three sets of plans were developed before all those involved were satisfied.[59] The interplay of verticals and horizontals figured strongly in the modeling of setbacks, especially on the 58th Street elevation that reveals the tower core (figs. 6.39 and 6.40). The building rises from a six-story base in which the piers were originally expressed with vertical fluting and the white marble spandrels were accent-

ed with round, stepped and layered applied plaques. Like 120 Wall Street, the balance of the building is sheathed in glazed white brick, and a single spandrel motif unifies the elevations. The terra-cotta decoration is of the same tone as the brick, creating an uninterrupted flow and integration of the masses. Adelson had announced his intention of making this building a "structure of architectural distinction," and that "beauty, as well as utility" was considered in its designing— a goal that was achieved by Kahn in the exterior

ABOVE
6.42 Squibb Building,
main entrance, 1930,
B&K

ABOVE RIGHT
6.43 Squibb Building,
outer vestibule, 1930,
B&K

and interior programs. The restrained exterior decoration was kept to a minimum and focused on the tower, where rectangular stepped and layered medallions (abstractions that recall those on the 261 Fifth Avenue building and earlier Wrightian ornament) and trios of prismatic pilasters crown the building (fig. 6.41).

An extruded and cast-nickel silver entrance canopy bearing the name of the building and surmounted by a geometric-patterned grille that emphasized verticality—the most reductive to

date by the firm (fig. 6.42)—greeted visitors and occupants who passed into the open vestibule, which was faced in St. Victor Rose marble and through the doorways, over which stepped and fluted metalwork formed a decorative border (fig. 6.43). The outstanding feature of the lobby, which has the same marble-faced walls—rising up to indirect cove lighting—and travertine floors, is the ceiling mural, a work on canvas by Arthur Covey, a leading muralist and president of the National Society of Mural Painters in 1929 (fig.

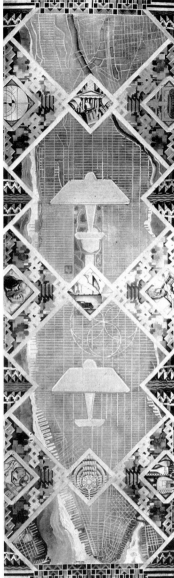

6.44). The mural depicts a map of Manhattan with two airplanes floating above it. In three panels along each side the artistic and scientific activities relating to the building and its location were represented emblematically: engineering, fine arts, and physics on the south side, and architecture, music and drama, and chemistry on the north (fig. 6.45).[60] Other aspects of city life, including the dynamic worlds of finance and industry, were depicted in three centered square panels. The subject of a smaller companion mural on the wall facing the entrance doors is the purchase of Manhattan from the Indians. The large number 24 in the painting probably represents the $24 purchase price. This mural, unlike that for the ceiling, is unsigned but is also the work of Covey. The elevator halls, in which the firm's penchant for elaborate molded plaster ceilings was eschewed, originally had planar light fixtures consisting of a rectilinear slab of embossed glass supported and suspended by metal rods close to the ceiling and over the source of light. The decora-

ABOVE LEFT
6.44 *Squibb Building, lobby, 1930, B&K*

ABOVE
6.45 *Squibb Building, Arthur Covey mural, 1930, B&K*

tive enrichment in this minimalist interior was focused on the radiator grilles, which evoke the stepped-back skyscraper (fig. 6.46), and on the elevator doors, which were commissioned from the Austrian émigré designer Vally Wieselthier. The doors were enlivened with playful animal and marine forms between bold stepped bands (fig. 6.47). In his memoirs Kahn recalled the transaction with Wieselthier: "I had arranged with a Viennese sculptor to carry out my own sketches to find after months of delay that the flat area of modeling clay remained untouched. In my usual anxiety to get results I proceeded to do my own modeling for better or worse!"[61]

The Squibb Building formally opened on May 1, 1930. Because of the stock market collapse in October 1929 and the ensuing recession,

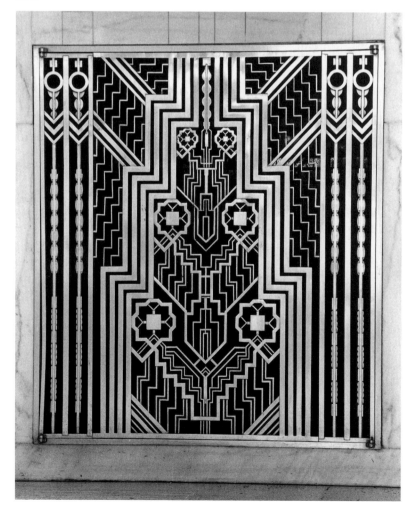

6.46 Squibb Building. Radiator Grille, 1930, B&K

it was only about 50 percent rented.[62] Many—and mixed—reviews were published in the architectural press. Most critics lauded the restraint of the building but differed in their opinion of other aspects of the design. George Sheppard Chappell (T-Square), the architectural critic of *The New Yorker* and one of the earliest to judge the building, was generally positive: "An admirable newcomer to this neighborhood is the huge Squibb Building, designed by Buchman & Kahn. They have done themselves proud. The cool white marble of the base courses is finely supplemented by the brickwork above, and the detail throughout is vigorous and restrained. There appears to be a little confusion in the relation of the setbacks, but the building as a whole has much beauty."[63] In the *Western Architect*, architect Arthur T. North discussed the Squibb Building in the context of the prevalence of brick clad structures in the city:

> New York has become essentially a brick town. Its largest, highest and most costly office building are made of brick. . . . Office buildings erected within the past few years show a marked tendency towards the all-brick structure with inconspicuous window sills and wall copings of metal. . . . Of the all-brick buildings that are especially notable are the Daily News, Squibb and Western Union Buildings—all noticeably different and decidedly individualistic of the designers. . . . The Squibb Building—the Office of Ely Jacques Kahn, Architects—is another white brick building with white marble in the lower stories. The brick is of such a fine quality that the transition from marble to brick is scarcely noticed. . . . The spandrels are of white brick, the faces of which are scarcely, though sufficiently accentuated by planes of very small projection. There is nothing to distract attention from the fine modeling of the masses of the building which alone is sufficient to attract and hold discriminating attention, giving way to sincere admiration. In distinguished company at 58th Street and Fifth Avenue, the Squibb Building easily maintains its artistic pre-eminence.[64]

Architect Harry Allan Jacobs was the only reviewer to take issue with the color of the Squibb Building: "In my opinion the Squibb

Building at 58th Street and Fifth Avenue would have been improved if the white brick had been relieved a little by bright colors, using terra cotta or different colored marbles."[65] Lewis Mumford wrote favorably of the Squibb Building but was critical of Kahn's differentiation of the base in other buildings: "If No. 2 Park Avenue is Mr. Ely Kahn's most successful attempt to use warm tones and full color in a large office building, perhaps the most satisfactory essay in color to be seen so far in New York, the Squibb Building, shows equally what can be done in pure white, when it is intelligently used. . . . It is a consistent piece of work, down to the fact that here Mr. Kahn almost parted with his deplorable practice of boldly differentiating the lower floors with their show windows from the main mass of the building. One congratulates the architect upon the general restraint and sincerity which characterize his whole handling of the problem."[66]

Hamlin critiqued the building differently: "The Squibb Building, New York, by the firm of Ely J. Kahn, is a beautiful glowing white mass, its setbacks composed effectively, but the lower portion is entirely unrelated to the upper, and the entrance and show window treatment look skimped and unreal."[67] Although John Cushman Fistere criticized Kahn in *Vanity Fair* for "his occasional tendency to sacrifice structural character for dramatic forms," he thought that Kahn had been inspired by the "quality of the architecture in the surrounding Plaza district" and that he had "contributed his best piece of work in the Squibb Building." Continuing, Fistere declared: "When he is at his best, Kahn is incomparable in the use of simple forms for striking effects."[68]

The Squibb Building was among Kahn's favorite works, and his involvement in the design and its execution was similar to that of the Park Avenue Building: "The Squibb Building had been and is one of my cherished creations. I had the fun of helping model details, working with the Squibb Company on their own area—mural painters on decoration, in the studio where terra cotta details were developed." Adelson, who took pride in this building, deferred to Kahn after it was completed and as long as he was the owner: "The one building where all changes were in my

hands was the Squibb Building. No alterations to the facade were permitted without my consent, and I was called in [afterward] to design what was needed."[69] The wittiest salute by Kahn to the Squibb Building occurred at the Society of Beaux-Arts Architects annual ball in 1931, held at the Hotel Astor in New York City. The theme

6.47 Squibb Building, Vally Wieselthier and Ely Jacques Kahn, elevator doors, 1930, B&K

6.48 "The Skyline of New York," Society of Beaux-Arts Architects Ball, 1931; from left: A. Stewart Walker (Fuller Building), Leonard Schultze (Waldorf-Astoria Hotel), Ely Jacques Kahn (Squibb Building), William Van Alen (Chrysler Building), Ralph Walker (One Wall Street) D. E. Ward (Metropolitan Tower), and J. H. Freedlander (Museum of the City of New York)

was "A Fête Moderne," and the entertainment, centered around modernism, the keynote, included a scene in which famous skyscrapers "came to life" in the form of a miniature skyline of widely known buildings formed by their architects in costume.[70] Among them were Kahn as the Squibb Building, Leonard Schultz as the Waldorf-Astoria Hotel, and William Van Alen as the Chrysler Building (fig. 6.48). Interviewed the following year, Kahn said he considered the Squibb Building "his masterpiece."[71]

The Bricken Casino Building: 1410 Broadway

In January 1929 Kahn started working on a huge project in the garment district: two buildings,

each thirty-five stories, 1400 and 1410 Broadway, which shared the east side block between 38th and 39th Streets (fig. 6.49). The Bricken Casino Building, as 1410 Broadway was called, was named for its builder and developer, Abraham Bricken, and for the demolished Casino Theatre, a venue for light opera and musical comedy that had occupied the site since the 1890s. The 1400 Broadway parcel, the larger of the two (which included the thirty-six-year-old Knickerbocker Theatre where Sarah Bernhardt had performed), was cobbled together by developer Abraham I. Gevirtz to form an L-shaped plot that wrapped around the Bricken Casino Building and required an idiosyncratic floor plan (fig. 6.50). The pairing made an awkward mix

6.49 1400 Broadway,
1931, B&K; and
Bricken Casino
Building, 1410
Broadway, 1931, EJK

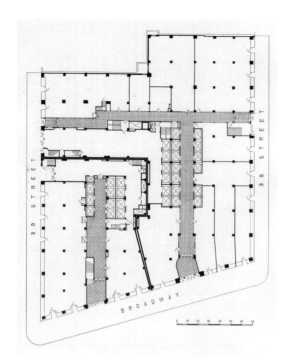

6.50 *1400 and 1410 Broadway, floor plan*

6.51 *Bricken Casino Building, tower, 1931, EJK*

and of the two, the smaller Bricken Casino stands out for its dramatic massing.[72] The new building application was the first filed by "The Firm of Ely Jacques Kahn." Albert Buchman retired in January 1930 and John Montfort and Kahn formed a joint partnership that was reported in the February issue of the *American Architect*[73] and formally announced by the new firm in a mailing dated June 1, 1930: "As Albert Buchman is retiring from practice the firm of Buchman & Kahn architects has been dissolved by mutual consent. Ely Jacques Kahn and John M. Montfort have formed a co-partnership under the name of The Firm of Ely Jacques Kahn and will continue the practice of the former firm with the same associates and organization at 2 Park Avenue, New York."[74]

Above its conventional four-story base and beginning at the twenty-first floor, a series of staggered setbacks, sloping back at an angle to appear faceted, were accented at the corner edges with angular applied white terra-cotta fins that jut upward. The setbacks soar telescopically and culminate in a tower, also finned (fig. 6.51). Verticality was emphatically expressed by alternating smooth white piers with dark brick spandrels to create a striking striped effect. Unique in Kahn's oeuvre, the Bricken Casino Building is his most expressionistic design. Ted Jacobsen, who worked on it, described the process: "The 1410 Broadway Building was a departure from previous designs—a further development of the New York setback code with emphasis on the dark spandrel to give a strong vertical . . . Yes—I worked on the 1410 Broadway Bldg.—my first job in the office and I recollect Mr. Kahn coming into the drafting room to announce—now this one will be vertical lines in black & white (and with towering set backs).' I was assigned to do the rendered perspective from his studies and I was proud & pleased that he accepted my drawings. In those days the designers used to argue (over a couple of fast ones at lunch) the theory and merits of horizontal or vertical treatments of the spandrels and piers and which should be light or dark."[75] The contrast between the four-story base, which was faced in black granite and had black glass and dark metal spandrels, with the rest of the building compro-

ABOVE LEFT
6.52 *Bricken Casino Building, lobby, 1931, EJK*

ABOVE
6.53 *Bricken Casino Building, elevator door, 1931, EJK*

mised the integration of the whole and was no doubt one example of the strategy that provoked Mumford's criticism of Kahn.

The entire entrance and lobby of the building have been completely remodeled. Period photographs reveal that, unlike the Squibb Building, the entrance vestibule was elaborate and had a ceiling mosaic and frieze similar to the Bricken Textile Building, located two blocks to the north on Broadway (see fig. 6.26). The lobby, however, featured abstract geometric patterns in the terrazzo floor that were mirrored in the ceiling light fixtures and a low horizontal banding of the walls (fig. 6.52). The wavy and flamelike motifs on the elevator doors were unusual for the firm (fig. 6.53). Kahn mentioned that the muralist Hildreth Meiere (1892–1961) contributed to the lobby.[76]

The Continental Building

It was a fitting finale to Kahn's work in the garment district that the client was Louis Adler, and that the forty-three-story building was his tallest skyscraper built pre–World War II. The property acquired by Adler in April 1928 was the site of the nine-story Continental Hotel, on the southeast corner of Broadway and 41st Street, which had catered chiefly to commercial travelers in recent years but was originally the Vendome, a leading family hotel erected about 1890.[77] To preserve the name recently associated with the site, Adler christened the new building the Continental. When demolition of the old hotel began in February 1930, a race was on between Adler, Bricken, and Gevirtz, the developers of three skyscrapers that were designed by Kahn and were located only three blocks apart in the Garment District. It was a heady moment for Kahn when the frenetic activity attracted the attention of the press: "Louis Adler joined the big skyscraper race on the Broadway Rialto yesterday, making it a threesome. With Bricken tearing down the old Casino on the 39th corner and Gevirtz doing likewise to old Knickerbocker Theatre adjoining at 38th Street, Adler will tackle the old Hotel Continental at the southeast corner of 41st Street to-morrow—all to rush up skyscrapers."[78] At forty-three stories the Continental Building, 1450 Broadway, was the tallest commercial edifice in the immediate Times Square area and overtopped Bricken's Casino and Textile Buildings and Gevirtz's building at 1400 Broadway. The commission provided Kahn with his first opportunity to produce a true tower. Unlike the Bricken and Gevirtz properties, the Continental has a slender presence of about 77 feet on Broadway. The slightly torqued tower that rises from the lower setbacks is only four

LEFT
6.54 Continental Building, early rendering, 1930, EJK

FACING PAGE LEFT
6.56 Continental Building, entrance, 1931, EJK

FACING PAGE RIGHT
6.55 Continental Building, 1931, EJK

window-bays deep on Broadway and eight deep on 41st Street—the main elevation that faces north on 41st Street, a much narrower thoroughfare than Broadway—thus making it difficult to view and photograph the full 173-foot expanse of the building. Two preliminary studies have survived. In a general sense the initial study was an elongation and evolution of the abandoned Sketch A for the twenty-five-story Park Avenue Building (fig. 6.54; see also fig. 5.10). The second Continental study, which is closer to the actual building, has a more subdued crown.[79] The expression of height (and therefore verticality) was foremost. In the final plan it was expressed by a greater simplification of the wall, the alternation of undecorated thick and thin piers and plain spandrels, the de-emphasis of parapet decoration, and a uniform color (fig. 6.55). There is a fine clarity to the massing of this white building. A special feature of the upper stories was the tiled terraces for some offices at the setbacks. It was said at the time that the "idea of a terrace just outside your office is a new one in New York and it is likely to be followed by architects when creating designs for new office building in the future."[80]

A massive clock of Benedict nickel in a matte finish distinguished the main entrance, which

6.57 *Continental Building, lobby, 1931, EJK*

was faced in Dover white marble (fig. 6.56). The lobby arcade of stores, originally L-shaped with entrances on both Broadway and 41st Street, was more elaborate than the exterior. A distinctive feature was the grand staircase of St. Victor Rose marble, with its streamlined railing and steps leading to the bank on the mezzanine. Like the Squibb and 120 Wall Street Buildings the marble-clad walls were smoothly faced, the floor patterning was geometric, and the elevator doors and letterbox were subdued. However, the ornate system of indirect lighting, heavily framed and gilded, was discordant with the elegant simplicity of the decor (fig. 6.57). When the interior was described as "modernistic," Kahn refuted the designation, declaring that the style was "not 'modernistic' but just modern."[81] Adler was a shrewd operator and businessman who capitalized on the proximity of the building to Times Square and four subway lines and on his personal renown in New York real estate (which generated publicity for his projects) as well as the status of his buildings and his successful dealings with tenants. These would be enormous assets in a depression market.

Wall Street Tower

Adler's flair for the spectacular reached its apogee on May 7, 1930, with the sensational purchase of an entire block, fronting on Wall, Water, Pine, and Pearl Streets, in the heart of the downtown Financial District, for a skyscraper of at least sixty-five stories, and possibly a hundred and five, to be ready for occupancy in the spring of 1932. The site, comprising fourteen plots belonging to various owners, had been assembled in record time by the Charles F. Noyes Company, a prominent real estate concern. Adler reportedly was the first individual to have bought an entire block on Wall Street.[82] During the construction of the Continental Building, on May 6, the day before Adler officially acquired the Wall Street block, Kahn noted in his diary: "Louis Adler Wall St—imminent." Less than a week later he excitedly wrote: "Adler Wall St nearly ready to start 65 stories whole block Pearl-Pine Wall!"[83] On July 17, 1930, Kahn filed the plans for the

760-foot high, sixty-five-story office building. In contrast to the estimate of $3,000,000 three months earlier for the Continental Building, $10,000,000 was the anticipated cost of the Wall Street skyscraper.[84] As late as January 14, 1931, the project was uncertain and it was reported that "no time has been set, as yet, for the beginning of construction work on the square block office building which Mr. Adler has in mind for the plottage bounded by Wall, Pine, Pearl, and Water St."[85] The high hopes of Adler and Kahn were dashed by the depressed economy. Exactly three years after the job appeared "imminent," Kahn sadly wrote in his diary: "Adler loses Wall St property."[86]

Unfortunately, the original plans filed for it are no longer extant, copies of them are not in Avery Library, and renderings and descriptions of the building have not come to light. Nor has research yielded such from the heirs of Louis Adler. It is surprising that Kahn did not preserve a record of a skyscraper design that represented the pinnacle of his work between the World Wars.

East Side Buildings

In 1930 before the depression deepened, Kahn designed three new buildings on the East Side of Manhattan: the Hudnut Building (with Eliel Saarinen) at 693 Fifth Avenue at 54th Street, the office building at 136 East 57th Street (the southeast corner of Lexington Avenue), and the Commerce Building at 155 East 44th Street (the northwest corner of Third Avenue) near Grand Central Terminal. Buchman & Fox had designed the twelve-story Bonwit Teller Building at 417 Fifth Avenue, which had been occupied by the store since 1910. When Bonwit Teller relocated uptown in 1930 by leasing the twelve-story Stewart & Company Building at 725 Fifth Avenue at 56th Street, designed by Warren & Wetmore, the merchants turned to Kahn for the renovation of the main entrance and the eight sales floors. His work was commended for the "accentuation of good taste, simplicity, and practicality," and the spacious main floor was described as "virtually a flood of space, white

lights, and coolness" with "white walls and exceedingly wide aisles."[87] The overly ornate Stewart facade was replaced with a restrained two-story entrance of metal and glass that allowed daylight to penetrate these floors (fig. 6.58). Teegen drew the design for the openwork grille of Benedict nickel silver.[88] With the exception of Mumford, who objected to the cool color of the grille, Kahn's overhaul of the Bonwit Teller facade was warmly received.[89] When the building was demolished in 1980 to make way for the sixty-two-story Trump Tower, the entrance grille was not preserved.

The collaboration of Kahn with Eliel Saarinen on the six-story building, which had a frontage of only twenty-five feet on Fifth Avenue, for the beauty salon of the Richard Hudnut cosmetic company, was a consequence of publicity from the 1929 Metropolitan Museum of Art industrial arts exhibition. According to Kahn, the men agreed to a harmonious division of labor on this project: "The only way we could separate our activities was to decide what area each would undertake with the complete understanding between us of what the results would be. A very handsome facade was the creation of

Saarinen (fig. 6.59)."[90] Hamlin admired the building in his summation of commercial work in 1930: "The Fifth Avenue Hudnut Building by E. J. Kahn and Eliel Saarinen . . . is one of the most charming small buildings on the Avenue; its square panels and square windows are both rich and delicate."[91] Just as the facade has touches of Kahn in the recessed layering that framed the windows and in the applied pilasters of the terminating parapet, the sophisticated interiors by Kahn, illustrated in depth in *Architectural Forum*, show the influence of Saarinen (fig. 6.60).[92]

The Tishman Realty and Construction Company leased the southwest corner site on 57th Street and Lexington Avenue in 1929 and developed the small plot, fifty by a hundred feet, as an office building. It became the location of its headquarters until 1947, when the company moved to its new air-conditioned building at 445 Park Avenue, designed by the Kahn and Jacobs firm and named the Universal Pictures Building (see Chapter Eight).[93] Kahn designed the apartment of Paul Tishman, one of the five sons of Julius Tishman, the founder of the company, and the commission for the office building may have

resulted from this relationship.[94] The organization of the elevations and fenestration was unique in Kahn's lexicon. From the second story to the first setback at the fourteenth, the window bays were completely glazed with intervening spandrels of black glass between the floors. On the exterior elevations the treatment created a striking pattern of large dark rectangles crisply banded in white and gave the impression that the building housed two-story studios (fig. 6.61). Mumford cited the building as an example of "how far 1931 edged away from picture-book romanticism," and he observed that the "Firm of Ely Jacques Kahn [has] actually concealed the columns on the ground floor behind mirrors, which give a maximum of invisibility." Furthermore, he lauded the effect of the window treatment and pronounced the building "worth more than a passing glance."[95]

Although the entrance to the building was pragmatic and unassuming, the small lobby was elegant. The details were mainly the work of Teegen, a key designer for three years after McMahon and Nadir left the firm in 1929. A cast-glass lighting fixture originally traversed the lobby ceiling (fig. 6.62). The design of the elevator doors is a distillation of earlier motifs that contrasted vertical and horizontal lines (fig. 6.63). The letterbox and radiator grilles followed suit and stand out against the dark marble walls (figs. 6.64 and 6.65).

THIS CAR NEXT

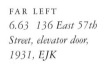

FAR LEFT
6.63 *136 East 57th Street, elevator door, 1931, EJK*

LEFT
6.64 *136 East 57th Street, letterbox, 1931, EJK*

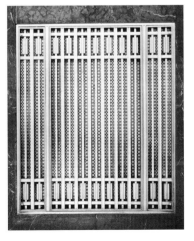

6.65 *136 East 57th Street, radiator grille, 1931, EJK*

The thirty-five-story Commerce Building at 155 East 44th Street—Kahn's last modernist skyscraper erected before World War II—opened early in the summer of 1931. The project was indicative of the expansion during 1929 of the Grand Central District east, toward and beyond Third Avenue. The client, the Grand Central Construction Corporation, a syndicate headed by Irving Judis and Joseph Silverson (with Arnold Gottlieb and Nathan Picket), had its office in Kahn's 271 Madison Avenue Building and knew how well a Kahn building worked.[96] The Commerce Building is located on the northwest corner of Third Avenue and fronts 170 feet on 44th Street and 100.5 feet on Third Avenue. The tower core rises to its summit in a series of harmoniously proportioned setbacks beginning at the fourteenth floor (fig. 6.66). Unlike the Squibb and Continental Buildings, the Commerce was faced in a warm, sand-colored brick above the imposing, six-story limestone base that includes a two-story transitional stage. Although three contrasting flat horizontal bands define the separation of base from shaft, verticality was forcefully expressed by the flat piers, which are unbroken by applied decoration (except for simple parapet railings). Single-window bays and identical spandrels unify the facades. The crowning tower reinforces the interplay of horizontals and verticals (fig. 6.67). The inspiration may have been the *Kölnische Zeitung* pavilion at the 1928 Pressa exposition in Germany (fig. 6.68). The recessed four-story main entrance is distinguished by its height and the simplicity of its grille (fig. 6.69). The flanking three-story bays above the store level originally contained black glass spandrels, a carryover from the building at 136 East 57th Street. Teegen has credited Allmon Fordyce (1900– 1972), the chief designer of the firm from October 1929 to February 1931, as the lead designer of this building.[97]

Like 136 East 57th Street, the lobby and elevator hall of the Commerce Building, now completely renovated, originally had smooth marble walls from floor to ceiling and cast-glass ceiling light fixtures, an effect similar to that in the

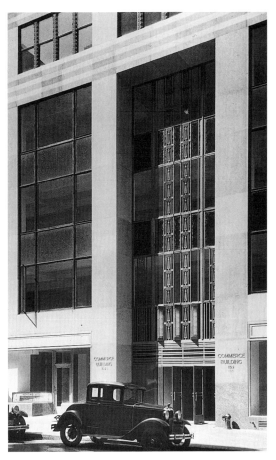

FACING PAGE
*6.66 Commerce
Building, 1931, EJK*

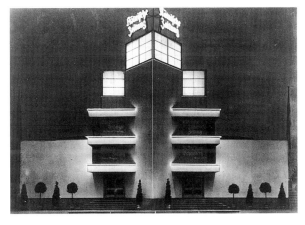

ABOVE LEFT
*6.67 Commerce
Building, tower, 1931,
EJK*

ABOVE RIGHT
*6.68 Commerce
Building, entrance,
1931, EJK*

LEFT
*6.69 Kôlnische Zeitung
pavilion, Pressa, 1928*

building at 530 Seventh Avenue. Kahn had discovered structural glass in Berlin in 1926 and investigated it further in France. A practical reason for using it here and in the earlier buildings was the elimination of the time-consuming "wet work" and painting required for ornamental plaster decoration.[98] A period photograph of the space shows that other than the lighting, decoration was minimal (fig. 6.70). Teegen was the main contributor to the lobby, and his initials are on most of the surviving drawings.[99] The smooth, clean surfaces and linearity that characterized the interior public space harmonized well with the exterior scheme of the Commerce Building. When built, the Commerce Building had an unobstructed view, from most of the floors above its base, of the Chrysler Building on Lexington Avenue at 42nd Street.

The dire economic conditions compromised the commercial success of this outstanding building. It was reported in January 1932 that, notwithstanding the "up-to-date" amenities and the proximity to Grand Central Terminal, renting had been slow and liens against the property had "pile(d) up" resulting in the foreclosure and auction of the building on December 24, 1931—about six months after its completion. In less than two weeks a client of the firm, Colonel Jacob Ruppert, a brewer and the owner of the New York Yankees baseball team, purchased the building from the high bidder in the foreclosure sale.[100]

Although the Commerce Building became a casualty of the depression, Mumford recognized the import of its minimalism and, coincidentally, just as the foreclosure proceeded and Ruppert's purchase was negotiated, he wrote glowingly in *The New Yorker* about the firm's accomplishment. Mumford thought the building was designed "in a fashion that must call forth praise, not perhaps so much for what is done, but for all the things that have happily been left undone or have been eliminated." He continued by analyzing the essence of a skyscraper office building:

> The shape of the Commerce Building is undistinguished: its setbacks seem plainly determined by the building regulations. The windows are undistinguished, too: they are a simple repetitive unit in a brick wall. It is just an office building, capable of being divided into a maximum number of cubicles. That is not much? In plan or in expression, I grant that it is not much, but in spirit the Commerce Building seems to me to tower miles above its competitors. First of all it is an office building, not a cathedral, an advertising symbol, a monument to prosperity, an unusable landing place for illusory dirigibles, or a pathological symptom of somebody's repressed desires. The lobby does not remind one of the nave of Winchester Cathedral or the foyer of the Roxy [theater]: its polished stone walls and its low glass ceiling merely mark it as a place where one may get in and out of elevators. It is scarcely fair to call undistinguished a building where the elements that have been left to the discretion of the architect have been carried through so handsomely. (Consider the imposing three-story entrance; which actually

6.70 Commerce Building, lobby, 1931, EJK

does not slice off more than three or four feet of usable depth.) But as a matter of fact, to call a business building undistinguished should be high praise: what we need is less individual fireworks and noise, and more quiet honesty, decency, and urbanity; more clever economy and less bombast and futile expense. The skyscraper as a form has encouraged every species of romantic extravagance; but the day of reckoning is now here, and such a return to sobriety as the Commerce Building indicates in its decorative aspects is a welcome sign.[101]

Even though Kahn looked intent, unperturbed, and debonair, seated at his desk in a public relations photograph from about 1932 (fig. 6.71), by the end of 1931 the toll from the depression on his clients who were developers, and consequently on him, would be devastating. Seriously affected were those projects that went forward in 1930 because developers whose financing was already in place before the stock market collapse in October 1929 were still optimistic. These speculative investments, like the Commerce Building, did not rent rapidly enough to offset the carrying costs. Adelson's Squibb Building, which opened in May 1930 and was only 50 percent rented, succumbed to foreclosure and was auctioned in January 1933.[102] Others, like the Bricken Textile Building, completed in January 1930, survived longer: In a foreclosure auction on April 9, 1935, it was bought by the Continental Bank and Trust Company, the plaintiff in the proceedings, for $100,000 and assumption of the debt.[103] A. E. Lefcourt, whose holdings in twenty buildings were estimated at $100 million in 1928, died suddenly on November 13, 1932 at age fifty-five, impoverished and broken by the depression.[104] In the summer of 1934 Adelson suffered another huge blow when the Park Avenue Building went on the block in a foreclosure sale.[105] Louis Adler was the only one of Kahn's major speculative clients who survived the depression relatively unscathed. Although he could not hold onto the Wall Street block, he managed to save the 530 and 550 Seventh Avenue Buildings and reportedly sold the Continental Building in 1933 to a private

6.71 *Ely Jacques Kahn, c. 1932*

investor, who sold it to the Johnson & Johnson pharmaceutical company in 1937.[106] Adler was a loyal client and would contribute to the success of the Kahn and Jacobs firm in the post–World War II period.

As the depression deepened, Hamlin framed the dramatically changed situation in American architecture. The issue that came to a head in the early 1930s was succinctly and presciently analyzed by him in his assessment of the year 1930: "Traditionalism was largely dead in the public and commercial field; the question facing America was whether in its place should be accepted the stark, austere, and limited alphabet of forms of the 'functionalist,' or the free inventiveness of those who feel that there is a place, even in the buildings of a machine age, for ornament, decoration, and a human lovableness."[107] The conflict would soon heat up, and Kahn would be in the middle of it.

CHAPTER SEVEN

THE 1930s

New Challenges and Opportunities

Like many American architects, Kahn found that his life and work went through tremendous upheaval during the depression years. The trajectory of the 1930s decade was entirely different from that of the 1920s, and Kahn struggled to survive professionally and economically. The momentum of his prolific career continued for about two years after the stock market crash of 1929, during which time fourteen of his large office buildings opened in Manhattan, including the Squibb Building, which he ranked among his personal favorites. By the spring of 1932, however, Kahn's fortunes, like those of most Americans, had declined and he was forced to reduce his office staff in the Park Avenue Building to a handful of key employees. Published reports of filed plans reveal that construction from 1932 to 1940 averaged less than $150,000 annually, which suggests that Kahn's office income was hovering between $5,000 and $10,000 per year at the most, far less than a commission on a single building during the boom years. Force of circumstance caused Kahn to transform himself professionally into a civic leader, educator, and writer.[1]

Kahn also experienced a personal evolution during this difficult period. As Clarence Stein, his close friend since their years at the Ecole des Beaux-Arts, wrote in 1933: "Ely has improved—he does not talk constantly about his architectural attainments—and he trys [*sic*] so hard not to blow himself up."[2] The modulation in attitude was accompanied by a major change in his personal life. His marriage to Elsie Kahn had been problematic from the start and, although they had three children and she eventually led the interior design department of Buchman & Kahn, the couple divorced in 1937. Elsie may have remained in the marriage as long as she did to see their youngest child Olivia, who turned seventeen in 1937, through her high school years. The incompatibility of Elsie and Ely led to an "arrangement" between them and to her affair, an "open secret," with Otto Mayer, a friend of Kahn's with whom he regularly played bridge, and the man she married after the divorce. At age fifty-four, Kahn found a more suitable partner in the socially and philanthropically active Beatrice Josephi Sulzberger (1890–1962) whom he married on November 23, 1938. Beatrice was the widow of Leo Sulzberger, the brother of Arthur Hays Sulzberger of the *New York Times*, and Kahn was welcomed into this prominent family. Although Kahn's children had a different view,

*7.1 Eero Saarinen,
"A Monumental Clock,"
design entry, Emerson
Prize competition, 1932*

friends called Beatrice and Ely an "agreeable pair" and commented on how meaningful it was to Kahn that he made Beatrice "so happy."[3]

1931 Annual Exhibition of the Architectural League

Kahn was named chairman of the influential Architectural League's Committee on Annual Exhibitions in 1931 to mark the league's fiftieth anniversary. He promised that the milestone exhibition would be "looking forward" rather than "backward" and would exhibit good "modern" architecture, which he considered to be akin to good clothing or good business: honest and clean.[4] Kahn wrote that "the function of architects is to clothe the machinery or purpose of a building: to facilitate the conduct of its business; to promote smoothness of operation."[5] His architectural criteria reflected values at the heart of American business instead of an allegiance to a particular style of architectural expression. The league's fiftieth anniversary exhibition proved a record-breaking success with the general public. Like past league shows, it featured the work of American architects, landscape architects, interior designers, sculptors, mural painters, and craftsmen. To reinforce his commitment to the forward direction of the show, Kahn urged critics to notice that it was "the 'progressives' and not the academician[s] in architecture [who] show the real 'Greek spirit'—even though they submit to the Greek orders."[6] When the show opened, *New York Times* critic Edward Alden Jewell commented that "the committee's slogan about looking forward applies, however, with a stirring oracular ring"—especially in the American exhibits, whose multiple visual languages he considered to be signs of its immaturity. For many, including Jewell, the League show had "virtually ignored" the new work of younger architects.[7]

The omission of George Howe and William Lescaze's Philadelphia Savings Fund Society Building (PSFS), then under construction, led the outraged young architecture critic Philip Johnson to organize a *Salon des Refusés* or "Rejected Architects" exhibit on Seventh Avenue and 57th Street to showcase the works of nine youthful designers, some of whom became well known later in their careers. In contrast to Kahn's primary concern with how buildings functioned, Johnson selected works that had physical attributes consistent with the work of such European modernists as Mies van der Rohe and Le Corbusier and unified his description "for convenience" under the newly coined term "the International Style." Johnson criticized Kahn and others for attempting "to justify everything about the completed building with cries of 'it is functional! Behold the result of conditions and clients!'"[8] To ensure that the enormous numbers of visitors to the league's show also saw the work of the younger architects, Johnson boldly placed a man outside its entrance wearing a sandwich board that proclaimed: "See really modern architecture, rejected by the League, at 903 Seventh Avenue."[9]

Kahn and Hood, the league's president, responded immediately to Johnson's provocation. Kahn, who had included Lawrence Kocher and Albert Frey's celebrated metal house and other works reflecting European modernism, defended the process of selection. He pronounced in the *New York Times* that "[r]ejections to the exhibition were not made on the basis of modernism, for the modernistic work in the exposition is fully as representative as the conservative work. The works of members of the Architectural League were rejected just as much as the works of outsiders." Hood, like Kahn, was often an apologist for new directions in American architecture against the grumbles of those who continued to work in conservative idioms. Johnson, however, successfully shifted their position from "progressives" to "conservatives" and pitted them against what some of their colleagues referred to as the "radical" modernists. Hood was perplexed by the shift and stated that by some the "league has been accused of being too modern. It's news that we are accused now of being too conservative. But honest differences of opinion are always good and I'm for them."[10]

In the months after the exhibition, the debate continued in a pair of articles published in *Creative Art*. Philip Johnson attacked Kahn's understanding of the International Style architects:

The day after the Rejected Architects opened their Salon des Refusés, Mr. Ely Jacques Kahn stated to the press that no models had been refused by the League because they were too modern. This is quite true. The Grand Central Palace contained work as modern as that displayed in the 57th Street Show. The official explanation, however, smacks too much of the smug rejection slip: "The number of exhibits submitted was so much greater than could be accommodated that the Committee selected what they considered the best work." Nevertheless, it is more than mere well-grounded rumor, that the officials believed these rejected models unqualifiedly bad—not architecture but unrealizable dreams. One may, therefore, question the critical ability of Mr. Kahn and his Committee.[11]

Confirming Johnson's suspicions, Kahn replied: "We are now in the position of facing, on one hand, the younger group of non-practicing radicals who are bringing over from Europe what they call the international style and which, having analyzed this work quite thoroughly abroad, may, or may not in my judgment at least, produce the architecture which will glorify this generation. Surely in our time, the flat stucco surfaces will leave something to be desired."[12]

Beaux-Arts Institute of Design Directorship

Kahn's opinion of the International Style remained remarkably consistent over the course of his career. He preferred that the designs of the younger generation of architects would engage color and texture and, above all, would pay attention to functionality and to innovations in mechanical systems. In an effort to help architecture students learn these lessons, Kahn accepted an offer to become the director of the Department of Architecture at the Beaux-Arts Institute of Design, the educational arm of the Society of Beaux-Arts Architects, an informal alumni association for American architects trained at the Ecole. The opportunity arose when Philip Allain Cusachs, who previously held the position and was a well-known designer of such Beaux-Arts

Balls as the "Birth of Modernism" (see fig. 6.48), died prematurely of a heart attack late in 1931. Although Kahn had had little contact with the institute while he was a busy practitioner in the 1920s, he reconnected with many of his fellow American alumni of the Ecole, including Kenneth Murchison and Harry Allan Jacobs, on a well-publicized two-week reunion voyage to Paris and the Colonial Exposition in early June 1931.[13] Kahn's social interaction with architects who were influential at the institute at this critical moment was probably a factor in his appointment as director of the Department of Architecture and as chairman of the Committee on Education later that year. Kahn held these positions until November 1935; Otto John Teegen, who had worked both for Kahn and Joseph Urban, succeeded him. Kahn reduced his level of involvement with the institute in November 1938, when International Style modernists Walter Gropius, Richard Neutra, and Albert Kahn joined the Committee on Education.[14]

The institute was composed of the Departments of Architecture, Mural Painting, and Sculpture, and followed the educational principles of the Ecole. By providing a "free school of architecture" for approximately 3,000 students across the United States, the institute helped to democratize American architectural education.[15] The institute's curricula featured national design competitions in which students from both architecture schools and ateliers competed for prizes. It offered Kahn a platform in discussions on the future of architectural education. Shortly after Kahn joined the institute, board chairman Benjamin Morris praised his "keen intelligence and devotion," which, Morris continued effusively, "have inspired his Committee and the students, while his spirit of adventure and cooperation has renewed the interest of the patrons and Schools of Architecture to a ruddy glow of comment, approval or even a healthy difference in opinion—this Department is a live wire."[16] Kahn's first published statement, in which he introduced students to his ideas on modern architecture, echoed his earlier response to Johnson's attack: "If modern architecture, by which we mean rational interpretation of new problems, is to be good we will be just as careful to avoid repetition of unpleasant modernistic detail as the cast incongruities of the Victorian Era. Modern architecture is not going to become a style based on Gropius or Taut; Wright or Corbusier. It will demand intelligent, clearly reasoned, solutions of plan—as ingenuous [sic] as you like, but, above all things simple, direct and honest in the expression of the particular problem."[17]

In order to effect change and introduce modern problems, Kahn initiated an "Illuminating Engineering Society Prize Competition," the first to be juried by both architects and engineers. Although the response from the engineers to the project was enthusiastic, the architects were ambivalent, and Kahn was often disappointed in the results from the competitions. In one review of projects, he chided the students for hiding "inconsistencies of plan or facade" behind the "brilliancy of presentation," and he complained that the "program requested architecture and not fireworks."[18] One of the exceptional students Kahn first noticed through the institute's program was Eliel Saarinen's son Eero Saarinen, a student at the Yale University School of Architecture, who, he fondly recalled, "walked away with high awards time after time"—one of which was received in the Emerson Prize competition for "A Monumental Clock," which Kahn juried in 1932 (fig. 7.1).[19] In his design Saarinen placed Raymond Hood's name at nine o'clock, that of the Swedish American sculptor Carl Milles at six o'clock, and the name Kahn, ambiguously referring either to Albert Kahn from Saarinen's city of Detroit or Ely Jacques Kahn, a close colleague of Hood and Milles, at three o'clock.

Kahn also dispensed negative critiques of students working in other institute departments, especially the Department of Mural Painting, and he condemned them publicly for exploring "superficial modernism" in painting, which he felt was as problematic as presenting the "tiresome repetition of accepted works."[20] He seemed impatient with students; once he commented somewhat smugly that no one assumed "that all of the students should produce masterpieces . . .

but it is reasonable to assume that even a small percentage would be qualified to indicate a solution that might be acceptable."[21] Kahn made it clear that building plans needed to express functionality, and during his tenure as director, he steered the curriculum of the Department of Architecture away from emphasizing the representational techniques of the Ecole and focused instead on practical issues and pragmatic solutions.

Kahn's association with the institute in the spring of 1932 fostered closer contact with Frank Lloyd Wright, whom he had met when the Architectural League held its first exhibition of Wright's work in the summer of 1930.[22] As Kahn noted, he had "much admired [Wright] for a long time;" Wright had been an important influence on Kahn's architectural decoration in the 1920s.[23] In the early years of the depression, Wright, like others in the field, lacked sufficient work, which led to his creation of a school, or cooperative design factory, at Taliesin in Spring Green, Wisconsin. He tried to fill the vacancies at Taliesin with "rebellious students" from the Beaux-Arts Institute, and with Kahn's help he secured the institution's mailing list. Wright attempted to rouse the interest of students in Taliesin by claiming that the institute had "betray[ed] modern architects."[24] The attack disturbed Kahn, who expressed his discontent in a carefully composed letter to the older architect:

In reading your original Diatribe to the Beaux-Arts students, I was inclined to become a little warm under the collar, because you shot a few bolts into me which seemed to be a bit sharper than necessary. I suspect, however, that you were smiling a little at the same time, for down deep, somewhere, you suspect that I am not quite as much of a ragamuffin as somebody might infer. The purpose of an answer to your letter is, that I am in entire sympathy with what you have in mind to do with your School. If the students now working under the Beaux-Arts system, or in many of our other schools, would have the advantage of personal contact with you and the inspiration of the men you draw about you, I feel that these students will learn something which they can adjust to their future work and there is no question but that such an experiment would be highly valuable. You would be surprised, I believe, if you really knew how much you are liked by the various men who you are at times inclined to jump on, and, in spite of our shortcomings, we are all interested in seeing the vigor of a new endeavor of this type which, if it can show the way, will undoubtedly be met with full enthusiasm.[25]

Kahn's diplomacy preserved the relationship and the two men visited each other in 1932 and 1933. In June 1933 Wright was still in financial difficulty and made several requests for lists of Kahn's professional contacts and materials. Kahn faithfully provided information to help the Taliesin Fellowship. In return, Wright shared his contacts in Japan with Kahn for his Carnegie grant abroad. In his 1935 book *Design in Art and Industry*, which resulted from the grant, Kahn praised Wright's teaching method: "Wright's personality is worth the student's interest, for he will discover that under the sparkle and brilliancy of the man is a wealth of sound judgment and experience. As his school develops, his students are expected to find broad opportunities for work in all of the arts, including music and painting, while actual labor on the erection of his buildings gives them knowledge of the handling of tools and materials."[26]

In the late 1930s, over a dinner for the National Association of Real Estate Boards, Kahn introduced Wright to the young novelist Ayn Rand. In preparation for her novel *The Fountainhead* (1943), Rand had worked in Kahn's office for five months to observe architectural practice. After meeting Wright through Kahn, she loosely based the character of Howard Rourke, the protagonist of *The Fountainhead*, on Wright himself. It was somewhat in the spirit of a scene from the book that Wright surveyed with Kahn the New York skyscrapers of the 1920s from a window in his office high above the city in the Park Avenue Building. In 1943 Kahn recounted the event in the *Architectural Record*: "Frank Lloyd Wright, standing at my office window a short time ago, looked at the mass of tall buildings north of 33rd Street and scornfully dismissed them all as evidence of disease. Perhaps he was more justified than he realized for they do represent the products of the unbridled competitive spirit for gain, ignoring as they do, each other's prerogative for light and air, to say nothing of omitting the slightest consideration of those highly practical long-term factors—density, circulation, demand. This is quite aside from their outward appearance—a most fantastically unrelated collection of curiously styled creations."[27] Although Kahn and Wright had very different personalities and career trajectories, they both had experienced the nineteenth and early twentieth centuries, and viewed the architectural and urban problems of midcentury America through this shared lens. They remained friends until Wright's death in 1959.

Exploration of Design Education at Home and Abroad

As director of the architecture program at the Beaux-Arts Institute, Kahn had been critical of the architectural establishment for producing too many architecture graduates and too few designers in other fields. He reinforced this observation while he was president of the Committee on Allied Arts of the American Institute of Architects, a position that allowed him to make his views more widely known. In December 1932, when his practice was at a low point, Kahn approached Frederick P. Keppel, the president of the Carnegie Corporation, with a proposal for "a book, or a report that, following investigation of the schools here and abroad, might present concrete suggestions."[28] Before accepting his application, Keppel asked William Emerson, an architect and professor at the Massachusetts Institute of Technology, to evaluate the proposal. Emerson, who was also the vice-chairman of the Education Committee of the American Institute of Architects, wrote Keppel that he valued Kahn "highly and his public spirited and intelligent cooperation in this and many other fields is of the greatest value."[29] Kahn emphasized the urgency for this study by pointing to the lack of adequately trained design students: "The startling thing is the realization that with over supply of theoretically trained people for the major arts, woeful lack of accomplishment in the field of design as it effects almost every detail of our buildings, our homes, our lives, we ignore the simple possibility of turning our efforts to help our young people and, at the same time, improve our standards in design."[30] Members of the Carnegie Corporation realized that Kahn's approach to the study of design in Europe and America could have a long-range impact on American leadership in the field and awarded him a $10,000 grant to explore "educational opportunities in the fields of crafts and industrial design."[31] As the trip became a reality, Kahn sought advice from the recent émigré Eugene Steinhof, a respected Viennese architect, artist, and educator who had taught at Josef Hoffmann's Kunstgewerbeschule in Vienna and who Kahn had invited to teach at the Institute. Surprisingly, Steinhof lamented that there was nothing new to be learned in Europe and that economic and political troubles on the continent had actually precipitated a decline in full-time students, lowered the quality of their work, and made the trip dangerous. Moreover, he argued that the "whole status of western European industrial production is to be found easily in the magazines. You know Europe and its magazines. This production has been entirely industrialized, mechanized and economized. In this fact lies the reason of the breakdown of the last Western European place of genuine industrial art work, the Wiener Werkstatte."

Steinhof convinced Kahn to explore Asia instead of Europe: "As your journey has to be made for the rebirth of the production and the education of the objects of the national industrial arts, I should think that you really ought to go where the genuine industrial arts are not mechanized, but still live in their natural freshness. Your ticket should lead you across the Pacific instead of the Atlantic."[32] Keppel initially responded with skepticism to Kahn's changed plans, and he expressed concern that the differences between Asian systems of production and conceptions of design and those of the United States were too radical to provide useful comparisons. Moreover, he felt that the greater distances

to travel might impair the effectiveness of the trip and would be too ambitious for the funds available.[33] Despite these obstacles, Kahn persuaded Keppel to support his decision to explore design education first in the United States and then in Asia.

In the summer and fall of 1933, Kahn completed his research on the East Coast and in the Midwest, with a stop at Taliesin to see Wright's school, which he coordinated with the opening of the Century of Progress Exposition in Chicago. Afterward Kahn flew from Newark to San Francisco and spent several weeks there before he sailed for Tokyo.[34] On the steamer Kahn happened to meet the Japanese expert on modern Asian crafts, Soetso Yanagi (1889–1961), the founder of a Korean folkcraft museum in Seoul, who had spent a year at Harvard University lecturing on the anonymous craftsmen of Japan and Korea. Yanagi urged Kahn to visit Korea and offered to escort him to provinces where, he claimed, "weaving and pottery [were] being developed on modern lines."[35] Kahn used Tokyo as a base from which to study crafts and design history in Japan, Korea, Beijing, and Hong Kong (fig. 7.2).[36] In October he left for Bali and the East Indies, and he spent the month of December in Burma, India, and Sri Lanka, where he concluded his journey by sailing for Genoa in January 1934. Kahn returned home on a steamer from Europe to direct the Department of Architecture at the institute in early February 1934 and was promptly elected to be a fellow of the American Institute of Architects.

Design in Art and Industry, the substantial book that detailed Kahn's astute observations and contained thirty-two photographs, most of them taken by Kahn, was purportedly written with the help of his son Ely Jacques Kahn Jr., a staff writer for *The New Yorker*, and promptly published by Charles Scribner's Sons in June 1935. The first chapters trace the history of craft and craft education in American schools, whereas the later chapters are a travelogue of sorts to schools in Japan, Korea, China, Polynesia, Cambodia, Indonesia, and India. Unexpectedly, Kahn discovered a model for American design education in the Cambodian city of Phnom-Penh. The school was supported by the French colonial government and operated on the master and apprentice system. It was free to all students, but only those who demonstrated talent were allowed to continue. The school maintained a strong relationship to regional materials and traditions, and although students copied examples found in a nearby museum, they were encouraged to experiment with variations on the originals. Kahn observed that there was "no concern with theory whatsoever, no philosophy," nor a "search for originality," and he noted positively that the Cambodian school, similarly to the Kunstgewerbe Schule in Vienna, operated "a sales office next to the museum proper, and a series of workshops or studios attached to the museum" that created objects for sale. After completing the two-year course of study, students were offered tools, models, and materials to advance their craft when they returned to their hometowns. Kahn contrasted the students in the Phnom-Penh system with those in the United States: "The students [in Phnom-Penh] were learning conventionalized forms, and, through actual experience, tending toward self-expression and originality. Our students, starting with self-expression and a definite desire to attain originality, arrive at standardization and actual conventionalization as they develop."[37]

Design in Art and Industry received limited critical attention and Kahn's intensive study did not ultimately have an impact in the United States. One reviewer for the *American Architect* called the book a "stimulant to creative thinking . . . a work which the philosophical as well as the practical educator and artist should possess."[38] In the *Art Digest*, Kahn was recognized as a "person ideally equipped to judge the tenor of modern times and to point out constructive means for the improvement of the quality of design as well as to alleviate artists from 'dignified starvation.'" His comments were dismissed, however, as "critical rather than factual," and the book was not considered an instruction manual on how to fix the American system of arts education.[39] The most insightful review, by Landon Warner in the *American Magazine of Art*, stated that Kahn "had caught something of the discontent that stirs us

7.2 Ely Jacques Kahn at the Great Amida (Daibutsu) of Kamakura, Japan, 1933

all today" about art training in the United States.[40] In 1935 the overwhelming response to such discontent, however, came from young architects advocating the International Style of their European mentors. It was the year Le Corbusier was invited by the Museum of Modern Art to make his first lecture tour of the United States (Kahn's future architecture partner, Robert Allan Jacobs, was Le Corbusier's translator and guide).[41] In early 1937 Walter Gropius arrived at Harvard, and shortly thereafter Mies van der Rohe began teaching at the Illinois Institute of Technology in Chicago. These architects and their followers had a significant impact on architecture and design in the United States, and on Kahn's own practice after World War II.

In the section of *Design in Art and Industry* titled "The Museum and Design," Kahn underscored the important role that exhibitions of everyday objects in museums, expositions, and especially department stores had played, and should continue to play, in the development of American industrial art. His own involvement, beginning in the 1920s, with decorative and industrial art exhibitions continued in the 1930s through his participation in Chicago's Century of Progress Exposition (1933) and the New York World's Fair (1939 and 1940). Other exhibitions of importance to Kahn were R. H. Macy's "Forward House" (1933), an exhibition of contemporary decorative arts at the 68th Annual Convention of the American Institute of Architects (1936), and two Contemporary American Industrial Art exhibitions at the Metropolitan Museum of Art (1934 and 1940). Kahn's contribution to these projects represented a significant portion of his work during the depression years and kept his designs in the public eye.

Chicago Century of Progress Exposition

Kahn's creative leadership in the 1920s and the extent of his building projects in New York City made him a logical choice for a prominent role in the Century of Progress Exposition. However, when the Architectural Commission was appointed in 1928 the members selected the two other "little Napoleons," Hood and Walker, but not Kahn, for the committee chaired by the New York architect Harvey Wiley Corbett. Kahn was not involved until January 1932, when he was named head of the newly created Industrial Arts

Section—where he immediately made it clear that there would be no "chaos masquerading as modern art."[42] Kahn envisioned the section as a showplace for contemporary American design side by side with competitive examples from foreign countries, a stance that was lauded by the editors of *Interior Architecture & Decoration*, who anointed Kahn the *arbiter elegantorum* and described him as a "wise and tolerant critic of the applied arts and crafts" who would determine the "acceptable standard" of quality in design.[43]

Kahn's design for the Home and Industrial Arts Building first appeared in the *New York Times* in April.[44] The unornamented, windowless, 550-foot-long L-shaped pavilion incorporated the larger Home Planning Hall at the north end that was connected by a colonnaded walkway to a Hall of Interior Decoration (fig. 7.3). A thirty-foot-high colonnade opened onto the "court of honor of building materials" that featured a cluster of fountains and pools decorated with colored terra-cotta tiles. Kahn designed the 300-foot-long colonnade to showcase a modern mural in marble mosaic on its back wall.

Only the northern wing of Kahn's original design for the Home Planning Building was realized, however. The reasons were complex but revolved, in part, around the lack of participants to fill the large hall as originally planned, and a month after the design was announced Kahn's contract was terminated. Another factor was Kahn's unusually strained relationship with J.

7.3 Industrial Arts Building, rendering, Century of Progress Exposition, Chicago, 1933, EJK. Photo: Van Anda Photos.

7.4 Johns–Manville
Building, Century of
Progress Exposition,
Chicago, 1933, EJK

Franklin Bell, the head of the Division of Applied Science and Industry and his supervisor on the project, whose scornful and possibly anti-Semitic comments disparaged Kahn's motives and skills: "Mr. Kahn has shown from the first that he is a chiseler trying to get all he can out of us and all he can out of exhibitors at the same time. He knows nothing about group planning and Mr. Skidmore had to do his work for him on that feature and on exhibits area layouts. Any concessions made to him will only lead to more demands. He will probably sue us but it would be better to let him sue as things now stand. He has already done about all the harm he can."[45] Instead of litigating, Kahn severed his relationship with the exposition organizers, and he notified them that "[l]ife is too short to look for trouble or to spend energy in these difficult days in being critical or looking back too far."[46] Kahn did not wish to burn bridges, for he had other commissions in process, including the design of the Johns-Manville and Kohler of Kohler buildings, each located in the Industrial Arts Section under Bell's watchful eye.

The building for Johns-Manville, in a simple semicircular drum shape and clad with unpainted transite board, was located near the Home Planning Building on Leif Erickson Drive, one of the main pedestrian boulevards on the exposition grounds (fig. 7.4). The surfaces of its two flanking wings had a distinctive light-and-dark checkerboard pattern. Four deep projecting rectilinear, fluted, and stepped-back pylons that recall classical details from Kahn's 1920s skyscrapers divided the entrance. These shared characteristics with the austere modern or "stripped" classicism that was emerging as a major design idiom of the 1930s, and Kahn was complimented by a contemporary critic for a composition created by the "refreshing use of vigorous and simple forms."[47] Around the base of the building, a light, one-story colonnade connected the wings and entrance. The pavilion was predominantly a grayish white, and the piers were yellow—colors purportedly selected to create a visual link between Urban's plan of brilliant colors for the main fairgrounds to the north and the predominant white he had selected for the buildings in the industrial areas to the south.

The New York–based Johns-Manville Corporation was an innovator in the creation of fireproofing and insulating materials, and Kahn emphasized the innovations in his design: "The building I am putting up for Johns-Manville will be all of their own composition material, fireproof, sound-proof, and heat-proof. Another feature of this new type structure will be the salvage; all these buildings can be swept away in a very short time and the parts may be used again."[48] The focus of the interior was dioramas that explained the company's operations, and an elaborate mural, *Give Us This Day Our Daily Light*, executed by the Viennese émigré artist Leo Katz. The mural featured huge, swirling nude figures, machines, and animals that depicted a world on the verge of chaos that only nature—and, by association, the materials produced by Johns-Manville—could control (fig. 7.5). Johns-Manville's administrators were unabashedly proud of both Katz and his artwork and proclaimed the building a showcase for the mural: "Be sure to see this amazing mural for which Johns-Manville constructed an entire building. In the Home and Industrial Arts Group stands an unusual building. It houses an unusual mural. Not just another thinly camouflaged commercial blurb, under the guise of Art—but the amazing message of an artist-philosopher to the people of this age."[49] The mural also received critical attention in the *Los Angeles Times* from Arthur Millier, who pronounced it nothing less than "the most important art work born during the depression."[50]

The Kohler Building, Kahn's other major commission, was located in the southern part of the industrial arts area near the Johns-Manville building (fig. 7.6). Kahn originally designed the building as a narrow rectangular bar that opened onto a garden through a 132-foot-long, three-story glazed wall and colonnade that brought light and views of the garden into the pavilion (fig. 7.7). In what may have been a nod to the work of Hoffmann, Kahn outlined the building's clean gray volumes with a narrow band of blue at the roofline.[51] The pavilion featured model bathrooms and various Kohler products along with a scale model, photographs, and dioramas of the Kohler Village in Wisconsin, not far from the Chicago fair. On an outside wall parallel to the main pedestrian walkway Kahn placed a long mural, *Far Flung Sources of Materials and Markets*, which depicted workers around the world mining materials used to manufacture Kohler products. It was designed and executed by members of the Mural Painting Atelier of New York. Critic Arthur Woltersdorf, writing in the *American Architect*, appreciated the Kohler building's "permanence," which he felt set it apart from the rest of the fair's "carnival architecture," and he praised Kahn for the cleverness of the simple, elegant forms and for escaping "the Urban brush" of garish color.[52] Kahn's opinion of Urban's color scheme for the fair, however, was favorable. He felt that the colors were "bold, fresh, and masculine" and accentuated the "solidity of buildings."[53] Yet, for Kahn, the external appearances of exposition buildings were less important than

7.5 Leo Katz, mural detail, Johns–Manville Building, Century of Progress Exposition, Chicago, 1933, EJK

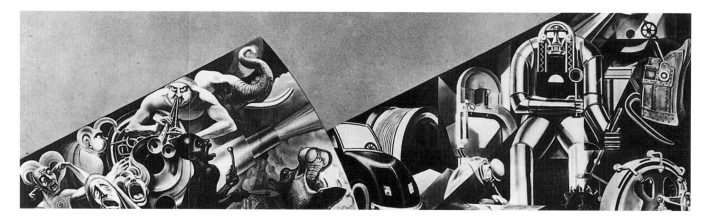

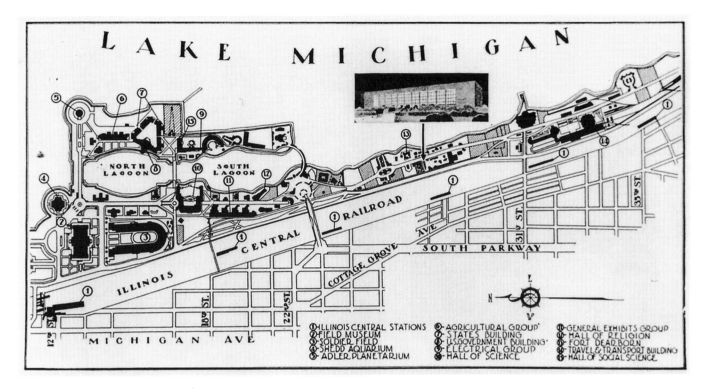

how the buildings functioned. In a lively interview with the *Yale Daily News*, Kahn reiterated this view: "Indeed, I shall be glad if people go through and say afterwards, 'Say, that was a peach of an exhibit, but, come to think of it, I don't believe I noticed what the building was like.' In other words, the buildings will be shells for the exhibits. We want to emphasize the exhibits, not the structures."[54]

During the fair in the summer of 1933, in one of his last projects before leaving for Asia, Kahn prepared a design for the Macy's "Forward House" exhibition that was sponsored in collaboration with *Architectural Forum*. The entire event was promoted by the department store as "the most dramatic and important exposition of the practical new arts of decoration and home equipment which New York has seen since [Macy's] Historic Art in Trade Expositions of 1927 and 1928." Thirty showrooms covered the fifth floor of the store's West Building, and everything in the exhibition was for sale, with the exception of architectural models and photographs. The eight

architectural models of modern houses designed by the "Great Eight," a term coined for the top designers of tall buildings in New York who were contributors to the exhibition (Walker, Hood, Corbett, Van Alen, Harmon, Schultze, White, and Kahn), were a small part of the enormous displays. Of the eight houses by the "Great Eight," none reflected the spirit of its designer in its

TOP
7.6 *Site of Kohler of Kohler Building on plan of Century of Progress Exposition, Chicago, 1933*

ABOVE
7.7 *Kohler of Kohler Building, Century of Progress Exposition, Chicago, 1933, EJK*

7.8 *Common Sense House, model, R. H. Macy's "Forward House" exhibition, 1933, EJK*

name more than Kahn's "Common Sense House" (fig. 7.8). In the text accompanying the exhibition, Kahn challenged the reader to ask: "Is this house modern? If being simple, efficient, and unpretentious demands the label of modern, so be it. The taste of the inhabitants of the house will promptly determine whether it will go 'modernistic,' which will be terrible, or rationally modern, which, in my judgment, connotes a simple working scheme adapted to the individual's taste and permitting him to flower in a setting that is not too prescribed."[55]

For Kahn, the label *modernism*, and its many variants in the 1930s, including the rigid aesthetic dogmatism of International Style acolytes, was rendered virtually meaningless. From his perspective, the most significant qualities of domestic architecture were simplicity and adaptability to the client—subjective criteria that were

always difficult for him to pin down in a clearly defined aesthetic vocabulary. The Common Sense House, however, was sarcastically attacked by Wright, who seemed to care little that Kahn was his friend or an important source of business contacts: "What better name to disarm criticism at the outset than 'Common Sense?' Great crimes have been committed in that name. But Ely's house is no great crime, it is just a 'little' house, he says, but must think so only because he builds so many huge loft-buildings. This little primrose invites you to 'bust in' between the garage and the lavatory into a 'Hall.' Is a Hall common sense in any small house? I ask you. Also, I am sorry I ever started the wrap-around corner window on its international career. It makes nonsense here. But, Ely, you know your women—that good second floor is proof."[56] Coming at a time when his marriage had soured, Kahn opened himself to

Wright's sarcasm by stating that his Common Sense house was a "delicate organism, the mysteries of which can be grasped only by the woman who appreciates closets or the height of a sink."[57] Kahn later expanded upon this relationship between women and the home in a 1941 radio show about relations between men and women called "We Men—We Women," in which he said that his primary professional contact with women was as clients for "country homes," and that his most significant problem with them was "finding out what they want."[58]

Industrial Arts Exhibitions

The next exhibition to which Kahn contributed was "Contemporary American Industrial Art" (1934) at the Metropolitan Museum of Art. He was among the architects and industrial designers on the Cooperating Committee that organized the exhibition of objects by more than two hundred designers and manufacturers. Kahn was the lead designer of the General Group and selected materials and designed the Textile Group in the West Gallery; he included fabrics of his own design for the DuPont Rayon Company, and he arranged a case displaying mass-produced metal objects fabricated in a variety of materials by the designer Walter von Nessen, who had fabricated the building number for 530 Seventh Avenue (see fig. C.9).[59]

In 1936, for an exhibition arranged by the Committee of Allied Arts for the sixty-eighth convention of the American Institute of Architects, held in the newly restored colonial town of Williamsburg in Virginia, Kahn, assisted by Ralph Walker, created "Design Trend: An Exhibit Which Investigates the Contemporary Market in Furniture, Materials, and Equipment for the Home Interior." For this exhibit they organized a series of eight rooms, including an entrance foyer, living room, drawing room, dining room, lounge, study, kitchen, and bathroom.[60] Henry Saylor referred to Kahn's involvement when he observed that the exhibits were put "together with all of the care in arrangement and lighting that marks the periodical exhibition of the crafts at the Metropolitan Museum."[61]

Kahn's final association with the Metropolitan Museum of Art exhibitions was in the "Contemporary American Industrial Art" exhibition of 1940, the fifteenth and last in the series. Kahn led in the unification of the Cooperating Committee, which consisted of twenty architects and designers divided into four groups. The ambitious show highlighted objects, designed by almost six hundred individuals, none of which was on the market yet. Kahn was credited with undertaking "the arduous task of unifying the exhibition," for which he demonstrated exceptional organizational skills. He also experimented with new materials.[62] For the exhibition Kahn designed a toiletry set and an ice bucket, which were among the earliest objects to utilize a new aluminum with a colored tint "baked into the metal" (fig. 7.9).[63] Times had changed and the Metropolitan show received mixed reviews. Writing for the *Forum*, Saylor expressed his disappointment: "An exhibition of this kind attempts as part of its chief purpose the recording of achievement in new materials, new ways of using them in design. Earlier efforts in the series, seen in retrospect, have been really stimulating in this regard."[64] Design critic Walter Rendell Storey disagreed with Saylor's assessment of the exhibition's historical importance and argued: "Certainly the show is more significant than the former ones held in 1929 and 1934, because a

7.9 *Ely Jacques Kahn, ice bucket, colored aluminum and Lucite, Bernard Rice's Sons, manufacturer, exhibited in "Contemporary American Industrial Art," Metropolitan Museum of Art, 1940*

larger proportion of the objects displayed are ready for general production and most of them will soon appear in the shops. The other exhibits had a considerably higher percentage of experimental designs made especially for them."[65] The 1940 "Contemporary American Industrial Art" exhibition had stiffer competition for public attention than earlier exhibitions. The 1940 New York World's Fair and the lurking threat of war abroad begged the question of the importance of American design in light of larger global issues.

New York World's Fair

In December 1935, less than two years after the Chicago fair had closed, a planning committee for the 1939 New York World's Fair was selected. Surprisingly, only one of the committee's ten members, Harvey Wiley Corbett, was an architect; the others were planners and designers. Although he was not on the planning committee, Kahn was commissioned to design several buildings, alone and in collaboration with others. These included the Marine Transportation Building with William Muschenheim and

7.10 Ely Jacques Kahn and William Muschenheim, Marine Transportation Building, New York World's Fair, 1939

Morrison Brounn, the Ballantine Inn with Irvin L. Scott and Otto John Teegen, and the White Owl Exhibit Building for the General Cigar Company, an independent commission.[66] The National Cash Register Building is often attributed to Kahn in collaboration with Walter Dorwin Teague, but there is little evidence of the nature or extent of Kahn's involvement with the project.[67] Kahn was the senior architect for the Marine Transportation Building, the first world's fair pavilion to focus exclusively on the subject. He opted to design the pavilion with the young architectural team of Muschenheim and Brounn, who had qualified to work at the fair by receiving an honorable mention in a competition for a "Typical Fair Building." In later correspondence Muschenheim reported that Kahn allowed the younger architects to design much of the structure: "Mr. Kahn came up with the idea of having the main entrance flanked by two simulated prows of large ships. The rest of the design was pretty much left to me and Morrison Brounn. Only half the scheme was built. The pond which was to have a lot of boats in it with a surrounding structure was omitted. The working drawings were handled by the office of Buchman & Kahn's [sic] and at the World's Fair."[68]

Kahn's idea for the ship prows developed from his determination that the building "suggest the sea and waterfront life to the public and at the same time give the impression of the tremendous power and size which one gets from our big ocean liners" (figs. 7.10 and C.10).[69] Kahn's literal representation of ship prows was enthusiastically endorsed by critic Eugene Du Bois: "The New York World's Fair, 1939, is full of architectural subtleties and abstractions, but there is one structure which is refreshingly obvious in its design: The Hall of Marine Transportation. Ely Jacques Kahn, the architect of this building, has been severely taken to task by the younger designers of the Fair for turning out such a matter-of-fact looking pavilion—one which doesn't require any guessing at all as to its purpose and contents. But Mr. Kahn sticks to his original surmise that the public doesn't want to be puzzled by abstracts and that a maritime building should look ship-shape."[70] To reinforce

the marine concept a mural by the surrealist painter Arshile Gorky (1904–48) was proposed for the two-hundred-foot exterior wall. Gorky's colorful mural featured a bubbling collage of devices associated with marine transportation, including ropes, helmets, horns and smoke stacks.[71] The fair administration rejected Gorky's concept for being too modern and instead chose a mural by the painter Lyonel Feininger, who initially expressed concern that the building was "already complete in its parts and rhythmic importance," and that a figurative mural "would have been a disfigurement."[72] Nonetheless, Feininger overcame his doubts and produced a mural constructed in five individual panels that became one of the most celebrated at the fair. The Marine Transportation Building was utilized as an exhibit hall only in 1939. For the second and last year, 1940, the exhibits were moved to the Communications Building and the Fair Corporation took over Kahn's building for its offices.

Kahn's Ballantine Inn, considered the fair's "first major restaurant concession," was designed in collaboration with the Scott & Teegen firm.[73]

During construction, the picturesque structure was nicknamed the "Three Ring" dining hall, a reference to the logo of Ballantine beer. For this facility, which handled over a thousand patrons at any given time, Kahn brought the expertise he had developed in the planning of large restaurant facilities, such as Longchamps in New York City (discussed below). At a time when Europe was at war, Kahn lightheartedly viewed his design as a return to a peaceful eighteenth-century Germany, which he associated with people "having a good time drinking beer."[74]

In contrast to the Ballantine Inn, the cylindrical White Owl Exhibit Building for the General Cigar Company had clean lines and was machine-like and functional (fig. 7.11). Visitors purchasing cigars could enjoy them in the air-conditioned smoking lounge that was outfitted with electric baseball scoreboards and watch a "Trans-Lux screen" that "flashed the latest world news from 10 A.M. to 10 P.M. daily."[75] The focus of the building was the Manufacturing Exhibit Hall where "pretty girls operate[d] two cigar making machines."[76] Near the production area, glass columns were filled with neat layers of cigars arranged in stunning patterns. A large wall mural by Dock Curtis depicted black men working the tobacco fields, women making the cigars in a factory, and white men standing at a bar consuming the finished product (fig. 7.12). The pavilion clearly catered to a male audience, and the atmosphere was that of a modern men's club.

Although radically different in form and style, each of Kahn's buildings at the 1939 New York World's Fair was well planned and functional. When confronted with questions about the consistency of his visual vocabulary at the fair, Kahn replied that he rejected a single set of aesthetic guidelines for architecture, as he had done previously in reference to the International Style, and that, to him, it was "all a matter of taste and mood of the moment. . . . One day you eat hamburgers and the next caviar. So it is with architecture. . . . I am against all designers who tell you 'This is what you are going to like' whether you like it or not."[77]

While Kahn was designing the fair pavilions, he was also planning Trailer Town, the "largest trailer camp in the world," to accommodate the thousands of visitors to the fair who were expected to arrive by automobile, with their mobile homes or tents in tow.[78] The location of the unrealized project was a site in the Throgs Neck section of the Bronx at the base of the Whitestone Bridge (fig. 7.13). Although similar camps already existed in New Jersey, near the George Washington Bridge, and also in the Bronx, Trailer Town was unique for the extent of its projected amenities: a library, playground, drugstore, tailor, beauty parlor, barber shop, and other retail establishments, which were promoted in the periodical *Trailer Town Topics*. Trailer Town had prominent backers, among them the mayor of New York, Fiorello LaGuardia, and the Bronx Borough president, James J. Lyons. LaGuardia initiated the search for a site and the builder Harry Rich Mooney, who was impressed with Kahn's "undisputed and prominent rank in his field," selected him to design the project. Kahn was upbeat about the planning: "No idea will be overlooked in the planning and construction of Trailer Town. It is our hope to build a complete 'city' so that trailer owners who come to see the World's Fair next year will find the largest trailer camp in the world, built to suit their every convenience and necessity."[79] However, New York City Parks Commissioner Robert Moses worried

7.12 *White Owl Cigar Exhibit Building interior, General Cigar Company, New York World's Fair, 1939, EJK*

7.13 Rendering of
Trailer Town, lower
right; 1939 New York
World's Fair across the
Whitestone Bridge, EJK

that the town would collect "trailer gypsies" who would become a "neighborhood nuisance" and "mar the architectural dignity of the [Whitestone] bridge" and sought to stop the project.[80] When a fire on the site mysteriously destroyed the Carl Knapp Mansion that was intended as the town's administration building, the plan was abandoned. Though a short-lived project, the Trailer Town reveals Kahn's emerging interest in urban planning and housing. In the mid-1930s he wrote about urban civic life organized around "Main Streets," a theme he would continue to pursue during the 1940s and 1950s as head of the Municipal Art Society in New York City and as a designer of public housing projects.[81]

Restaurants, Showrooms, Apartments, Theaters

In the second half of the 1930s, the little commercial work that trickled in, with the exception of the Pix Movie Theater on 42nd Street, was primarily for interiors of restaurants, shops, and show-rooms. The most important restaurants were for the Longchamps chain, and the grandest of these was the 30,000-square-foot facility in the Paragon Building, 253 Broadway. This Longchamps, the largest restaurant in New York City, boasted 2,000 square feet of murals by Winold Reiss that depicted "the types, customs and costumes of the nations of the world."[82] The space was organized behind a three-story glass block wall as a series of terraces with the dining areas offering views below. Kahn refined the dining experience with indirect lighting, special acoustical treatment, and conditioned and ionized air. The success of this theatrical space led to a five-level design for Longchamps in the Empire State Building, with multiple curved dining platforms and stairs of mirrored glass. Completed in 1938 as the economy improved, Kahn's new restaurant in the sky-scraper was considered by many to be a positive sign of the recovery of Fifth Avenue from the depression.[83] Kahn's role in the Fifth Avenue "revival" also included a minor renovation of the Hudnut Building and additions to the Bonwit

*7.14 Hazel Kolman
showroom, 1936, EJK*

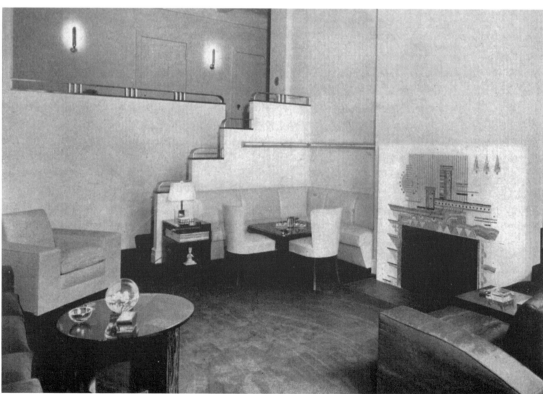

*7.15 F. H. Greenevaum,
Jr. apartment, 1936,
EJK*

192 CHAPTER SEVEN

Teller store, both former clients. To accommodate increased sales for Bonwit Teller, Kahn added two stories to their existing store and renovated an adjacent seven-story structure fronting on East 56th Street. Kahn's success with clients was evident and this project led to his commission to design the new Bonwit Teller White Plains (1941), one of the first suburban branch stores in the New York area. Kahn's reputation as a designer of shops was also enhanced by two other projects with "connoisseur appeal:" a shop selling Mme. T. Azeez's antique jewelry, and a lingerie and fashion boutique for Hazel Kolman (fig. 7.14).[84] The clean modern design for the Kolman showroom, with its dark wood details, chrome furniture, and indirect lighting, conveyed a quiet sense of contemporary luxury characteristic of Kahn's domestic and retail interiors of this period. This approach is evident in his apartment for Mr. and Mrs. F. H. Greenevaum, Jr. (1936) on Manhattan's Upper East Side.[85] With its elegant white walls, minimal, tailored furniture, and curved metal handrails, the design reveals Kahn's adroit ability to interpret the "streamlined" modernism of the decade (fig. 7.15). Opportunities such as this and the Kolman interior were rare in the 1930s, but when he received one, Kahn produced designs as sophisticated and polished as the interiors he had created in the 1920s.

One of the few buildings in New York City designed by Kahn from the ground up during the 1930s was the 850-seat Pix Movie Theater, on 42nd Street between Broadway and Sixth Avenue, for the Brandt Theater Circuit. When it opened in December 1939, the Pix, like other "little" movie theaters of the period, exhibited French and other foreign films. It had the distinction, however, of being the first one constructed to the new theater safety codes, and the first purpose-built one for movies on 42nd Street. Developing the scheme with project designer Arthur Frappier, Kahn described the streamlined modern forms in the Pix as "clean cut" (fig. 7.16).[86] For the comfort of patrons he devised novel "anemostats"—mechanisms that integrated the air-conditioning ducts and lighting units. Continuing his interest in interior lighting from the 1920s, Kahn designed fixtures considered "in line with the character of

the building—simple, functional and as interesting as budget allowances permitted."[87] The Pix Theater project offered Kahn the only opportunity during the 1930s to design a new building for a new type of program. Kahn's career would be propelled in the coming years by his sharper focus on such practical issues as functionality, comfort, and the latest mechanical systems.

7.16 *Pix Theater, interior, 1939, EJK*

KAHN AND JACOBS

1940–50

The decade of the 1940s in America began and ended with the specter of a war: World War II and the Korean War. As early as 1938, when war broke out in Europe, supplies of steel and concrete became limited and construction in New York City came to a near standstill. At the end of the 1930s, Kahn noted that "work [had] never [been] so dull" and that "[w]ar in Europe has construction demoralized— at least as far as I'm concerned. What's ahead [is] a pure guess."[1] As America's involvement in the war became imminent and the government slowed private building, the firm's future was "touch and go," a fear that Kahn recorded in his diary.[2] Once the nation entered World War II in December 1941, however, Kahn and his new wife Beatrice energetically engaged in positions of leadership in the war effort: Kahn became the president of the Municipal Art Society and assumed an active role in wartime housing and planning, and Beatrice accepted the demanding chairmanship of the Greater New York Army and Navy Board Club of the Jewish Welfare Board. In a 1941 article, "Talk If You Must—But Act!," Kahn encouraged his colleagues to follow his lead by pursuing contracts for government projects that had been awarded almost exclusively to

engineers.[3] The same year, he optimistically predicted that postwar building would be "adapted to modern needs," and anticipated the postwar recovery by maintaining contact with prewar clients, developers, and builders.[4] Kahn's efforts paid off; his work on stores, industrial buildings, and restaurants, including a new Longchamps on Madison Avenue, continued during the war, and he expanded his practice to include large housing projects. Perhaps most important, in the 1940s, Kahn once again received commissions for large speculative office buildings, and his firm designed 445 Park Avenue (1947), the first major postwar example in New York City.

Partnership with Robert Allan Jacobs

One of Kahn's most important professional decisions during this period was to make Robert Allan "Bob" Jacobs [1905–88] a partner in the firm.[5] Kahn would have known Jacobs because Jacobs was the son of a friend and close professional colleague, the late New York architect Harry Allan Jacobs (1872–1932). Jacobs was a 1934 graduate of the Columbia University School of Architecture and the recipient of a coveted Hamlin Prize for design. After he received

8.2 *Municipal Asphalt
Plant, Hugh Ferriss,
rendering, c. 1941, K&J*

his professional degree, Jacobs married Frances Nathan Cullman and promptly set off for Paris in the hope of finding work with the famous Swiss architect, Le Corbusier. Although Le Corbusier could not place him that summer, he was invited to return for the fall and winter of 1934–35. During the six months that Jacobs spent in Le Corbusier's office he worked—the only American and without pay—on a proposal for the 1937 Paris Exposition Internationale des Arts et des Techniques dans la Vie Moderne and a competition for the Musées de la Ville et de L'Etat, also in Paris. On Le Corbusier's first American lecture tour the next year, Jacobs served as his translator, guide, photographer, and, on one occasion in Chicago, a resource for sexual favors from women. Le Corbusier referred to Jacobs as his "faithful shadow" and he remained a strong influence on the younger architect throughout his career.[6]

In late 1935, after his tour with Le Corbusier, Jacobs joined the New York firm of Harrison & Fouilhoux as a designer and draftsman. Jacobs had dined with Wallace Harrison and Le Corbusier during the tour and may have met him in school when Harrison was a professor at Columbia. During Jacobs's tenure with this firm, Harrison & Fouilhoux completed a variety of work including the Rockefeller Apartments in

New York (1935–37), a competition entry for the Goucher College Campus (1938), and several buildings for the 1939 New York World's Fair, including the iconic theme buildings, the Trylon and Perisphere. With these projects largely designed and work in the office coming to a standstill, Jacobs was laid off from Harrison & Fouilhoux. Jacobs recalled that in April 1938 Kahn had offered him a job on a train they both happened to be taking back from Lake Placid to New York City. Jacobs accepted Kahn's offer and received a salary of thirty-five dollars per week to work on the design of a new apartment for Kahn and Beatrice at 970 Park Avenue.[7] Just as Buchman had expected Kahn's in-laws to generate business for his firm, Kahn correctly assumed that this would be the case with Jacobs. Shortly after they filed building plans together for a five-story residence on Riverview Terrace in 1939, Kahn offered Jacobs a 15 percent junior partnership for $5,000. In December 1941, with less than a handful of employees in the firm, Jacobs insisted on being made a full, 50 percent partner with no additional financial investment. Throughout the more than three decades of its existence, the partnership was exclusively professional and generally cordial, with intermittent explosive disagreements (sometimes spaced years apart) that Kahn began to note in his diary in the 1950s and which became more frequent near his retirement in the 1960s. Kahn rarely, if ever, socialized with Jacobs. The impression of Sheldon Fox, a later partner, was that Kahn never thought of the younger Jacobs as "an architectural designer equal to himself."[8]

Kahn and his new partner immediately undertook one of the firm's most publicized commissions of the decade: the design of the exterior of the Municipal Asphalt Plant along the East River Drive in New York City (1941). An early rendering of the project by Hugh Ferriss—executed before the project was completed—envisions the Asphalt Plant as part of the future Public Works Administration (PWA) plan to beautify the Upper East Side along the East River. The plan was for the parkway to accommodate pedestrians, automobiles, cranes, and trucks, captured by Ferriss in a night scene illuminated by street lights, the glow of the ramp to the sanitation dump, and a full moon over the East River (fig. 8.2).[9] Kahn brought the project into the office through his connection with the borough president Stanley Isaacs.[10] The issue of whether the city streets should be paved with asphalt—modern and relatively inexpensive—or with traditional and expensive cobblestones, had become a hot political topic. Isaacs, who favored the modern method, requested the renovation and improvement of an existing asphalt-making facility at the east end of 90th Street, which had convenient access to the East River for transport of materials. Kahn and Jacobs were technically the consulting architects to the office of the borough president and were supervised by Walker D. Binger, the commissioner for public works. Their challenge was to create an enclosure for the new machinery in a "dustless, smokeless, and odorless" facility that had a "pleasing design" and satisfied Binger's functional requirements.[11] Working with Shamoon Nadir, the designer employed by Kahn in the late 1920s who had returned to the office after a stint in England, Jacobs may be credited with designing the four ninety-foot-high parabolic arches cast around light, prefabricated steel trusses that enclose the asphalt-mixing facility (fig. 8.3). Although Kahn

noted his own involvement with the project in his diary, Jacobs later claimed that he had designed it after seeing the French engineer Eugene Freyssinet's extraordinary concrete parabolic airship hangars (1921–23) in Orly, on his trip to France to work with Le Corbusier.[12] The arches were a radical formal departure from any of Kahn's earlier work, making the attribution to Jacobs likely. Yet the building retained several qualities typical of Kahn's industrial structures that point to a collaborative effort, including an innovative fabrication process that allowed the plant's heavy equipment to be installed during construction, and cast-in-place concrete panels between the arches that produced a seamless roof structure and reduced costs. The soaring form of the Municipal Asphalt Plant became a dramatic architectural highlight for vehicular traffic driving south on East River Drive (fig. 8.4).

On Halloween Day in 1941, Mayor Fiorello LaGuardia presided over the unveiling of a plaque on the plant that commemorated the participants in its realization. Kahn stood next to Isaacs and Jacobs near LaGuardia in a photograph taken of the ceremony (fig. 8.1). Despite the satisfaction of LaGuardia and Isaacs and the popular and critical success of the project, Robert Moses, the New York City parks commissioner, called

8.3 Municipal Asphalt Plant, under construction, 1941, K&J

8.4 *Municipal Asphalt Plant, 1941, K&J*

the plant a "cathedral" and attacked its design as a "freakish experiment." Ironically, he echoed Kahn's earlier critiques of student work at the Beaux-Arts Institute of Design by charging that although "modern architects" were capable of making "lovely renderings, their talents ended there."[13] Perhaps in response to Moses's public denunciation of modern architecture, Elizabeth Mock, Philip Johnson's temporary replacement at the Museum of Modern Art, inserted the building, which had not previously been considered for the show, into the architecture section of the museum's critically acclaimed fifteenth anniversary exhibition, "Art in Progress."[14] Only three other New York City buildings were exhibited: the Edward A. Norman House (1941) on East 70th Street by William Lescaze, Rockefeller Center (1932–40), and, not surprisingly, the Museum's own building by Philip Goodwin and Edward D. Stone (1938–39). In the exhibition

catalogue, Mock commented on how this industrial building produced an "exciting experience for motorists on the adjacent super-highway."[15] Other publications sang the building's praises in design and construction. For example, *Architectural Forum* noted that the building would be improved once "wartime shortages permit[ed] the installation of the Monel metal covering planned for the barrel roof and diagonal conveyor belt enclosure."[16]

The Municipal Asphalt Plant remained unfinished but in full service until 1968, when all plants were centralized in Queens. The plant received the Landmarks Preservation Commission designation in early 1976 and the rehabilitation of it as a neighborhood athletic facility was planned. Kahn and Jacobs/Hellmuth, Obata & Kassabaum, the successor firm to Kahn and Jacobs, joined forces with the young firm of Pasanella + Klein for the redesign. At the time of its historic designation, *New York Times* critic Paul Goldberger cited Kahn and Jacobs's "fresh rethinking" of materials in a period when there were few examples of such concrete construction in the United States, and none in New York City. He noted, too, that the plant was a "crucial modern monument in the city . . . [that] had been doing unofficial landmark duty for a long time."[17]

The War, Public Housing, and Refugees

Just as the Municipal Asphalt Plant was nearing completion, Kahn capped his five years on the board of directors of the Municipal Art Society by succeeding Ralph Walker as its president in 1941. In this capacity Kahn's attention shifted to the stewardship of the city's parks and open spaces and, after the country entered World War II, to wartime conditions and postwar planning. As president of the Municipal Art Society, Kahn found himself on the losing side of several issues with Robert Moses. For example, he unsuccessfully fought efforts by Moses and others to widen and straighten the Bronx River Parkway, arguing that the existing roadway was a "work of art." Likewise, he battled the Moses plan to tear down the historic aquarium located in Battery Park. Nor was Moses inclined to support Kahn's controversial and short-lived proposal to have the city's least artistically worthy public statues "do a double service—to the war and to art—by being transformed into tanks and torpedoes."[18] In his capacity as head of the Municipal Art Society and chairman of the Committee of Civic Design of the New York chapter of the American Institute of Architects, during the war Kahn was frequently asked to advise on the city's defenses. With little research on the subject, he assured residents that steel, concrete, and stone buildings, including skyscrapers, were "natural air raid shelters," but expressed concern that the substandard neighborhoods of "East-side cold water flats" were wartime liabilities.[19] Motivated by the need to make the city less vulnerable to attack, Kahn proposed an eccentric plan that he called "ideal housing," which would replace these tenements on a checkerboard of Lower East Side blocks with parks set above elaborate subterranean bomb shelters (fig. 8.5). These rectangular sites were referred to by Kahn as "war-and-peace villages" that could contain "new municipal markets, theaters, skating rinks, swimming pools, gymnasiums, auditoriums, and schools" in their vast underground expanses.[20] Kahn rejected criticism that his scheme was "visionary or radical." For him, the buildings on the Lower East Side were "not only eyesores but economic headaches" that could be easily torn down to create a "new order of things." Expressing little acknowledgment of the immigrant communities he would be displacing, Kahn viewed his scheme as substituting defensible open spaces for easily targeted density; a substitution that would also realize his "wider vision of a beautiful and more practical city."[21] Critic Bruce Bliven writing in the *New Republic* situated Kahn's proposal in the context of Le Corbusier's unrealized Plan Voisin (1925) for Paris and dismissed both as financially and politically impractical.[22] If Kahn could not convince city officials to tear down blocks of low-income neighborhoods to make room for middle-class tenants, then he could encourage constructing middle-class housing in other parts of the city. He recognized the need to improve housing opportunities for families who were being squeezed out by New Yorkers who could afford expensive housing, and for low-income families, whose needs were being addressed through publicly financed projects. He argued that the critical mass of new middle-class housing should be located in new neighborhoods along the edges of Manhattan, like the one he helped create around the new Municipal Asphalt Plant.

Kahn's prominence in the areas of public art and buildings and his close political contacts led to valuable government contracts for public housing. His engagement with housing had been greatly accelerated in November 1938, when he was named a "special consultant of the United States Housing Authority" on policies affecting housing design and construction, and on the relationship between national and statewide housing organizations.[23] Beatrice was instrumental in elevating Kahn's public political stature among both Democrats and Republicans, and particularly

8.5 "Ideal Housing,"
Arthur Frappier,
rendering of scheme,
1941, K&J

among Jewish organizations—all of which
enhanced his professional opportunities. When
she married Kahn in 1938, Beatrice was the president of the New York section of the National
Council of Jewish Women and worked closely
with Mrs. Nathan Strauss, wife of the head of the
United States Housing Authority, to raise money
for Council House, a community center in the
Bronx. At the time an architecture firm was being
selected for the Municipal Asphalt Plant, Beatrice
invited Stanley M. Isaacs, to be the keynote speaker at the center's opening. At the same time,
Kahn, as president of the program committee of
the New York Building Congress, invited Senator
Robert F. Wagner, author of the Wagner Steagall
Act of 1937 that created the United States
Housing Authority, to speak to the group. Kahn
shared much of the senator's enthusiasm for public housing. (When the senator's son, Robert F.
Wagner Jr., became mayor of the city of New

York in 1954, Kahn's firm was awarded lucrative
commissions for the design of the Frederick
Douglas Houses (1957) and the Carver Houses
(1957) projects.) Concerned more with policy
than with party politics, Kahn supported the
reelections of Republican Thomas E. Dewey in
1937, Democrat Franklin Delano Roosevelt in
1940, and Democratic Governor Herbert H.
Lehman in 1949. Beatrice, although a long-time
Democrat, was vice-president of the women's
division of the citizens committee to reelect
LaGuardia, a Republican, in 1941. Immediately
following World War II, she served on the influential executive committee of the American
Council for Judaism, an organization that opposed
Zionism "in favor of the integration of Jews in the
country of which they are citizens."[24]

It was not surprising, therefore, that despite
its small size and nearly a decade without large
projects, the firm of Kahn and Jacobs was placed

on Mayor LaGuardia's list of one hundred firms allowed to undertake public projects of $100,000 or more, and appointed as lead architect, with William Hohauser and Ethan Allen Dennison, on the design of section II of the enormous Fort Greene Housing project that extended from the New York Navy Yards south to Myrtle Avenue in Brooklyn. The project consisted of 3,500 apartments and was referred to at the time as "America's Biggest Low-Rent Housing Colony."[25] Kahn's section demonstrated his Beaux-Arts planning in the axial arrangement of buildings along a central spine (fig. 8.6).[26] On the north side of the site, Kahn's team placed the three tallest buildings, which protected the site from the strong northerly winds and allowed the largest number of units to enjoy direct southern sunlight. After the Fort Greene Houses opened in 1942, Kahn joined the design team of the Gowanus Houses in Brooklyn, one of the first housing projects opened after the war. Announced in July 1943, the project was composed of over a thousand apartment units. But Kahn's involvement with New York City hous-

ing was relatively short lived. Even though Kahn had testified against the city in a court case and had simply confirmed what he claimed to be public information, Mayor LaGuardia exercised his authority to remove the firm from the list of architects qualified to undertake large city projects. Kahn publicly admonished the mayor for being "high-handed" in his actions.[27] Kahn and Jacobs, however, approached housing in ways that revealed their diverse approaches to architecture. These differences were best expressed in a 1950s cartoon that depicted Jacobs as Don Quixote on a horse, jousting with windmills, and Kahn, his Sancho Panza, riding on a donkey at his side. In the caption Jacobs challenges Kahn: "Let's show the N.Y. Housing Authority how to build housing!" To which Kahn replies: "But, Bob, those are just windmills."[28] With Jacobs depicted as the dreamer and Kahn the pragmatist, the cartoon exchange may apply to much, but certainly not all of each man's life and work during their decades of partnership.

During the war Kahn and Jacobs designed several federal public housing projects, a major

8.6 Kahn and Jacobs, William Hohauser, Ethan Allen Dennison, Fort Greene Houses, rendering, section II outlined, c. 1941

8.7 *United Service Organizations (USO) clubhouse, interior rendering, 1942, K&J*

source of revenue. The first, which was designed in 1942 and spearheaded by Jacobs, was located near Mineville in upstate New York and consisted of 200 temporary and 230 permanent units to house the influx of workers needed to operate the nearby plant of the Republic Steel Corporation, which was converted to round-the-clock wartime production. The largest such housing project in northern New York, the facilities included a community building with an auditorium, offices, workshops, and a nursery. In 1943 Kahn and Jacobs were awarded an additional commission for two wartime projects in Maryland: 250 trailer units in Jarboesville and 150 permanent dwellings in Cedar Point. The main concept in planning here was the clustering of three homes in a group around a central courtyard. Small windows tucked under the low eaves in the front of the houses contrasted with the higher roofs, large overhangs, and glass openings in the facades at the rear. There were no provisions for parking.

In addition to Kahn's role as an advisor to the United States Housing Authority, he was a special consultant to the Federal Security Agency, which was responsible for building recreation centers for the armed forces, and in 1941 the firm received a commission from the United Service Organizations (USO) to design club buildings for enlisted men and women across the country. Kahn and Jacobs designed three models, each with large lounges and social halls for the entertainment and relaxation of servicemen and civilian personnel.[29] One spacious model had high ceilings, clean, geometric lines, a soaring room divider with a mural surrounding a fireplace, and simplified contemporary seating (fig. 8.7).

Another consequence of the war at the firm was the influx of refugees from Europe, notably the famous German Jewish architect and Kahn's contemporary Erich Mendelsohn (1887–1953), who arrived in the United States from Jerusalem in 1941, and the talented Latvian architect Elsa

Gidoni (1901–78), who joined the firm in 1943. Kahn was instrumental in helping Mendelsohn by providing him with free office space and staff support from at least October 1941 until July 1943. At one point the possibility of Mendelsohn joining Kahn's firm was discussed.[30] Mendelsohn appreciated Kahn's empathy with his plight, but found life in New York too unsettling. Despite their fondness for one another, the German modernist realized that he and his American host had very different ideas about architecture. Mendelsohn considered Kahn "a splendid, refreshing man" who, he noted, was fond of the early modern Berlin architect "[Alfred] Messel and who in his heart of hearts—his architectural heart—is quite adverse to me, but certainly sympathizes with me."[31]

Buchman & Kahn in the late 1920s had over one hundred employees, but diminished to just a few in the late 1930s. By the mid-1940s Kahn and Jacobs was a highly efficient group of about twelve. These included James Newman, who had been the office manager of the firm in the 1920s; the French-born designer Pierre "Pete" Bezy, who had distinguished himself during his architectural education at Columbia by winning a coveted "Second Medal" in the 1931 Paris Prize Competition and entered the firm in 1943; Arthur Frappier, who left the firm after the Pix Theater and returned around 1940; the skilled draftsman Shamoon Nadir, who had contributed outstanding architectural decoration to Kahn's late 1920s office buildings; and Elsa Gidoni. The chain-smoking Gidoni, whose drawings were commonly noted for their cigarette burns, was one of the designers-in-charge of several Kahn and Jacobs projects, including the Thalhimers Department Store (1945), 445 Park Avenue (1947), 1407 Broadway (1950), Connecticut Light and Power (1959), Travelers Insurance Company (1960), 700 Park Avenue (1961).[32] Kahn and his wife helped Gidoni, Mendelsohn and others rebuild their lives in New York by sharing their professional and personal resources. Shortly after the war the firm added the Polish refugee Fred Land, Delbert D. Ehresman (who later was the chief draftsman responsible for hiring Sheldon Fox), and Theodore Smith-Miller, an accomplished

Chilean architect and graduate of Columbia University, who had worked in the design department of Corning Glass Works and had designed the Chilean Building at the 1939 New York World's Fair, and a residence and studio for Russell Wright in New York City. Jacobs later fondly referred to the office at this time as a "potpourri" of talents and nationalities that would help to build the city skyline after the war.[33]

445 Park Avenue

Near the end of 1942, Kahn and Jacobs began talks with David Tishman, the president of the Tishman Realty and Construction Company, about a project at 445 Park Avenue (fig. 8.8). Tishman was negotiating the purchase of a complete blockfront on the east side of Park Avenue, between 57th and 58th Streets, owned by the well-known New York lawyer and author Edward Larocque Tinker and his wife Frances, who had removed tenants from their apartments on the block by ending their leases before rent control went into effect on November 1, 1943. Although the site was uncomplicated by renters, negotiations were drawn out and Tishman did not purchase the property until December 1945. Tishman planned this significant post-war building to be a "monument," which he first envisioned as a modern luxury apartment building in keeping with the residential character of Park Avenue. When financing proved difficult and the need for modern postwar office space became evident, Tishman decided to "invade residential Park Avenue with an office building."[34] He turned to Kahn, who had designed the company headquarters at 136 East 57th Street in 1930, and whom he could trust for the most efficient space planning and the latest mechanical and lighting technologies. The efficiency of Kahn and Jacobs made it possible for Tishman to have the site cleared, contracts awarded, and most building materials purchased in record time by March 1946.

The advanced state of the project was critical to overcoming the biggest obstacle: the new Civilian Production Administration (CPA), established to stabilize the transition to a peacetime economy. Beginning in March 1946 the

CPA authorized only "essential and non-deferrable" projects and those "substantially in progress."[35] Although the CPA rejected outright hundreds of proposals in Manhattan, it held a special appeal hearing in Washington, D.C., on the future of 445 Park Avenue. In May Tishman's gamble paid off: 445 Park Avenue was deemed "essential" based on its advanced state of progress and on the assessment that "existing office and commercial space in New York City were inadequate to the demand."[36] When CPA approval was made public in July, Tishman announced that "the first and most significant" lease in post-war

Manhattan had been signed by the Universal Pictures Company for eight floors at 445 Park Avenue, for which the building was renamed. As Tishman had hoped, other big leases quickly followed, and the building was completely filled by October 1947 when Lever Brothers leased half of the fourteenth floor.

Elsa Gidoni, the project architect for 445 Park Avenue, was highly attuned to the International Style work of Erich Mendelsohn.[37] With her training in 1920s Berlin and experience building modern structures in Tel Aviv, she designed 445 Park Avenue with a bold expression of horizontality, in which serial windows alternated with flat banding. Setting the structural columns back from the facade and hanging the curtain wall off the floor slabs made this system possible. The setbacks, which begin at the twelfth floor, were taken in one-story increments that maintained the horizontal pattern of the elevations. The new zoning regulations of 1943, which reduced the legal height of the first setback from two to one-and-one-half times the width of Park Avenue, still produced what critics, including Lewis Mumford, considered massive volume.[38] Kahn and Jacobs utilized the setbacks for outdoor terraces, a strategy that Kahn had initiated in the Continental Building (1930) and which was evolved later by Hood as terrace gardens in Rockefeller Center. Within the bands of fenestration, every other window was operable. The windows were set on a module of four feet ten inches, a ratio convenient for office layouts and one that became an industry standard. Between the windows, heating risers and air returns were threaded through the narrow vertical columns that had been modeled with a center indentation to achieve a light appearance. Kahn and Jacobs would have probably been familiar with a similar structural system employed by Hood in the McGraw-Hill Building (1931) and pointed out by Mumford in his *New Yorker* critique.[39] To reinforce the continuity of the exterior treatment and to harmonize with it, the lobby featured a series of exposed fluorescent light fixtures, set into reflective waves that covered the ceiling and created rhythmic undulations of light and shadow on the dark marble walls and light-colored floors of the otherwise

8.8 Universal Pictures Building, 1947, K&J

understated space (fig. 8.9). This treatment recalls Kahn's penchant for covering lobby ceilings with cast-glass fixtures, as he had done in Tishman's building at 136 East 57th Street (1931; see fig. 6.63) and others of the period. Kahn and Jacobs benefited from lucrative contracts to design the interiors for tenants, among them, Ford, Lehn & Fink, and Monsanto (fig. 8.10). The firm's spare interior designs often featured simple undecorated surfaces, flexible partitions, recessed lighting, and fluid spaces that were accented with modern artwork.

Tishman believed that the fully air-conditioned Universal Pictures Building, the first in New York City, with its large floors artificially lit, pointed to the future of office space. The horizontal system, it was argued in a marketing brochure, enhanced the amount of light penetrating the interior of the offices and kept the workers from feeling "'entombed' by the heavy masonry" of prewar buildings.[40] Likewise, Mumford was enthusiastic about the lightness of the horizontal windows and wrote that the wall system was "so adroit that one regrets that we have had to wait so long for it." He pronounced the environmental systems "the best

8.9 Universal Pictures Building, lobby, 1947, K&J

8.10 Monsanto Chemical Company offices, Universal Pictures Building, 1947, K&J

8.11 Lane Bryant Store,
maternity center, 1947,
K&J

answer to the year-round problem of lighting
and heating that has yet been worked out for a
New York building . . . 445 is a technical milestone."[41] The building became symbolic of the
postwar resurgence of New York. In 1947, the
Britannica Book of the Year hailed the Universal
Pictures Building at 445 Park Avenue along
with the Fuller House by Buckminster Fuller,
the famous chapel of St. Francis in Pampulha by
the Brazilian architect Oscar Niemeyer, the
Baker House dormitory at the Massachusetts
Institute of Technology by the Finnish architect
Alvar Aalto, and the United Nations Secretariat
by Wallace K. Harrison, Le Corbusier, and others as examples of the best postwar architecture
worldwide.[42]

Lane Bryant and Crawford Clothing Stores

In addition to the Universal Pictures Building,
among the first projects Kahn and Jacobs completed after the war were two major clothing
stores, Lane Bryant and Crawford, both of which

opened in early 1947. For many New Yorkers,
the stores symbolized the rebirth of postwar retail
construction that played "a considerable part in
shaping the direction of New York's growth."[43]
As the first new women's apparel store on Fifth
Avenue in fifteen years—an interval that had witnessed a depression and a world war—Lane
Bryant received special notice. City Council
President Vincent R. Impellitteri gushed that the
new store was "a monument to democratic
achievement and a real contribution to the great
tradition of Fifth Avenue and the reputation New
York City enjoys as the greatest retail center in
the world."[44] Located on the corner of Fifth
Avenue and 40th Street, the new quarters provided Lane Bryant with 50 percent more space and
enabled the sixty-year-old company to expand its
retail sales lines. Kahn and Jacobs added air conditioning throughout the ten-story building and
upgraded the lighting with a combination of fluorescent and incandescent ceiling fixtures, play-
fully alternating them in circular and rectilinear
openings. The lighting scheme was carried

throughout the six merchandising floors, which included an unusual waiting room and library for "expectant fathers" and a much-heralded "maternity center" with twenty-seven fitting rooms (fig. 8.11).[45]

At the request of the client, Kahn and Jacobs's design of the new Crawford Store and headquarters, on the street level of the McAlpin Hotel on Broadway and 34th Street at Herald Square, was somewhat more experimental than that for Lane Bryant. Kahn had seen the 1943 "Brazil Builds" exhibition at the Museum of Modern Art, and was inspired by the buildings that had been constructed using what he called Le Corbusier's "pet theories" of raising them up on columns to create a habitable space on the ground level. Kahn noted that "to the conventional builder" this concept seemed "wildly radical," but he appreciated the potential it presented of a new shopping environment where "stores could be reached under a protected space" created by raising "buildings on stilts."[46] Kahn and Jacobs explored this idea in the design of the new store for Crawford (fig. 8.12). Unifying what was once seven stores into one continuously undulating series of display windows, Kahn and Jacobs pushed the show windows back and forfeited floor space to create a protected outdoor arcade for window shoppers.[47] Customers entering the curved glass-front doors were met with a block-long double-height streamlined interior replete with curved clothing racks along one wall and shining aluminum balustrades. The effect was advertised as the "ultra-modern atmosphere of the Store of Tomorrow" and a "new milestone in the parade of progress."[48] The Kahn and Jacobs "Store of Tomorrow" anticipated the covered arcades of outdoor suburban shopping malls.

8.12 *Crawford Store, arcade, 1947, K&J*

8.13 *Mt. Sinai Hospital, Klingenstein Maternity Pavilion, Atran Laboratory, and Berg Institute of Research, 1951, K&J*

FACING PAGE
8.14 *Mt. Sinai Hospital, Klingenstein Maternity Pavilion, 1951, K&J*

Mt. Sinai Hospital

The Kahn and Jacobs additions to Mt. Sinai Hospital had programmatic, if not formal, precedence in the nearby Hospital for Joint Diseases (1923), designed by Kahn on Madison Avenue at 123rd Street, and a design for the Manhattan General Hospital, 149–157 East 90th Street (1934, unrealized). In June 1944 the firm began discussions with administrators of the Mt. Sinai Hospital for the design of three research buildings, part of the hospital's plan to become one of the most important postgraduate medical facilities for doctors following the destruction of many of the most advanced hospitals in Europe and "the backbone of the country's medical profession in the next generation."[49] Working with York & Sawyer as consulting architects, Kahn and Jacobs designed the facility for a parcel of land running between Fifth Avenue and Madison Avenue from 98th to 99th Streets. The plans included the Magdalene and Charles Klingenstein Maternity Pavilion on Fifth

Avenue as part of the Institute for Biogenetics, and the Atran Laboratory and the Berg Institute of Research on Madison Avenue.

Kahn and Jacobs was awarded the job for many reasons. Perhaps most important was the influence of Joseph F. Cullman Jr., Bob Jacobs's father-in-law, and a trustee and treasurer of the hospital. The firm filed plans for the building in September 1947, but lack of funding stalled construction until early 1949, when the Federation of Jewish Philanthropies of New York, with whom Kahn and his wife had close ties, bailed out the project.

The maternity ward and research laboratories were designed in an inverted "L" plan that connected Fifth Avenue to Madison Avenue, with an open garden area running parallel along the north side (fig. 8.13). Entry routes for most pedestrians and automobiles were located on Fifth Avenue, and a circular off-street driveway was designed for efficient loading and unloading (fig. 8.14). On the Fifth Avenue facade a white frame carried

brick infill panels set below operable windows. Top-floor windows were designed to be higher and wider, affording spectacular views of Central Park from the maternity suites. On the elevations of the research laboratory the continuous horizontal bands of brick and windows share an affinity with 445 Park Avenue, designed in the office at the same time. In fact, the research laboratory shared with 445 Park Avenue the concave outer faces of its vertical mullions as well as the system of setting the columns back from the facade. The outstanding construction feature was the entirely welded steel frame, the largest example to date in the city. This welded steel frame would be a feature of the construction of the firm's later build-

ing at 20 Broad Street (see Chapter Nine). Although the technique had been developed in 1926, it was not used in tall buildings until 1949, after the building code changed to allow it.[50] The method was not only cost-effective; it was quieter and well-suited to a hospital environment.

The Mt. Sinai additions reveal the diversity of the firm's work and the increasing ability of Jacobs to help Kahn generate lucrative institutional business, which included the Neustadter Convalescent Home in Yonkers (1949), the Shelter for Delinquent Boys and Youth House (1957), the New York State Hospital in Rochester (1959), and the High School of Industrial Art and Public School 59 (1960).

1407 Broadway

Optimism for an imminent end to World War II in Europe rose to new heights in early June 1944, shortly after Allied troops invaded Normandy on the much-anticipated D-Day. That was the month Kahn's firm began talks with Mt. Sinai and Louis W. Abrons, president of the General Realty and Utilities Corporation, with "real estate merchandiser" Samuel M. Hirsch, who announced that Kahn and Jacobs, in association with Sydney Goldstone, were to be the architects of the first postwar office and showroom skyscraper in the garment district. The new building, at 1407 Broadway between 38th and 39th Streets would be directly across from Kahn's prewar Bricken Casino and 1400 Broadway buildings, which were completed in 1931. Earlier in 1944 Abrons had purchased the site known as the Wendel site, which was named after its last owner Ella Wendel—the youngest daughter of the renowned New York "millionaire hermit," John Gottlieb Wendel.[51] When plans for a fully air-conditioned, forty-two-story building were announced later that year, they won instant recognition as heralding the "first major addition to the garment district" since the 1930s and sparked optimism that "New York will continue to grow as a fashion and trade center after the war."[52]

The property formed an L-shape around architect Henry Oser's Fashion Center Building

(1925) with the long arm on 39th Street and the short arm on Broadway. From the outset the schemes rejected the expressed verticality of 1400 and 1410 Broadway (Bricken Casino) across the street in favor of a horizontality similar to that of 445 Park Avenue. Like most developers, Abrons and Hirsch insisted on having the greatest possible rentable space, and Jacobs complained that the demand made the building "a sheer wedding cake."[53] He successfully argued for a taller and slimmer building with less space but that would command higher rents for its superior light and views (fig. 8.15). Kahn and Jacobs worked on the design of 1407 Broadway without a contract for nearly four years (due to constraints on building immediately following the war and the owners' financial difficulties) before the site was cleared in July 1948. At that time, Abrons aggressively promoted the building with full-page advertisements in local newspapers. The ads, however, did not yield the desired result and young William Zeckendorf (1905–71) was brought into the venture—the first of its kind in his career.[54] Zeckendorf had the energy and charisma to help the building rent successfully and, as the young architectural critic Jane Jacobs later observed, 1407 Broadway became so successful that it took less than a decade for it and other new buildings following it in the area to virtually empty Worth Street of its textile houses.[55] In contrast to Tishman's argument for the large floors that covered the entire site of the Universal Pictures Building, Zeckendorf and Hirsch took Jacobs's advice and argued that "the trend is toward higher buildings occupying only 65 per cent of the plot or less," a ratio of building to site that anticipated the Seagram Building (1958; see Chapter Nine) and others.[56] The developers were also among the earliest to alleviate congestion by dedicating two floors for indoor parking, and they provided off-street loading docks. According to Zeckendorf, the most important feature was the air-conditioning system.[57] The flexibility provided by the air-conditioning and the space allowed for work spaces to be expanded or contracted as needed along a "vast expanse of glass, with no heavy columns or blank walls between the window units."[58]

8.16 *1407 Broadway, lobby, 1950, K&J*

Fortune proclaimed that the building, which topped out at forty-two stories on New Years Day 1950, "promises to be the best-looking of the new skyscrapers in New York."[59] In contrast to the Universal Pictures Building, the lobby of 1407 Broadway was a luxurious and more complex design, with curved walls of white marble acting as counterpoints to walls of horizontally striated metal bathed in indirect lighting. The play of light and dark, of various planes on different levels, and the variety of materials brings to mind the attention to detail in the lobbies that characterized Kahn's great garment district buildings of the 1920s and early 1930s (fig. 8.16). The interior details were reinforced on the building exterior by the V-shaped profiles of the vertical mullions, painted vermilion on the surfaces facing the street and dark green on either side. The effect renders the mullions as a sharp vertical ribbon of red woven across the horizontal bands of deep green and dark window glass. The decorative elements, interior spaces, and massing of the building proved to be very popular with tenants and by the end of the year 1407 Broadway was completely rented. Although Mumford liked the building's serpent-green brick facade and vermilion mullions as one of the first examples of "real color in a big structure since the McGraw-Hill Building," he considered

8.17 *"Kahn and Jacobs Architects,"* brochure cover, c. 1963

FACING PAGE
8.18 *100 Park Avenue, vertical scheme, 1944, K&J*

KAHN
and
JACOBS
architects

the impact lost on such a massive building. Mumford disliked the "irregular shape" and erroneously claimed it had been constructed to maximize the rentable space allowed by law.[60] On this very important point, Jacobs, Zeckendorf, and others immediately corrected him, and Mumford apologized to Jacobs personally and in *The New Yorker* for being "deplorably inaccurate." In his public apology, Mumford commended the owners of 1407 Broadway for taking Kahn and Jacobs's "farsighted" advice "not to sacrifice quality to maximum coverage."[61]

1407 Broadway was an important marker for Kahn and Jacobs. Architect Robert A. M. Stern called the design "remarkably vivacious," and critic David Dunlap recognized it as "one of the best post-war buildings on Broadway."[62] Architectural historian Carol Krinsky called it "exceptional for its time" but otherwise "bulky."[63] A pinwheel collage of a rotated photograph, taken looking up at the crisp setbacks of 1407 Broadway, was the cover image of the Kahn and Jacobs's 1963 brochure, created more than a decade after the building opened, and indicates the importance of the design to the identity of the firm (fig. 8.17). The building also demonstrates the ability of the firm to reconnect with the garment district after World War II, the area where Kahn established his reputation in the 1920s.

100 Park Avenue

A few months after D-Day, anticipating a rapid end to the war, Kahn and Jacobs filed plans in October 1944 for the firm's third large project to date, a building at 100 Park Avenue, located south of Grand Central Station between 40th and 41st Streets. As an early rendering by Nadir reveals, the massing of the building was to step up in two wings flush with the sidewalk and have a recessed entrance (fig. 8.18). The volumes filled the allowable envelope in a series of symmetrical setbacks. Single window bays stretched uniformly across the facades in a pattern whose verticality was emphasized by the piers, a feature often found in Kahn's earlier work. The client, accountant Samuel D. Leidesdorf, who owned the

site (which included the old Murray Hill Hotel), a developer and a friend of Kahn, brought the commission into the office.[64] The project was one of the first major commissions Kahn worked on with Pete Bezy, who brought to the firm his experience designing the interiors of Lucio Costa's Brazilian Pavilion at the 1939 New York World's Fair. As Jacobs later recalled, Bezy, who became the firm's principal designer and a partner, was a "brilliant architect."[65] Bezy had the important distinction of being able to work equally well with both senior partners, Kahn and Jacobs, and reportedly formed the "cement" between the two.[66]

Postwar building conditions kept the 100 Park Avenue project dormant until 1946, when Leidesdorf partnered with Louis Adler, Kahn's progressive prewar client. After contracting with the George A. Fuller Construction Company, Leidesdorf and Adler increased the height of the building to thirty-six floors, which made 100 Park Avenue, when completed, the tallest and most expensive postwar office building constructed in New York City and the first new office building in the Grand Central District since the early 1930s.[67] Nadir redrew the enlarged project as a more massive version of 1407 Broadway, with its primary glass-enclosed entrance placed on the corner of Park Avenue and 41st Street (fig. 8.19). Kahn, however, continued to experiment with another scheme—probably at the behest of Leidesdorf, who reportedly had the last word in the design of the building—through drawings and a model (fig. 8.20). In this blocky version that recalls the massing of the Park Avenue Building, which Leidesdorf may have wanted to emulate, Kahn reduced the size of the entrance and returned it to its central position on the Park Avenue elevation. The dark color of the base was repeated in the spandrels between the paired windows that were set off by white piers regularly spaced across the facade. By December 1948, the team and clients had agreed on a final vertical scheme that incorporated and improved upon aspects of the earlier designs (fig. 8.21). In this built version, the elevations were reorganized into multiple and varied window bays, and greater emphasis was placed on widened vertical

piers that alternated with narrower, light members. This arrangement created a rhythm that alleviated the heaviness of the massing. Separated above and below by gray extruded aluminum spandrels that give the effect of vertical bars in relief, the windows and spandrels together form darker vertical bands across the elevations. The base of the building is faced in gray granite to harmonize with the spandrels. Views of the Park Avenue entrance are somewhat compromised by the southern ramp leading to Warren & Wetmore's New York Central Building, which straddles Park Avenue. The sheered setbacks created a massing that critics, including Mumford, thought recalled the "wedding cake" style of the 1920s.[68] At first only on the crowning setback facing Grand Central Station and then on both the north and south sides was placed an enormous stainless steel "100," whose combination of

numerals was one of the first to form an office building's identifying logo and foreshadowed the new postwar computerized world of business (fig. 8.22).

During excavation of the site in January 1949, Adler and Leidesdorf hired leasing agents Cushman & Wakefield. They moved aggressively to rent the 660,000 square feet of space, which was divided into floors as large as 32,000 square feet in the main block, and a standard 7,700 square feet in the tower. Leases proceeded quickly; two of the biggest tenants, American Airlines and Philip Morris, hired Kahn and Jacobs to plan and design their office interiors. The Philip Morris interiors, which critics noted for their efficient use of the twenty-nine-foot window bays, and the John Hancock Mutual Life Insurance Company building in Boston shared the title of "Office of the Year," bestowed by *Office Manage-*

FACING PAGE
*8.22 100 Park Avenue,
1950, K&J*

LEFT
*8.23 Philip Morris
Offices, interior, 100
Park Avenue, 1950,
K&J*

ment and Equipment magazine in 1950 (fig. 8.23).[69] A remarkable feature of the leases, and one that revived Adler's restriction of the 1920s, required that all tenants, with the exception of those on the ground floor, lease at least one entire floor. Kahn was proud of having matched the spaces to the needs of tenants. The success of the building can be attributed, in part, to the multiple connections of Kahn and Jacobs. For example, Philip Morris may have taken space in the building because Joseph F. Cullman Jr., the head of Cullman Brothers, a tobacco concern that later purchased Philip Morris, was Jacobs' father-in-law.[70]

Most contemporary descriptions of the building remarked upon the innovative configuration of its first floor plan (fig. 8.24). Kahn and Jacobs essentially brought the sidewalk into the building by setting the revolving doors of the main entrance ten feet back from the building line and formed a large area protected from the

inclement weather. On the south side of the lobby, tenants could enter a branch of the elegant Brass Rail restaurant, and on the north side of the building the Chemical Bank and Trust offered them financial services. The lobby extended sixty feet across the front of the building on Park Avenue and was forty feet deep, grander in scale than any of Kahn's earlier buildings (fig. 8.25). It had floor to ceiling travertine walls and a terrazzo floor and revealed Kahn's characteristic engagement with lighting. He included a striking luminous ceiling of alternating sixty-foot bands of dark bronze indirect lighting fixtures set between arched aluminum reflectors. The rhythmic waves of light directed visitors to the twenty elevators that were simply framed in bronze.

Whereas the Fifth Avenue Association pronounced 100 Park Avenue the "best new building over six-stories" to be built in 1950 and 1951, Mumford offered a more nuanced impres-

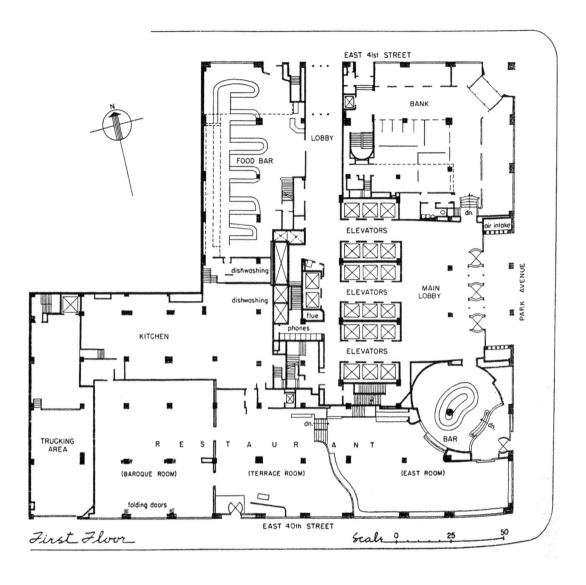

8.24 100 Park Avenue,
ground floor plan, 1950,
K&J

sion of the building.[71] He voiced serious reservations about the construction of new office buildings in midtown and called those involved, including Adler, Liedesdorf, and Kahn and Jacobs, "sleepwalkers," unaware of either the problems of the "obsolete city" or advances in architecture. Therefore, in order to discuss any individual building, he felt it necessary to "relax all practical and functional standards of judgment." He considered 100 Park Avenue a satisfying combination of the vertical "ticker-tape" and horizontal "layer cake" styles. After acknowledging his difficulty in describing exactly what he found satisfactory about the design, he said it was "rigorous, making no attempt at decorative emphasis." Perhaps he was most pleased by the building's "many little departures from uniformity," which he concluded, somewhat pessimistically, were "about all that is left to the architect to relieve the emptiness of modern design." Mumford particularly noted the lobby: he called it "inhumanly cold," but thought it appropriate for corporate America. He concluded that "the general flawlessness of such architecture must itself give one pause; it begins to look like the housing for mechanically perfect electronic computing machines. What are mere human beings doing on the premises?"[72]

Critic Thomas Creighton wrote in *Progressive Architecture* that 100 Park Avenue was the "best of the new office buildings that has yet been erected in New York or in most other cities." Notwithstanding this praise, he said, that did not necessarily make it a good building. In fact, he pointed out, "100 Park Avenue is as bad as any of its brothers of today or its cousins of the '20s.'" He blamed neither the architects nor their clients for trying to maximize rentable space, but rather the city planners for not controlling issues of population density, particularly around Grand Central Station and the new United Nations facility. Creighton felt 100 Park Avenue "came off well" technologically, but was "no better than its neighbors" in many respects. The outstanding feature of the building, he opined, was its excellent space planning. Referring specifically to Kahn, he called the firm "past masters" of efficient office planning and acknowledged that "100 Park Avenue represents the result of their

study and experiment to date." After noting that the building did not challenge the setback or structural conventions, as had the Lever House or the Empire State Building, Creighton concluded that 100 Park Avenue was simply "a frank statement, by capable people, of a commercial structure straining at the setback limitations."[73] Kahn, on the other hand, considered an office building to be "an effective administrative instrument and a potent public relations tool," inseparable from the business itself.[74] According to him, a well-designed work environment replete with modern environmental technologies had the potential to foster good relations between corporate America and its employees, to bring life to a city, and to balance form, function, and finance.[75] The lengthy and rich process of design experimentation that was required for 100 Park Avenue built upon a body of research that Kahn would utilize in a variety of ways in each of the firm's subsequent postwar office buildings in the city.

8.25 100 Park Avenue, lobby, 1950, K&J

CHAPTER NINE

FROM MIDTOWN
TO WALL STREET

1950–65

FACING PAGE
*9.1 View south on Park
Avenue from 57th Street,
Kahn and Jacobs
brochure, c. 1973*

Park Avenue was the center of Kahn's life and work in the 1950s and 1960s. After making his home at number 970 for fifteen years, the seventy-year-old Kahn and his wife moved to a larger apartment at 1185 Park Avenue, eleven blocks to the north.[1] Kahn's sixty-block commute from his new home to his office in the Park Avenue Building at 32nd Street provided him with an impressive review of more than $80,000,000 of construction that had come into the office after World War II. Often completed in association with other architects, these buildings included a luxury apartment complex at 700 Park Avenue (1961); the offices at 445 Park Avenue (1947); 425 Park Avenue (1957), 399 Park Avenue (1961, with Carson & Lundin); the Seagram Building, 375 Park Avenue (1958, Mies van der Rohe, design architect), and 100 Park Avenue (1950); and the apartment building at 80 Park Avenue (1955, with Paul Resnick). Between 52nd and 56th Streets on the east side of Park Avenue, Kahn's stamp was on an office building on every block but one (fig. 9.1).

425 Park Avenue

A speculative office building at 425 Park Avenue (1957), on a block front between 55th and 56th

Streets, was the large project that followed the Universal Pictures Building, 1407 Broadway, and 100 Park Avenue (fig. 9.2). Like several other sites on Park Avenue, this project had been assembled and was owned by Robert Walton Goelet, a leading force in the transformation of the area. Kahn and Lou Crandall, president of the George A. Fuller Construction Company discussed building a structure on the site in March 1953. With characteristic efficiency the firm produced the drawings that enticed a major tenant—a condition required for financing—in fewer than four months. Before plans had been filed, the National Biscuit Company signed a promise to lease six of the proposed thirty-one floors. The company's relocation from its former headquarters of fifty years on 14th Street and Ninth Avenue was an effort to gain access to new clients uptown in the corporate epicenter of the city and to expand production by moving the bakeries to a larger facility out of the city. After financing had been secured, the existing buildings were demolished and Fuller proceeded with construction. The building rented rapidly during construction; among the international array of tenants who leased entire floors was one of Kahn and Jacobs's competitors, the firm of Carson & Lundin, the architects of the Esso Building at 75

221

Rockefeller Center (1942), and the Sinclair Oil Building at 600 Fifth Avenue and 48th Street (1952).

Kahn was the partner-in-charge of 425 Park Avenue and Arthur Frappier was the project manager. The design expressed many of Kahn's ideas for the contemporary office building and in

9.2 *425 Park Avenue, 1957, K&J*

a rare moment of praise for his own work, he commented in his diary that it had been a "good job."[2] Instead of the wide vertical piers of white brick that Kahn appreciated above all other materials and had employed for 100 Park Avenue, he introduced here a rigorous yet lighter rhythm of protruding narrow white brick piers that advance up the three main elevations from a granite base in single window bays with no differentiation of load-bearing piers and are in dramatic contrast to the strident horizontality of the Universal Pictures Building on the block to the north.[3] The vertical rhythm recalls the linearity and massing of Hood's Daily News Building (1929), and it may have been a precedent for Kahn. The Park Avenue elevation is symmetrically organized. Above the first twelve-story block, 425 Park Avenue rises in proportioned setbacks that reveal the sheer tower. The light curtain wall continues to the top of the tower, where it forms a screen over the mechanical systems. Attached to the east elevation in the rear is a solid white elevator-and-service core. When viewed from the sidewalks, the vertical members visually shimmer across the facade into a finely articulated fabric of white brick wall surface, which may be considered a reinterpretation of the intricate surfaces of Kahn's late 1920s buildings in a simplified modern vocabulary. From his earlier work, he also carried over a careful consideration of light and shadow on facades and the punctuation of setbacks with dormers. The interior public spaces contain the flow of traffic within sensuous curves that contrast with the rigorous orthogonal geometry of its facade and plan. The rounded ceiling, walls, and columns of the lobby entry were faced with a uniform blanket of small, almost all white, mosaic tesserae (fig. 9.3).

Team Play at Kahn and Jacobs

Despite the claims of Bob Jacobs to the contrary later in his life, and their differing viewpoints on design, he and Ely Kahn shared some similar approaches to architecture. Nowhere was this similarity more evident than in the first of four articles Jacobs was invited to write about the firm in the *Christian Science Monitor* on the occasion of

9.3 *425 Park Avenue, entrance, 1957, K&J*

the opening of the Travelers Insurance Company Building (1960) in Boston's burgeoning Office Building District (fig. 9.22). Titled "Team Play Guides Today's Architects," the article contained ideas about the relationship between architectural design and business that evoked Kahn's essays "Economics of the Skyscraper" in the *Architectural Record* (1928) and "Skyscrapers of Manhattan" in the *Christian Science Monitor* (1934).[4] Jacobs pointed out that the building industry had become so complex that his firm required a group of specialists to work together on a project and that this procedure was a far cry from the popular image of the "artist–architect–builder" epitomized by Frank Lloyd Wright. Jacobs claimed that members of his firm considered themselves "shirtsleeves architects" because they "think of architecture as a quasi-business."[5] He claimed that the diversity of modern projects led to greater specialization in the office. The article

closed with a description of how Kahn and Jacobs brought "prestige" to their clients. By Jacob's account, the firm accorded this prestige independently and in association with "leading architects" and engineers, including Mies van der Rohe and Phillip Johnson on the Seagram Building (1957); I. M. Pei on the Mile High Center in Denver (1952); Welton Beckett on the Remington Rand and Massachusetts Mutual Life Insurance Company Building in Los Angeles (1950); and Abbott, Merkt & Co. on department stores and shopping centers. "In these and many other projects," he contended, "Kahn and Jacobs prides itself on achieving beauty, imagination, and taste on the one hand and a realistic approach to cost factors on the other." Jacobs concluded that by balancing these polarities that become "symbols of a company," the firm's "hall mark [was] stamped upon each one of the many structures which it designs."[6]

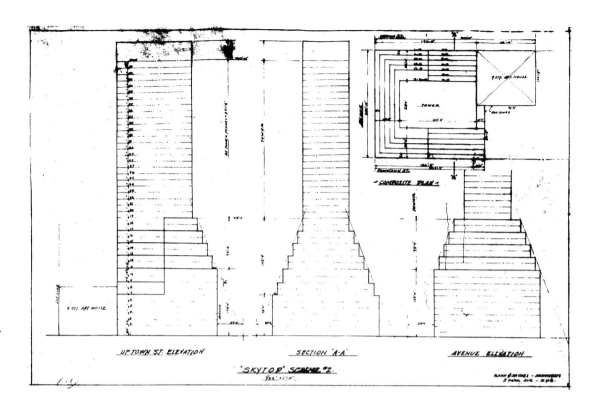

UPTOWN ST. ELEVATION   SECTION 'A-A'   AVENUE ELEVATION

"SKYTOP" SCHEME #2.
1/32" = 1'-0"

9.4 "Operation Skytop," scheme 2, 375 Park Avenue, plan and elevations, K&J

Sheldon Fox, one of the promising young architects hired by the firm during the flush 1950s, recalled that Jacobs was particularly concerned with disseminating information about the firm's activities through brochures and other forms of publicity.[7] Around 1950 Jacobs created the first design portfolio of Kahn and Jacobs's work, and in the 1960s he initiated the position of public relations officer in the firm.[8] Indicative of the evolution of the firm in the mid 1960s was the elevation of Lloyd Doughty, Sheldon Fox, and Irving Kaplan to junior partners.

Seagram Building

An iconic modernist skyscraper of the twentieth century involved Kahn and Jacobs when, in July 1951, shortly after Samuel Bronfman, the president of Joseph E. Seagram & Sons, had secured the property for a new building at 375 Park Avenue, Kahn sent Bronfman a brochure with a cover letter requesting a meeting. Kahn directed Bronfman to the developer Samuel Leidesdorf, who could provide him with "information as to

how 100 Park Avenue was successfully finished." In closing, Kahn noted that his firm had a "thoroughly trained staff that could analyze the preliminary steps" before action was taken.[9] That day Kahn enthusiastically, and perhaps, optimistically, entered in his diary: "Bronfman possibility 375 Park!"[10] Kahn and Jacobs also convinced the influential lawyer and client Alfred L. Rose to add a good word on their behalf. Writing in August 1951, Rose assured Bronfman that he "highly recommended both men" from the "standpoint of ability and integrity," for Kahn had "ranked among the top architects of the City for a generation," and Jacobs was "making quite a name for himself today." Rose mentioned how satisfied he was with Kahn's "architectural and decorative work" on the 1942 renovation of his penthouse apartment in the city, and later with Jacobs's design of his vacation home in Lake Placid, New York. He pointed out their work on Mt. Sinai Hospital, on 100 and 445 Park Avenue, and made special mention of Kahn's Squibb Building as examples of "their architectural ability."[11]

Kahn joined Crandall and a group of prominent rental agents to develop sketches of building massing options under existing zoning restrictions that they called "Operation Skytop" on the Seagram site (figs. 9.4 and 9.5). "Scheme 2," the only option preserved in sketches, reveals a bulky, symmetrical building set as close to Park Avenue as possible with evenly spaced setbacks leading up to a heavy tower. The setback design that followed the pattern of Kahn and Jacobs's 445 Park Avenue and 100 Park Avenue, did not satisfy Bronfman's desire for a grand monument to the House of Seagram to celebrate its hundredth anniversary in 1957. In June 1954 he invited the former president of Lever Brothers, Charles Luckman, who was an architect, to discuss the project. At their first meeting Bronfman confided in Luckman that he wanted a thirty-five-story office tower with galleries for art exhibits and a Venetian fireplace in the boardroom. According to Luckman's account, Bronfman intended to crown the tower with an English castle he had already arranged to purchase and transport to New York.[12] Within three weeks Luckman came back with a scheme that featured a facade of vertical piers of marble, bronze, and dark glass that rose from a low base. A week later, after discussions with his daughter Phyllis Lambert, who had studied modern art at Vassar and had a strong interest in the project, Bronfman rejected the scheme. At this point, Crandall, the builder, suggested to Bronfman that Lambert undertake a selection process for a new architect. Through Marie Alexander, a college friend who worked at the Museum of Modern Art, Lambert met Philip Johnson, the head of the Department of Architecture and Design.[13] In search of an architect and with the help of Johnson and Crandall, Lambert visited the offices of Walter Gropius, I. M. Pei, Paul Rudolph, Minoru Yamasaki, Eero Saarinen, Frank Lloyd Wright, Marcel Breuer, Harrison & Abramovitz, Kahn and Jacobs, and Mies van der Rohe.

In November 1954, when it became clear that Mies van der Rohe, who was nearly Kahn's age, had been selected and that Mies had asked to work with Philip Johnson, who had not yet built a skyscraper, Crandall persuaded Bronfman that the project needed a "competent" associated architect.[14] Kahn quickly agreed to that role and became an active participant in the process that led to the final design (fig. 9.6). He went as far as presenting his own design scheme for the project, and in his diary on April 26, 1955, he wrote that he was "waiting to see what happens to van der Rohe suggestions and ours."[15] Kahn's introduc-

9.5 *"Operation Skytop," scheme 2, 375 Park Avenue, perspective, K&J*

9.6 Mies van der Rohe, Philip Johnson, and Kahn and Jacobs, associate architects, Seagram Building, 375 Park Avenue, 1958

tion of his own ideas caused tension. Phyllis Lambert felt that Kahn was "undermining Mies's decisions" by extending his influence beyond the acceptable purview of associate architects—which is usually limited to the production of documents and supervision of construction—and by suggesting changes that would have profoundly altered the massing of Mies's building.[16] Although Kahn found the situation with Mies "amusing," he accepted the decision to build Mies's design and demolition on the site began soon thereafter in September 1955.[17]

According to Kahn's diary, the Seagram project suffered some delays in April 1956 and again in July 1957, when Kahn entered in his diary that "violent changes" to the building and their cost were discussed.[18] Kahn, however, grew to appreciate Mies's "attractive approach" across the open plaza to the Seagram Building and tried a similar strategy in his next building at 399 Park Avenue.[19] Apparently, pleased with Kahn's contributions to the building process, Bronfman mentioned to Crandall the possibility of bringing the team together again under Mies's leadership to design a new, but eventually unrealized, headquarters for Seagram in Chicago.

Astor Plaza, First National City Bank, and Citicorp Center

While working on his own scheme for the Seagram Building in April 1955, Kahn began discussions with engineer and real estate developer Joseph P. Blitz for a new building at 399 Park Avenue, on the block north of the Seagram Building and across the street to the east of Lever House. Bounded by Lexington and Park Avenues, and 53rd and 54th Streets, the full block was leased by Vincent Astor from the estate of William Waldorf Astor, which was controlled by the British branch of the family. With its two already well-publicized neighbors, Astor planned to develop a "prestige" building of his own, to be called Astor Plaza.[20] He began to assemble the site in 1953 with the intent of developing a forty-six-story skyscraper with Fuller as the contractor and the Hanover Bank and Newsweek, both controlled by Astor, as the primary tenants.

Astor offered William S. Paley and Frank Stanton, chairman of the board and president, respectively, of the Columbia Broadcasting System (CBS), a combined 15 percent interest in the enormous project. Although there was no discussion of CBS moving into the new building, Astor had grandiose visions of it being a "city within a city"—large enough to rival Rockefeller Center, with a sunken garden, helicopter landing, and tunnels connecting to other Park Avenue buildings.[21] However, Astor lacked the experience required to develop a project of this magnitude. In fact, this would have been the first construction venture in the one-hundred-and-fifty-year history of the Astor family in the city.[22] Although contemporary accounts vary, Astor seems to have had difficulty securing a mortgage from both financial institutions and from the estate of his British-based family members in control of the William Waldorf Astor Estate. When he was unable to find a lender, he partnered with Blitz, who asked Kahn and Jacobs to develop a scheme for a forty-three-story office building. They worked on the scheme until Astor's financial crisis in September 1956. In his diary at the time Kahn realized that he would be collaborating with Carson & Lundin, who had presumably been working independently with Astor.[23] Plans filed in November listed the two firms together as the architects.

The architects produced several schemes, each of which responded to the powerful presence of the Seagram Building to the south and the Lever House to the west. One proposed setting the building back from Park Avenue to align with the Seagram Building and provide a tree-filled plaza on Mies's grid (fig. 9.7). Another moved a narrower tower close to the street, where it hovered on heavy concrete supports set into a plaza filled with gardens and walkways (fig. 9.8). Clad in white panels with nearly square windows, the building had proportions that were compatible with the Lever House. The plan exposed a stark white slab-shaped service core on its south elevation, a light counterpoint to the dark bronze of Mies's adjacent building.

By May 1957 Blitz had abandoned the Astor deal. He may have become frustrated by Astor's

inability to assemble the entire property because of a holdout, the Michels family, operators of a pharmacy on Lexington Avenue. Backed into a corner, Astor agreed to lease his property to First National City Bank, the parent company of City Bank Farmers Trust Company, the trustee of the William Waldorf Astor Estate. The bank succeeded in acquiring the Michels property and consolidated the site. Kahn and Jacobs and Carson & Lundin were engaged to reconfigure the original plans to the bank's more utilitarian needs (fig. 9.9). The narrow side of the tower retained its orientation to Lever House, but in order to maximize rental space the tower and its flanking blocks covered the entire Park Avenue street front, and the plaza was reduced to an entry-level arcade. Following the lead of the Lever House and

the Seagram Building—both of which appeared reflected in the building's mirrored glass windows—399 Park Avenue displays a complex interplay of vertical and horizontal members that helps to dematerialize the heavy massing in the lower stories. Unlike the Lever House or the Seagram Building, however, 399 Park Avenue articulates its structure clearly on the exterior of the building through light colored load-bearing piers that are balanced by slender vertical mullions interwoven with darker, nonreflective spandrel panels set in horizontal bands across the facade. Construction of the steel skeleton began in April 1959 under the supervision of Fuller. Notwithstanding the relatively economical facade, the forty-one-story building was one of the largest and most expensive office buildings

9.9 *Kahn and Jacobs and Carson & Lundin, Astor Plaza Building, 1961*

9.10 Hippodrome Building, five-story stage, c. 1952, K&J

Kahn and Jacobs ever produced. After the building was completed in 1961, the bank decided to maintain its historic downtown headquarters on Wall Street and to create a distinguished uptown headquarters. The bank assembled a site to the east of 399 Park Avenue and built the new Citicorp Center (1977) on Lexington Avenue.

Hippodrome Building

Kahn and Jacobs were also critical players in the early redevelopment of corporate Sixth Avenue in the 1960s. A well-known historic building was on the site of one such speculative office project: the heavily ornamented Hippodrome, also known as "the world's largest playhouse," located on the east side of Sixth Avenue between 43rd and 44th Streets.[24] In 1929 developer Fred F. French had purchased the site for the erection of a skyscraper in competition with, and higher than, the Chrysler Building and the proposed Empire State

Building. French's plans were laid to rest during the depression, when the property was foreclosed in 1932. After years of neglect, the Hippodrome was torn down in August 1939. A plan to build a low-rise structure designed to cover the cost of the site ("taxpayer") failed to materialize, and the site was cleared for a parking lot to accommodate the growing numbers of automobiles in the city.[25] In 1948 the textile manufacturer G. A. Horvath purchased the site and turned to Kahn and Jacobs for the design of a three-story building that combined stores, office space, and a parking garage. Ultimately, Kahn and Jacobs built a five-story structure with an additional floor below ground for parking (fig. 9.10). Vertical aluminum members that protruded from the white limestone facade extend above and below the windows to frame each bay. The ribbed gray aluminum spandrels were similar to those at 100 Park Avenue. Anticipating an increase in building materials after the Korean War, the firm designed the foundations strong enough to accommodate a twenty-story structure and brought the white elevator core above the roofline to a height of eight stories.

Finding tenants for the Hippodrome Building was difficult. The location had neither the prestige of Park Avenue nor the visual impact and space availability of taller buildings. It was, however, a highly desireable and successful parking garage. Because of its location between Grand Central Station and the *New York Times* Building the fate of the Hippodrome Building was more frequently discussed in the "Topics of the Times" section of that newspaper than many more pressing issues.[26] In November 1955, the owners decided to add the eight additional stories Kahn and Jacobs had originally planned. In a feat of acrobatics worthy of the building's name, Kahn and Jacobs and their contractors developed a construction method for the additional floors that ensured the minimum disruption for tenants. The *Real Estate Record and Builders Guide* proclaimed the expansion to be "the largest addition to an existing building which will remain completely tenanted throughout the operation."[27] Materials were brought into the building from cranes outside, and protective bridges were built over the sidewalks to maintain access to stores and restaurants on the street level. The facade retained its heavy white piers set between bays of single-hung windows and light vertical members (fig. 9.11). The design of the facade made a clear reference to the more prestigious 100 Park Avenue, located only a few blocks to the east, and their efforts to cash in on this association paid off: The expanded Hippodrome Building contributed to the increased prestige of Sixth Avenue, which was renamed "Avenue of the Americas" in 1960. To capitalize on this distinction, the address of the building was changed from 50 West 44th Street to 1120 Avenue of the Americas. Even before construction began on the additional floors, Socony Mobil Company had signed a long-term lease for the seventh floor and Eastern Airlines had committed to lease a large portion of the eighth. The rental success—General Electric among others became new tenants—led to the third stage in 1961: the firm's completion of the project to the original specifications, by topping it off with a twelve-story tower that brought the building to twenty stories. Office amenities were upgraded to include individually controlled air-conditioning systems, recessed lighting, and high-speed automatic elevators. At the same time the firm redesigned the lobby with white marble and mosaic walls, pools, and sculptural groups.

Union Dime Bank Building

Kahn and Jacobs were also pioneers in the growth of the "New Sixth Avenue" through their construction of the Union Dime Bank Building, 111

9.11 Hippodrome Building, twenty-story final stage, rendering, c. 1961, K&J

West 40th Street, on Sixth Avenue across from Bryant Park.[28] The bank had occupied a three-story Renaissance-revival style building (1910) by Alfred H. Taylor across the street from a prominent Buchman and Fox Building. Founded by a group of men involved in the textile industry, the bank had close ties to tenants in many of Kahn's buildings in the nearby garment district. Buchman & Kahn had maintained a presence in the area and, after the demolition of the Sixth Avenue El in the late 1930s and the end of World War II, in the mid-1940s, Kahn and Jacobs partnered with Sydney Goldstone to bring together banking and textile interests in a single high-rise

building on its site. The new building, designed by Kahn, was the first one to go up on Bryant Park in thirty years.

Aware of the success this team had with 1407 Broadway, executives at Union Dime turned for advice to its owner, Edmund F. Wagner, president of General Realty and Utilities Corporation, who recommended the architectural team again. Although he was listed as an architect on the plans, Goldstone appears to have played little or no role in the design of the Union Dime Bank Building. Sheldon Fox, who worked on the project, never recalled meeting Goldstone, but pointed to the important roles played by Kahn and one of his chief designers, Riva Ferrucci.[29] The earliest published sketches (February 1955) of the thirty-story building show a clean, undecorated, light-colored building with a dark three-story entrance base, uniform bays, and setbacks reminiscent of 1400 Broadway and other Kahn buildings from the late 1920s, and a tower suggestive of 100 Park Avenue in its massing (fig. 9.12). However, within three months the design was altered significantly (fig. 9.13). Above the dark three-story base, the uniformity of the grid was changed to favor the expression of verticality instead of horizontality by emphasizing the load-bearing piers with colossal white pilasters. Like 1407 Broadway, another L-shaped building, it had an interior shopping arcade that connected the entrances. In an advertisement General Realty proudly announced that the building would be the "largest and most strategically located structure in the important uptown Textile Center," and that its tenants, the "leading textile and business concerns," would be provided with "every facility for the efficient conduct of business."[30] The rental campaign was effective, and tenants rushed to lease space in the new building.

The design as built, however, was revised again. The height of the building was increased slightly and the facade was modified into single-window bays articulated by piers that reprised the strong verticality of 425 Park Avenue and organized the elevations into a tight, uniform, stepped-back grid (fig. 9.14). Kahn designed a new entrance on Sixth Avenue, a sixty-foot-wide double-height glass wall for the bank that overlooked Bryant Park and another expanse for the grand 40th Street entrance. Reminiscent of the work of Josef Hoffmann and of Kahn's treatment of the 1933 Kohler fair pavilion, the base featured walls outlined with dark stone. Kahn referred back to his own 1920s work when he commissioned a mural by Max Spivak, a New York artist popular for his mosaics in the 1940s and 1950s. Kahn commissioned Spivak to design a mural eighteen feet high by forty feet long to "relieve the grayness of the lobby" and to be "symbolic of the spindle and loom" associated with the

9.15 *Union Dime Bank Building, Max Spivak (shown standing), entrance mural, 1958*

FACING PAGE
9.16 *20 Broad Street, 1957, K&J*

textile trade (fig. 9.15).[31] The colorful abstract mosaic, which evoked the craft of fabric production, originally faced the visitor at the 40th Street entrance. It was the last large-scale mosaic mural in a Kahn office building. Kahn further referenced his earlier work by cladding the slim vertical members in six miles of extruded white terra cotta that contrast with the beige, evenly stacked brick spandrels. Critics immediately noted that this was the first major use of terra cotta in a skyscraper since Raymond Hood's McGraw-Hill Building of 1931.[32]

New York Stock Exchange Expansion

Following the crash of 1929, the New York Stock Exchange embarked on a highly successful campaign to renew the American public's faith in its ability to sustain the economic health of the nation. To help achieve this goal, a small visitors gallery was opened to educate nonmembers about the inner workings of the exchange. In 1951, after a period of closure during World War II, the gallery was expanded into an informal "school" that offered the public lessons on the economy. Located next door to the New York Stock Exchange, in the imposing Commercial Cable Building (1898) at 20 Broad Street, the school featured exhibits by such industrial giants as the American Telephone and Telegraph Company, General Electric, Standard Oil, and the Association of American Railroads. These exhibits were accompanied by the film *Money at Work* and later by the popular animated cartoon *What Makes Us Tick.*[33]

By the early 1950s, the exchange needed additional space to accommodate its growth. It was not feasible to modernize the adjacent buildings, and in 1954 the decision was made to replace them with a new building, to be called 20 Broad Street—the first new construction of its kind in the Wall Street District since the erection of the forty-eight-story building at 30 Broad Street (1931). General Realty, which had played a role in the development of 30 Broad Street and had been instrumental in securing the 1407 Broadway job, was the link to the commission Kahn and Jacobs received for 20 Broad Street. In his diary Kahn mentioned working on the project in the summer of 1953.[34] Kahn and Jacobs, in association with Sydney Goldstone, produced the first published images in July 1954 when the building was announced.[35] The building would have three basements, a column-free space from the second to the fifth floors for the expansion of the existing trading floor, and modern amenities such as air-conditioning and high-speed elevators (rare at that time in the Wall Street area).

Although Crandall was the experienced general contractor, unforeseen obstacles arose. In contrast to the relative ease of acquiring tenants, demolition and construction at 20 Broad Street involved complications rarely encountered at uptown locations. The demolition of the Blair and Cable Buildings for the construction of 20 Broad Street proved to be the "most difficult and costly . . . ever undertaken in the city."[36] The density of the area worsened the problems and had an impact on the financial feasibility of the project. In an effort to reduce construction noise, the steel skeleton was welded together instead of riveted. Transporting the enormous trusses through the narrow, winding streets in the vicinity, however, created another set of problems.

When 20 Broad Street opened in early 1957, it was said to have "changed completely" the "Wall Street Picture" (fig. 9.16).[37] The building housed a new exhibit hall and visitors' center to accommodate the 300,000 visitors expected annually, a number on a par with the visitors to the Statue of Liberty and the new United Nations buildings. Among the most advanced exhibits were a model of a nuclear power plant and the "latest styles in space suits."[38] Although some architecture critics found the building bulky and

the exterior treatment was not innovative, Kahn's design brought to the Wall Street area a building whose setback massing, flexible plan, and facade of ridged aluminum spandrels, white brick, and glass had become synonymous with midcentury corporate America—which was, after all, the essence of the exchange itself. [39]

9.17 477 Madison Avenue, early scheme, c. 1952, K&J

477 *Madison Avenue*

In midtown, Kahn and Jacobs designed two speculative office buildings for critical locations on Madison Avenue. The first was 477 Madison Avenue, on the southeast corner at 51st Street, which, until 1950 had been the site of an elegant three-story Italian Renaissance-revival villa built in 1908 for William K. Vanderbilt, and a center of New York social life. In recent years the mansion had been transformed into an administration facility for the Archdiocese of New York. When the church purchased the Villard Houses across the street to the south in 1949, the Vanderbilt villa and adjacent structures on the property were sold to the Simon Brothers, builders of luxury apartment and office buildings in the city, who hired Kahn and Jacobs to "improve" the lot with a new twenty-two-story office building. [40]

The Korean War and labor union unrest stalled construction after the site was cleared, and it was then temporarily used as a parking lot. The steel strike was settled in the late summer of 1952, and the project resumed. Although steel was still scarce and expensive and labor costs were soaring, the promise of lucrative corporate leases propelled the Simon Brothers forward. By August Kahn and Jacobs had produced renderings of the proposed twenty-three-story structure. Its elevators and air-conditioning units were situated in an enlarged tower core located at the pinnacle of the series of setbacks. The unornamented facade had suggested both factory and office building by combining a grid similar to Kahn's 1400 Broadway with the strong horizontality found in 445 Park Avenue (fig. 9.17). By the time construction began in 1953, the horizontal ribbon windows in the upper stories had been eliminated, leaving a smooth white brick building with a complex configuration of setbacks that were reminiscent of Kahn's prewar buildings. He used a formula common in the 1920s to create facades of white brick with gray mullions organized into four- and three-window bays that lacked any articulation of the underlying steel frame but included balconies on upper floors with railings (fig. 9.18). The simplification of the fenestration and of the storefronts on 51st Street were probably measures to make the building more profitable in light of the high construction costs. The stringent economizing created a building that appears to have been unqualified for illustration in the firm's brochures.

The Ford Foundation's early lease of eight floors, and other leases that soon followed, ensured the financing of construction and 477 Madison Avenue formally opened in April 1954. Cardinal Spellman dedicated the building because the site had previously been the home of the Catholic Charities, which was affiliated with St. Patrick's Cathedral on the Fifth Avenue block between 50th and 51st Streets. The Ford Foundation had spectacular views of the cathedral, Rockefeller Center, the Empire State Building, and beyond— precisely the civic and corporate landscape it wished to influence. Interestingly, when the Ford Foundation moved to its own headquarters in 1967, the *New York Times* architecture critic, Ada Louise Huxtable, contrasted the new building for the foundation with "the typical speculative office building on Madison Avenue" by Kahn and Jacobs it had inhabited.[41] Huxtable, however, neglected to place adequate emphasis on the changing nature of the foundation itself. The speculative office building at 477 Madison Avenue offered the spatial and technological ease the foundation required at the time it was focused on establishing its organizational roots and addressing a new community. Later, its new headquarters at 342 East 42nd Street were intended to provide a forceful physical statement of the Ford Foundation's place in the city and mark a clear departure from its previous anonymity. Like the Lever Brothers and Citibank before it, the Ford Foundation used its office space, efficiently designed by Kahn and Jacobs, as an economically viable springboard for a future landmark building of its own.

330 Madison Avenue

It was a time of transition for Kahn. Beatrice died in 1962, and he remarried two years later. Beatrice and Ely Kahn had befriended Liselotte Hirschmann Myller and Dr. Ernst Myller,

German-Jewish refugees, whom they had first met in the spring of 1942, through mutual friends, during a serendipitous encounter in Rena Rosenthal's shop on Madison Avenue.[42] They had remained in contact with Liselotte after Ernst's death in 1953, and in the mid-1950s Liselotte

9.18 *477 Madison Avenue, 1954, K&J*

9.19 *330 Madison Avenue, view from below, 1963, K&J*

FACING PAGE
9.20 *330 Madison Avenue, rendering, c. 1962, K&J*

provided professional interior design service for the new Kahn apartment at 1185 Park Avenue.[43] After Beatrice died, the two widowed partners became closer. They were married early in 1964, and Liselotte brought her vivacious, good-natured, and intelligent companionship into Kahn's retirement years. After his death, she became a devoted and stalwart supporter of Kahn's legacy.

One of the last Manhattan office buildings to bear Kahn's signature, 330 Madison Avenue, was constructed when he was seventy-eight years old, shortly before his retirement. The building, located on the west side of Madison Avenue between 42nd and 43rd Streets, was alternatively known as the Sperry & Hutchinson Building (for the creators of S & H Green Stamps, who leased five floors) and by its address (fig. 9.19). Of the several historic buildings on the site, the largest was the fifteen-story Manhattan Hotel (1896), which had been converted to an office building in 1921 by the First National City Bank. The corner site was located near Grand Central Station, at 42nd Street, set among the many midtown offices, which made 330 Madison Avenue one of the most valuable properties in the country. It was a neighbor to William Lescaze's eighteen-story office building at 300 East 42nd Street (1963); Harrison & Abramovitz's forty-two-story Socony Mobil Building at 150 East 42nd Street (1956); and Lacey, Roche, & Dinkeloo with Eero Saarinen's, Ford Foundation, 321 East 42nd Street, (1966).[44]

Anticipating the development of this choice plot after the real estate investors Fuller and Reynolds purchased it, Kahn had the design almost finished before they completed the transaction. His design for the thirty-nine-story office building was a variation of the highly successful 100 Park Avenue (fig. 9.20). It emphasized verticality with window bays placed between strong vertical piers that rise the full height of each setback. These and the intervening narrow, non-load-bearing members continue up to the narrow, slightly projecting string courses that delineate each of the parapets. Here, in contrast to 100 Park Avenue, Kahn achieved a dramatic patterned effect by inverting the relationship of

light to dark. He emphasized the load-bearing piers by using black brick to frame the window bays in each mass. The building's dark brick corners, contrasting with lighter-color bays, were visually strengthened by the massive black granite piers at the entrance. The bold white, gray, and black color scheme recalls Kahn's 1410 Broadway, in which white piers contrasted with black brick spandrels (see fig. 6.50). Kahn established a visual rhythm across the wider Madison Avenue elevation by alternating crisp three- and four-window bays with inoperable windows. Within the three-story entrance base was a soaring retail space with large windows along Madison Avenue. A T-shaped lobby, similar to those for the Union Dime Bank Building and 1407 Broadway, connecting Madison Avenue with 42nd and 43rd Streets, was clad in white marble with highlights in gray over the elevator doors. The floors were predominantly white with black bands for accent. Olivia Kahn, Ely's youngest daughter and an artist, recalled that at her father's invitation, she had worked for a year on designs for a mural to be located in the build-ing's lobby; representatives of the Catholic Church ultimately rejected her mural for its level of abstraction.[45]

The stark contrast between white and black on the facades was a departure from Kahn's post-war work and strikingly different from most buildings in midtown. In an interview Kahn stated that "his firm wanted to design a building with character and color contrast," and in a surprising rejection of the celebrated whiteness of the Squibb Building, he asserted that "an all-white building would be unimaginatively monotonous, and one constructed of entirely dark materials could be morbid and formidable."[46] However, he had to persuade the uncertain clients first. Kahn employed the successful strategy he had utilized for the polychrome treatment of the Park Avenue building: He reportedly had a 25- by 50-foot model constructed to his specifications for the clients' review. Despite the light downturn in the rental market in the early 1960s, the building was filled quickly, and when five full floors were leased in 1964 to Sperry & Hutchinson, the building was given the company's name. Kahn's scheme may have inspired Shreve, Lamb & Harmon's black and white, forty-four-story office tower of 1966, 245 Park Avenue, at 46th Street.

A Building Goes Up

In 1969, Kahn produced a children's book titled *A Building Goes Up*.[47] Rather than a survey of historical styles, a discussion of design concepts, or even an overview of the role of architecture in cities, the book is a "nuts and bolts" description of the process of constructing a tall office building. On the front cover Corbusian lettering suggests both a general relationship to architectural practice and a more specific affinity to modernism. On the other hand, the sketch of a building under construction by Cal A. Sacks, with its simple, Miesian massing, has little in common with any building by Kahn. The back cover, however, showcases the floor plan of the Mutual of New York Building (1966) by Kahn and Jacobs, erected in Syracuse, New York (fig. 9.21), for which Eugene Kohn was the project architect. Kahn fictionalized the building's location in a

9.21 Mutual of New York Building, Syracuse, New York, 1966, K&J

9.22 *Travelers Insurance Company Building, Boston, Massachusetts, 1960, K&J*

small city called Middleburg, New York, as well as the client, the Amalgamated Insurance Company.

In Kahn's story, John Brown of Amalgamated is placed in charge of the new building operations. His first task is to select an architect. To implement this task, Brown "went to Middleburg and spent several days examining other buildings of the general type that he thought his company wanted." Kahn's fictional client is most concerned that the architect he chooses will be able to complete the project. He visits the offices of the architects who interest him "so that he would have some idea of the size and general competence of their organizations." He quickly chooses a fictional architect named Trowbridge Barclay.[48] Brown tells Barclay that he wants a "fine building" of a quality "in keeping with the company's national reputation" and one which the "citizens of Middleburg could be proud of."[49] Barclay begins designing the building immediately, with an emphasis on building codes, costs, and the size of the rentable space. He selects steel for the flexibility it offers his client. Based upon Kahn's own way of doing business, Barclay selects the structural and mechanical engineers because he has worked with them previously, and he sidesteps the bidding process by selecting a contractor with whom he already has a good working relationship. Before beginning construction, the real estate agent approves the building's overall size, the layout of its offices, and suggests the specific "luxuries" that might be justified.

Kahn's Mr. Barclay evaluates his design of the building by using small-scale site models and a full-scale, two-story painted wood model of a single window module. A very important component of the design is the lobby, which Barclay decides to cover in marble because it is a "durable and attractive material."[50] The floor is a pink Tennessee marble that "harmonized with the white marble walls.[51] The ceiling is covered in a fireproof material made from weaving steel, copper, and aluminum into a new metal textile that filters light from above to produce an "unusual effect" on the marble walls.[52] Because "a person's introduction to a building" is important, the elevator cabs have teak laminate walls and stainless steel doors.[53] After these and other details of the design and construction are completed, Kahn concludes the story with a happy ending: "When the bank floors were completed, the Amalgamated Insurance Company building was finally finished. The officers of the insurance company were pleased. They had a building of their own and tenants of whom they could be proud. Mr. Barclay and Mr. McBride [the builders] were happy too, for as part of a team they had helped produce a beautiful building that would be a contribution to the welfare of the city. They had a working, successful building, and a satisfied client as well."[54]

This was the story of architecture Kahn wished to tell and the one he lived. For him, building was an economic proposition that enhanced not only the lives of the clients and the end users, but also the city as a whole. Pragmatism had formed the core of Kahn's practice, and was, he believed, the essential component in the process of building tall speculative office buildings in America. In his view and in his work, however, the aesthetic was inseparable from the pragmatic. The artistic treatment of surfaces, especially of facades, entrances, and lobbies to attract tenants, increases a building's value. To give visual pleasure had been from the beginning of his practice a standard, one that continued until he retired. Although a vocal exponent of pragmatism, Kahn produced richly sensuous buildings.

After Kahn retired in 1965 the specialization continued, and large projects included one of the firm's most dramatic buildings during this period, One Astor Place (1971), a fifty-five-story office and theater complex on Broadway, between 44th and 45th Streets, designed by project architect Der Scutt with Bezy, for builders Sam Minskoff & Sons and the Lehman Brothers (fig. 9.23). When Jacobs prepared to retire from the firm in 1972, the year of Kahn's death, the three young partners, Doughty, Kaplan, and Fox, offered to buy his share in the firm.[55] Jacobs rejected their offer and instead sold the firm to Hellmuth, Obata & Kassabaum (HOK), a St. Louis–based firm with offices in Washington, D.C., Dallas, San Francisco, Anchorage, Alaska, and Belleville, Indiana. The new firm, called Kahn and Jacobs/Hellmuth, Obata & Kassabaum agreed to retain Doughty, Kaplan, and Fox for five years, although each man subsequently pursued his own course. By 1977, the name Kahn and Jacobs was dropped.

9.23 *One Astor Place,
rendering, c. 1970, K&J*

CODA

On September 6, 1972, the *New York Times* published Ely Jacques Kahn's obituary. Included was an image of him smoking a pipe and another of the Bergdorf Goodman Building (1927) on Fifth Avenue between 57th and 58th Streets. The staff writer deemed Kahn "an exceptionally prolific representative of a period, although not an innovator," and described Kahn's buildings as "of modern classical design, which evolved from the Beaux Arts tradition" and were "notable for their clean lines and their basic simplicity."[1] While the article provided a concise assessment of some of Kahn's achievements and outlined the variety of his work with exhibition designs, publications, and public service, it did not adequately address the architect's legacy.

In the last decades of his life Kahn's early skyscrapers, which made his name in the 1920s, were out of favor with critics and largely neglected. The situation was changing when Robert Venturi's groundbreaking book *Complexity and Contradiction in Architecture* was published in 1966 and "post-modern" architecture began to appear.[2] Architectural historians reexamined and revised the prevailing devaluation of the architec-

tural decoration that distinguished the 1920s "art deco" skyscrapers by Kahn, buildings that did not conform to the canon of International Style modernism. By 1975, three years after his death, the seminal study *Skyscraper Style: Art Deco, New York*, by Cervin Robinson and Rosemarie Haag Bletter, reintroduced the work of Kahn and others.[3] Since then, the color, surface decoration, and massing characteristic of Kahn's oeuvre have been reconsidered as valid alternatives to International Style modernism. Two buildings in particular, the AT&T Building (1984) and the "Lipstick" Building (1986), both by Philip Johnson, were postmodern provocations to challenge the glass box—which Kahn never fully accepted—as the quintessential form of the New York skyscraper. In 1987, shortly after their completion, Robert A. M. Stern and his co-authors honored Kahn, Raymond Hood, and Ralph Walker in a separate chapter titled "Three Modern Masters" in their *New York 1930: Architecture and Urbanism Between the Two World Wars*.[4] Had Kahn lived another decade or so he would have relished the new publications that featured his pre–World War II setback buildings and revived interest in them and in his polychrome facades.

Kahn's legacy, like his practice, has multiple, interrelated components. He not only contributed to the fabric of the city over fifty buildings still extant. He forcefully expressed their times. The sensuous rhythms of the architectural decoration in Kahn's setback skyscrapers of the 1920s epitomized the energy of the Jazz Age, and his postwar buildings identified a burgeoning corporate culture. Moreover, these buildings functioned well and demonstrated his grasp of modern commercial requirements.

In his practice, Kahn influenced a younger generation of architects. He instilled in his youthful colleagues the importance of surface detail and the investigation of new materials. In regard to the business of architecture, he stressed the satisfaction of the client and the dependability of the architecture product. Several junior partners he and Robert Allen Jacobs mentored assumed leadership positions in the firm. One, Sheldon Fox, with Eugene Kohn (who was briefly in Kahn and Jacobs), and William Pedersen, formed a successor firm named Kohn Pedersen Fox Architects (KPF). Der Scutt is another architect who worked for Kahn and Jacobs early in his career and then became a prominent skyscraper architect on his own.

Kahn's ability to resolve the conflict between historicism and modernity, a conflict that was a hallmark of his generation of architects trained at the Ecole des Beaux Arts, was a personal legacy. For example, in 1971, Kahn wrote a letter to the editor of the New York Times expressing his disappointment in the Metropolitan Museum of Art's proposed fountains to face Fifth Avenue. Kahn believed that these fountains should embody the "vibrant evidence of history" that characterized such fountains in Florence and Rome. In keeping with the modern era he suggested for the commission the celebrated contemporary sculptor Isamu Noguchi, who, Kahn asserted would unite "imagination with the knowledge of material."[5] Kahn's respect for history and creativity, his openness to experiment, and his receptivity to new materials and technologies, defined his vast body of work. In many ways, these same qualities defined the dynamic production of commercial architecture in New York City during the twentieth century.

SELECTED BUILDINGS AND PROJECTS

Wherever possible, the building date indicates the year of completion recorded in the dockets of the New York City Department of Buildings.

1919

Cusack Building, 1122 Broadway

Lehn & Fink Building, 635 Greenwich Street

1920

Armion Building, 469 Seventh Avenue

Jay-Thorpe Building, 24 West 57th Street

1922

Borden Building, 350 Madison Avenue

Ludwig Baumann Building, 500 Eighth Avenue

1923

Montefiore Hospital of for Joint Diseases, 1901 Madison Avenue

Kahn and Feldman Silk Throwing Mill, 360 Suydam Street, Brooklyn

1924

Rubin Building, 501 Seventh Avenue

1925

Arsenal Building, 463 Seventh Avenue

Bomzon Building, 49--53 West 38th Street

Banco Building, 253--259 West 35th Street

550 Seventh Avenue

Scientific American Building, 24 West 40th Street

Furniture Exchange Building, 206 Lexington Avenue

Lefcourt Madison Building, 16--22 East 34th Street and 15–19 East 33rd Street

(with Blum & Blum) Street

Millinery Center, 1040 Sixth Avenue (formerly, 680 Sixth Avenue)

79 Madison Avenue

1926

15–19 West 39th Street

306–308 West 38th Street

424 Madison Avenue

1001 Sixth Avenue (101 West 37th Street)

247 West 35th Street

Lefcourt Empire Building, 989 Sixth Avenue (formerly, 625 Sixth Avenue)

Rutley's Restaurant, Broadway at 40th Street

Victor Riesenfeld apartment, 1050 Park Avenue

1927

Ed. Pinaud Factory, 214 East 21st Street

Insurance Center Building, 80 John Street

Court Square Building, 2 Lafayette Street

58–60 Broad Street

Park-Murray Building, 11 Park Place

271 Madison Avenue

Park Avenue Building, 2 Park Avenue

Bergdorf Goodman Building, 754 Fifth Avenue

Grand Central Terminal Building, 42 West 39th Street

1928

Lefcourt Clothing Center, 275 Seventh Avenue

United States Appraisers Building, 201 Varick Street

Federation Building, 71 West 47th Street

International Telephone and Telegraph Building, 67 Broad Street (formerly Lefcourt-Exchange)

Lefcourt State Building, 1375 Broadway

"Exposition of Modern French Decorative Art," Lord & Taylor

1929

261 Fifth Avenue

Allied Arts Building, 304 East 45th Street

Film Center Building, 630 Ninth Avenue

111 John Street

530 Seventh Avenue

Proposed 23-story building for Abraham Bricken, 66 Pine Street

Jay-Thorpe Building, 25–27 West 56th Street (separate building addition)

Gross Building, 330 Seventh Avenue (connected to 1923 Schwartz & Gross building)

Broadmoor Pharmacy and Restaurant, in Lefcourt Colonial Building, 40 East 41st Street

"The Architect and the Industrial Arts," (Backyard Garden; and Bath and Dressing Room), Metropolitan Museum of Art

Yardley & Company, 452 Fifth Avenue

Van Cleef & Arpels, jewelry store, 671 Fifth Avenue

Shelton Looms showrooms, 1 Park Avenue

Alfred I. Rose apartment, 1009 Park Avenue

Louis Tishman apartment, 888 Park Avenue

1930

Bricken Textile Building, 1441 Broadway

Holland Plaza Building, 431 Canal Street

Rolls Royce Building, 32 East 57th Street

Squibb Building, 745 Fifth Avenue

Bonwit Teller, 725 Fifth Avenue (renovation of Stewart & Company Building by Warren & Wetmore)

Proposed 65-story building at 80 Wall Street for Louis Adler

Charles J. Liebman apartment, 907 Fifth Avenue

Maurice S. Benjamin apartment, 211 Central Park West

1931

1400 Broadway

Bricken Casino Building, 1410 Broadway

Continental Building, 1450 Broadway

Commerce Building, 155 East 44th Street

136 East 57th Street

Richard Hudnut Building, 693 Fifth Avenue (demolished)

Paramount Publix Warehouse, 521 West 43rd Street

120 Wall Street

Léron, linen and lingerie shop, 745 Fifth Avenue

1933

Home Planning Building, Chicago Century of Progress Exposition

Johns-Manville Building, Chicago Century of Progress Exposition

Kohler Building, Chicago Century of Progress Exposition

Common Sense House, in "Forward House" exhibition, R. H. Macy's department store, New York

1934

"Contemporary American Industrial Art," (General Group, West Gallery Unit), Metropolitan Museum of Art

Yardley & Company Shop, British Empire Building, Rockefeller Center

1935

Yardley & Company showrooms

Linden House Apartments, West 230th Street and Spuyten Duyvil Parkway, Riverdale, New York (with Kenneth Franzheim)

1936

Hazel Kolman showroom, 509 Madison Avenue

Mme. T. Azeez Jewelry Shop, 380–96 Park Avenue

F. H. Greenevaum Jr. apartment, Upper East Side

1938

Longchamps Restaurants, (with Winold Reiss and Charles Schweizer), Empire

State Building, 350 Fifth Avenue and Paragon Building, 253 Broadway (with Winold Reiss and Charles Schweizer)

1939

Bonwit Teller department store expansion, 7 East 56th Street

Trailer Town (unrealized), The Bronx, New York,

White Owl Exhibit Building,. 1939 New York World's Fair

Ballantine Inn, (with Scott & Teegen), 1939 New York World's Fair

Marine Transportation Building, (with Muschenheim & Brounn), 1939 New York World's Fair

Pix Theater, 121 West 42nd Street

1940

"Contemporary American Industrial Art," (Metals and Glass Section), Metropolitan Museum of Art

1941

Bonwit Teller department store, 42 South Broadway, White Plains, New York

Municipal Asphalt Plant, 555 East 90th Street

1942

Fort Greene Houses, Myrtle Avenue, Brooklyn, New York (with William Hohauser and Ethan Allen Dennison)

Federal Public Housing, Mineville, New York

1943

Longchamps Restaurant, 1015 Madison Avenue

Federal Public Housing, Cedar Point and Jarboesville, Maryland

1944

Federal Public Housing, Rome, New York

1945

Thalhimer Brothers department store, Richmond, Virginia

1947

Universal Pictures Building, 445 Park Avenue

Office interiors for Monsanto Company, Lehn & Fink Company, Ford Motor Company, Universal Pictures Building

Crawford store, McAlpin Hotel, 1282 Broadway

Lane Bryant store, 461 Fifth Avenue

1948

R. J. Reynolds apartment, 1 Beekman Place

Trifari showrooms, Sixth Avenue and 30th Street

1949

855 Sixth Avenue, (with William J. Minogue)

Bloomingdales, Harding Boulevard and 188th Street, Fresh Meadows, Queens, New York

Gowanus Houses, Brooklyn (with Rosario Candela and William T. McCarthy)

1950

100 Park Avenue

Office interiors for Philip Morris, Gottesman & Company, Duplan Corporation, 100 Park Avenue

1407 Broadway

Office and showroom interiors for Burlington Mills, Pacific Mill, 1407 Broadway

Hudson Manor Apartments (Douglas Park), Riverdale, New York (with Rosario Candela and Paul Resnick)

1951

B. Altman department store, Westchester Avenue and Bloomingdale Road, White Plains, New York

1952

Charles Klingenstein Maternity Pavilion, Atran Laboratory, Berg Institute of Research, Central Kitchen, Central Sterile Supply, Mt. Sinai Hospital, Fifth Avenue and 98th Street

Hippodrome Building (five stories), 50 West 40th Street (later 1120 Sixth Avenue) (eight stories, 1957; twenty stories, 1961)

Mile High Center by I. M. Pei (Kahn and Jacobs, Associate Architects), 1700 Broadway, Denver, Colorado

1953

Remington Rand Building, 2601 Wilshire Boulevard, Los Angeles, California (with Welton Beckett and Associates)

1954

477 Madison Avenue

Saks Fifth Avenue, Bloomingdale Road and Greene Place, White Plains, New York

Prentice-Hall Publishing Plant, Englewood Cliffs, New Jersey

1955

Scandinavian Airlines Systems Office Building, 138-02 Jamaica, Queens, New York

80 Park Avenue, apartment house (with Paul Resnick)

1956

Carver Houses, Madison to Park Avenue, East 99th to East 104th Streets

1957

20 Broad Street

National Biscuit Company Building, 425 Park Avenue

Frederick Douglass Houses, Amsterdam and Manhattan Avenues, 100th to 104th Streets

Saks Fifth Avenue, Milburn, New Jersey (with Abbott, Merkt & Company)

1958

Seagram Building, 375 Park Avenue by Ludwig Mies van der Rohe and Philip Johnson (Kahn and Jacobs, Associate Architects)

Union Dime Bank Building, 111 West 40th Street (with Sydney Goldstone)

1959

Rochester State Hospital, Rochester, New York

Monmouth Shopping Center, Eatontown, New Jersey (with Abbott, Merkt & Company)

1960

High School of Industrial Art , 1075 Second Avenue; and PS 59, 228 East 57th Street (with William Lescaze)

American Airline Passenger Terminal, JFK International Airport, New York

Travelers Insurance Company, High and Pearl Streets, Boston, Massachusetts

Connecticut Light and Power Company Plant, Manresa Island, Norwalk, Connecticut

University Towers, apartment house, 100 York Street, New Haven, Connecticut

1961

First National City Bank Building, 399 Park Avenue (with Carson & Lundin)

700 Park Avenue, apartment house

1962

Sperry & Hutchinson Building, 330 Madison Avenue

1963

City Squire Motor Inn, 784 Seventh Avenue

1964

New York Telephone Company Switching Center, 811 Tenth Avenue (with Voorhees, Walker, Smith, Smith & Haines)

Lighthouse for the Blind, 111 East 59th Street

Greyhound Corporation pavilion, 1964 New York World's Fair

Rheingold pavilion, 1964 New York World's Fair

Travelers Insurance Company pavilion, (with Donald Deskey), 1964 New York World's Fair

African pavilion, 1964 New York World's Fair, by Tom John, Graham Associates (Kahn and Jacobs, architects of record)

Eastman Kodak pavilion, 1964 New York World's Fair, by Will Burtin, Inc. (Kahn and Jacobs, architects of record)

1965

Central Synagogue community house and religious school, 125 East 55th Street

NOTES

CHAPTER ONE

1. Kahn's birth date was registered May 31, 1884 on his birth certificate, but all other references cited June 1, 1884. Eli Kahn Birth Return #398563, June 1, 1884, Department of Records and Information Services, Municipal Archives, New York City. Kahn died on Sept. 5, 1972 in New York.

2. Lewis Mumford, *The Brown Decades; A Study of the Arts in America 1865–1895* (New York: Dover Publications, 1931).

3. All historical information on Kahn family in Hohenems from A. Tänzer, *Die Geschichte der Juden in Hohenems*, parts 1 and 2 of *Die Geschichte der Juden in Tirol und Vorarlberg* (Meran, Austria: F. W. Ellmenreich's Verlag, 1905); Josef Jank, "Hohenems" (Hohenems, Austria: Verkehrsverein der Stadt Hohenems, n.d.), courtesy of Otto Amann, Bürgermeister, Hohenems; Otto Amann, letter to Jewel Stern, Mar. 24, 1984; and Paul Reitzer, secretary, Israelite *Kultus-Gemeinde* Innsbruck, Austria, letter to Jewel Stern, Dec. 15, 1988.

4. Ely Jacques Kahn, Autobiographical Memorandum, Feb. 7, 1962, p. 1 of 2, Special Collections Research Center, Syracuse University Library.

5. Jacques Kahn Certificate of Death #48969, Aug. 17, 1918, New York State Department of Health. In a later source Jacques Kahn's arrival was dated 1868. It is doubtful that he left Austria at age 13. See *National Cyclopaedia of American Biography*, 1934 ed., s.v. "Ely Jacques Kahn."

6. Eugenie Maximilian and Jacques Kahn, Certificate of Marriage Registration #4277, July 16, 1879, Office of the City Clerk, City of New York.

7. Unless otherwise noted, all information on the Maximilian family from Adèle Maximilian, "All about Us." (New York: Unpublished Manuscript, 1977), courtesy of Adèle Maximilian.

8. For the French *tapissier* in the nineteenth century, see "The Reign of the Upholsterer," in Siegfried Giedion, *Mechanization Takes Command* (New York: Oxford University Press, 1948), 364–65.

9. Adèle Maximilian, interview by Jewel Stern, Aug. 1, 1983. See also, patent application, M. K. Maximilian, "Sofa Bed," Agency of the Scientific American Patent Office, Mar. 7, 1871. Maximilian died on June 7, 1871.

10. Ely Jacques Kahn manuscript, 1970, Ch. I of XI, p. 1, Avery.

11. Jean McDonald, interview by Jewel Stern, Merritt Island, Florida, Oct. 13, 1983. Jean McDonald, the daughter of Eugenie's niece, Rosalie Maximilian Campbell, was Kahn's second cousin.

12. Ferdinand Maximilian, U. S. Patent 477135, June 14, 1892, and U. S. Patent 1083119, Dec. 30, 1913.

13. H. E. Winlock, Director, Metropolitan Museum of Art, letter to Rosomax Campbell, Jan. 11, 1935; and W. M. Ivins, Jr., Acting Director, Metropolitan Museum of Art, letter to Rosomax Campbell, Dec. 7, 1939, courtesy of Jean McDonald.

14. Kahn memorandum, p. 1 of 2.

15. Ibid.

16. "Jacques Kahn, mirrors, 191 Worth, h. 221 East 60," *New York City Directory*, 1883–1884; and "Jacques Kahn, mirrors, 27 Bleecker," *New York City Directory*, 1889–1890. The architect of 27–31 Bleecker Street was Albert Buchman (probably a coincidence). See, NB 1477, July 27, 1887, *New Buildings Docket*, 1886–1887, Department of Buildings, City of New York, 250.

17. Jacques Kahn letterheads from the 1890s, courtesy of Adèle Maximilian; and "Jacques Kahn, mirror," listed at 533 West 37th Street from 1905 to 1927 in *New York City Directory*.

18. Ely Jacques Kahn, draft, "Autobiography," n.d., p. 1 of 13, Avery.

19. Kahn memorandum, p. 2 of 2.

20. Kahn manuscript, 1970, Ch. I of XI, p. 4, Avery.

21. Rena and Rudolf Rosenthal, Certificate of Marriage Registration #18233, Oct. 16, 1901, Office of the City Clerk, City of New York.

22. Kahn-Rosenthal wedding, Maximilian interview, Aug. 1, 1983.

23. Kahn started in Public School Number 18 on East 51st Street and transferred to Public School Number 6 at 85th Street and Madison Avenue. Kahn manuscript, 1970, Ch. I of XI, p. 4 Avery. For Dr. Sachs's School, see Ronald Steel, *Walter Lippmann and the American Century* (Boston: Little, Brown, 1980), 6.

24. Kahn draft, "Autobiography," p. 2 of 13, Avery.

25. Kahn memorandum, p. 1 of 2.

26. Kahn's record at Columbia College determined from Ely J. Kahn, Official Transcript #1184, 1899–1903, Columbia College, New York, courtesy of Columbia University.

27. Kahn memorandum, p. 2 of 2.

28. Kahn's extracurricular activities determined from "Ely Jacques Kahn," *Columbia Yearbook* (New York: Columbia, 1903), 282; and Paul R. Palmer, Curator of Columbiana Collection, letter to Jewel Stern, Oct. 25, 1983.

29. Ibid., *Columbia Yearbook*.

30. Ely Jacques Kahn, draft, Ch. II, n.d., p. 31 of 39, Avery.

31. Carl E. Schorske, *Fin-de-Siècle Vienna: Politics and Culture* (New York: Knopf, 1980), 148–49.

32. Phyllis Ellen Funke, "Luxembourg," *Hadassah Magazine* 70 (Nov. 1988): 326. Hirsch led Luxembourg's small Jewish community from 1843 to 1866.

33. Reitzer, letter to Stern, Dec. 15, 1988.

34. Kahn, Certificate of Marriage Registration #4277; Kahn, Birth Return #398563; and 221 East 60th Street, 1890 Census, Department of Records and Information Services, Municipal Archives, New York City; Rosenthal, Certificate of Marriage Registration #18233; Ely J. Kahn, Official Transcript #1184, Columbia College; and Ely Jacques Kahn, Official Transcript #89, 1903–1912, Columbia University School of Architecture.

35. No mention of religion has been found in Kahn's memoirs.

36. Kahn manuscript, 1970, Ch. I of XI, p. 5, Avery.

37. Ibid.

38. See Kahn, Official Transcript #89 and "Classbook 1903–1904," Columbiana Departmental Records, Architecture Roll Books 1889–1932, Rare Book and Manuscript Library, Columbia University, New York.

39. Kahn draft, Ch. II, p. 28 of 39, Avery. Kahn's transcript indicated that he received a high mark the following year in "Theory of professional practice—Professional relations, contracts, competitions, conduct of office," a one-hour course listed as "Architecture 55" in the *Catalogue and General Announcement 1905–1906*, Columbia University, 44.

40. "Report of the Committee on Education," *Proceedings* of the American Institute of Architects, Fortieth Annual Convention, 1907, 28, quoted in Arthur Clason Weatherhead, "The History of Collegiate Education in Architecture in the United States" (Ph.D. dissertation, Columbia University, 1941), 150.

41. "The Work of Messrs. Carrère & Hastings," *Architectural Record* 27 (Jan. 1910): 1, 3, 96–98.

42. "General Statement," *Year-Book of the Columbia University School of Architecture 1905–1906* (New York: The Architectural Society, 1906), 10.

43. "Messrs. Carrère & Hastings," *Architectural Record*, 36–37. See also, William H. Jordy, *American Buildings and Their Architects; Progressive and Academic Ideals at the Turn of the Twentieth Century* (Garden City, NY: Doubleday, 1972), 373–75.

44. Robert S. Peabody, "A Tribute," *Brickbuilder* 19 (Feb. 1910): 55.

45. For a full account, see Mardges Bacon, "The French School Comes to America," in *Ernest Flagg* (New York: Architectural History Foundation and Cambridge, Massachusetts: MIT Press, 1986), 49–74.

46. My thanks to Sara Vos, Columbia University Central Files, for direction to this source.

47. See, for example, Thomas Hastings, "Architecture and Modern Life," *Harpers New Monthly Magazine* 94 (Feb. 1897): 402–8.

48. "Classbook 1905–1906."

49. A. D. F. Hamlin, "Architectural Education in America," *Journal of the Royal Institute of British Architects* 17 (Dec. 18, 1909): 150.

50. Full texts of "How and Where to Begin a Design" and "Detail Ornament or Decoration," both undated and footnoted as "A lecture to architectural students," in David Gray, *Thomas Hastings, Architect; Collected Writings Together with a Memoir* (Boston: Houghton Mifflin, 1933).

51. A. D. F. Hamlin, "The Atelier System in Architectural Teaching," *Columbia University Quarterly* 11 (June 1909): 324.

52. Curtis Channing Blake, "The Architecture of Carrère and Hastings" (Ph.D. dissertation, Columbia University, 1976), 14; and Thomas Hastings, "Principles of Architectural Composition," in Gray, *Thomas Hastings*, 118–46 (footnoted: "read before the Chicago Institute of Art, Mar. 16, 1915," 118).

53. For André, Richard Chafee, "The Teaching of Architecture at the Ecole des Beaux-Arts," in Arthur Drexler, ed., *The Architecture of the Ecole des Beaux-Arts* (New York: Museum of Modern Art, 1977), 96.

54. Determined by Jewel Stern from class rolls in "Classbook 1905–1909."

55. Thomas Hastings, "High Buildings and Good Architecture," *American Architecture and Building News* 46 (Nov. 17, 1894): 68.

56. Ely Jacques Kahn, "On What Is Modern," in *Ely Jacques Kahn*, Contemporary American Architects Series (New York: Whittlesey House, 1931), 12–15 passim.

57. For Kahn's salute of Hastings in his memoirs see, Ely Jacques Kahn, draft, "Introduction," n.d., p. 3 of 7, Avery.

58. John Vredenburgh Van Pelt, *A Discussion of Composition Especially as Applied to Architecture* (New York: Macmillan Company, 1902), 36.

59. John Vredenburgh Van Pelt, letter to Henry H. Saylor, Mar. 2, 1946, American Institute of Architects, Washington, D.C.; and *American Architects Directory*, 1956 ed., s.v. "John Vredenburgh Van Pelt"; E. Delaire, *Les Architectes élèves de l'Ecole des Beaux-Arts 1793–1907* (Paris: *Librairie de la Construction Moderne*, 1907), "Van Pelt," 419.

60. Weatherhead, "The History of Collegiate Education," 35.

61. Van Pelt, *Discussion of Composition*, vi.

62. Colin Rowe, review of Talbot Hamlin, ed., *Forms and Functions of Twentieth Century Architecture in Art Bulletin* 35 (1953): 170. Guadet's principles enumerated in Paul Cret, "The Ecole des Beaux-Arts: What Its Architecture Really Means," *Architectural Record* 23 (April 1908): 371.

63. Determined from class rolls in "Classbook 1905–1909."

64. Alfred Dwight Foster Hamlin was appointed acting head of the school after Ware's removal. From about 1904 to 1911, Hamlin's title was executive head; in 1911 he became director. Austin W. Lord succeeded Hamlin in 1912.

65. A. D. F. Hamlin, *A Text-Book of the History of Architecture*, College Histories of Art Series, John C. Van Dyke, gen. ed. (New York: Longmans, Green, 1896).

66. Kahn draft, "Introduction," p. 1 of 7, Avery.

67. Ely Jacques Kahn, interview by Richard Chafee, tape recording, New York City, Sept. 24, 1971, typed transcript, 22–23. Special thanks to Richard Chafee for this valuable document. Class grades in Hamlin's Modern Ornament course in "Classbook 1905–1909."

68. A. D. F. Hamlin, "An Appreciation of Otto Wagner," *Architectural Record* 31 (May 1912): 485.

69. Peter S. Kaufman, "American Architectural Writing, Beaux-Arts Style: The Lives and Works of Alfred Dwight Foster Hamlin and Talbot Faulkner Hamlin" (Ph.D. dissertation, Cornell University, 1986), 45; and Irving K. Pond, "German Arts and Crafts at St. Louis," *Architectural Record* 17 (Feb. 1905): 119–25.

70. The thesis project was described in A. D. F. Hamlin, "General Statement," *Yearbook of the Columbia University School of Architecture 1906–1907* (New York: The Architectural Society, 1907), 10.

71. The two illustrations in the 1906–7 yearbook are the only surviving documents of Kahn's thesis. See also, Harvey A. Kantor, "The City Beautiful in New York," *New York Historical Society Bulletin* 57 (April 1973): 149–71.

72. "Wins a Trip to Rome," *New York Times*, June 14, 1905, p. 16; "McKim Fellowship, Columbia University," *Architecture* 12 (Aug. 15, 1905): 120–21; and Robert A.M. Stern, Gregory Gilmartin, and John Masssengale, *New York 1900: Metropolitan Architecture and Urbanism 1890-1915* (New York: Rizzoli, 1983), 156.

73. "The Morningside," in *Columbia Yearbook*, 1904, 63; and "The Columbia Jester," in *Columbia Yearbook*, 1907, 165.

74. *Year-book of the Columbia University School of Architecture 1905–1906*, 5.

75. Kahn, interview, Chafee, transcript, 20; and *Biographical Dictionary of American Architects (Deceased)*, 1956 ed., s.v. "William Schickel."

76. Schickel's home address, 52 East 83rd Street, in William

Schickel, Certificate of Death #19800, June 14, 1907, Municipal Archives, New York City.

77. H[arold] Van Buren Magonigle, "A Half Century of Architecture, 7," *Pencil Points* 15 (Nov. 1934): 564. Magonigle was head designer when Kahn worked in the firm.

78. *Catalogue and General Announcement 1904–1905, Columbia University*, 316; and "General Statement," *Year-book of the Columbia University School of Architecture 1905–1906*, 10–.

79. Kahn draft, "Autobiography," pp. 2–3 of 13; and Kahn manuscript, 1970, Ch. I of XI, pp. 5–6, both Avery.

80. Ely Jacques Kahn, "Backyard Garden," in "The Architect and the Industrial Arts," *American Magazine of Art* 20 (April 1929): 205.

CHAPTER TWO

1. Thomas Hastings, "The Influence of the Ecole des Beaux-Arts upon American Architecture," *Architectural Record*, The Beaux-Arts Number (Jan. 1901): 82.

2. Ely Jacques Kahn, draft, "The Paris of the Trilby days is far, far away," Sep. 9, 1942, p. 1 of 13, courtesy of Liselotte Kahn.

3. For matriculation of American students at the Ecole, see Bacon, *Ernest Flagg*, 32. The number of American students in the 1870s and 1880s calculated from the "Chronological List" in James Noffsinger, *The Influence of the Ecole des Beaux-Arts on the Architects of the United States* (Washington D. C.: Catholic University Press, 1955), 106; see also Chafee, "Teaching of Architecture" in *Architecture of the Ecole*, 104–6.

4. Montgomery Schuyler, "Schools of Architecture and the Paris School" (1898), in William H. Jordy and Ralph Coe, eds., *American Architecture and Other Writings by Montgomery Schuyler*, vol. 2 (Cambridge, Mass.: Belknap Press of Harvard University Press, 1961), 576.

5. Bacon, *Ernest Flagg*, 33.

6. Kahn manuscript, 1970, Ch. II of XI, p. 2; Address, 22 rue Jacob, on Ely Jacques Kahn, *Atelier Chifflot* Identification Card, Kahn scrapbook 1, Avery.

7. For 50 rue Jacob address, Henry White, L'Ambassadeur des Etats Unis, letter to Le Directeur de l'Ecole Nationale des Beaux Arts, June 3, 1907, Ely Jacques Kahn Dossier, AJ 52 425, National Archives, Paris. For autographs, Kahn interview, Chafee transcript, 17–18; and *Ely Jacques Kahn Sketchbook 1907–1908*, verso of "Chartres, North Porch," Avery.

8. Kahn draft, "Paris of the Trilby days," p. 5 of 13.

9. Henry White, letter to Ecole.

10. J[ulien] Guadet, "Concours d'Admission du Lundi 9 Décembre 1907," Section d'Architecture, Ecole Nationale des Beaux–Arts, courtesy of National Archives, Paris.

11. Unidentified and undated newspaper clipping in Kahn scrapbook 1, Avery. Date of Kahn's formal admission in Kahn, Dossier, "Feuille de Renseignements," National Archives, Paris.

12. C. S. Stein, letter to his parents, Jan. 6, 1908, Cornell CSP, Box 29. See also Anne Boyer Cotten, "Clarence

Stein, Architect First, Planner Second," (M.A. thesis, Cornell University, 1986). Although Stein's descriptive correspondence to his parents cannot stand in for Kahn's thoughts and reactions, it does provide a valuable and vivid sense of the activities and concerns of Kahn while at the Ecole.

13. C. S Stein, letters to his parents, Dec. 3, 1907 to June 16, 1911, Cornell CSP, Box 29.

14. Kahn manuscript, 1970, Ch. II of XI, p. 6, Avery; and Kahn interview, Chafee transcript, 3.

15. Description of atelier Redon from Kahn manuscript, 1970, Ch. II of XI, p. 5, Avery.

16. Kahn interview, Chafee transcript, 4.

17. Ibid.; 11; and Kahn manuscript, 1970, Ch. II of XI, p. 6, Avery.

18. Kahn draft, Ch. I, "11/22/66," p. 20 of 50.

19. Ely Jacques Kahn, "The Province of Decoration in Modern Design," *Creative Art* 5 (Dec. 1929): 886.

20. Ely Jacques Kahn, letter to James Philip Noffsinger, April 19, 1955, quoted in Noffsinger, *Influence of the Ecole,* 82.

21. Albert Laprade, *"Exposition des Oeuvres de Gaston Redon,"* catalogue of an exhibition organized by the Ancien Elèves of the Atelier Redon, November 14 to 30, 1957, Ecole Nationale Supérieure des Beaux-Arts, Paris, p. 3, courtesy of Liselotte Kahn.

22. Kahn manuscript, 1970, Ch. II of XI, p. 5, Avery.

23. Kahn interview, Chafee transcript, 6.

24. Delaire, *Les Architectes élèves,* "Hastings," 289–90; "Redon," 384; "Deglane," 232; and "Van Pelt," 419.

25. Verso of "Chartres," Kahn Sketchbook, Avery Library. The "O. K." was a takeoff on Shepard's middle initials, V. K.

26. William Edwar Groben Dossier, AJ 52 423, "Feuille de Renseignements," National Archives, Paris; C. S. Stein, letter to his parents, Sept. 20, 1907, Cornell CSP, Box 29; No dossier for William V. K. Shepard exists in the Ecole des Beaux-Arts Section of the Naitonal Archives, Paris. F. Giacomoni, Archives de France, letter to Jewel Stern, Feb. 29, 1984.

27. Description of 7 rue Corneille in Kahn manuscript, 1970, Ch. II of XI, p. 8.

28. C. S. Stein, letter to his parents, Nov. 20, 1908, Cornell CSP, Box 29. Stein's mention of the "Rochesterian" was the sole clue to the identity of Kahn's roommate. Walter Henry Cassebeer, the only student from Rochester, New York, to attend Columbia School of Architecture during these years, lived at 7 rue Corneille. See, Walter H. Cassebeer Dossier, AJ 52 417, National Archives, Paris.

29. Emily Cassebeer, Rochester, NY (daughter-in-law of Cassebeer), telephone conversation with Jewel Stern, May 29, 1984. No mention of Cassebeer has been found in Kahn's papers. "Lithographs of Rochester," 25/35, a portfolio in Kahn's library signed by Cassebeer and dated 1916, is the only evidence of a continuing friendship.

30. Kahn interview, Chafee transcript, 22; and Aline McMahon Stein, interview by Jewel Stern, New York City, April 29, 1983.

31. Kahn manuscript, 1970, Ch. II of XI, pp. 3–4, Avery.

32. Kahn draft. "Paris of the Trilby days," pp. 2–3 of 13.

33. Lee Simonson, *Part of a Lifetime* (New York: Duell, Sloan & Pearce, 1943), 22.

34. Simonson referred to himself as a *"habitué"* of the Stein salon in *Part of a Lifetime,* 14. Kahn did not name the friend who invited him to the Stein salon, but he noted that that friend knew of his interest in Leo Stein's writing. Kahn manuscript, 1970, Ch. II of XI, p. 15, Avery.

35. Ely Jacques Kahn, draft, Ecole des Beaux-Arts, p. 1 of 5, courtesy of Liselotte Kahn.

36. Ibid., pp. 1–2 of 5.

37. Kahn, interview, Chafee transcript, 23.

38. Peter Collins, *Concrete: The Vision of a New Architecture* (New York: Horizon Press, 1959), 188–89.

39. William J. R. Curtis, *Le Corbusier: Ideas and Forms* (Oxford, U.K.: Phaedon Press, 1986), 27–29.

40. Kahn interview, Chafee transcript, 5.

41. Annie Jacques, Le Conservateur de la Bibliothèque et des Collections de l'Ecole Nationale Supérieure des Beaux-Arts, letter to Jewel Stern, Jan. 18, 1988.

42. Laprade, *"Exposition des Oeuvres de Gaston Redon,"* p. 3.

43. Drawings in Kahn Sketchbook, Avery; see also, Kahn draft, "Paris of the Trilby days," p. 9 of 13.

44. Kahn sketches in leather album monogrammed "E. J. K." on cover, Cooper-Hewitt, National Design Museum, New York. See also, Kahn manuscript, 1970, Ch. XI of XI, p. 5, Avery.

45. Kahn manuscript, 1970, Ch. II of XI, p. 16, Avery.

46. Kahn draft, "Autobiography," p. 13 of 13, Avery; and Kahn manuscript, 1970, Ch. XI of XI, p. 7, Avery. Drawings from the trip are in Ely Jacques Kahn Sketchbook, [n.d.], courtesy of Rolf Myller (Liselotte Kahn's son), New York.

47. Kahn draft, Ch. II, p. 25 of 39, Avery.

48. Kahn draft, Ch. I, "11/22/66," p. 25 of 50.

49. Ely Jacques Kahn, "Sources of Inspiration," *Architecture* 60 (Nov. 1929): 252–53.

50. Kahn draft, Ch. I, "11/22/66," pp. 24–25 of 50.

51. Ibid.

52. C. S. Stein, letter to his parents, Nov. 20, 1908, Cornell CSP, Box 29.

53. Louis Vauxcelles, "Le Salon d'Automne de 1910," *L'Art Décoratif* 14 (Oct. 1910): 113–22.

54. Kahn draft, Ch. I, "11/22/66," p. 26 of 50.

55. Ibid., p. 23, 26 of 50.

56. Kahn manuscript, 1970, Ch. II of XI, p. 16, Avery.

57. Ibid., Ch. V of XI, p. 13.

58. Kahn draft, "Autobiography," p. 6 of 13, Avery; and Kahn interview, Chafee transcript, 20.

59. C. S. Stein, letter to his parents, Dec. 30, 1910, Cornell CSP, Box 29; Van Alen atelier in *Macmillan Encyclopedia of Architects,* s.v. "William Van Alen," by Steven McLeod Bedford. Kahn fraternized with *élèves* of other *patrons,* but it was taboo to visit other ateliers. Kahn interview, Chafee transcript, 4–5.

60. "Wins Beaux Arts Prize," *NYT,* Feb. 5, 1911, sec. II, p. 10; and "Concours Ed. Labarre," in *Ecole Nationale des Beaux-Arts: Les Concours d'Architecture de l'Année Scolaire 1910–1911,* 3–4, for Expert and Laprade.

61. Program in "Concours Ed. Labarre 1910–1911," 3. Kahn's Prix Labarre interpreted from the program,

Kahn's general plan, and description of latter in A. Gelbert, "Ecole des Beaux-Arts, Jugement du Concours Labarre," *La Construction Moderne* (Jan. 28, 1911), 207.

62. Gelbert. "Jugement du Concours Labarre," 207.

63. Francis Swales, "Notes from Europe," *American Architect* 99 (May 24, 1911): 1847. Kahn's general plan was illustrated.

64. "The Ellis Island Immigrant Station, Boring & Tilton, Architects," *Architects' and Builders' Magazine* 2 (July 1901): 345.

65. Kahn manuscript, 1970, Ch. II of XI, p. 7, Avery; Melle J. Gueris, Le Commissaire Général of the Société des Artistes Français, to Jewel Stern, Dec. 27, 1977; and "Les Recompenses du Salon," [n.d.], n.p. Kahn scrapbook 1, Avery.

66. Kahn interview, Chafee transcript, 8.

67. Kahn manuscript, 1970, Ch. XI of XI, p. 2, Avery.

68. C. S. Stein, letter to his parents, Mar. 17, 1911, Cornell CSP, Box 29; and Delaire, *Les Architectes élèves*, "Guidetti," 285.

69. Kahn manuscript, 1970, Ch. XI of XI, p. 1; and Kahn draft, "Autobiography," p. 10 of 13, both Avery.

70. Kahn interview, Chafee transcript, 21.

71. Kahn dossier, "Feuille de Valeurs," National Archives, Paris.

72. Kahn interview, Chafee transcript, 23.

73. Unless otherwise cited, all descriptions of Kahn and Stein's final six-week trip together is from C. S. Stein, letters to his parents, July 17, 1911 to Sept. 21, 1911, Cornell CSP, Box 29.

74. "The Exhibitions in Rome," *Nation* 92 (June 29, 1911): 655–56.

75. Eduard F. Sekler, *Josef Hoffmann: The Architectural Work* (Princeton, NJ: Princeton University Press, 1985), 140.

76. C. S. Stein, letter to his parents, Aug. 20, 1911, Cornell CSP, Box 29.

77. Stein and Cassebeer were on the "List or Manifest of Alien Passengers for the United States Immigration Officer at Port of Arrival," SS *Rochambeau* sailing from Le Havre Oct. 14, 1911, National Archives and Records Service, Washington, D. C., "Cassebeer," 1; "Stein," 3.

78. "Ely J. Kahn Returns with Diploma," *NYT*, Dec. 3, 1911, p. 15.

79. Stein, "Autobiographical Notebook," Cornell CSP, Box 1, Folder 1.

CHAPTER THREE

1. Kahn draft, "Introduction," pp. 2–3 of 7, Avery.

2. Kahn draft, "Autobiography," pp. 8–9 of 13, Avery.

3. Kahn and Lamb were enrolled in Advanced Design (A21.4) with Hastings in 1905–6, "Classbook 1905–1909." Both men passed the December 9, 1907 admission examination to the Ecole. Lamb chose the atelier Deglane. Their grades were almost equivalent, but Lamb entered and received a 3rd *médaille* in the Grand Prix de Rome competition, whereas Kahn competed for and won the Prix Labarre. William Frederick Lamb Dossier, AJ 52 426, National Archives, Paris. For Lamb's entry into Carrère & Hastings, William F. Lamb Membership Application, American Institute of Architects, Jan. 22, 1921, American Institute of Architects, Washington, D.C.; see also William Lamb in "Death List of a Day," *NYT*, Oct. 4, 1903, p. 7; and "William F. Lamb, 68, Architect, is Dead," *NYT*, Sept. 9, 1952, p. 31.

4. Simonson, a Jew, wrote of discrimination at Harvard in the January 1908 *Advocate*.

5. Carey McWilliams, *A Mask for Privilege: Anti-Semitism in America* (Boston: Little, Brown, 1948), 19. "Patrician intellectuals in the East" were one of three groups that harbored deep anti-Jewish feelings in late nineteenth-century America, according to John Higham in *Send These to Me: Immigrants in Urban America*, rev. ed. (Baltimore: Johns Hopkins University Press, 1984), 109.

6. Moses Rischin, *The Promised City: New York's Jews 1870–1914* (Cambridge, Mass.: Harvard University Press, 1962), 265.

7. Kahn draft, "Autobiography," p. 8 of 13, Avery.

8. *The New International Yearbook for the Year 1912*, s.v. "Architecture," by A. D. F. Hamlin.

9. *The New International Yearbook for the Year 1913*, s.v. "Architecture," by A. D. F. Hamlin.

10. Percentage computed by Jewel Stern from figures in *The New International Yearbook for the Years 1914 and 1915*, s.v. "Building Operations."

11. The only building photograph Kahn saved from these years was of the Alfred Library entrance elevation, which he identified as his first job in 1911. Photograph in Kahn scrapbook 1, Avery.

12. Kahn draft, "Introduction," pp. 3–4 of 7, Avery. *National Cyclopaedia of American Biography* 1934, s.v. "Ely Jacques Kahn"; and bound portfolio "Kahn and Jacobs New York City Architect-Engineers," December 1950, n.p., Robert Allan Jacobs Archive, Avery.

13. Kahn draft, "Introduction," p. 4 of 7, Avery. *Yearbook of the Society of Beaux-Arts Architects*, 1916, 38, for year of Kahn's membership election.

14. "Index of Exhibits," in the catalogues of the Architectural League of New York Annual Exhibitions, 1912–1914, n.p.

15. Henry H. Saylor, "Ely Jacques Kahn." *Architecture*, 64 (Aug. 1931): 65.

16. Horace J. Bridges, Stanton Coit, G. E. O'Dell, and Harry Snell, *The Ethical Movement; Its Principles and Aims*, Horace J. Bridges, ed. (London: The Union of Ethical Societies, 1912), 125–27. Families belonging to the New York Society for Ethical Culture who became Kahn's clients were Younker, Baumann, Oppenheim, Blumenthal, Karelson, and Leidesdorf.

17. Mrs. Robert (Margaret) Bookman, interview by Jewel Stern, New York City, May 17, 1983. Margaret Bookman, Kahn's sister-in-law, was the former wife of Robert Plaut, Elsie Plaut Kahn's brother. For Elsie Plaut Kahn, *Columbia University Alumni Register 1754–1931* (New York: Columbia University Press, 1932), 457.

18. Ely Jacques Kahn and Elsie Plaut, Certificate and Record of Marriage #11823, May 16, 1913, City of New York Department of Health; and "List or Manifest of Alien

Passengers for the United States Immigration Officer at Port of Arrival," SS *Imperator* sailing from Hamburg July 30, 1913, National Archives and Records Service, Washington, D.C., List 2.

19. Review by Jewel Stern of *New Buildings Dockets,* 1913–15; and "The Building Department," *NYT,* May 22, 1914, p. 22. The blueprint of the plan of the building, which was only 10 by 20 feet, is in Kahn scrapbook 1, Avery.

20. Clarence A. Martin, director, College of Architecture, Cornell University, letter to Ely Jacques Kahn, Sept. 15, 1914, Kahn scrapbook 1, Avery; and signature illegible, secretary of the Board of Trustees, Cornell University, letter to Ely Jacques Kahn, Nov. 10, 1914, Kahn scrapbook 1, Avery. Kahn was not contractually required to be in Ithaca on weekends.

21. Cram to Kahn, Sept. 25, 1914.

22. For challenge, Ely Jacques Kahn, Ithaca, New York, letter to Clarence S. Stein, n.d., Cornell CSP. For student tribute, Kahn scrapbook 1, Avery.

23. "I fear that my 'persistence' in this matter may tend to annoy you, but our need of you is so great and our desire so sincere that I trust you will let them counteract any possible annoyance." Clarence A. Martin, letter to Ely Jacques Kahn, Aug. 20, 1915, Kahn scrapbook 1, Avery. See also, Kahn Manuscript, 1970, Ch. II of XI, p. 2, Avery.

24. Hamlin, "Twenty-five Years of American Architecture," *Architectural Record,* 40 (July 1916): 2. For economic conditions, see also, Frederick Lewis Allen, *The Lords of Creation: The Story of the Great Age of American Finance* (London: Hamish Hamilton Ltd., 1935), 195–96.

25. Kahn was listed at 381 Fourth Avenue in the 1915–16 *New York City Directory.* In the 1916–17 and 1917–18 editions, Kahn was listed at 373 Fourth Avenue.

26. The name of the Plaut estate, Knolltop, location of Kahn cottage, and information on Younker family from Bookman interview. Kahn referred to the Plaut remodeling in Kahn draft, "Introduction," p. 4 of 7, Avery. The Kahn cottage, dated 1918, and Herman Younker house, dated 1919, illustrated in *Ely Jacques Kahn,* (Whittlesey), 30, 32; and in H. I. Brock, "When the Architect Builds His Own Home," *NYT,* Aug. 2, 1931, sec. V, p. 12. The Herman Younker house was featured in plan and elevation in "A Group of Three Houses Near New York," *House & Garden* 39 (Feb. 1921): 40. There are no Elmsford plans in Avery Library.

27. Fox left architecture to join his father's bank. See "M. J. Fox in Columbia Bank," *NYT,* Oct. 14, 1917, sec. IX, p. 2. For the role of Kahn's father-in-law, see Kahn manuscript, 1970, Ch. III of XI, p. 2; Kahn draft, "Autobiography," p. 9 of 13; and Kahn draft Ch. II, p. 26 of 39, Avery. Also Robert Allan Jacobs, telephone conversation with Jewel Stern, April 20, 1984.

28. Review by Jewel Stern of Buchman & Fox entries in *New Buildings Dockets,* 1912–18.

29. Kahn draft, "Autobiography," p. 9 of 13, Avery.

30. Ely Jacques Kahn, "American Office Practice," *Journal of the Royal Institute of British Architects,* 64 (Sept. 1957): 443.

31. Jacobs, telephone conversation, April 20, 1984. Jacobs (Kahn and Jacobs) remembered hearing that a 30 percent interest in the firm was bought for Kahn. No record of the 1917 agreement with Buchman survives.

32. The history of the firm has never been accurately documented. Incorrect, confused, and often contradictory information has been reported in Kahn's memoirs and these Kahn and Jacobs brochures: "Kahn and Jacobs," typed resume, 1941–42; "Kahn and Jacobs Architects," catalogue, 1959; and "Kahn and Jacobs Architects," catalogue, 1967, courtesy of Liselotte Kahn. See also, Kahn draft, "Autobiography," p. 9 of 13. Other errors were published in Saylor, "Ely Jacques Kahn," 66.

33. The best biographical source for Schwarzmann is John Maass, *The Glorious Enterprise, The Centennial Exhibition of 1876 and H. J. Schwarzmann, Architect-in-Chief* (Watkins Glen, New York: American Life Foundation, 1973). For Tribune Building, Hermann J. Schwarzmann, architect, in *New York City Directory,* 1880–1889, and Dennis S. Francis, *Architects in Practice, New York City, 1840–1900,* p. 68. For Schwarzmann clientele, review by Jewel Stern of *New Buildings Dockets,* 1881–1887; and Maass, *The Glorious Enterprise,* p. 135. The Liederkranz Clubhouse, 111–19 East 58th Street, has been demolished.

34. Non-Jews have been partners: John Miller Montfort in Buchman & Kahn and The Firm of Ely Jacques Kahn, and Lloyd Doughty and Pierre A. Bezy in Kahn and Jacobs.

35. Buchman biography compiled from these sources: Albert Buchman, Certificate of Death #9764, April 16, 1936, City of New York Department of Health; "Deaths, Albert Buchman," *American Architect* 148 (June 1936): 132; "Albert Buchman, Architect, 76, Dies," *NYT,* April 17, 1936, p. 21; "Prominent Architects of the Day, Buchman & Deisler," in *A History of Real Estate, Building and Architecture in New York City* (New York: Real Estate Record Association, 1898; reprint ed., New York, Arno Press, 1967), 697; and Maryalice Cleary, Assistant Registrar, Cornell University, to Jewel Stern, Nov. 7, 1983. Volume of work determined from *New Buildings Dockets,* 1883–84, 1884–85, and 1885–86.

36. For Deisler, Paul Deisler, Houston, Texas, telephone conversation with Jewel Stern, Oct. 2, 1983; and Gustav Francis Deisler, Certificate of Death #7501, Mar. 21, 1927, City of New York Department of Health. See also, "Buchman & Deisler," in *A History of Real Estate,* 697.

37. "Buchman & Deisler," in *A History of Real Estate,* 697.

38. "Leaders in the Building Trade, Jeremiah C. Lyons," *A History of Real Estate,* 311; and review by Jewel Stern of *New Buildings Dockets,* 1895–1900.

39. Bloomingdale's addition, NB 955, July 5, 1893, *New Buildings Docket,* 1892–93, 226. Four Buchman & Deisler buildings on Broadway, numbers 491–93, 580–90, 594–96, and 714, are extant. Others include a six-story building, northeast corner of Waverly Place and Green Street; the northeast and northwest corners of Prince and Wooster Streets; and an apartment house at 100 West 80th Street.

40. Moses King, *Notable New Yorkers 1896–1899* (New York: Orr Press, 1899), 395. Special thanks to John Maass for

bringing this to my attention; John Maass, letter to Jewel Stern, Sept. 8, 1983. Deisler was listed as a "contractor" in the *New York City Telephone Directory Manhattan White Pages* until his death in 1927.

41. Fox's years with Buchman were dated 1895–1917 in *Who's Who in New York (City and State)*, 8th ed., 1924, s.v. "Mortimer J. Fox."

42. "Fox-Morgenthau Wedding," *NYT*, April 8, 1906, p. 9.

43. *Some Recent Work of Buchman & Fox* (New York: Architectural Catalog Company, L. Lawrence Stern, Publishers, c. 1914), courtesy of Mortimer J. Fox, Jr.; and review by Jewel Stern of *New Buildings Dockets*, 1899–1917.

44. Thomas C. Cochran, "The City's Business," in Allan Nevins and John A. Krout, eds., *The Greater City: New York, 1889–1948* eds. (New York: Columbia University Press, 1948): 148–49.

45. "$250,000. The Cost of a Convenient Road Home," *New York Sun*, Aug. 10, 1913, p. 1, courtesy of Mortimer J. Fox, Jr.

46. "Architects and Hotel Men,"in *Empire State Notables 1914* (New York: Hartwell Stafford, 1914), 556.

47. Buchman & Fox, 30 East 42nd Street, *New York City Directory*, 1917–18; "Buchman & Kahn (Albert Buchman, Ely J. Kahn) architects," 56 West 45th Street, *New York City Directory*, 1918–19.

48. Jacques Kahn, Certificate of Death #48969, Aug. 17, 1918, New York State Department of Health. Kahn's inheritance, if any, is not of record because his father left no will. Petition for Letters of Administration on the Goods, Chattels and Credits of Jacques Kahn, Deceased, to the Surrogates' Court, County of New York, Sept. 19, 1918. Kahn watercolor at Dordrecht in collection of Cooper-Hewitt, National Design Museum.

49. In the 1920–21 *New York City Directory* under Jacques Kahn, Inc., 533 West 37th Street, Eugenie Kahn is listed president, Louis Kahn, vice-president, and Ferdinand Kahn Maximilian, secretary. Two letters from Rudolf Rosenthal to his nephew, Jean M. Heyman, dated Feb. 18, 1921 and Sept. 15, 1921, document Rudolf's role in the business. Letters, courtesy of Jean M. Heyman, Brussels. For sale of the business, Maximilian interview, Sept. 22, 1983.

50. Three Lehn & Fink commissions in "Kahn and Jacobs," typed resume, c. 1941, n.p., courtesy of Liselotte Kahn.

51. Kahn draft, "Autobiography," p. 10 of 13, Avery.

52. NB 337, Nov. 29, 1919, *New Buildings Docket*, 1919, n.p; and "5th Av. Building Medals," *NYT*, Nov. 11, 1920, p. 25.

53. Ely Jacques Kahn, "Essential Details in Store Designing," *Architectural Forum* 40 (June 1924): pl. 81.

54. Ibid., 245–48 for all quotes.

55. "Mill Building of Kahn & Feldman, Brooklyn," *Architectural Forum* 39 (Sept. 23): 90, pl. 52. The client seems to be unrelated to Kahn. The Kahn and Feldman factory, 360 Suydam Avenue, building permit application E.S.6780, May 24, 1921, courtesy of Building Department, Brooklyn, New York.

56. Sheldon Cheney, *The New World Architecture* (New York: Tudor Publishing Company, 1930), 295. The book fea-

tured eleven images of Kahn's work, attributed solely to him, not to Buchman & Kahn. From the captions accompanying these images and his comments in the text, Cheney's admiration of Kahn's body of work is apparent.

57. "Mill Building, Brooklyn," *Architectural Forum*, pl. 52; and Eugene Clute, *The Practical Requirements of Modern Buildings* (New York: Pencil Points Press, 1928), 170.

58. Lewis Mumford, "Our Modern Style," *Journal of the American Institute of Architects* 12 (Jan. 1924): 26.

59. Talbot F. Hamlin, *The American Spirit in Architecture, The Pageant of America Series*, Ralph Gabriel, ed., vol. 13 (New Haven, Conn.: Yale University Press, 1926), 197.

60. Ely Jacques Kahn, "Our Skyscrapers Take Simple Forms," *NYT*, May 2, 1926, sec. IV, pp. 11, 22.

61. Mel Scott, *American City Planning Since 1890* (Berkeley and Los Angeles: University of California Press, 1969), 156.

62. "Map of Borough of Manhattan Showing Use, Height and Area Districts," in George B. Ford, *New York City Building Zone Resolution* (New York: New York Title and Mortgage Company, 1917), n.p.

63. Colonel William A. Starrett, *Skyscrapers and the Men Who Build Them* (New York: Charles Scribner's Sons, 1928), 102.

64. Kahn addressed this issue in detail in his articles "The Office Building Problem in New York," *Architectural Forum* 41 (Sept. 1924): 94–96; and "Economics of the Skyscraper," *Architectural Record* 63 (April 1928): 298–301. See also, Carol Willis, *Form Follows Finance* (New York: Princeton Architectural Press, 1995): 67–88.

65. Alfred C. Bossom, "America's National Architecture," *American Architect* 128 (July 29, 1925): 78.

66. Alfred C. Bossom, "Fifty Years' Progress Toward an American Style in Architecture," *American Architect* 129 (Jan. 5, 1926): 49.

67. Francisco Mujica, *History of the Skyscraper* (Paris: Archaeology & Architecture Press, 1929): 19, 35, 67.

68. Ely Jacques Kahn, "What Is Modern Architecture?" *Architecture* 59 (Jan. 1929): 1.

69. See, for example, Donald Harris Dwyer, "Modernistic Architecture, America's Contribution to Art Deco," in "Art Deco and Its Origins," exh. cat., Heckscher Museum, Huntington, New York, 1974, 17; and Elayne H. Varian, "American Art Deco Architecture," exh. cat., Finch College Museum of Art, New York, 1974–1975, n.p.

70. Rosemary Haag Bletter, "The Art Deco Style" in Cervin Robinson and Rosemarie Haag Bletter, *Skyscraper Style: Art Deco, New York* (New York: Oxford University Press, 1975): 80 (n. 86).

71. "Borden Company Plans $4,000,000 Office Building in Grand Central Terminal Zone," *NYT*, June 27, 1920, sec. VIII, p. 8; see also, Borden Building, NB 211, June 11, 1920, *New Buildings Docket*, 1920, n.p.; and *New International Yearbook for the Year 1921*, s.v. "Architecture," by C. Matlack Price. The Borden Company would occupy ten floors of the rental office building.

72. For the Aronson Building and other office buildings, see John Taylor Boyd Jr., "The New York Zoning Resolution

and Its Influence upon Design," *Architectural Record* 48 (Sept. 1920): 193–217; and Aymar Embury II, "New York's New Architecture; The Effect of the Zoning Law on High Buildings," *Architectural Forum* 35 (Oct. 1921): 119–24.

73. "Lease May Cause Delay," NYT, Jan. 16, 1921, sec. VIII, p. 1. The thirty-foot site on 45th Street was later acquired and the court filled in to the fifth floor, consistent with the Buchman & Kahn design. For the Borden Building construction saga, see Andrew Alpern and Seymour Durst, *Holdouts!* with a Foreword by John V. Lindsay (New York: Mc Graw-Hill, 1984), 54–62.

74. Harvey Wiley Corbett, "The Influence of Zoning on New York's Skyline," *American Architect* 123 (Jan. 3, 1923): 2.

75. "Tapestry" was the trademark of the Fiske Company, a Boston and New York manufacturer of the variegated face and fire brick popular in the 1920s.

76. Kenneth Frampton and Yukio Futagawa, *Modern Architecture 1920–1945* (New York: Rizzoli, 1983), 211, 213.

77. Ely Jacques Kahn, manuscript, fragment "II," [n.d.], n.p., courtesy of Liselotte Kahn. Membership lists were published in the annual *Yearbook of the Architectural League of New York*. In the 1920 edition, Kahn's election year was erroneously reported as 1919.

78. Walter H. Kilham, *Raymond Hood, Architect* (New York: Architectural Book Publishing Company, 1973), 81, 79. See also Allene Talmey, "Profiles: Man against the Sky," *The New Yorker* 7 (April 11, 1931): 24.

79. *Yearbook of the Architectural League of New York Thirty-sixth Annual Exhibition*, 1921, n.p.

80. The four studies were illustrated in the league's 1922 yearbook and explained by Ferriss in "The New Architecture," *NYT*, Mar. 19, 1922, sec. II, p. 7.

81. Only three renderings for Buchman & Kahn were entered in Hugh Ferriss's Job Book 1922–62, Hugh Ferriss Papers, Avery Library, Columbia University, New York: (1) 1924, Office Building [Scientific American Building]; (2) 1925, Office Building 28th and Madison [79 Madison Avenue Building]; and (3) 1925, Office Building near Municipal Building [Court Square Building]. See Schell Lewis and Francis Keally renderings, Museum of the City of New York; and J. Floyd Yewell renderings, Cooper-Hewitt, National Design Museum, New York.

82. Nancy Hadley, American Institute of Architects, electronic communication to John A. Stuart, June 28, 2004.

CHAPTER FOUR

1. James C. Young, "Titanic Forces Rear a New Sky Line," *NYT*, Nov. 15, 1925, sec. 4, pp. 6, 19.

2. *NYT*, Jan. 30, 1916, sec. I, p. 16; J. H. Burton, "Effect of the 'Save New York' Movement," *Real Estate Record and Builder's Guide* 99 (Feb. 3, 1917): 22–23, 25; "'Save New York Committee' Plans New Factory Centre for Needle Trades," *NYT*, Mar. 24, 1918, sec. III, p. 14. See also chapter "New York Saved" in Seymour I. Toll, *Zoned American* (New York: Grossman, 1969).

3. Willford I. King, "The Building Outlook for 1925," *Architectural Record* 57 (Jan. 1925): 89. Determined by Stern from Chart 1: "The Volume of Construction of Residential and Business Buildings and the Course of Interest Rates, 1915–1924."

4. Unless otherwise noted, all data in this paragraph are from the New Year's issue of the *New York Times* Sunday Real Estate Section or the first January issue of *The Real Estate Record and Builder's Guide*. The January issues of *Architectural Record* and *Architectural Forum* are another source.

5. Shultz and Simmons, *Offices in the Sky*, 162–63.

6. S. W. Straus, in Alan Rabinowitz, *The Real Estate Gamble; Lessons from 50 Years of Boom and Bust* (New York: AMACOM, 1980): 42.

7. C. H. Blackall, "American Architecture Since the War," *American Architect* 138 (Jan. 5, 1928): 2–3.

8. Ely Jacques Kahn, "Our Skyscrapers Take Simple Forms," *NYT*, May 2, 1926, pp. 11, 22.

9. "Big Building For Garment Centre," *NYT*, Sept. 1, 1922, p. 1.

10. Documentation of Gregory's relationship to the firm is uneven. He was employed at times between 1918 and 1930. From 1926 to 1930 he was compensated for commissions brought into the office. See "Memo for Mr. Gregory," May 28, 1926; and "Agreement of Jan. 1, 1928," Buchman & Kahn Account Book, 1928–1929, Avery. Kahn never mentioned Gregory in his writings.

11. For a Buchman & Kahn plot solution diagram and for examples of the firm's lot analyses, see James B. Newman, "Factors in Office Building Planning," *Architectural Forum* 52 (June 1930): 881–82, 884–86.

12. Ely Jacques Kahn, "The Office Building Problem in New York," *Architectural Forum* 41 (Sept. 1924): 95.

13. Ely Jacques Kahn, "The Architecture of Industrial Buildings," *Architectural Forum* 51 (Sept. 1929): 276.

14. Determined by Stern from review of floor plans.

15. Frances Borsi and Ezio Godolit, *Vienna 1900; Architecture and Design* (New York: Rizzoli, 1986): 171, 216–17.

16. *New International Yearbook for the Year 1924*, s.v. "Architecture," by Talbot F. Hamlin.

17. Leon V. Solon, "The Viennese Method for Artistic Display; New York Galleries of the Wiener Werkstätte of America," *Architectural Record* 53 (Mar. 1923): 266–71.

18. H. Van Buren Magonigle, quoted from his speech "Plagiarism as a Fine Art," in *Journal of Proceedings of the 57th Annual Convention of the American Institute of Architects* (Washington D. C.: American Institute of Architects, 1924), 69: See also "Bowery Savings Bank, New York City," *Architecture and Building* 55 (Aug. 1923): 81–82.

19. "Sale of Old State Arsenal Creates Interest in Adjacent Values," *Real Estate Record and Builder's Guide* 112 (July 28, 1923): 103

20. NB 562, Nov. 9, 1923, *New Buildings Docket*, 1923, n.p. See also, "Increased Values in Garment Centre," *NYT*, July 22, 1923, sec. VIII, p. 1.

21. "The Arsenal Building, New York City," *Architecture and Building* 57 (April 1925): 32.

22. William F. Lamb, "Office Building Vestibules," *Architectural Forum* 41 (Sept. 1924): 105.

23. C. H. Blackall, "American Architecture Since the War," *American Architect* 133 (Jan. 5, 1928): 2.

24. Kahn, "Our Skyscrapers Take Simple Forms," 11. For the Shelton's impact on professionals, see Robert A.M. Stern, Gregory Gilmartin, Thomas Mellins, *New York 1930: Architecture and Urbanism Between the Two World Wars* (New York: Rizzoli, 1984), 208–12.

25. Fiske Kimball, "What Is Modern Architecture?" *Nation* 119 (July 1924): 129. See also, Fiske Kimball, "Three Centuries of American Architecture," *Architectural Record* 57 (June 1925): 562.

26. H. I. Brock, "From Flat Roofs To Towers and Slats; The Architectural League Has Seen a Revolution in Its Fifty Years," *NYT*, April 27, 1931, sec. V, p. 7.

27. Kahn, "Office Building Problem," 96.

28. *New International Yearbook for the Year 1923*, s.v. "Architecture," by C. Matlack Price.

29. "Arsenal Building, Seventh Avenue, New York," *American Architect* 129 (June 5, 1926): pls. 129–32; and Parker Morse Hooper, "Office Buildings of Today and Tomorrow," *Architectural Forum* 48 (Jan. 1928): 5.

30. "Romance in Lives of City Builders," *NYT*, Feb. 24, 1929, sec. XII, p. 3; and Charles F. Noyes, "Cites Garment Men in City's Realty Growth," *Women's Wear Daily*, Oct. 11, 1929, sec. 4, p. 20.

31. W. Parker Chase, *New York: The Wonder City* (New York: Wonder City Publishing Company, 1932): 110.

32. Kahn draft, Ch. II, p. 7 of 39.

33. Chase, *The Wonder City*, 110–11.

34. For Adler biography, Robert Liberman (Louis Adler's grandson), interview by Jewel Stern, New York City, Nov. 30, 1990; Joseph K. Foster, "Louis Adler Proves Again That—Success Is Theirs Who Do and Dare," *Jewish Tribune*, [n.d.], pp. 14, 29, clipping, c. 1930, in Louis Adler Scrapbook, courtesy of Robert Liberman, The Muss-Tankoos Corporation; and "Romance in the Lives," *NYT*.

35. "Trade Takes Site of Gothic Chapel," *NYT*, Jan. 20, 1924, sec. 9, p. 1.

36. Kahn draft, Ch. II, pp. 8–9 of 39.

37. "44-Story Building to Rise in 5th Av.," *NYT*, June 22, 1928, p. 41; "Romance in Lives," *NYT*; "Adelson's 58th St. Projects Financed for $8,000,000," *NYT*, May 25, 1929, p. 35; Noyes, "Cites Garment Men," and "Abe Adelson Buys Broadway Building," *NYT*, Oct. 16, 1929, p. 56.

38. Kahn draft, Ch. II, p. 16 of 39.

39. "Trade Takes Site," *NYT*.

40. "Romance in Lives," *NYT*.

41. "$3,500,000 Millinery Center Project for Sixth Avenue," *Real Estate Record and Builder's Guide*, 115 (April 25, 1925): 9.

42. Kahn, "Our Skyscrapers Take Simple Forms," 11.

43. Newman, "Office Building Planning," 881.

44. Corbett, "The Influence of Zoning on New York's Skyline," *American Architect*, 58 (Jan. 3, 1923): 1. Corbett claimed to have introduced shadow brick on sidewalls in Helmle & Corbett's Bush Terminal Building (1918), 130 West 42nd Street.

45. Erich Mendelsohn, *Amerika* (Berlin: Rudolf Mosse Buchverlag, 1928), 76, 193.

46. Cheney, *New World Architecture*, 141. Cheney also illustrated the upper stories of the loft building on Sixth Avenue and 37th Street and noted its uncommon "box forms." Ibid., 143.

47. For de Bazel, J. P. Mieras, and F. R. Yerbury, *Hollandische Architektur des 20. Jahrhunderts* (Berlin: Verlag Ernst Wasmuth, 1926), viii, ix. The elevations were completed by 1925. A vintage copy of the book was in Kahn's library at the time of his death.

48. Kahn manuscript, 1970, Ch. XI of XI, pp. 7–8.

49. Detail photograph of 550 Seventh Avenue frieze by Keck in "The Zoning Laws in New York and the Development of a New Commercial Center," *American Architect* 128 (Aug. 26, 1925): 189.

50. Description of original Millinery Center vestibule and entrance and photograph of elevator hall in "Building at 39th Street and Sixth Avenue," *Architecture and Building* 58 (Feb. 1926): 18. Photographs of the original building entrance and vestibule have not been found.

51. Lewis Mumford, "American Architecture To-day," Part III, *Architecture* 58 (Oct. 1928): 191.

52. Kahn draft, Ch. II, p. 8 of 39; and "Gaston Lachaise," exh. cat. Los Angeles County Museum of Art, 1963–1964, n.p.

53. Millinery Center doors illustrated in "Metals and Methods," Part II, *Metal Arts* 2 (Jan. 1929): 19–21.

54. Walter L. Creese, letter to Ely Jacques Kahn, Nov. 2, 1949, courtesy of Walter L. Creese.

55. Ely Jacques Kahn, letter to Walter L. Creese, Nov. 9, 1949, courtesy of Walter L. Creese.

56. Compiled and analyzed by Jewel Stern from *New Buildings Dockets 1917–1926*.

57. Maximilian Zipkes (dates unknown), a practicing architect, headed Natanson's "Managing Department" and was associated with Buchman & Kahn on the Furniture Exchange.

58. "Work Begun on $3,500,000 Project in New Silk Center," *Real Estate Record and Builder's Guide*, 116 (July 4, 1925): 7.

59. Kahn draft, Ch. II, pp. 27–28 of 39.

CHAPTER FIVE

1. Charles R. Richards, Henry Creange, and Frank Graham Homes, *Report of Commission Appointed by the Secretary of Commerce to Visit and Report upon the International Exposition of Modern Decorative and Industrial Art in Paris 1925*, (Washington, D.C.: U.S. Government Printing Office, 1926), pp. 17, 16, 6–10.

2. Notations "Europe Modern Exposition Dec. Arts," Sept. 5, 1925 and "back from Europe," Ely J. Kahn diary, Oct. 5, 1925, courtesy of Liselotte Kahn.

3. Kahn draft, Chapter II, pp. 31–32 of 39, Avery. Actually, Germany was not represented. Kahn was probably referring to German architect Peter Behrens's glass structure, which was attached to the Austrian pavilion. See also, Kahn draft, "Autobiography," p. 11 of 13, Avery.

4. Helen Appleton Read, "International Exposition of Decorative Arts in Paris Has Practical Background for

Display of the Bizarre and Exotic Atmosphere of Luxury," *Brooklyn Daily Eagle*, Aug. 23, 1925, Archives of American Art, Helen Appleton Reed Papers [hereafter AAA, Read Papers], reel N736, frame 113.

5. Helen Appleton Read, "New Architecture at the International Exposition of Decorative Arts in Paris Illustrating the Use of Reinforced Concrete; Strange Geometric Shapes," *Brooklyn Daily Eagle*, Aug. 16, 1925, [AAA, Read Papers], reel N736, frame 112.

6. Alfred C. Bossom, "The Rebirth of Art and Architecture in Europe: A Review of the International Exposition at Paris," *American Architect* 128 (Aug. 26, 1925): 161–66; and "Exhibits from Paris to be Shown Here," *NYT*, Jan. 2, 1926, p. 4.

7. W. Francklyn Paris, "The International Exposition of Modern Industrial and Decorative Art in Paris," Part II. General Features, *Architectural Record* 58 (Oct. 1925): 379, 384.

8. "Mr. Murchison Says—," *Architect* 5 (Nov. 1925): 207. Murchison wrote this spicy column from July 1924 to November 1929.

9. "Exhibits from Paris to Be Shown Here," *NYT*, Jan. 3, 1926, sec. 10, p. 4; and *Yearbook of the Forty-first Annual Exhibition of the Architectural League of New York*, 1926, n.p.

10. "Changing Styles in Architecture," *NYT*, Feb. 21, 1926, sec. 10, p. 2.

11. Ely Jacques Kahn, "The Architectural League Exhibition of 1926," *Architectural Record* 59 (Mar. 1926): 226–27.

12. Kahn diary, Dec. 21, 1926.

13. Donald Deskey, Vero Beach, Florida, telephone conversation with Jewel Stern, May 30, 1983.

14. Helen Appleton Read, "Selections from French Exposition Come to Metropolitan Museum," *Brooklyn Daily Eagle*, Feb. 21, 1926, [AAA, Read Papers], reel 736, frame 138.

15. *New International Yearbook for the Year 1925*, s.v. "Architecture," by Talbot F. Hamlin.

16. Eugene Clute, "Modernism and Tradition," *Pencil Points* 6 (Sept. 1925): 41.

17. Deborah Frances Pokinski, *The Development of the American Modern Style* (Ann Arbor, Mich.: UMI Research Press, 1984), 57. This volume is an excellent source on the subject. For contemporary articles see: Ralph T. Walker, "A New Architecture," *Architectural Forum* 48 (Jan. 1928): 3–4; Henry H. Saylor, "Editorial Comment," *Architecture* (Oct. 1928): 209; Louis Leonard, "What Is Modernism?" *American Architect* 136 (Nov. 1929): 22–25; Royal Cortissoz, "The Vitality of Tradition," *Architectural Forum* 52 (May 1930): 635–36; and George Howe, C. Howard Walker, and Ralph T. Walker, "Modernist and Traditionalist," *Architectural Forum* 53 (July 1930): 49–50. Howell Lewis Shay, "Modern Architecture and Tradition," *T-Square Club Journal* 1 (Jan. 1931): 12–15; Dwight James Baum, "Modern Traditionalism," *T-Square Club Journal* 1 (April 1931): 14–15; H. I. Brock, "From Flat Roofs to Towers and Slats," *NYT*, April 19, 1931, sec. 5, pp. 6–7; and Philip N. Youtz, "American Architecture Emerges from the Stone Age," *Creative Art* 10 (Jan. 1932): 17–21.

18. *New International Yearbook for the Year 1926*, s.v. "Architecture," by Talbot F. Hamlin.

19. Kahn, "The Office Building Problem in New York," 96. *Books* here referred to the practice of copying the historical styles directly from architectural reference books.

20. Stern, Gilmartin, and Mellins, *New York 1930*, 554. A plan in Avery Library of the front elevation of 15–19 West 39th Street, dated April 14, 1925, gives a good indication of the final massing and decorative scheme. All that is known of the client is his name: "owner, J. Ackerman Coles of Scotch Plains, New Jersey," NB 217, April 3, 1925, *New Buildings Docket*.

21. Newman, "Factors in Office Building Planning," 885. See also, "Loft Buildings on Side Streets," *Architecture and Building* 58 (Mar. 1926): 40–41 and pls. 55–58.

22. "Office Buildings of Today and Tomorrow," 7, pl. 4; and Meyer Liberman Jr., conversation with Jewel Stern, Miami, Florida, Nov. 24, 1988.

23. "Harry H. Uris, 73, Realty Operator," *NYT*, May 8, 1945, p. 19.

24. "Skyscraper Builder Says City Wants Best and Is Not Overdone," *New York Sun*, Feb. 13, 1927, Real Estate and Apartment Section, p. 1.

25. "Court Square Building, New York City," *Architecture and Building* 59 (May 1927): 147; and "Monumental Edifice, 21 Stories High, for Civic Center," *Real Estate Record and Builder's Guide* 116 (Nov. 28, 1925): 9.

26. Court Square lobby illustrated in *Architecture and Building* 59 (May 1927): pl. 102; and lobby bracket and Kahn's own apartment illustrated in Walter W. Kantack, "Present Tendencies: Lights and Lighting," *Good Furniture and Decoration* 36 (Feb. 1931): 83, 84.

27. "Insurance Building on Historic Site," *NYT*, Feb. 7, 1926, sec. RE, p. 1. For names of developers of Insurance Center, NB 718, Nov. 20, 1925, *New Buildings* Docket.

28. "Machine-Age Exposition," exh. cat., organized by *The Little Review*, 1927, 119 West 57th Street, New York, 3.

29. *Yearbook of the 41st Annual Exhibition of the Architectural League of New York, 1926*, n.p. For Berlin exhibition, see Cervin Robinson, "Buildings and Architects," in Cervin Robinson and Rosemarie Haag Bletter, *Skyscraper Style: Art Deco, New York* (New York: Oxford University Press, 1975), 12–13, n. 23, 31. The source cited was the exhibition catalogue: *Ausstellung neuer amerikanischer Baukunst, Januar 1926*, Berlin, Im Verlage der Akademie der Kunste zu Berlin.

30. Kahn, "Our Skyscrapers Take Simple Forms," 11.

31. "Park Ave Hotel site bought by Abe Adelson—sketches started," Kahn diary, April 20, 1926.

32. "Skyscraper to Replace Famous Park Avenue Hotel," *NYT*, Aug. 29, 1926, sec. 10, p. 1.

33. Kahn, "Economics of the Skyscraper," 298.

34. Ibid., 300.

35. Joan Jones, "Minton's fling," n.d., n.p., courtesy of Carole A. Berk, Bethesda, Maryland.

36. Compiled by Jewel Stern from *Readers Guide to Periodical Literature*, vols. 3–7 (1910–1928).

37. Leon V. Solon, "The Philadelphia Museum of Art Fairmount Park, Philadelphia," *Architectural Record* 60 (Aug. 1926): 97–99, 101.

38. Herbert Croly, "Notes and Comments: A New Dimension in Architectural Effects," *Architectural Record* 57 (June 1925): 94.

39. "Administration Buildings for Industrial Plants by Prof. Dr. Peter Behrens," *American Architect* 128 (Aug. 1925): 174, pl. 226.

40. "Skyscraper to Replace Famous Park Avenue Hotel," *NYT*; and "$9,000, 000 Project to Replace Old Park Avenue Hotel," *Real Estate Record and Builder's Guide* 118 (Aug. 28, 1926): 7.

41. Leon V. Solon, "Modernism in Architecture," *Architectural Record* 60 (Sept. 1926): 200.

42. Kahn draft, Ch. II, pp. 4–5 of 39, Avery.

43. Ibid., 5.

44. "Big Splashes of Color to Adorn Skyscrapers," *New York World*, Jan. 23, 1927, p. 8.

45. Karl Schriftgiesser, "Architecture Succumbs to the Influence of Jazz," *Boston Evening Transcript*, Feb. 23, 1927, sec. 3, p. 1. See also, Ralph Flint, "Freedom in Skyscraper Styles Noted in Architectural Show," *Christian Science Monitor*, Feb. 28, 1927, p. 5.

46. "Wants Color in Buildings," *NYT*, Feb. 23, 1927, p. 18.

47. "Hail Jazz Era," *New York World*, July 3, 1927, Real Estate and Apartment Section, p. 1; and "Gay Buildings Seen in Artistic Trend," *NYT*, July 10, 1927, sec. 10, p.12. See also, "Color Splashes in the City's Drabness," *NYT Magazine*, Oct. 9, 1927, pp. 8–9, 23.

48. "Office Buildings of Today and Tomorrow," p. 8.

49. Parker Morse Hooper, "Modern Architectural Decoration," *Architectural Forum* 48 (Feb. 1928): 159.

50. Solon, "The Park Avenue Building," *Architectural Record* 63 (April 1928): 296.

51. Susan Tunick, "Architectural Terra Cotta: Its Impact on New York," *Sites* 18 (1986): pp. 9, 15–17.

52. Ibid., 28; French Building, NB 518, Aug. 25, 1925, *New Buildings Docket*; and "The French Building, New York City," *Architecture and Building* 59 (Oct. 1927): 320.

53. For color illustrations and description see, Susan Tunick, *Terra-Cotta Skyline: New York's Architectural Ornament* (New York: Princeton Architectural Press, 1997), 79–80.

54. "Office Buildings of Today and Tomorrow," 7; Fiske Kimball, "The Family Tree of the Skyscraper," *Forum* 79 (Mar. 1928): 403; Repard Leirum, "About the House; Ambitions in Architecture," *The New Yorker* 3 (Mar. 19, 1928): 72; Lewis Mumford, "American Architecture To-day," *Architecture* 57 (April 1928): 183, 185–186; Randolph William Sexton, *American Commercial Buildings of Today* (New York: Architectural Book Publishing Company, 1928), 19–33; *New International Encyclopedia for the Year 1927*, s.v. "Architecture," by Talbot Hamlin.

55. M. A. Mikkelsen letter to Mr. Ely J. Kahn, July 8, 1927, Kahn scrapbook 1, Avery.

56. "Portfolio of Current Architecture," *Architectural Record* 63 (April 1928): 305–26; and Solon, "The Park Avenue Building," 289–97.

57. Michael A. Mikkelsen, "Color Experiments," in "Expansion of the *Architectural Record* for 1930," editorial, *Architectural Record* 66 (Nov. 1929): 502.

58. Robert A. M. Stern, "Relevance of the Decade," *Journal of the Society of Architectural Historians* 24 (Mar. 1965): 9.

59. Four articles by Kahn were published in the *Record* from 1926 through 1928: "The Architectural League Exhibition of 1926," 59 (Mar. 1926): 227–28; "The Ziegfeld Theatre, New York," *Architectural Record* 61 (May 1927): 385–93; "Economics of the Skyscraper," 63 (April 1928): 298–301; and "Exhibition of French Decorative Art," 63 (May 1928): 462.

60. In addition to those in the notes above, see T-Square, "The Sky Line: Smaller Buildings—Gothic Revivals and Satisfying Facades," *The New Yorker* 3 (Oct. 15, 1927): 87; Lewis Mumford, "Modernist Furniture," *New Republic* 54 (Mar. 21, 1928): 155; Mujica, *History of the Skyscraper*, 67, pls. 94–97; Fiske Kimball, *American Architecture* (New York: Bobbs-Merrill, 1928), 213–14; Henry-Russell Hitchcock Jr., *Modern Architecture: Romanticism and Reintegration* (New York, Payson & Clarke, 1929), 201; James Henry Sullivan, "The New Architect," *Architectural Progress* 4 (Jan. 1930): 13; "An 8-Page Section of Decorative Glass," *American Architect* 13 (Feb. 1930): 41; R. L and C. A. Glassgold, eds., *Modern American Design* (New York: Ives Washburn, 1930), 114–15; "Portfolio of Mail-Chute Boxes," *Architecture* 63 (June 1931): 384; and "Portfolio of Interior Clocks," *Architecture* 65 (Feb. 1932): 113.

61. Lewis Mumford, "American Architecture To-day," 185–86.

62. Kahn draft, Ch. II, p. 1 of 39, Avery; and Otto John Teegen, interview by Jewel Stern, New York City, Dec. 7, 1976.

63. The source of all biographical information on Nadir in this paragraph is from his response to Jewel Stern's questionnaire, Bridgeport, Connecticut, Jan. 9, 1977.

64. Shamoon Nadir, letter to Jewel Stern, May 16, 1978. Although Nadir's part in the design was extensive—thirteen drawings of details with his initials survive in Avery Library—he was not the sole contributor.

65. *Who Was Who in American Art*, s.v. "Bart Van Der Woerd"; and Kees Somer, Amsterdam, letter to Jewel Stern, June 30, 1992.

66. List or Manifest of Alien Passengers for the United States Immigration Officer at Port of Arrival, SS *Rijndam*, sailing from Rotterdam, Sept. 1, 1926, List 6.

67. Nadir questionnaire. Teegen concurred with Nadir on Van der Woerd's ability and added that the Dutchman had a distinctive style, but was personally uncommunicative. Otto John Teegen, letter to Jewel Stern, May 12, 1978.

68. John Theodore Jacobsen's response to Jewel Stern's questionnaire, Honolulu, Hawaii, Dec. 1977.

69. Nadir questionnaire.

70. "Note of Agreement of December 31, 1925, between Buchman, Kahn and Montfort," Avery.

71. Kahn and Jacobs, typed brochure, c. 1941, n.p., courtesy of Liselotte Kahn.

72. Saylor, "Ely Jacques Kahn," pp. 65, 66, 70.

73. Newman, "Factors in Office Building Planning," pp. 881, 889–90.

74. Nadir questionnaire.

75. Saylor, "Ely Jacques Kahn," 66.

76. Although Buchman & Kahn drew the plans and filed

them for the Lefcourt-Madison Building, Lefcourt insisted that George and Edward Blum, the firm that had designed the Lefcourt-Marlborough Building, 1351 Broadway, be associated on the project. Lefcourt-Madison Building: NB 177, Mar. 20, 1925, *New Buildings Docket*.

77. C. G. Poore, "Skyscraper Builder Began as a Newsboy," *NYT*, Jan. 20, 1929, sec. IX, p. 5. For Lefcourt biography, see also, "Owns the Corner Where He Once Sold Papers; Lefcourt to Build on Hotel Normandie Site," *NYT*, Jan. 5, 1926, 1; "'Sweat Shop' Ended, Trade Leader Says," *NYT*, Mar. 13, 1926, p. 6; Percy Winner, "New York Skyline Becomes a Monument to Memory of Successful Men," *NYT*, Nov. 17, 1928, sec. III, p. 1; "Romance in Lives," *NYT*, p. 3; and Marolyn Davenport, "Abraham E. Lefcourt," research for Real Estate Board of New York, courtesy of Davenport.

78. "Demand for Broadway Space Shown by Leasing Volume," *NYT*, Nov. 13, 1927, sec. 12, p. 2.

79. "Frederick Brown Makes Munificent Gift to Jewish Charities," *Real Estate Record and Builder's Guide* 115 (May 9, 1925): 6; for biography, see "Romance in Lives," *NYT*, 3.

80. Kahn draft, Ch. II, p. 2 of 39, Avery.

81. "Furniture Exchange Building, New York City," *Architecture and Building* 58 (Feb. 1926): 27; and "Loft Buildings on Side Streets," *Architecture and Building* 58 (Mar. 1926): 41.

82. Kahn draft, Ch. II, p. 2 of 39, Avery.

83. Kahn, "Economics of the Skyscraper," 300–1. A ninth-story residence for Edwin Goodman was added to the Bergdorf store on the 58th Street corner.

84. Illustrations in "The Bergdorf-Goodman Building, New York City," *Architecture and Building* 60 (April 1928): 107–8, pls. 79–82. Hofstatter noted as interior designer in "5th Av. Building Opened," *NYT*, Mar. 11, 1928, sec. 11, p. 1.

85. Milton M. Blumental, president of 42–44 West 39th Street Inc., owner, in NB 145, Oct. 14, 1926, *New Buildings Docket*. See also, "M. M. Blumenthal Dies at Dinner Here," *NYT*, Dec. 22, 1942, p. 17. For the Federation Building, "Jewish Federation to Dedicate Home," *NYT*, May 13, 1928, sec. 2, p. 2.

86. Teegen interview.

87. "Consolidated Stock Exchange Home Sold, $10,000,000 Skyscraper to Displace It," *NYT*, June 23, 1926, p. 1; "Starting Broad Beaver for Lefcourt," Kahn diary, Aug. 26, 1926; and "New Building Projects in Manhattan and Brooklyn," *NYT*, Oct. 31, 1926, sec. 11, p. 1.

88. "Oppose Skyscraper in Financial District," *NYT*, Jan. 19, 1927, p. 3. The case was heard in the New York Supreme Court in January 1927.

89. Lefcourt Exchange original plan: NB 427, Sept. 7, 1926, *New Buildings Docket*; revised plan: NB 388, Aug. 24, 1927, *New Buildings Docket*. International Telephone & Telegraph architect, Louis S. Weeks, a consultant, has sometimes been mistakenly credited with the design. Weeks supervised construction of the building.

90. Kahn draft, Ch. II, p. 14 of 39, Avery.

91. T-Square, "The Skyline: Romance in Brick—Lotus and Scarabaeus—The Gateway Again," *The New Yorker* 4 (Sept. 8, 1928): 67.

92. "Historic Site Being Cleared For $8,000,000 U.S. Building," *NYT*, Nov. 6, 1927, sec. 12, p. 1.

93. Joseph K. Foster, "Louis Adler proves again that - Success Is Theirs Who Do and Care," *Jewish Tribune*, n.d., p. 14, clipping in Louis Adler scrapbook.

94. "Saves Government $400,000 on Record-Time Job," *NYT*, Dec. 2, 1928, sec.13, p. 1.

95. "Historic Site Being Cleared," *NYT*.

96. Stern, "Relevance of the Decade," 8.

97. "Praise Architect Show; Authorities Hold Modernists Have Ceased to be Underdogs," *NYT*, Mar. 6, 1927, p. 23.

98. Helen Appleton Read, "Art-in-Trade Exposition Stresses the Modern Note," *Brooklyn Daily Eagle*, May 8, 1927 [AAA, Read Papers], reel N736, frame 183. Kahn's friend Lee Simonson designed the Macy's installation.

99. Herbert Lippman, *Arts* 11 (1927): 324–26. Cited in Stern, "Relevance of the Decade," 9, note 21. Hugh Ferriss selected the American architecture section.

100. "Machine-Age Exposition," exh. cat., pp. 3, 6.

101. Kahn, "The Ziegfeld Theatre, New York," 386.

102. "P. Hoffmann working on Decorations," Kahn diary, Oct. 23, 1927.

103. Kahn diary, Dec. 19, 1927.

CHAPTER SIX

1. Lewis Mumford, "Modernist Furniture," *New Republic* 54 (March 21, 1928): 154–55. Mumford referred to the "Golden Portal" of Adler and Sullivan's Transportation Building for the 1893 World's Columbian Exposition in Chicago. See also, *An Exposition of Modern French Decorative Art*, organized by Dorothy Shaver in collaboration with Lucien Vogel and Ely Jacques Kahn, Lord & Taylor, New York, exh. cat., Feb. 1928; Ely J. Kahn, "Exhibition of French Decorative Art" *Architectural Record* 63 (May 1928): 462–68; and "French Art Moderne Exposition in New York," *Good Furniture Magazine* 30 (Mar. 1928): 119–22.

2. "Architects Take Two Floors In Tower at 2 Park Avenue," *NYT*, Aug. 30, 1927, p. 40.

3. "New Fifty-sixth Street Addition to the Jay-Thorpe Building at 24 West Fifty-seventh Street," *NYT*, Dec. 4, 1927, sec. 13, p. 1; and "Jay-Thorpe Shop, New York," *Architectural Forum* 50 (June 1929): pls. 164–65. The *Forum* attributed the interiors to "Whitman & Goodman, Architects," designers of an art moderne salon for Saks Fifth Avenue.

4. "Maillard's Restaurant and Tea Room, 385 Madison Avenue, New York City" *Architecture and Building* 55 (May 1923): 49–50, pl. 118. The firm also designed the Chicago Maillard's. See "Interior Architecture: Maillard's Restaurant, Chicago, Ill.," *American Architect* 127 (June 17, 1925): 545–52.

5. For Wolfgang Hoffmann, C. Adolph Glassgold, "The Modern Note in Decorative Arts," Part 2, *The Arts* 13 (April 1928): 234–35.

6. "The Editor's Diary," *Architecture* 60 (Dec. 1929): 375. For images, see "Jewelry Store of Van Cleef & Arpels,

Inc., Fifth Avenue, New York City," *Architecture* 61 (Mar. 1930): 137–40.

7. *The Architect and the Industrial Arts*, exh. cat., Metropolitan Museum of Art, New York, 1929, 14–15.

8. "The First Exposition of Modern American Decorative and Industrial Art," exh. cat., January 17, 1929, Mandel Brothers, n.p. My thanks to Marilyn F. Friedman for this information.

9. Jeannette Kilham, "New Aims in Decorating," *Junior League Magazine* (Jan. 1930): 95. Shamoon Nadir was the lead designer for the bath and dressing room. Nadir questionnaire.

10. Kahn diary, July 16, 1928; and Kahn draft, Ch. II, p. 38 of 39, Avery.

11. Sidney Blumenthal, "Art in Manufacture," *American Magazine of Art* 21 (Aug. 1930): 441; and Kahn draft, "Autobiography," p. 11 of 13, Avery.

12. For Kohler, Kahn diary, July 16, 1928; Metropolitan Museum of Art, *The Architect and the Industrial Arts*, exh. cat., 1929, p. 65; Kahn draft, Ch. II, p. 38 of 39, Avery; and "Ely Jacque Kahn Designs New Kohler Showroom," *Kohler of Kohler News*, 16 (Mar. 1932): 2–13.

13. T-Square (George Sheppard Chappell), "The Sky Line: Glass Houses, Houses Like Golf Balls, and Some on Wheels," *The New Yorker* 4 (April 14, 1928): 79.

14. "Glass Skyscraper Next for 5th Avenue," *The World*, Mar. 18, 1928, n.p., clipping, Kahn scrapbook 1, Avery.

15. Teegen interview; and Nadir questionnaire.

16. "261 Fifth Avenue," *Architecture and Building* 61 (Feb. 1929): 41.

17. R. W. Sexton, "Lighting Fixtures of To-day," *Architecture* 61 (June 1930): 323.

18. "Features of the American Designers' Gallery Exhibition," *Metal Arts* 1 (Dec. 1928): 84; and "Exposition of American Contemporary Art," American Designers' Gallery advertisement, *Metal Arts* 1 (Dec. 1928): vi.

19. R. L. Leonard and C. A. Glassgold, eds., American Union of Decorative Artists and Craftsmen, *Annual of American Design 1931* (New York: Ives Washburn, 1930), 114–15.

20. "Buys Ninth Av. Block for a Film Exchange," *NYT*, Mar. 29, 1928, p. 48.

21. "Film Center Building Tenants Reflect Change of Movie Industry," *Real Estate Record and Builders Guide* 187 (April 29, 1961): 4; and "Film Center: Buchman and Kahn, Architects," *Architectural Record* 66 (Oct. 1929): 307–8.

22. Teegen interview. McMahon was a nonmatriculating student in the Columbia University Extension Program, 1922–23, and his initials first appear on Buchman & Kahn plans in 1924. On his application to the American Institute of Architects he stated that he studied at Pennsylvania State College, the Cooper-Union and the atelier of Harvey Wiley Corbett (both in New York City), as well as the Pratt Institute in Brooklyn.

23. Nadir questionnaire.

24. "John St. Blockfront to Have Tall Offices," *NYT*, May 20, 1928, p. 153.

25. NB 271, April 28, 1928, *New Buildings Docket*.

26. "Work Started on John Street Insurance Building," *Real Estate Record and Builder's Guide* 121 (May 19, 1928): 7.

27. "Building Rented before Finished," *New York Sun*, June 8, 1929," clipping, Louis Adler scrapbook.

28. $2,000,000 Building to Go Next Week," *NYT*, Sept. 16, 1928, p. 169.

29. "Soaring Values Force Buildings Skyward," *Real Estate Magazine of New York*, Aug. 1928, and "Louis Adler Plans New Building," *New York Evening Journal*, Jan. 19, 1929, clippings, Louis Adler scrapbook; and "Midtown Skyscraper Leased from Plans," *NYT*, Feb. 10, 1929, p. 165.

30. "Architecture Used Overcame All Problems; Structure, Designed by Buchman & Kahn, Provides for All Needs, with No Special Type Followed." *Women's Wear Daily*, Dec. 17, 1929, sec. IV, clipping in Louis Adler scrapbook.

31. "Proposed 33-Story Bricken Textile Bldg. For Broadway, 41st Street and 7th Ave.," *Women's Wear Daily*, Dec. 14, 1928, sec. 1, p. 8. An early rendering was illustrated, but the final massing changed.

32. *New International Yearbook for the Year 1930*, s.v. "Architecture," by Talbot F. Hamlin.

33. "Varick Street Industrial Centre is Expanding Rapidly," *NYT*, Nov. 10, 1929, sec. RE, p. 1.

34. "New Building Planned for United States Appraisers," *NYT*, July 11, 1926, sec. X, p.1; and Trinity Leases Site at Holland Tunnel," *NYT*, Nov. 29, 1928, p. 17.

35. NB 79, Feb. 13, 1929, *New Buildings Docket*. There are no plans or drawings of the Holland Plaza Building in Avery.

36. "Rising on Varick Street," *NYT*, Mar. 17, 1929, sec. W, p. 19.

37. Ely Jacque Kahn, "The Holland Plaza Building, New York," *Architecture* 62 (Sept. 1930): 133.

38. "Skyscraper Builders," *NYT*, Jan. 5, 1929, sec. RE, p. 4; and "31-Story Skyscraper to Rise in Wall Street," *NYT*, Dec. 9, 1928, p. 1.

39. "Mark Spot Where Washington Landed; Bronze Tablet Will Be Placed on New Building at Foot of Wall Street," *NYT*, Feb. 23, 1930, p. 181.

40. NB 80, Feb. 13, 1929, *New Buildings Docket*; and "Tall Building for Lower Wall Street," *NYT*, Mar. 10, 1929, p. 177.

41. "Fifty-one Caissons for Wall St. Edifice," *NYT*, Aug. 11. 1929, sec. RE, p.2.

42. Newman, "Office Building Planning," 889. This article is a good technical source for 120 Wall Street. For Newman biography, see *American Architects Directory*, 1956, s.v. "James B(laine) Newman. Newman entered Buchman & Kahn in 1924 and continued through The Firm of Ely Jacque Kahn and Kahn and Jacobs. His name is on the firm's letterhead as a partner in 1965. For an image of 120 Wall Street with the World Trade Center towers in the background, see Daniel M. Abramson, *Skyscraper Rivals: The AIG Building and the Architecture of Wall Street* (New York: Princeton Architectural Press, 2001), 186.

43. Nadir questionnaire and Teegen letter to Stern, May 12, 1978. For quotation, Teegen interview. Teegen initially worked closely with Nadir, who left the firm at the end of 1929. The drawings, dated from June 18, 1929 to

Sept. 13, 1929, for the directory board, elevator doors, east elevator vestibule, ceiling, Wall Street entrance, South Street entrance, and Wall Street vestibule all have Teegen's initials. Drawings in the collection of Carola Teegen Walton and Guy Walton, reviewed by Jewel Stern, Nov. 18, 1991, Panther Valley, New Jersey.

44. Ernst A. Plischke, *Ein Leben mit Architektur* (Vienna: Locker Verlag, 1989), 107–18. My thanks to Edith Hudson for the translation.

45. Nadir questionnaire.

46. "Office Building at 120 Wall Street, New York City," *Architecture and Building* 62 (Dec. 1930): 336.

47. Brinley mural illustrated in Arthur S. Covey, "The Office-Building Lobby," *Architecture* 63 (May 1931): 258.

48. "Wall St. District Showing Activity," *NYT*, Oct. 26, 1930, sec. RE, p.1.

49. "Skyscraper Site of Century Theatre," *NYT*, May 29, 1929, p. 1.

50. Kahn diary, May 28, 1929.

51. Ibid., June 14, 1929.

52. "French Plan Centre on the Century Site," *NYT*, Aug. 13, 1929, p. 4; see also, "N.Y. French Centre to Rise 65 Floors," *The World*, Aug. 13, 1929, p. 1.

53. Kahn diary, Aug. 18, 1929.

54. Kahn diary, Jan. 20, 1930.

55. "6,500,000 Loan on Century Site," *NYT*, Oct. 24, 1930, p. 43.

56. K. G. S., "Architect's Work on View," *NYT*, April 19, 1932, p. 24.

57. "Preparing to Raze Mason Apartment," *NYT*, Feb. 10, 1929, p. 165.

58. "Squibb & Sons Lease on Upper 5th Avenue," *NYT*, July 9, 1929, p. 54.

59. Newman,"Office Building Planning," 887–88. Two of the three floor plans are illustrated.

60. The published study for the mural was altered. The panel that originally represented fashion on the left side was changed to physics, and all three panels on the left side were shifted to the right side and those on the right moved to the left side. See Anne Lee, "Contemporary American Murals," *Architectural Forum* 54 (April 1931): 479; and "Ceiling of Main Lobby, Squibb Building, New York City," *Architecture* 63 (May 1931): 260.

61. Kahn draft, Ch. II, p. 3 of 39, Avery.

62. "Squibb Building Opened," *NYT*, May 2, 1930, p. 46.

63. T-Square, "The Sky Line Ecclesiastical and Domestic—A Modern Fifty-seventh Street—With a Personnel to Match," *The New Yorker* 6 (April 12, 1930): 118.

64. Arthur T. North, "The Passing Show," *Western Architect* (Oct. 1930): 166, Kahn scrapbook 1, Avery.

65. Harry Allan Jacobs, "Color in Architecture," *NYT*, Dec. 28, 1930, p. 2.

66. Lewis Mumford, "Notes on Modern Architecture: The Squibb Building," *New Republic* 66 (Mar. 18, 1931): 121.

67. Hamlin, *Yearbook* 1930.

68. John Cushman Fistere, "Poets in Steel," *Vanity Fair* 37 (Dec. 1931): 59.

69. Kahn draft, Ch. II, p. 3 of 39, Avery.

70. "Beaux-Arts Ball Festival of Color," *NYT*, Jan. 24, 1931, p. 18.

71. K. G. S., "Architect's Work on View."

72. "The Knickerbocker to Be Torn Down," *NYT*, July 19, 1929, p. 21. For illustrations of the entrance and lobby of 1400 Broadway, see "A Group of New York Office Buildings," *Architecture* 66 (Sept. 1932): 157–62.

73. "What Architects Are Talking About," *American Architect* 137 (Feb. 1930): 118. See also, 1410 Broadway, NB 27, Feb. 13, 1930, *New Buildings Docket*.

74. Announcement card, June 1, 1930, courtesy of Liselotte Kahn.

75. Jacobsen questionnaire, Dec. 1977; and John Theodore Jacobsen, letter to Jewel Stern, Mar. 9, 1978.

76. Ely Jacques Kahn draft, "II League," p. 2 of 2, courtesy of Liselotte Kahn.

77. "Louis Adler Buys Broadway Corner," *NYT*, April 21, 1928, p. 31; and "Louis Adler to Improve Hotel Continental Site with 45-Story Building," *NYT*, Feb. 9, 1930, sec. 11, p.1.

78. "Three in Broadway Skyscraper Race," *The World*, Feb. 9, 1930, clipping in Louis Adler scrapbook.

79. "Architectural News in Photographs: Proposed Continental Bldg.," *Architecture* 61 (May 1930): 280; "New 44-Story Office Building to Be Erected by Louis Adler at 1450 Broadway," *Women's Wear Daily*, Mar. 7, 1930, clipping in Louis Adler scrapbook, and "The Continental Building," *NYT*, Mar. 9, 1930, sec. XII, p. 1.

80. "The Continental Building, New York City," *Architecture and Building* (April 1931): 86.

81. "Entrance to Continental Building," *NYT*, April 5, 1931, p. 146.

82. "Wall Street Skyscraper May Rise 105 Stories," *NYT*, May 8, 1930, p. 1. The deal was also announced in the *New York Sun*, *New York Telegram*, *The World*, *New York American*, *New York Herald Tribune*, *New York Daily News*, and the *Real Estate Record and Builder's Guide*.

83. Kahn diary, May 6, 1930 and May 12, 1930.

84. Continental Building, NB 199, *New Buildings Docket*, July 17, 1930.

85. J. P. Lohman, "Speaking of Real Estate," *New York American*, Jan. 14, 1931, clipping in Louis Adler scrapbook.

86. Kahn diary, May 6, 1933.

87. "Quiet Taste Keynote of New Bonwit Teller's," *Women's Wear Daily*, Sept. 15, 1930, sec. 1, p. 1. See also, "In Eight Months They Changed It; Which Do You Prefer?" *American Architect* 138 (Nov. 1930): 30–31.

88. The Teegen drawing is in the Metropolitan Museum of Art in New York, accession number 1986.1187.10.

89. Lewis Mumford, "Notes on Modern Architecture: The Bonwit Teller Building," *Architecture* 66 (Mar. 18, 1931): 120.

90. Kahn draft, Ch. II, p. 33 of 39, Avery.

91. *New International Yearbook for the Year 1931*, s.v. "Architecture," by Talbot F. Hamlin.

92. "The Hudnut Building New York, N.Y., Ely Jacques Kahn and Eliel Saarinen, Associated Architects, *Architectural Forum* 55 (Oct. 1931): 415–22. In 1955 the entire façade and the upper three floors were removed to accommodate a new women's shoe store. See "5th Ave.

Lease Closed," *NYT*, Mar. 11, 1955, p. 41. The building was later demolished.

93. "Lexington Av. Corner Leased By Tishmans," *NYT*, July 4, 1929, p. 28; and "Leasing Features Realty Activity," *NYT*, Apr. 14, 1931, p. 52; and "Leasehold Is Sold By Tishman Realty," *NYT*, April 8, 1952, p. 50.

94. Kahn diary, June 14, 1929.

95. Lewis Mumford, "The Sky Line: From the Palace of the Popes—The Cantilevered Front—Return to Sobriety," *The New Yorker*, 52 (Jan. 2, 1932): 43–44.

96. "Loans Placed Here Total $13,000,000," *NYT*," June 13, 1930, p. 47.

97. Teegen Interview and Teegen letter to Stern, May 12, 1978. For Fordyce, see *American Architects Directory*, 1956, s.v. "Allmon Fordyce."

98. Dock Curtis, "Give Us Facts: Says Ely Jacques Kahn," *Modern Plastics*, 12 (May 1935): 12–13.

99. Drawings in the collection of Carola Teegen Walton and Guy Walton.

100. "Pays $3,500,00 for Skyscraper," *NYT*, Jan. 6, 1932, p. 39. Kahn designed an eleven-story warehouse at 91st Street and Third Avenue (demolished) for Ruppert. See, "Ruppert to Build Annex to Brewery," *NYT*, Dec. 30, 1932, p. 32.

101. Mumford, "The Sky Line," 44.

102. "Creditors Bid in Squibb Building," *NYT*, Jan. 4, 1933, p. 35.

103. "23 Parcels Bid in at Auction Sales," *NYT*, April 10, 1935, p. 39.

104. "A. E. Lefcourt Left $2,500, No Realty," *NYT*, Dec. 15, 1932, p. 9.

105. "Foreclosure Sale on 2 Park Avenue," *NYT*, Aug. 26, 1934, p. RE I; and "Realty Auctioned under New Ruling," *NYT*, Aug. 31, 1934, p. 32.

106. "Louis Adler Buys 7th Avenue Corner," *NYT*, Dec. 16, 1933, p. 31; and "Skyscraper Set to Begin New Life," *NYT*, Oct. 24, 1965, p. R 1.

107. Hamlin, *Yearbook* 1930.

CHAPTER SEVEN

1. Teegen letter to Stern, May 12, 1978. Kahn's income was estimated from reports of plans filed in the *NYT* between 1930 and 1940.

2. Clarence Stein, letter to Aline MacMahon, July 6, 1933. Cornell CSP.

3. Aline MacMahon Stein interview, Apr. 29, 1983; Bookman interview, May 17, 1983; Ely Jacques Kahn Jr., letter to Stern, Oct. 16, 1983; Kahn diary, Nov. 1, 1929; Olivia Kahn, letter to Stern, Apr. 13, 1992; Olivia Kahn, interview by Jewel Stern, New York City, Nov. 14, 2005; and "Mrs. L. Sulzberger Wed to Architect," *NYT*, Nov. 24, 1938, p. 34.

4. *NYT*, Jan. 25, 1931, p. N4; Ely Jacques Kahn, "Do Architects Want Criticism?" *American Architect* 137 (Apr. 1930): 59, 92.

5. Hamilton M. Wright, "Contemporary Architecture as Mr. Kahn Sees It," *Western Architect Current Architecture* 40 (Feb. 1931): 7–8.

6. Brock, "Flat Roofs to Towers," p. 81.

7. Edward Alden Jewell, "Architectural League" *NYT*, Apr. 19, 1931, p. 136; and Jewell, "Panorama of Current Week of Art in New York," *NYT*, Apr. 26, 1931, p. 10 X.

8. Philip Johnson Interview, Oral History Project, 1991, p. 15. Museum of Modern Art Archives, New York. Included were Alfred Clauss and George Daub, Walter Baermann and Richard Wood with Hazen Sise, Oscar Stonorov and Herbert Morgan, William Muschenheim; and Elroy Webber. For quotations see Jewell, "Panorama," *NYT*.

9. "Rejected," *Art Digest* 5 (May 1, 1931): 16.

10. For quotes by Hood and Kahn, see "Young Architects Stage Rival Show," *NYT*, Apr. 21, 1931, p. 5.

11. Philip Johnson, "Rejected Architects," *Creative Art* 8 (June 1931): 433.

12. "Points of View," *Creative Art* 8 (June 1931): 469.

13. "Artists Return to Paris," *NYT*, May 21, 1931, p. 25; and "Architects Return from Paris Reunion," *NYT*, July 4, 1931, p. 30. See also *The Beaux-Arts Boys on the Boulevard; or, The Invasion of Paris in 1931*, photographs by Carl Reimers, illustrations by Tony Sarg, and with a foreword by Henry Saylor (1933), in Avery Library Rare Books Collection.

14. *B.B.A.I.D.* 10 (May 1934): 1; *B.B.A.I.D.* 15 (Nov. 1938): back cover.

15. "A Free School of Architecture," *NYT*, Aug. 1, 1920, p. 46.

16. Annual Report 1932 of the Beaux-Arts Institute of Design. Incorporated 1916, 304 East 44th Street, New York, p. 4.

17. "Beaux-Arts Institute of Design. Department of Architecture. School Year 1931–1932. Notice to Students and Correspondents," In *B.B.A.I.D.* 8 (May 1932): 1.

18. *B.B.A.I.D.* 8 (Aug., 1932): 2.

19. Kahn Manuscript, 1970, Ch. V of XI, p. 2; Eero Saarinen received a "mention" in the Emerson Prize competition. See also *B.B.A.I.D.* 9 (Dec. 1932), 9–10.

20. *B.B.A.I.D.* 9 (Nov., 1932): 3–4.

21. *B.B.A.I.D.* 9 (Apr., 1933): 3.

22. H. I. Brock, "A Pioneer in Architecture That Is Called Modern," *NYT*, June 29, 1930, p. 77.

23. Kahn to Wright, Aug. 20, 1930. Frank Lloyd Wright Foundation [hereafter FLWF].

24. Letter reprinted as "To the Students of the Beaux-Arts Institute of Design," *Architecture* 66 (Oct. 1932): 230.

25. Kahn to Wright, Sept. 1, 1932. FLWF.

26. Ely Jacques Kahn, *Design in Art and Industry* (New York: Charles Scribner's Sons, 1935), 191–92.

27. Ely Jacques Kahn, "Commercial Centers, Prewar vs. Postwar," *Architectural Record. Office and Loft Buildings* 93 (Apr. 1943): 75.

28. Kahn to Keppel, Dec. 2, 1932. Carnegie Corporation Archives. Rare Book & Manuscript Library, Butler Library, Columbia University, CCNY Series III. A (Grant Files), Box 30, Folder 7 [hereafter Carnegie Archives].

29. Emerson to Keppel, Dec. 22, 1932, Carnegie Archives.

30. Statement dated Dec. 28, 1932, Carnegie Archives.

31. Resolution X966, Carnegie Archives.

32. Steinhof to Kahn, Apr. 29, 1933, Carnegie Archives.

33. Keppel to EJK, June 2, 1933, Carnegie Archives.

34. "Itinerary and Information for Mr. Ely Jacques Kahn," Anglo-American Travel Service. Avery.

35. Kahn to Keppel, Sept. 26, 1933, Carnegie Archives.

36. See the humorous account of Kahn's journey in Kenneth Murchison, "Hors de Concours," *Architectural Forum* 60 (April 1934): 293.

37. Ely Jacques Kahn, *Design in Art and Industry*, 129, 132, 135–36.

38. *American Architect* 147 (Aug. 1935): 4.

39. "Kahn on Training," *Art Digest* 10 (Jan. 1, 1936): 25.

40. Langdon Warner, "New Books on Art," *American Magazine of Art* 28 (August 1935): 503.

41. For the best account of Jacobs's role in Le Corbusier's lecture tour, see Mardges Bacon, *Le Corbusier in America: Travels in the Land of the Timid* (Cambridge, Mass., and London: MIT Press, 2001).

42. "Chicago Fair Plans for Industrial Art," *NYT*, Jan. 26, 1932, p. 41.

43. "Chief of the Section of Industrial Art," *Interior Architecture & Decoration* combined with *Good Furniture and Decoration* 38 (Feb. 1932): 29.

44. "Design For Industrial Arts Building At Fair," *NYT*, Apr. 24, 1932, sec. II, p. 6.

45. Kahn to Lohr, with notes in the margins signed by J. Franklin Bell, Nov. 14, 1932, University of Illinois at Chicago [UIC] Special Collections.

46. Kahn to Lohr, Dec. 5, 1932, UIC Special Collections.

47. Almus Pratt Evans, "Exposition Architecture 1893 versus 1933," *Parnassus* 5 (May 1933): 20.

48. "Archaic Ideas Have Been Discarded by World Fair Architects," *Yale Daily News*, Apr. 8, 1933. Kahn scrapbook 2, Avery.

49. *Official Guide. Book of the Fair 1933* (Chicago: Century of Progress Administration Building, 1933), 172.

50. Arthur Millier, "Leo Katz Mural Outstanding Art Work of Depression Era," *Los Angeles Times*, Jan. 21, 1934, p. A1.

51. Compare Hoffmann's concert auditorium design published in *Architectural Forum* 49 (Nov. 1928): 712.

52. See Arthur F. Woltersdorf, "Carnival Architecture," *American Architect* 143 (July 1933): 10, 13–15.

53. Ely Jacques Kahn, "Close-up Comments on the Fair," *Architectural Forum* 59 (July 1933): 23.

54. "Archaic Ideas have Been Discarded by World Fair Architects," *Yale Daily News*, Apr. 8, 1933, Kahn scrapbook 2, Avery.

55. Ely Jacques Kahn, "Common Sense House," *Forward House* 1933, n.p.

56. Frank Lloyd Wright, "In the Show Window at Macy's," *Architectural Forum* 59 (Nov. 1933): 419–20.

57. Kahn, "Common Sense House."

58. Paul R. Milton, "We Men—We Women," Episode #31, 2, 4. Kahn scrapbook 3, Avery.

59. Walter Rendell Storey, "Modern Trends in Decorative Art," *NYT*, Nov. 11, 1934, p. SM12; "Exhibition of Contemporary American Industrial Art," exh. cat., Metropolitan Museum of Art, 1934, 16–17.

60. Untitled Exhibition Pamphlet, Kahn scrapbook 3, Avery.

61. Henry Saylor, "Diary," *American Architect and Architecture* 148 (May 1936): 68.

62. Edward Alden Jewell, "A Melange of Current Exhibitions," *NYT*, May 5, 1940, p. 162.

63. "Glass-like Wares Shown for Home," *NYT*, Apr. 30, 1940, p. 33.

64. Henry H. Saylor "Diary," *Architectural Forum* 72 (June 1940): 435: and "Forum of Events. Contemporary Industrial Art," *Architectural Forum* 72 (June 1940): 9–14.

65. Walter Rendell Storey, "Decorative Art: Modern Design," *NYT*, May 5, 1940, p. 61.

66. Kahn diary entries for May 27, 1938 and Aug. 19, 1938.

67. Stern, *New York 1930*, 747. Kahn does not mention this project in his diary.

68. William Muschenheim letter to Jewel Stern, Oct. 1, 1988.

69. "Vast Marine Hall Planned for Fair," *NYT*, Jan. 24, 1938, p. 25.

70. Eugene Du Bois, "Building the Fair," *Brooklyn Daily Eagle*, Feb. 3, 1939, Kahn scrapbook 3, Avery.

71. A sketch for this mural is now in the National Gallery of Art, Washington, D.C. Acquisition no. 1971.59.1.

72. "Critic Glimpses Mural at the Fair, *World Telegram*, [n.d.] n.p., clipping Kahn scrapbook 3, Avery.

73. "New Building and Statue Designed for World's Fair," *NYT*, Aug. 12, 1938, p. 19.

74. Eugene Du Bois, "Building the Fair."

75. "Your White Owl Exhibit Building," *Long Ash* (June 1939): 25, Kahn scrapbook 3, Avery.

76. Ibid.

77. Eugene Du Bois, "Building the Fair."

78. *Trailer Town Topics* 1 (Nov. 1938): 4. Kahn scrapbook 3, Avery; Christopher Janus, "All Roads to Lead to the Fair," *NYT*, Mar. 5, 1939, p. XX1.

79. *Trailer Town Topics* 1 (Nov. 1938): 4, Kahn scrapbook 3, Avery.

80. "Literary Lyons Swings His Axis at Moses over Trailer Town," *NYT*, Apr. 11, 1939, p. 20.

81. See Ely Jacques Kahn, "Main Streets across the Continent," *Art and Decoration* 45 (Sept. 1936): 19–21, 49, 51.

82. "Restaurant System to Open New Branch," *NYT*, July 21, 1937, p. 40; and "Longchamps Restaurant," *Architectural Forum* 69 (Oct. 1938): 265–69.

83. "Fifth Ave. Section Undergoes Change," *NYT*, Oct. 23, 1938, p. 183.

84. See "It's the Front that Counts. Architect Kahn Tells of the New Ideas Illustrated in Milady's Shops," *New York Sun*, Dec. 18, 1937. Kahn scrapbook 3, Avery. "Showroom for Hazel Kolman New York City," *Architectural Record* 80 (Aug. 1936): 115.

85. Anne Claiborne, "A Musical Modern Décor," *Arts & Decoration* 45 (Nov. 1936): 22–24.

86. See program for the Pix Theater, Kahn scrapbook 3, Avery.

87. "Fluorescent Lamps Solve Lighting Problem in New York's Pix Theater," *Magazine of Light Published by General Electric* 9 (May 8, 1940): 24–25.

CHAPTER EIGHT

1. Kahn Diary, Oct. 1, 1939.

2. Kahn Diary, Oct. 9, 1941.

3. Ely Jacques Kahn, "Talk If You Must – But Act!" *Pencil Points* 22 (Feb. 1941): 74.

4. Ely Jacques Kahn, "New Architecture Reign Foreseen in Post-War Era," *Herald Tribune*, Apr. 13, 1941. Kahn scrapbook 3, Avery.

5. "Joins Ely Jacques Kahn Firm," *NYT*, Feb. 21, 1941, p. 39.

6. Mardges Bacon, *Le Corbusier in America* (Cambridge, Mass., and London: The MIT Press, 2001), ix, 72, 121–122.

7. Jacobs interview, Nov. 5, 1989. See drawings of Kahn's apartment at 970 Park Avenue signed by Jacobs in Avery.

8. Written responses from Sheldon Fox, Mar. 15, 2005.

9. See also Neil Bingham, *Wright to Gehry: Drawings from the Collection of Barbara Pine* (London: Sir John Soane's Museum, 2005), 32.

10. Robert Allan Jacobs, response to Stern questionnaire, Apr. 4, 1984.

11. "City Plant to be Streamlined. Replacing of Unsightly One is Authorized by Board at Isaac's Urging," *NYT*, Mar. 28, 1941, p. 25.

12. Jacobs claimed the design was his in a telephone conversation with Jewel Stern, Mar. 28, 1984, and in her interview with him, Nov. 5, 1989.

13. Robert Moses, "Mr. Moses Surveys the City Statues," *NYT*, Nov. 21, 1943, p. SM18.

14. "List from Which 50 Selections Are to be Made," Nov. 8, 1943, Department of Architecture and Design, Exhibition Files, Exh. 258C. MOMA Archives, New York.

15. Elizabeth Mock, ed., *Built in USA Since 1932* (New York: Museum of Modern Art, 1944), 99.

16. "Municipal Asphalt Plant," *Architectural Forum* 80 (Mar. 1944): 110.

17. Paul Goldberger, "Asphalt Plant Into Gymnasium," *NYT*, Jan. 27, 1976, p. 32.

18. Bronze Generals Sought as Scrap," *NYT*, Nov. 1, 1942, p. 31.

19. *Home Information Service* 4 (Feb. 1941): 1.

20. "Are Skyscrapers Bombproof?" *Popular Science* 138 (May 1941): 84.

21. Lee E. Cooper, "Clearing of Slums Urged as Step in Defense Plan," *NYT*, May 11, 1941, p. RE1.

22. Bruce Bliven, "Science Creates a New World," *New Republic* 104 (Feb. 17, 1941): 204.

23. "To Advise USHA on Policy," *NYT*, Nov. 15, 1938, p. 12.

24. "Anti-Zionists Form Unit," *NYT*, Sept. 30, 1945, p. 39.

25. "More Plans Filed by Housing Agency," *NYT*, Oct. 8, 1940, p. 45. Other architects working on Fort Greene Houses included William F. R. Ballard, consulting architect of the New York City Housing Authority, Harrison & Fouilhoux, Rosario Candela, Albert Mayer, Clarence S. Stein, Charles Butler, Robert D. Kohn, and Henry S. Churchill. "Largest Public Housing Project Taking Form in Brooklyn," *NYT*, June 21, 1942, p. RE1. See also

Daily News, Brooklyn section, Apr. 2, 1941, p. B27.

26. "More Plans Filed by Housing Agency," *NYT*, Oct. 8, 1940, p. 45.

27. "Kahn, Architect, Off City Work List," *NYT*, Nov. 18, 1944, p. 15.

28. "Kahn and Jacobs Loose Items from Scrapbooks 1940s–1960s," in RAJ Avery.

29. "Streamlined Recreational Clubs for Men in the Service," *NYT*, Apr. 28, 1941, p. 13; and "USO Buildings," *Architectural Forum* 77 (July 1942): 89.

30. Kathleen James, *Erich Mendelsohn and the Architecture of German Modernism* (New York: Cambridge University Press, 1997), 241, 333.

31. Ita Heinze-Greenberg "'Around noon land in sight' Travels to Holland, Palestine, the United States, and Russia," in *Erich Mendelsohn: Architect 1887–1953*, Regina Stephan, ed., (New York: Monacelli Press, Inc., 1999), 67.

32. See Despina Stratigakos, "Reconstructing a Lost History: Exiled Jewish Women Architects in America," *Aufbau* 22 (Thursday, October 31, 2002): 14. Thomas W. Ennis, "Women Gain Role in Architecture," *NYT*, Mar. 13, 1960, p. R1.

33. Jacobs interview, Nov. 5, 1989.

34. "Office Building Bonanza," *Fortune* 41 (Jan. 1950): 84–86, 127–30.

35. "Spurt in Building of Homes Due Here," *NYT*, Mar. 27, 1946, p. 18.

36. "Tishman Building gets CPA Sanction," *NYT*, July 17, 1946, p. 37.

37. Elsa Gidoni, "So Now They Are Sending Us Female Architects," unpublished manuscript, Gidoni Archive, Prints and Photographs Division, Library of Congress; "Elsa Gidoni, A.I.A.," *Architectural Record* 103 (Mar. 1948): 106.

38. Lewis Mumford, "The Sky Line: Skin Treatment and New Wrinkles," *The New Yorker* (Oct. 23, 1954): 134.

39. Lewis Mumford, "The Best Is Yet to Come," *The New Yorker* (Dec. 13, 1947): 74–81.

40. Marketing brochure [n.d.], RAJ Avery.

41. "The Best Is Yet To Come," *The New Yorker*, (Dec. 13, 1947): 79–80.

42. Walter Yust, ed., *1947 Britannica Book of the Year*, (Chicago, London, Toronto: Encyclopaedia Britannica, 1947), 72; and Yust, ed., *1948 Britannica Book of the Year*, 65.

43. "Fifth Avenue Opening," Editorial, *NYT*, Apr. 17, 1947, p. 26.

44. "Crowd at Opening Hails Lane Bryant," *NYT*, Feb. 4, 1947, p. 29.

45. "New Store is Exhibited," *NYT*, Jan. 20, 1947, p. 22.

46. Kahn, "Commercial Centers, Prewar vs. Postwar," "Architectural Record. Office and Loft Buildings 93 (Apr. 1943): 76.

47. "Miracle (and Mecca) on 34th Street," *Architectural Record* 102 (July 1947): 90–95.

48. Display advertisement for Crawford Clothing, *NYT*, Jan. 16, 1947, p. 21.

49. "Mt. Sinai Establishes 2 New Posts In Post-War Expansion Program," *NYT*, Mar. 26, 1944, p. 36.

50. "Welding to Save on Hospital Cost," *NYT*, Feb. 17, 1950, p. 42.

51. "Ella Wendel Dies; Last of her Family," *NYT*, Mar. 15, 1931, p. 1.

52. "37-Story Edifice for Garment Zone," *NYT*, June 17, 1944, p. 23.

53. "Office Building Bonanza," *Fortune* 41 (Jan. 1950): 86.

54. "1407," *Wall Street Journal*, Mar. 9, 1948, p. 6; William Zeckendorf and Edward McCreary, *The Autobiography of William Zeckendorf*, (New York: Holt, Rinehart and Winston, 1970), 84.

55. Jane Jacobs, "New York's Office Boom," *Architectural Forum* 106 (Mar. 1957): 110.

56. "Demand is Seen for Tower Space," *NYT*, July 2, 1950, p. R4

57. "Find New System Conserves Space," *NYT*, Aug. 7, 1949, p. R8.

58. "Unusual Features on Wendel Site," *NYT*, Dec. 5, 1948, p. R1.

59. "Building Bonanza," *Fortune*, 86.

60. Lewis Mumford, "More Pelion, More Ossa," *The New Yorker*, 26 (Feb. 3, 1951): 76, 79, 82.

61. Lewis Mumford to Robert Allan Jacobs, Feb. 11, 1951. RAJ Avery. See also Lewis Mumford, "The Sky Line: Artful Blight," *The New Yorker* 27 (May 5, 1951): 89.

62. Stern *New York 1960*, p. 434–35, and David W. Dunlap, *On Broadway: A Journey Uptown Over Time* (New York: Rizzoli, 1990), p. 158.

63. Carol Krinsky, "Architecture in New York City," in Leonard Wallock, ed., *New York: Culture Capital of the World, 1940–1965* (New York: Rizzoli, 1988), p. 98.

64. See "Large Unit Rented on the East Side," *NYT*, Oct. 18, 1940, p. 40.

65. Jacobs telephone conversation with Jewel Stern, Mar. 28, 1984.

66. Written responses from Sheldon Fox, Mar. 15, 2005.

67. "New York Office Building Reverts to Vertical Style," *Architectural Forum* 90 (Jan. 1949): 15.

68. Jacobs later dismissed the building as yet another example of Kahn's "wedding cake" style. Jacobs interview, Nov. 5, 1989.

69. See "Success Tied to Attractive Buildings," *Building Line* (Nov. 9, 1950): 6; "100 Park Avenue: New York, N.Y.," *Progressive Architecture* 32 (May 1951): 64.

70. Joseph F. Cullman, Jr. *I'm A Lucky Guy*, (New York: Philip Morris, 1998), 14, 82.

71. "Next President gets Trade Plea," *NYT*, Oct. 1, 1952, p. 57.

72. Mumford "More Pelion," 76.

73. Thomas Creighton, "100 Park Avenue," *Progressive Architecture*, 32 (May 1951): 54.

74. "Success Tied to Attractive Buildings," *Building Line* (Nov. 9, 1950): 6. "Kahn and Jacobs Scrapbooks Brochures 1940s–70s," RAJ Avery.

75. Carol Willis, *Form Follows Finance* (New York: Princeton Architectural Press, 1995).

CHAPTER NINE

1. Kahn Diary, Nov. 1, 1954.

2. Kahn Diary, Feb. 10, 1957.

3. Ely Jacques Kahn, "American Office Practice," *Royal Institute of British Architects Journal* (Sept. 1957): 448.

4. Ely Jacques Kahn, "Economics of the Skyscraper," Architectural Record 63 (April 1928): 298–301," and Ely Jacques Kahn, "Skyscrapers of Manhattan," *Christian Science Monitor*, Mar. 14, 1934, Weekly Magazine Section, p. 4–5.

5. Robert Allan Jacobs, "Team Play Guides Today's Architects," *Christian Science Monitor*, Aug. 24, 1960, p. 11.

6. Jacobs, "Team Play," p. 11.

7. Written responses from Sheldon Fox, Mar. 15, 2005.

8. Kahn and Jacobs Architects, company portfolio, [n.d.], [n.p.], c.1963. RAJ Avery. Milton J. Hofflin, a family friend, was hired for the job of public relations officer.

9. Kahn letter to Samuel Bronfman, July 2, 1951, Phyllis Lambert Fonds, CCA Archives, Box 08–L–515.

10. Kahn Diary, July 2, 1951.

11. Alfred L. Rose letter to Samuel Bronfman, Aug. 2, 1951, Lambert Fonds, CCA Archives.

12. Charles Luckman, *Twice in a Lifetime: From Soap to Skyscrapers* (New York: W. W. Norton & Co., 1988), 323–25.

13. Phyllis Bronfman Lambert, "How a Building Gets Built," *Vassar Alumni Magazine* 44 (Feb. 1959): 13–20.

14. Doughty telephone conversation with Jewel Stern, Apr. 12, 1984.

15. Kahn Diary, Apr. 26, 1955.

16. Phyllis Lambert, ed., *Mies in America* (New York: Abrams, 2001), 587, n.7.

17. Kahn Diary, June 21, 1955.

18. Kahn Diary, Apr. 27, 1956; Kahn Diary, July 8, 1957.

19. Ely Jacques Kahn, "Tall Buildings in New York," *Royal Institute of British Architects Journal* 67 (Oct. 1960): 452.

20. "Vincent Astor Dies In His Home at 67," *NYT*, Feb. 4, 1959, p. 1.

21. "Astor Planning for $75,000,000 Building Project," *Los Angeles Times*, Sept. 20, 1956, p. 26; and "Skyscraper Rival for Rockefeller Center is Planned," *Chicago Daily Tribune*, Sept. 19, 1956, p. C9.

22. Glenn Fowler, "Astor Building May Be Resumed," *NYT*, Mar. 8, 1958, p. 35.

23. Kahn Diary, Sept. 19, 1956 and Sept. 24, 1956.

24. "Hippodrome Gets 3-Story Successor," *NYT*, July 6, 1951, p. 11.

25. "Hippodrome Nears End," *NYT*, Aug. 15, 1939, p. 40.

26. "Topics of the Times," *NYT*, Nov. 20, 1956, p. 22.

27. "Contracts for Tower Addition To Midtown Building Awarded," *Real Estate Record and Builders Guide* 188 (July 29, 1961): 4.

28. "6th Avenue Area Between Rockefeller Center and Bryant Park Springing to Life as Office Boom Moves Southward," *Real Estate Record and Building Guide* 189 (Apr. 21, 1962): 2.

29. Sheldon Fox, interview with John Stuart, May 10, 2005.

30. "Display Ad," *NYT*, May 5, 1955, p. 68.

31. "Popularity of Mosaic Increases in Housing and Business Units," *NYT*, Sept. 9, 1956, p. R1.

32. John P. Callahan, "New Machine Puts Terra Cotta Back on the New York Skyline," *NYT*, Dec. 8, 1957, p. W1.

33. "Exchange is Opening Its 'School' In U.S. Economy for All Investors," *NYT*, Dec. 20, 1951, p. 58; "Stock Exchange Takes a Plunge and Lands in Movie Business to Show How It 'Ticks,'" *NYT*, Apr. 30, 1952, p. 39.

34. Kahn Diary, July 11, 1953. Negotiations for the skyscraper began earlier that year. "Building to Rise Near Stock Mart," *NYT*, July 1, 1954, p. 42; "Wall Street's Other Boom," *Fortune* 54 (Oct. 1956): p. 163; and "Funston Proposes New Construction," *NYT*, Feb. 12, 1952, p. 35.

35. "Building to Rise Near Stock Mart," *NYT*, July 1, 1954, p. 42.

36. "Site Clearance Finished for New Structure at 20 Broad Street," *Real Estate Record and Builders Guide* 175 (June 25, 1955): 3.

37. "20 Broad Street 100% Rented at Early Construction Stage," *Real Estate Record and Builders Guide* 177 (June 9, 1956): 3. *Fortune* magazine concurred: "Today, in a dramatic turnabout, Wall Street is in the midst of a building boom . . . Gray stone will give way to shining metal and glass." See, "Wall Street's Other Boom," *Fortune* 54 (Oct. 1956): 163.

38. Burton Crane, "Big Board Pictures What a Buyer of Securities Gets for His Money," *NYT*, Feb. 24, 1957, p. 149.

39. Stern, *New York 1960*, 170.

40. "Builders Acquire Madison Ave. Plot," *NYT*, Oct. 18, 1949, p. 48; "David Simon, 69, A Builder Here," *NYT*, May 21, 1961, p. 87.

41. Ada Louise Huxtable, "Bold Plan for Building Unveiled," *NYT*, Sept. 29, 1964, p. 45.

42. Liselotte Kahn, *The Memoirs of Liselotte Kahn* (New York: Cato Publishers, 1996), 102–03.

43. Ibid., 137.

44. "Demolition Started at 42nd and Madison To Prepare For 39-story Skyscraper," *Real Estate Record and Builders Guide* 187 (June 24, 1961): 2.

45. Olivia Kahn interview with John Stuart, Jul. 29, 2005.

46. "Tower to Blend Black and White," *NYT*, Sept. 29, 1963, p. 338.

47. Ely Jacques Kahn with illustrations by Cal Sacks, *A Building Goes Up* (New York: Simon & Schuster, 1969).

48. Kahn, *A Building Goes Up*, 13. The choice of the name "Trowbridge" may refer to New York architect Samuel Beck Parkman Trowbridge (1862–1925) of the firm Trowbridge & Livingston. Trowbridge may have been a historical ideal for Kahn, because he had been trained both as an engineer at Columbia School of Mines and as an architect at the American School of Classical Studies in Athens and at the Ecole des Beaux-Arts in Paris.

49. Ibid., 12.

50. Ibid., 40.

51. Ibid., 44.

52. Ibid., 47.

53. Ibid., 46.

54. Ibid., 60.

55. Written responses from Sheldon Fox, Mar. 15, 2005.

SELECTED BIBLIOGRAPHY

Abbreviations for Frequently Cited References

Avery   Ely Jacques Kahn Collection, Drawings and
                 Archives, Avery Architectural and Fine Arts
                 Library, Columbia University
RAJ Avery   Robert Allan Jacobs Collection, Drawings
                 and Archives, Avery Architectural and Fine
                 Arts Library, Columbia University
Cornell CSP   Clarence Stein Papers, Division of Rare and
                 Manuscript Collections, Cornell University
                 Library
NYT   New York Times

Dissertations

Blake, Curtis Channing. "the Architecture of Carrère and
    Hastings." Ph.D. diss. Columbia University, 1976.
Canato, Mario. "Pragmatic thinking in the ideas of the sky-
    scraper architects of the 1920s." Ph.D. diss. University of
    Pennsylvania, 1992.
Cotten, Anne Boyer. "Clarence S. Stein and His Commitment
    to Beauty: Architect First, Community Planner Second."
    M. A. thesis, Cornell University, 1987.
Creese, Walter Littlefield. "American Architecture from 1918
    to 1933 With Special Emphasis on European Influence."
    Ph.D. diss. Harvard University, 1949.
Gray, Lee Edward. "The Office Building in New York City,
    1850–1880." Ph.D. diss. Cornell University, 1993.
Kaufman, Peter S. "American Architectural Writing, Beaux
    Arts Style: The Lives and Works of Alfred Dwight Foster
    Hamlin and Talbot Faulkner Hamlin." Ph.D. diss. Cornell
    University, 1986.
Lehman, Arnold. "The New York Skyscraper: A History of its
    Development, 1870–1939." Ph.D. diss. Yale University, 1974.
Radde, Bruce F. "Esthetic and Socio-Economic Factors of
    Skyscraper Design: 1880–1930." Ph.D. diss. University of
    California, Berkeley, 1975.
Samson, Miles David. "German-American dialogues and the
    Modern Movement before the 'Design Migration,'
    1910–1933." Ph.D. diss. Harvard University, 1988.

Books

Abramson, Daniel M. Skyscraper Rivals: The AIG Building and
    the Architecture of Wall Street. New York: Princeton
    Architectural Press, 2001.
Bennet, Robert. Deconstructing Post–WWII New York City: The
    Literature, Art, Jazz, and Architecture of an Emerging Global
    Capital. New York: Routledge, 2003.
Blake, Peter. No Place Like Utopia: Modern Architecture and the
    Company We Kept. New York: W. W. Norton, 1991.
Bressi, Todd W. Planning and Zoning New York City: Yesterday,
    Today and Tomorrow. New Brunswick, NJ: Center for
    Urban Policy Research, 1993.
Bruegmann, Robert. The Architects and the City: Holabird &
    Roche of Chicago, 1880–1918. Chicago: University of
    Chicago Press, 1997.
Chase, W. Parker. New York: The Wonder City. New York:
    Wonder City Publishing Co., 1932.
Cheney, Sheldon. The New World Architecture. New York: Tudor
    Publishing Co., 1930.
Cheney, Sheldon, and Martha Candler Cheney. Art and the
    Machine: An Account of Industrial Design in 20th-century
    America. New York and London: Whittlesey House, 1936.
Christen, Barbara S., and Seven Flanders, eds. Cass Gilbert, Life
    and Work: Architect of the Public Domain. New York: W. W.
    Norton & Co., 2001.
Clausen, Meredith. The Pan Am Building and the Shattering of
    the Modernist Dream. Cambridge, Mass.: MIT Press, 2005.
_____. Pietro Belluschi: Modern American Architect.
    Cambridge, Mass.: MIT Press, 1994.
Dolkart, Andrew. Morningside Heights: A History of Its

Architecture and Development. New York: Columbia University Press, 1998.

Douglas, Ann. *Terrible Honesty: Mongrel Manhattan in the 1920s*. New York: Noonday Press; Farrar, Straus, and Giroux, 1996.

Douglas, George H. *Skyscrapers: A Social History of the Very Tall Building in America*. Jefferson, NC and London: McFarland & Co., 1996.

Drexler, Arthur, ed. *The Architecture of the Ecole des Beaux-Arts*. New York: Museum of Modern Art, 1977.

Edgell, George Harold. *The American Architecture of To-day*. New York: Charles Scribner's Sons, 1928.

Ferris, Hugh. *The Metropolis of Tomorrow*. New York: Ives Washburn, 1929.

Gibbs, Kenneth Turney. *Business Architectural Imagery in America, 1870–1930*. Ann Arbor, Michigan: UMI Research Press, 1984/1976.

Goldberger, Paul. *The Skyscraper*. London: Allen Lane, 1981.

Heilbrun, Margaret. *Inventing the Skyline: The Architecture of Cass Gilbert*. New York: Columbia University Press, 2000.

Hitchcock, Henry-Russell, and Arthur Drexler, ed. *Built in USA: Post-War Architecture*. New York: The Museum of Modern Art, 1952.

Hitchcock, Henry-Russell, and Philip Johnson. *The International Style: Architecture Since 1922*. W. W. Norton & Company, New York, 1932.

Huxtable, Ada Louise. *The Tall Building Artistically Reconsidered: The Search for a Skyscraper Style*. New York: Pantheon Books, 1984.

Kahn, Ely Jacques. *Ely Jacques Kahn. Contemporary American Architects Series*. Foreword by Arthur Tappan North. New York: Whittlesey House, 1931.

_____. *Design in Art and Industry*. New York: Charles Scribner's Sons, 1935.

_____. *A Building Goes Up*. New York: Simon & Schuster, 1969.

Kilham, Walter H. *Raymond Hood, Architect*. New York: Architectural Book Publishing Co., 1973.

Kimball, Fiske. *American Architecture*. Indianapolis and New York: Bobbs-Merrill Co., 1928.

Landau, Sarah Bradford. *Rise of the New York Skyscraper, 1865–1913*. New Haven: Yale University Press, 1996.

Lepik, Andres. *Sky Scrapers*. Munich and New York: Prestel, 2004.

Lowe, David. *Beaux Arts New York*. New York: Whitney Library of Design, 1998.

_____. *Art Deco New York*. New York: Watson-Guptill Publications, 2004.

Maas, John. *The Glorious Enterprise, The Centennial Exhibition of 1876 and H. J. Schwarzmann, Architect-in-Chief*. Watkins Glen, NY: American Life Foundation, 1973.

Martin, Reinhold. *The Organizational Complex: Architecture, Media, and Corporate Space*. Cambridge, Mass.: MIT Press, 2003.

Messler, Norbert. *The Art Deco Skyscraper in New York*. New York: P. Lang, 1986.

Mock, Elizabeth, ed. *Built in USA: Since 1932*. New York: The Museum of Modern Art, 1944.

Moudry, Roberta. *The American Skyscraper: Cultural Histories*. Cambridge: Cambridge University Press, 2005.

Mujica, Francisco. *History of the Skyscraper*. New York: Archaeology & Architecture Press, 1930.

Mumford, Lewis, and Robert Wojtowicz. *Sidewalk Critic: Lewis Mumford's Writings on New York*. New York: Princeton Architectural Press, 1998.

Nash, Eric Peter, and Norman McGrath. *Manhattan Skyscrapers*. New York: Princeton Architectural Press, 1999.

Neumann, Dietrich, ed. *Architecture of the Night: The Illuminated Building*. New York: Prestel, 2002.

Nofsinger, James. *The Influence of the Ecole des Beaux-Arts on the Architects of the United States*. Washington D.C.: Catholic University Press, 1955.

Nye, David E. *American Technological Sublime*. Cambridge, Mass.: MIT Press, 1994.

Okrent, Daniel. *Great Fortune: The Epic of Rockefeller Center*. New York: Viking, 2003.

Park, Edwin Avery. *New Backgrounds for a New Age*. New York: Harcourt, Brace and Co., 1927.

Plunz, Richard. *A History of Housing in New York City: Dwelling Type and Social Change in the American Metropolis*. New York: Columbia University Press, 1990.

Pokinski, Deborah Frances. *The Development of the American Modern Style*. Ann Arbor, Michigan: UMI Research Press, 1984/1982.

Robinson, Cervin, and Rosemarie Haag Bletter. *Skyscraper Style: Art Deco, New York*. New York: Oxford University Press, 1975.

Ruttenbaum, Steven. *Mansions in the Clouds: The Skyscraper Palazzi of Emery Roth*. New York: Balsam Press, 1986.

Sexton, R. W. *American Commercial Buildings of Today*. New York: Architectural Book Publishing Co., 1928.

_____. *The Logic of Modern Architecture*. New York: Architectural Book Publishing Co., 1929.

Shultz, Earle, and Walter Simmons. *Offices in the Sky*. Indianapolis: Bobbs-Merrill, 1959.

Solomonson, Katherine. *The Chicago Tribune Tower Competition: Skyscraper Design and Cultural Change in the 1920s*. New York: Cambridge University Press, 2001.

Solon, Leon Victor. *Polychromy*. New York: The Architectural Record, 1924.

Starrett, William Aiken. *Skyscrapers and the Men Who Build Them*. New York: Scribner, 1928.

Stern, Robert A. M. *George Howe; Toward a Modern American Architecture*. New Haven and London: Yale University Press, 1975.

Stern, Robert A. M, Gregory Gilmartin, John Massengale. *New York 1900: Metropolitan Architecture and Urbanism 1890–1915*. New York: Rizzoli, 1983.

Stern, Robert A. M., Gregory Gilmartin, Thomas Mellins. *New York 1930: Architecture and Urbanism Between the Two World Wars*. New York: Rizzoli, 1984.

Stern, Robert A. M., Thomas Mellins, David Fishman. *New York 1960: Architecture and Urbanism between the Second World War and the Bicentennial*. New York: Monacelli Press, 1995.

Susman, Warren I. "Culture and Civilization: The Nineteen-Twenties," in *Culture As History: The Transformation of American Society in the Twentieth Century*. New York: Pantheon Books, 1973/1984.

Tallmadge, Thomas E. *The Story of Architecture in America*. New York: W. W. Norton & Co., 1927.

Tunick, Susan. *Terra-Cotta Skyline: New York's Architectural Ornament*. New York: Princeton Architectural Press, 1997.

Van Leeuwen, Thomas A. P. *The Skyward Trend of Thought: The Metaphysics of the American Skyscraper*. Cambridge, Mass.: MIT Press, 1988.

Vlack, Don. *Art Deco Architecture in New York 1920–1940*. New York: Harper and Row, 1974.

Willis, Carol. *Form Follows Finance: Skyscrapers and Skylines in New York and Chicago*. New York: Princeton Architectural Press, 1995.

Willis, Carol, and Donald Friedman. *Building the Empire State*. New York: W. W. Norton in association with the Skyscraper Museum, 1998.

ARTICLES

"American Industrial Art Exhibited at the Metropolitan Museum of Art." *American Architect* 135 (Mar. 5, 1929): 315–22.

"Architecture Used Overcame All Problems." *Women's Wear Daily*, Dec. 17, 1929, sec. 4, p. 4.

Benson, Robert. "Douglas Haskell and the Modern Movement in American Architecture." *Journal of Architectural Education* 36 (summer 1983): 2–9.

Blackall, D. H. "American Architecture Since the War." *American Architect* 133 (Jan. 5, 1928): 1–11.

Bossom, Alfred C. "Fifty Years' Progress Toward an American Style in Architecture," *American Architect* 129 (Jan. 5, 1926): 43–49.

Brock, H. I. "From Flat Roofs to Towers and Slats: The Architectural "League Has Seen a Revolution in Its Fifty Years." *NYT Magazine*. April 19, 1931, pp. 6–7, 16.

"Built-in Air Conditioning," *Architectural Record* 102 (Oct. 1947), 147–48.

"City of Color," Dominion (New Zealand), Apr. 7, 1931, n.p., clipping, Kahn scrapbook 1, Avery.

Clute, Eugene. "Modernism and Tradition." *Pencil Points* 6 (Sept. 1925): 41.

"Decorative Work Replaces Cornices."*NYT*, Mar. 27, 1929, sec. 10, p. 16.

Hamlin, Talbot F. "Some Restaurants and Recent Shops." *Pencil Points* 20 (Aug. 1939): 485–92.

Hastings, Thomas. "Architecture and Modern Life." *Harpers New Monthly Magazine* 94 (Feb. 1897): 402–8.

"High-rise Office Buildings." *Progressive Architecture* 38 (June 1957): 159–91.

Hitchcock, Henry-Russell. "Modern Architecture I. The Traditionalists and the New Tradition." *Architectural Record* 63 (April 1928): 337–49.

_____. "Modern Architecture II. The New Pioneers." *Architectural Record* 63 (May 1928): 453–60.

Hornbeck, James S. "Office Buildings: A Review of the New Skyscraper." *Architectural Record* 121 (Mar. 1957): 228–50.

Jacobs, Jane. "New York's Office Boom." *Architectural Forum* 107 (Mar. 1957): 105–13.

Johnson, Philip. "The Skyscraper School of Architecture." *Arts* 17 (May 1931): 569–75.

Kimball, Fiske. "What Is Modern Architecture?" *The Nation* 119 (July 1924): 128–29.

Leonard, Louis. "What Is Modernism?" *American Architect* 136 (Nov. 1929): 22–25, 112.

Mumford, Lewis. "American Architecture To-day." *Architecture* 57 (April 1928): 181–188.

Mumford, Lewis. "The Skyline: From the Palace of the Popes—The Cantilevered Front—Return to Sobriety." *The New Yorker* 52 (Jan. 2, 1932): 43–44.

"New York Skyline Gets a Facelifting." *Business Week* (May 21, 1949): 23–25.

Newman, James B. "Factors in Office Building Planning." *Architectural Forum* 52 (June 1930): 881–890.

"Office Building Bonanza." *Fortune* 41 (Jan. 1950): 84–86, 127–30.

"Office Buildings." *Architectural Record* 115 (April 1954): 186–209.

Pond, DeWitt Clinton. "Treatment of the 'Set-Back.'" *Architecture* 54 (Oct. 1926): 293–97.

"Portfolio of Current Architecture: Park Avenue Building." *Architectural Record* 63 (April 1928): 305–326.

Price, C. Matlack. "The Trend of Architectural Thought In America." *Century Magazine* 102 (Sept. 1921): 709–22.

"Reconstruction and Revival." *American Architect and Architecture* 150 (Apr. 1937): 144.

Saylor, Henry H. "Ely Jacques Kahn." *Architecture* 64 (Aug. 1931): 65–70.

Solon, Leon. "The Park Avenue Building, New York City." *Architectural Record* 63 (Apr. 1928): 289–97.

Swan, Herbert S. "Making the New York Zoning Ordinance Better." *Architectural Forum* 35 (Oct. 1921): 125–30.

Tafuri, Manfredo. "The Disenchanted Mountain: The Skyscraper and the City." In *The American City: From the Civil War to the New Deal*, trans. Barbara Luigia La Penta. London: Granada, 1980.

Watkin, William Ward. "Whence Comes This Modernism?" *American Architect* 142 (Sept. 1932): 22–23, 88.

Willis Carol, Zoning and Zeitgeist: The Skyscraper City in the 1920s." *Journal of the Society of Architectural Historians* 45 (Mar. 1986): 47–59.

Wright, Hamilton M. "Contemporary Architecture as Mr. Kahn Sees It." *Western Architect; Current Architecture* 40 (Feb. 1931): 7.

Young, James C. "Titanic Forces Rear a New Sky Line." *NYT Magazine*, Nov. 15, 1925, p. 6.

ARTICLES BY ELY JACQUES KAHN
listed in chronological order

"Essential Details in Store Designing." *Architectural Forum* 40 (June 1924): 245–48.

"The Office Building Problem in New York." *Architectural Forum* 41 (Sept. 1924): 94–96.

"The Architectural League Exhibition of 1926." *Architectural Record* 59 (Mar. 1926): 226–27.

"Our Skyscrapers Take Simple Forms." *NYT*, May 2, 1926, sec. IV, pp. 11, 26.

"The Ziegfeld Theatre, New York." *Architectural Record* 61 (May 1927): 385–93.

"Economics of the Skyscraper." *Architectural Record* 63 (Apr. 1928): 298–301.

"Exhibition of French Decorative Art." *Architectural Record* 63 (May 1928): 462.

"Whittlings." *Pencil Points* 9 (Oct. 1928): 661."

"Contemporary Design." *Quarto Club Papers* 2 (1928): 53–61.

"What is Modern Architecture?" *Architecture* 59 (Jan. 1929): 3–4.

"Modernism in Metal Work." *Metal Arts* 2 (Jan. 1929): 9.

"Backyard Garden." *Pencil Points* 10(March 1929): sup.108.

"The Modern European Shop and Store." *Architectural Forum* 50 (June 1929): 795–804.

"The Architecture of Industrial Buildings." *Architectural Forum* 51 (Sept. 1929): 273–77.

"Sources of Inspiration." *Architecture* 60 (Nov. 1929): 249–56.

"The Province of Decoration in Modern Design." *Creative Art* 5 (Dec. 1929): 885–86.

"Do Architects Want Criticism?" *American Architect* 137 (Apr. 1930): 59, 92.

"Civilized Architecture." *Architectural Forum* 52 (June 1930): 785.

"Modern Lighting Departs Radically From the Methods of the Past." *House & Garden* 58 (Aug. 1930): 42–47.

"The Holland Plaza Building, New York." *Architecture* 62 (Sept. 1930): 133–38.

"Redesigning the Bonwit Teller Store." *Architectural Forum* 53 (Nov. 1930): 571.

"Decoration as a Merchandising Background." *Interior Architecture and Decoration* 1 (June 1931): 135–39.

"Points of View." (Letter to the Editor, May 4, 1931) *Creative Art* 8 (June 1931): 469.

"This Modernism." *T-Square Journal of Philadelphia* 1 (Sept. 1931): 5.

"Architectural Planning." *New Republic* 68 (Oct. 14, 1931): 237.

"Impressions of the Paris Colonial Exposition." *American Architect and Architecture* 140 (Oct. 1931): 34–9+.

"Let Us Know What is Being Done." *T-Square Journal* 2 (Feb. 1932): 31–33.

"Architectural Education." ("Notice to Students and Correspondents." reprinted from *The Bulletin of the Beaux-Arts Institute of Design*, May 1932) *Architecture* 66 (Oct. 1932): 229–30

"Close-up Comments on the Fair." *Architectural Forum* 59 (July 1933): 23–24.

"Common Sense House." in "Forward House." *Architectural Forum* 59 (Oct. 1933): 283.

"Skyscrapers of Manhattan." *Christian Science Monitor*, Mar. 14, 1934, Weekly Magazine Section, pp. 4–5.

"Note by the Chairman of the West Gallery Unit," in "Contemporary American Industrial Art: 1934." *Bulletin of the Metropolitan Museum of Art* 29 (Dec. 1934): 204–05.

"'Give Us Facts' says Ely Jacques Kahn" an interview by Dock Curtis. *Modern Plastics* 12 (May 1935): 9–13, 61, 62.

"Design Trends." *Architectural Forum* 64 (June 1936): 469.

"Main Streets Across the Continent." *Arts and Architecture* 45 (Sept. 1936): 19–21, 49, 51.

"Lighting in Design Procedure." *Interior Design and Decoration* 9 (July 1937): 73

"Professional Discussions." *Pencil Points* 19 (July 1938): 433–35.

"Talk If You Must—But Act! *Pencil Points* 22 (Feb. 1941): 74.

"We Men—We Women: A Radio Interview with Ely Jacques Kahn" by Paul R. Milton. (Apr. 15, 1941). Transcript, Kahn scrapbook 3, Avery.

"Commercial Centers, Prewar vs. Postwar." *Architectural Record* 93 (Apr. 1943): 74–77.

Ely Jacques Kahn and Robert Allan Jacobs. "Home Loan Headquarters; Office for a typical 'Savings and Loan.'" *Architectural Record* 97 (Jan. 1945): 90–91.

Encyclopaedia Britannica. 1946 ed., s.v. "Colour in Architecture."

"The Policy of the Journal," in "Architects Read and Write." *Journal of the American Institute of Architecture* 7 (May 1947): 250–51.

"Contemporary Design in Architecture." *Journal of the American Institute of Architects* 9 (Apr. 1948): 159–167.

"The Time is Ripe." *Craft Horizons* 16 (May/June 1956): 20–24.

"American Office Practice." *Journal of the Royal Institute of British Architects* 64 (Sept. 1957): 443–51.

"Tall Buildings in New York." *Journal of the Royal Institute of British Architects* 67 (Oct. 1960): 451–55.

INDEX

Page numbers in *italic* type refer to illustrations. References to colorplates are preceded by "C."

PHOTO CREDITS

Abbreviations of Frequently Cited Credits

Avery Ely Jacques Kahn Collection, Drawings and Archives, Avery Architectural and Fine Arts Library, Columbia University
RAJ Avery Robert Allan Jacobs Collection, Drawings and Archives, Avery Architectural and Fine Arts Library, Columbia University
Fischer LOC Sigurd Fischer Archive, Prints and Photographs Division, Library of Congress
MCNY Museum of the City of New York, Ely Jacques Kahn Collection
Whittlesey Ely Jacques Kahn. Contemporary American Architects Series, New York: Whittlesey House, 1931

C.1 The Metropolitan Museum of Art, Gift of the artist, 1972 (1972.41); Photograph ©2005 Metropolitan Mueum of Art
C.2 Liselotte Kahn and *Architectural Record* 63 (April 1928): 288
C.3 © Peter Mauss/ESTO
C.4–C.7 Photo: Peter Mauss, Collection of the Friend of Terra Cotta
C.8 © Cervin Robinson
C.9 © Jewel Stern
C.10 Liselotte Kahn
Frontispiece: Jean M. Heyman and Jewel Stern
1.1–1.3 Adèle Maximilian and Jewel Stern
1.4 Jean M. Heyman and Jewel Stern
1.5–1.6 Yearbook of the Columbia School of Architecture 1907
1.7 ©Léon & Levy/Roger-Viollet
2.1 *Design for Several Bays for a Public Building*, 1907, graphite, brush and gray wash on Bristol illustration board, 23⅞ x 17⁹⁄₁₆ in. (606 x 446 mm), Cooper-Hewitt, National Design Museum, Smithsonian Institution, gift of Ely Jacques Kahn, 1952-86-3
2.2–2.6 Avery
2.7 Emily Cassebeer
2.8 Clarence Stein Papers, courtesy of the Division of Rare and Manuscript Collections, Cornell University Library
2.9 Avery
2.10 Carcassonne, February 19, 1909, graphite on brown wove paper, 11 3/8 x 8 1/16 in. (289 x 205 mm), Cooper-Hewitt, National Design Museum, Smithsonian Institution, gift of Mrs. Ely Jacques Kahn, 1977-122-1
2.11 Rolf Myller
2.12 Ecole Nationale Supérieure des Beaux-Arts, Paris
2.13 *Architects and Builders Magazine* 2 (July 1901): 345
2.14 The Wolfsonian-Florida International University, The Mitchell Wolfson, Jr. Collection; Photo: Silvia Ros
3.1 Liselotte Kahn
3.2 Avery
3.3 James Dabney McCabe, *The Illustrated History of the Centennial Exhibition*, 1876
3.4 R. M. De Leeuw, *Both Sides of Broadway: From Bowling Green to Central Park, New York City*, 1910
3.5 Bloomingdale Properties, Inc.
3.6 Buchman & Fox firm brochure, c.1914, courtesy of Mortimer J. Fox Jr.
3.7 Buchman & Fox firm brochure, c.1914, courtesy of Mortimer J. Fox Jr.
3.8 Empire State Notables 1914
3.9–3.11 ©Jacob Getz, 1983

3.12 Fischer LOC, Job No. 279
3.13 Sheldon Cheney, *The New World Architecture* (New York: Tudor Publishing Co., 1935)
3.14 *Architectural Forum* 39 (Sept. 1923): pl. 52
3.15 *Architectural Forum* 35 (Oct. 1921): 129
3.16 Liselotte Kahn and *New York Times*, June 27, 1920, sec. VIII, p. 8
3.17 *Architecture and Building* 53 (April 1921): pl. 54
3.18 Avery
3.19 ©Jacob Getz, 1983
3.20 Rolf Myller
3.21 ©Jacob Getz, 1983
3.22 Avery
4.1 ©1976, 2006. CBS Outdoor Inc. All Rights Reserved
4.2 John A. Stuart, adapted from *New York Times*, March 24, 1918, sec. III, p. 14
4.3–4.4 *Architecture and Building* 56 (June 1924): pl. 130
4.5 Avery
4.6 ©Jacob Getz, 1983
4.7 Rolf Myller
4.8 Franco Borsi and Ezio Godoli, *Vienna 1900: Architecture and Design* (New York: Rizzoli, 1986) © 1986 Marc Vokaer
4.9 *American Architect and Architectural Review* 124 (Aug. 1, 1923): pl. 2425
4.10–4.11 Fischer LOC, Job No. 47
4.12 Fischer LOC, Job No. 10
4.13 R. W. Sexton, *American Commercial Buildings of Today*, Architectural Book Publishing Co., 1928
4.14 Fischer LOC, Job No. 80
4.15 Fischer LOC, Job No. 174
4.16 *Architectural Forum* 50 (Jan. 1929): 26.
4.17 Fischer LOC, Job No. 80
4.18 Cranbrook Archives, Saarinen Family Papers, #5169; photo: Atelier Apollo.
4.19 Fischer LOC, Job No. 174
4.20 Aug. M. J. Sevenhuijsen, *Nieuwe Bouwkunst In Nederland*, Blaricum Waelburgh, c. 1928
4.21 Avery
4.22–4.23 Fischer LOC, Job No. 38
4.24 Fischer LOC, Job No. 174
4.25 ©Jewel Stern
4.26 Fischer LOC, Job No.
4.27 The Wolfsonian-Florida International University, The Mitchell Wolfson, Jr. Collection; Photo: Silvia Ros
5.1 *Architecture and Building* 58 (March 1926): pl. 58
5.2 ©Jacob Getz, 1983
5.3 *Architecture and Building* 58 (March 1926): pl. 58
5.4a–5.4b ©Jacob Getz, 1983
5.5 *Architectural Forum* 48 (Jan. 1928): pl. 4
5.6 *Architecture and Building* 59 (May 1927) pl. 102
5.7 ©Jacob Getz, 1983
5.8–5.9 Fischer LOC, Job No. 168
5.10–5.11 Liselotte Kahn and *Architectural Record* 63 (April 1928): 292
5.12–5.13 Liselotte Kahn and *Architectural Record* 63 (April 1928): 293
5.14–5.15 Fischer LOC, Job No. 243
5.16–5.17 ©Jewel Stern
5.18 *Architecture and Building* 60 (May 1928): pl. 91
5.19 Fischer LOC, Job No. 243
5.20–5.21 ©Jewel Stern
5.22 Avery
5.23 Fischer LOC, Job No. 244
5.24 *Architecture and Building* 60 (April 1928): pl. 79
5.25 Fischer LOC, Job No. 264
5.26 Fischer LOC, Job No. 273
5.27 Fischer LOC, Job No. 271
5.28 Fischer LOC, Job No. 302

5.29 ©Jewel Stern
5.30 Fischer LOC, Job No. 315
5.31–5.32 ©Jewel Stern
6.1 Fischer LOC, Job No. 255
6.2 Fischer LOC, Job No. 313
6.3 Fischer LOC, Job No. 364
6.4 Whittlesey
6.5 *Architecture and Building* 61 (Feb. 1929): pl. 26
6.6 Ezra Stoller ©Esto and Department of Special Collections, Spencer Research Library, University of Kansas Libraries
6.7 Frank Lloyd Wright Foundation
6.8 Henry-Russell Hitchcock, *In the Nature of Materials* (New York: Duell, Sloan and Pearce, 1942)
6.9 Fischer LOC, Job No. 294
6.10 *Architecture and Building* 61 (Feb. 1929): pl. 28
6.11–6.12 ©Jewel Stern
6.13 Fischer LOC, Job No. 294
6.14 Fischer LOC, Job No. 298
6.15–6.16 ©Jewel Stern
6.17 Rendering: Schell Lewis; R. W. Sexton, *American Commercial Buildings of Today*, Architectural Book Publishing Co., 1928
6.18–6.19 ©Jewel Stern
6.20–6.21 Fischer LOC, Job No. 385
6.22–6.23 ©Jewel Stern
6.24 Rendering: Schell Lewis; *Architectural Forum* (June 1930): 813
6.25 MCNY; Photo: Sigurd Fischer
6.26 Fischer LOC, Job No. 386
6.27–6.28 ©Jewel Stern
6.29 Whittlesey
6.30 Fischer LOC, Job No. 387
6.31 ©Jewel Stern
6.32 *Architectural Record* 69 (April 1931): 315
6.33 Fischer LOC, Job No. 394
6.34 *Architecture and Building* 62 (Dec. 1930): 344
6.35–6.36 ©Jewel Stern
6.37 Skyscraper, 1930, graphite and fixative on tracing paper mounted on paper laminate, 24⅝ x 15¾ in. (625 x 400 mm), Cooper-Hewitt, National Design Museum, Smithsonian Institution, gift of Ely Jacques Kahn, 1952-15-13
6.38 Hugh Ferris, *The Metropolis of Tomorrow*, 1929
6.39 Liselotte Kahn and *Vanity Fair* 37 (Dec. 1931): 59
6.40 Photo: Lawrence Cashman
6.4–6.441 Fischer LOC, Job No. 391
6.45 Peter A. Juley & Son Collection, Smithsonian American Art Museum, J0008692
6.46–6.47 Photo: Lawrence Cashman
6.48 Avery
6.49 Fischer LOC, Job No. 437
6.50 Whittlesey
6.51–6.53 Fischer LOC, Job No. 437
6.54 MCNY
6.55–6.57 Fischer LOC, Job No. 447
6.58 Fischer LOC, Job No. 412
6.59 Fay S. Lincoln Photograph Collection, Historical Collections and Labor Archives, Special Collections Library, The Pennsylvania State University, University Park, Pennsylvania.
6.60 Fay S. Lincoln Photograph Collection, Historical Collections and Labor Archives, Special Collections Library, The Pennsylvania State University, University Park, Pennsylvania
6.61–6.62 Fischer LOC, Job No. 449
6.63–6.65 ©Jewel Stern
6.66–6.67 Fischer LOC, Job No. 456
6.68 Rheinisches Bildarchiv Köln
6.69–6.70 MCNY; Photo: Sigurd Fischer
6.71 Photo: Blank & Stoller; *Architectural Forum* 58 (June 1933): 31
7.1 Courtesy of The Detroit Institute of Art; Photo: Joseph Szaszfai
7.2 Avery

7.3 *Architectural Forum* 57 (Oct. 1932): 303; Photo: Van Anda Photos
7.4–7.5 Avery
7.6 Kohler News (May 1933): 3
7.7–7.8 Avery
7.9 *Architectural Forum* 72 (June 1940): 9
7.10–7.13 Avery
7.14 *Architectural Record* 80 (Aug. 1936): 115. Photo: Ben Schnall
7.15 *Arts & Decoration* 45 (Nov. 1936): 23. Photo: Ben Schnall
7.16 *Pencil Points* 22 (Mar. 1941): 163. Photo: William Ward
8.1 Courtesy of Liselotte Kahn
8.2 Courtesy of the Collection of Barbara G. Pine. Rendering: Hugh Ferriss
8.3 *Architectural Forum* 80 (March 1944): 112
8.4 RAJ Avery; Kahn and Jacobs brochure, c.1963, p. 35
8.5 Avery Architectural and Fine Arts Library, Columbia University. Rendering: Arthur Frappier
8.6 RAJ Avery; Kahn and Jacobs brochure, c.1950, p. 14
8.7 *Architectural Forum* 77 (July 1942): 89. Rendering: Andre Remonart
8.8–8.9 RAJ Avery; Kahn and Jacobs brochure, c.1950, p. 9
8.10 MCNY
8.11 MCNY, Photo: Erich Kastan
8.12 *Architectural Record* 102 (July 1947): 90. Photo: Ben Schnall
8.13–8.14 RAJ Avery; Kahn and Jacobs brochure, c.1963, p. 51
8.15–8.16 RAJ Avery; Kahn and Jacobs brochure, c.1950, p. 11
8.17 RAJ Avery; Kahn and Jacobs brochure, c.1963, cover
8.18 MCNY
8.19 MCNY, Rendering: Nadir
8.20 MCNY
8.21 MCNY, Photo: I.N.P.
8.22 RAJ Avery; Kahn and Jacobs brochure, c.1963, p. 14
8.23 *Progressive Architecture* 32 (May 1951): 64. Photo: Lionel Freedman
8.24 *Progressive Architecture* 32 (May 1951): 56
8.25 *Progressive Architecture* 32 (May 1951): 62. Photo: Lionel Freedman
9.1 RAJ Avery; Kahn and Jacobs brochure, c.1973, p. 24. Photo: attributed to Norman McGrath
9.2 RAJ Avery; Kahn and Jacobs brochure, c.1963, p. 18
9.3 Photo: John A. Stuart
9.4–9.5 Courtesy of the Hagley Museum and Library
9.6 RAJ Avery; Kahn and Jacobs brochure, c.1963, p. 22
9.7–9.8 RAJ Avery
9.9 RAJ Avery; Kahn and Jacobs brochure, c.1963, p. 9
9.10 MCNY, Photo: Felix Gilbert
9.11 RAJ Avery
9.12–9.13 Rendering: Kahn and Jacobs
9.14 RAJ Avery; Kahn and Jacobs brochure, c.1963, p. 19
9.15 Max Spivak photographs, 1938 – [ca.1967], Archives of American Art, Smithsonian Institution; Photo: J. Alex Langley
9.16 RAJ Avery; Kahn and Jacobs brochure, c.1963, p. 20
9.17 Rendering: Kahn and Jacobs
9. 18 Photo: John A. Stuart
9.19 RAJ Avery; Kahn and Jacobs brochure, c.1970, p. 30
9.20 RAJ Avery; Kahn and Jacobs brochure, c.1963, p. 21
9.21 RAJ Avery; Kahn and Jacobs brochure, c.1970, p. 19
9.22 RAJ Avery; Kahn and Jacobs brochure, c.1963, p. 8
9.23 RAJ Avery; Kahn and Jacobs brochure, c.1970, p. 12.